THE PERSONALITY OF THE DOG

THE PERSONALITY
OF THE DOG

Edited by Brandt Aymar
and Edward Sagarin

WINGS BOOKS
New York • Avenel, New Jersey

Copyright © 1964 by Crown Publishers, Inc.
Further acknowledgements are listed at the back of the book.

This 1995 edition is published by Wings Books,
distributed by Random House Value Publishing, Inc.,
40 Engelhard Avenue. Avenel, New Jersey 07001,
by arrangement with Crown Publishers, Inc.

Random House
New York • Toronto • London • Sydney • Auckland

Printed and bound in the United States of America

Library of Congress Cataloging-in-Publication Data
The Personality of the dog / edited by Brandt Aymar and Edward Sagarin.
    p. cm.
    Originally published : New York : Bonanza Books, 1964.
    ISBN 0–517–14665–7
    1. Dogs—Literary collections. 2. Literature, Modern. I. Aymar, Brandt.
II. Sagarin, Edward, 1913–
PN6071.D6P47   1995
808.8'036—dc20   95–16058
                                             CIP

8 7 6 5 4 3 2 1

TABLE OF CONTENTS

ILLUSTRATIONS

INTRODUCTION

THE LITERATURE that mankind has created about dogs is vast, but if one can imagine a canine art form in which dogs communicate their thoughts to one another through the world of smells and sights, how much vaster would be the dog's literature about man. And whereas, in their poetry and short stories, their novels and their biographies, men have generally imputed to dogs some of the most glorious of human traits, one must shrink with horror to imagine how dogs would portray humans. They would find them cruel and lascivious, ferocious and selfish, stupid and irrational: in fact, they would probably find them beastly and inhuman, but—assuming that the dogs had mastered the symbolism of language—they would prefer not to use these terms, but rather to say that men are unbeastly and undoglike.

This collection is, in a sense, just such an effort: a dog's-eye view of the world, or, in many instances, a dog's-nose smell of man. And if it is not entirely flattering, let us understand that these portraits are painted by men, as they imagine the world of dogs to be.

Over and over again, in these stories, men show their affection for dogs by addressing them as "Boy." They will say to a dog, male or female, regardless of the name, "Here, boy," and it is almost the kindest word they can use. By contrast, consider an ordinary expression that a man will use when heaping insult and invective on another man: "He's a dog!"

Perhaps the two characteristics for which most dogs are known—known to men that is, if not to other dogs—are love and loyalty. To what incredible lengths a dog will go—at least in the literature, and probably in the world of reality as well—to protect the well-being and earn the accolades of the master.

This is the subject of story after story, in almost every language of the world that has a form of writing, and spoken in the myths and folklore of those peoples whose tongues have not yet been reduced to written form. Fortunately, the variations are many, and dog lovers never tire of them.

In the selection of material for this anthology, we have attempted to choose those stories from dog literature which emphasize the individual personality of the dog as the protagonist of the tale. We have chosen from many styles and periods: from the essentially revolutionary literature of Alexander Kuprin and the world of Russian czarism; from the now melodramatic works of Jack London, which still bring a tear to the eye of many readers; from the humorous satire on romantic love—canine and human—of G. B. Stern, who offers us a Cyrano devoid of a large nose, but not an effective one; from the amazing tour-de-force achieved in Sheila Burnford's story of the white dogs of the Ojibways. The same superhuman (or supercanine) courage is evident in many of these stories; the same spirit of tenacity; the same ability of man, the artist, to use the dog as a vehicle through which he sees and smells man's world—and it is sometimes not a pretty world, at that.

Love breeds many ramifications, even in a dog's life. Elizabeth Barrett's dog Flush turns his undying love for her into biting jealousy for Robert Browning, in Virginia Woolf's delicate biography. What a study in contrast to read Flush's account of the romance of these two poets, and then John Held, Jr.'s story of MacDunald, as he watches and seeks to understand the breakup of the marriage of his master.

Loyalty breeds courage, where the feats of the smallest setter match those of the largest malemute. But courage is a two-edged weapon, and in Yehuda Yaari's story of the shepherd dog who came to live on an Israeli *kibbutz*, it is courage that drives the dog to feats of loyalty and then, finally, to his own doom.

Ours is a world in which much is said of rejection, and of the nefarious effects of non-acceptance on the life of a child. But what happens to a rejected dog, the bewilderment which he feels, is shown in a sensitive story by Corey Ford, "Home Is the Hero." What Ford achieves here is something that repeats throughout this anthology: namely, the ability of a reader (at least the human reader) to identify with the dog.

The editors have sought those stories and poems, as well as works of visual art, which seemed best to portray personality traits, temperament, characteristics of dogs, thus following a pattern that was set in two previous collections, *The Personality of the Cat* and *The Personality of the Horse*. But here there was a second effort. The editors searched through numerous anthologies, many long out of print and others more recent; many in paperback that were sold for but a short time and others that remained on the market for a much longer period. And, to our dismay, we found the same stories, repeated over and over. While attempting to remain true to the main theme of this collection, namely the choice of outstanding literary and artistic material that demonstrates the personality traits, the editors have further made an effort to include a maximum number of pieces never before anthologized in dog or animal books. To our knowledge and on the basis of considerable research, there appear for the first time in a collection of this type the stories, among others, of Virginia Woolf, Sarah Addington, Sholom Aleichem, Havilah Babcock, Sheila Burnford, Mazo de la Roche, Corey Ford, John Gautier, John Held Jr., Michael Komroff, Alexander Kuprin, C. G. Learoyd Farley Mowat, Olive Schreiner G. B. Stern, Mary Wilkins, Friedebert Tuglas, and Yehuda Yaari.

So that, if any reader complains that much of our material has been used before, we must retort that he is barking up the wrong troo.

Brandt Aymar
Edward Sagarin

January
1964

TINY TIM

BY *Mazo de la Roche*

H E WAS UNACCOMPANIED and he was going out to America as a Christmas present to a young lady. He was nine months old but looked on himself as grown-up. His legs were short and straight, his body sensitive, alive, as tense as a fiddle-string, and he had a square muzzle, a hysterical tail and a black spot over one eye. His pedigree was as long as his days were short.

In England he had been the pet of a young man and an old lady. When one of them was not making much of him, the other was. There was not a corner of the house, from attic to basement kitchen, where he was not welcome. The maids let him kiss them or even bite them if he chose. His kisses were swift, moist licks; his bites mumbling, gnawing, long-drawn-out worryings that left a good deal of slobber but no pain.

But his favorite dream was the way he would have bitten cats, if he could have caught them. He would wake from this dream gnashing his small teeth and spring to his feet and stare about him.

"Cats, is it?" the old lady would inquire, and she would hobble to the door and let him out into the garden. He would rage up and down it, screaming of his desire to catch a cat.

The old lady had been most untidy. Three maids and a tidy grown-up grandson could not keep the house from looking as though it had been stirred up with a spoon. It was an exquisitely happy home for Tiny Tim because, no matter what he did in it, he could never do wrong.

So the first nine months of his life passed and then the untidy old lady died.

Tim missed her a good deal. She had made a delightful cushion to lie on when he was tired from play and she had always been ready to hobble to the door to let him in or out. In fact, letting Tim in or out was the chief excitement of her day. No one else could do it so satisfactorily because the wheeziness of her breath always contributed to Tim's gusto in rushing out or bounding in.

But what he missed most, perhaps, was her untidiness. Now, if he worried the corner of a rug, it was soon laid back in place. If he tore the filling out of a cushion, the rent was at once mended and he was rebuked. Old shoes, old bones, which he had loved to keep handy on the drawing-room rug, were taken away where he could not find them. There had always been at least four dishes of food and drink on the floor of the room. Every time he barked at the sugar basin she had given him a lump. He always had the jam spoon to lick. It was useless for her grandson to tell the old lady that Tim would die if she kept on like this. She knew better. She knew that it was she herself who was most likely to die.

So, when she died and the young man was given a post in the East, he decided to send Tim as a Christmas present to a young lady in America. And Tim was to carry all the young man's love with him. Some day, it was hoped, those three would live together.

When Tim found himself in a small cage in a small room on board ship he felt more curious than alarmed. His only companion was an immense Irish wolfhound whose name was Oona and who was accompanied by a grim and silent master. Oona utterly ignored Tim. When they were let out of their cages for exercise, he tried to make up to her at once. It had always been so easy for him to make friends that he thought all he had to do was to stand on his hind legs, put his nose against her muzzle, and beam at her out of his hazel eyes. The next moment she would be rolling over and over with him, pawing him quietly, racing with him round and round the room.

But Oona did nothing of the sort. She looked straight through him with a sombre gaze. She stood as a rock while his small paws padded against her like little waves. But when he gave her a warm lick with his tongue, she lifted her long velvety lip and snarled.

He made several attempts to win her. He brought his ball and his rubber bone to show her. He got directly in her way, looking up in her face ingratiatingly. But she turned her head away from ball and bone and, when he stood in her path, she stepped over him.

He would stand under her, looking out from between her powerful legs as between pillars, her rough body looming above him like a cloud. He was exquisitely clean and dainty. She was unkempt, strong-smelling. She had an immense attraction for him.

He would sit gazing at her by the hour, nervous shivers running along his spine and through his legs. He never seemed to sit solidly down. His thin little stern hovered shudderingly above the heaving deck.

It was a bad voyage. From the first day out they encountered fog, rough seas, gales. Oona became more and more melancholy. She began by being very sick and, after that, she refused all food but a mouthful or two of dry biscuit. This she would turn over and over in her mouth while Tim watched her in rapt attention; then sometimes she would spit it out again, turn it over on the floor with an expression of disgust, and finally bolt it as though to be rid of the disgusting sight of it.

No sort of weather affected Tim's stomach. He crunched his biscuit with his square little muzzle turned up to the face of Grierson, his keeper. He swept the dish clean of his soft meal in three gulps. In between he wondered what had become of the innumerable little snacks he used to enjoy. He wondered what had become of the house where he had romped, the garden where he had chased imaginary cats, the large soft lap where he had snuggled, the two strong young hands that had snatched him up and stroked him or put on his lead or sometimes cuffed him. To do justice to Tim it must be said that he missed the kindly lap, the strong hands, more than the delicious titbits.

He was constantly on the lookout for love. Those who came to the kennels were friendly. They scratched him behind the ears sometimes, but they were all alike, and none of them was like his old lady or his young man.

Oona's master was as unfriendly as Oona herself. Twice daily he took her for a walk. They stalked out, stalked round the deck, and stalked back again, without looking in the direction of anyone else.

When Tim saw Oona's lead being snapped to her collar he

was wild with excitement, wild to go with her to the deck. He danced about on his toes and filled the air with his pleadings. But he might not have existed as far as Oona and her master were concerned.

Tim had the feeling that if he could go for a walk he might find his old lady or his young man. Sometimes he had such a burden of love in him that he felt he must find somewhere to deposit it. At others he felt strangely full of hate, growling for no reason at all.

But on the third morning something happened. A young man and a young lady, having nothing better to do, came to look at the dogs and decided to take Tim for a walk on deck.

It seemed too good to be true. Tim was *so* frantic when they really set off. He so strained against the collar that he had a fit of coughing and the young couple thought he was going to be sick and all but took him back to the kennels.

His feet scarcely touched the deck. He bounced in an ecstasy of hope. Surely now he might find his own house, his own garden, his own old lady.

But he found none of them. The young couple, whose names were Jean and John, held him so closely on his lead that he became quite tired and ceased to strain. He walked sedately, with wistful looks into the faces of all he met.

Everyone was *so* kind to him and it became the thing for Jean and John to take him for walks. Everyone knew him by name and bits of cake and sweets constantly came his way. Jean usually led him because he was so becoming to her, and she held his lead so short that he always felt as though he were about to choke. They often passed Oona and her master, looking gloomier and more aloof as the days went on.

In this new world of Tim's there were only two dogs, himself and Oona, and Oona would not look at him, would not exchange sniff for sniff or lick for lick. The more he saw of John and Jean the less he liked them. There was no one on board for him to love. He gobbled up all the food that was offered him and grew thinner and thinner. At night he dug into the straw of his cage and tried to dig through the floor itself. He lay curled up in a little shivering heap. He longed to obliterate himself.

Then on his rocking horizon appeared a new old lady. She was even more solid, more impressive, more comfortable, than his own old lady. She came up the steps from the tourist class, hanging on firmly to the brass rail, and promenaded solidly around the deck leaning on her ebony stick and peering through windows and doors with an air of dignified curiosity.

One of the deck stewards came up to her apologetically.

"I'm very sorry, Madame," he said, "but this deck is reserved for the cabin passengers."

She stared at him.

"Can't I walk about and look at it?" she asked.

"I am afraid not," he returned, still more apologetically.

"Well, well, I'm sorry I have come where I shouldn't, but when one is on one's first sea voyage one likes to look about."

"Of course." The steward spoke deferentially. "It's quite natural and I'm very sorry indeed — "

"It's your duty," she interrupted and turned back towards the stairs.

The steward assisted her down them and, returning, met John with Tim on the lead. They were waiting for Jean.

"Did you see that old lady?" asked the steward.

"Yes," answered John, without interest.

"Well, she's one of the Mount-Dyce-Mounts."

"One of the Mount-Dyce-Mounts!" echoed John, unbelievingly.

"Yes, and it's her first trip. She's going out to see a married daughter in British Columbia. Traveling alone. I hated terribly to turn her back off this deck. But I couldn't help it. She's a lovely old lady, she is indeed."

"And a Mount-Dyce-Mount!" exclaimed John, and forgetting all about Jean hurried down the steps dragging Tim after him and went up to where the old lady had settled herself in her chair. The sun had come out, the sea calmed, and it was fine for the time of year.

John introduced himself, with a charming air, to old Mrs. Mount-Dyce-Mount and begged her to let him know if he could be of the slightest service to her.

She thanked him kindly and was interested in Tim. She patted her lap and he sprang on to it. His nostrils quivered over the stuff of her dress. Then he looked long and earnestly into her face. He swiftly touched her cheek with his tongue. He gave a joyous bark. It seemed too good to be true. He had found another old lady.

He saw a good deal of her, though not half as much as he

desired. John took him to the tourist deck to call on her twice every day. If John went without him she asked at once for the little dog. The trouble was that the call was short and what Tim longed to do was to stay close by her side, forever and ever, as long as this strange heaving world lasted.

When John, knowing that Jean was waiting impatiently for him to play deck tennis with her, dragged Tim away to the kennels, Tim dug his nails into the deck, made his small body rigid, and turned up his hazel eyes full of pleading and hate for John.

Once the old lady said: "Do let him stay!" And Tim curled up on her lap for an hour of supremest content. When John came to fetch him Tim snapped at him and, when they were alone together, John hit him with the end of the lead.

There was a fog off Newfoundland. The ship lay motionless in the sullen ice-cold water while all night long the warning whistle sounded. Tim lay curled up tightly, shivering through all his tender being. That day John and Jean had become engaged and they lay awake planning for their future. Old Mrs. Mount-Dyce-Mount lay awake too, thinking of the past and dreading the long rail journey to British Columbia and wondering if her daughter-in-law really wanted her.

Towards morning the engines started. All the passengers who were awake gave sighs of relief and thought, "Thank goodness, we're off."

The ship moved through the sullen water very quietly, as though feeling her way. But an iceberg submerged in the depths collided with her in a shock so terrible that those who slept were soon awake, wild with fear. A heavy sea was rolling.

The attendant let Tim and Oona out of their cages. Oona was unmoved by the excitement about her, but when her master appeared she went to him with a slow wag of the tail and a sombre light in her eyes.

Tim capered over the decks, a new hope possessing him. Perhaps this strange world of the ship was about to disappear and he would find his way back to his own house and garden. He liked the peculiar listing of the deck which the humans found so terrifying. He dug in his little nails, cocked his ears, and investigated places where John and Jean had never permitted him to go.

Presently he saw them rushing frantically, hand in hand, their life preservers on askew, Jean's silk pyjamas fluttering in the icy wind. He flew after them barking.

It was not one of those shipwrecks in which people behave with fortitude, though heroic deeds were afterwards recounted in the newspapers. Perhaps there were too many on board like John and Jean, who fought their way hysterically to the best places, not giving a second thought to old Mrs. Mount-Dyce-Mount.

Tim loved the sight of these pyjamaed legs. He had always longed to bite them and now he darted after them, nipping first one and then the other. Jean shrieked terribly.

"Oh, oh," she screamed, "he's gone mad!"

John screamed and kicked out at Tim and shouted: "Somebody kill this dog! He's gone mad!"

Women screamed in a new terror and a man unexpectedly whipped out an automatic from his pocket and fired at Tim. The boat listed still more. There was pandemonium aboard.

Tim had not liked the revolver shot at all. He skulked down a stairway and trotted, one ear pricked and the other lopping, along a deserted passage.

He sat down and licked the spot where John had kicked him. Then he scratched and the thumping of his elbow on the floor sounded like an imperative knocking.

"Go away!" A harsh old voice came from within.

It was the voice of the old lady. Tim was galvanized by it into joyous activity. He tore at the door and it swung open. Mrs. Mount-Dyce-Mount was revealed sunk on a seat beneath the closed porthole which showed nothing beyond but gray-green water. The luggage in the cabin had slid to one side. The toilet articles were on the floor.

Tim saw nothing of this. He only saw his dear old lady and he leaped into her lap and began ecstatically to lick her face, whimpering with joy as he did so.

"Timmie, Timmie, oh, you naughty little boy!" she murmured, and for a moment she hugged him to her. Then she said, "But you should not have done this. You should not have done this!"

But Tim thought he should. He began to investigate the cabin. He became even more worked up, for he smelled Oona in it. He leaped back into his old friend's lap and informed her with hysterical barkings that Oona had been here.

"But you should not have done it," she repeated. "Poor little Tim, you should not have done it. Perhaps if you go up on deck someone will save you. Go away, now! Naughty boy! Oh, dear, I wish you would go!"

Her voice broke and she began to cry.

Tim curled up in a tight ball and began to shiver from head to tail. But, almost instantly he uncurled and stood tense on the slanting floor, listening. He heard Oona and her master coming. They were creeping cautiously along the passage, which was becoming more and more difficult to negotiate.

When Oona's master opened the door he gave a start of astonishment.

"Why, why," he stammered, "I thought this was my cabin."

"I dare say it is," returned Mrs. Mount-Dyce-Mount. "I'm just staying in it for the time being."

"But, my God—don't you know we're going down?"

"Of course I do," she returned, irritably; "that's why I said for the time being."

"But you can't stay here! You'll drown! Don't you realize that? Where is your life preserver?"

"I couldn't get it on. I'm not the right shape. I just couldn't get it on. Then everybody was jostling so I got my ankle turned and some young people almost knocked me over and I was frightened and I came in here. But—this dear little dog—I wish you could save him!"

Oona's master took her by the arm and lifted her to her feet.

"You must come at once!" he said, sternly.

The old lady clung to his shoulder and began to cry a little. He quickly opened a drawer and took out a packet he had come back for.

"Would you mind," he asked, "sending this to the address written on it—if you have the opportunity?"

"Certainly I shall," she answered, and put the packet into her handbag.

Tim paid no heed to these proceedings. He was occupied by Oona's sudden condescension towards him. She, who had never given him a glance, was now delicately sniffing him all over. Her strong tail was wagging approval of him. When she thrust her muzzle under his chest she lifted him off his feet. She uttered a low whine of pleasure.

The Captain and his officers had been able to quiet the hysterical passengers. The second last of the lifeboats was about to be lowered into a sun-gilded sea. A dozen hands reached out to help Mrs. Mount-Dyce-Mount.

The vessel was sinking fast. There was not a moment to spare. Oona's master picked up Tim and dropped him into the old lady's lap.

He perched on her knees, alert in every nerve. His restricted life of the past week had been opened up to an almost over-powering breadth. There was so much to see. All that was needed to make his exhilaration complete was cats!

Still he could see Jean and John clinging together in a boat quite near and he began to bark at them loudly, vindictively, with a kind of strangling snarl between each explosion. John called out:—

"Mrs. Mount! Throw that dog out! He's mad! It's not safe for you to hold him!"

"Yes, he's quite mad!" cried Jean. "He'll bite you!"

Tiny Tim barked the louder and Mrs. Mount-Dyce-Mount held him close.

The last lifeboat was lowered. The Captain, some sailors, a stoker, and Oona and her master were in it. He had refused to leave her and they found room for her in the boat. The waves were mounting higher, a sudden squall broke, and the ship, shaken as though by a great convulsion, rolled over and sank. A driving storm of sleet and snow blurred the vision, so that the occupants of the lifeboats became isolated and felt small and weak and afraid.

All but Tim.

He stood tiny, shivering, indomitable, on Mrs. Mount-Dyce-Mount's lap. With his bright eyes he strove to pierce the blurring, icy flakes. His instinct was directed towards Oona and all his eager senses sought to search her out. When a bitter wave slashed across the lap where he was braced, he lifted a paw and stood shivering on three legs.

The squall passed and the sun rose ruddy and beautiful for Christmas morning. The ship had disappeared and two of the lifeboats had been swamped. The waves were romping with the wreckage and with the bodies of those who clung to it.

Tim soon discovered John and Jean clinging together in the sea, more dead than alive. He showed his little teeth in rage at their nearness and gave out such a volley of barks as almost threw him overboard.

Then he saw Oona and his barking ceased. She was swimming round and round as though searching for something. Her grand rugged head looked grander still, rising out of the foam. Tim strained towards her, trembling, uttering little plaintive whimpers.

The SOS had been heard and another ship was already coming to the rescue. The wind fell, the sun rose, and a feeble cheer was raised.

John and Jean were the first to be picked up. The Captain, the sailors, the stoker, all those who had been in that last lifeboat were saved—all but Oona and her master. And she might have been saved but, when they tried to reach her, she swam out of their way, her gaunt head raised, her sombre eyes searching the waves.

THE ROMANTIC DOG

VOLTAIRE, TONO AND DULCIBEL

BY *G. B. Stern*

VOLTAIRE HAD NO ILLUSIONS. Bitterly honest when in session with himself, he admitted what had happened to him. He had fallen for Dulcibel. He had no illusions about her, either. His eyes were wide open. She was without grace of birth, breeding or ancestry to recommend her; and, worst of all, she had no brains to redeem her from utter mediocrity. Her points were all wrong; her Legs was all wrong; and although nowadays no animal would be narrow-minded enough to blame another for going on the films, Voltaire was convinced that she had no talent, only a vulgar desire for celluloid publicity. No; vain, silly, bogus little mongrel lady-dog, not worthy of the name of bitch, that was Dulcibel; that was his enchantress.

He let his beard grow long, and spent many lonely hours in the dank shut-off corner he had dug out for himself, away from the villa and the other dogs. And always, writhing in self-contempt, he reached the same conclusion. He was helpless. He was humiliated. He could not free himself from thrall. Canine nature being what it is, he had known from the first whiff what he was in for. "I will be worse before I am better," he growled:

> *"O toi, qui vois la honte où je suis descendue,*
> *Implacable Vénus, suis-je assez confondue!*
> *Tu ne saurais plus loin pousser ta cruauté.*
> *Ton triomphe est parfait."*

How he longed to tear at her wide white ruff, worry it, draggle it . . . *la volupté.* . . . And, thus musing, he caught cold. It was a *very* dank corner of the garden, and a dog who was also a philosopher should have known better than to select it for his hermitage. The Relative Legs, returning from Florence, immediately clapped him into a warm flannel coat, bottle-green, and confined him to the villa or the hottest patch of sunshine on the terrace. Thus he was present at the first encounter between the Relative Legs and the Highly Insured Legs; an encounter conducted with freezing politeness on the one side, and a sulky annoyance, barely concealed, on the other. For the Highly Insured Legs obviously preferred a villa full of males; and suffered, moreover, from the pretty delusion that the Supreme Legs had a special tenderness for herself.

Suddenly those few sentences were spoken which were Voltaire's doom:

"You have such a dear little dog, my brother tells me. A Pomeranian. Where is he?"

"She," corrected the Highly Insured Legs. "She's down at the Casetta. I've had to shut her up."

"Tomorrow, perhaps," said Tono, trying to cheer him. It was unusual for the griffon to be in despair. Usually his mood never varied from a detached but cheerful cynicism.

"*Mais je te dis*, we shall not see her up here tomorrow, nor the day after, nor for a long, long while. And I cannot bear it; my whole system is poisoned; till the poison is out . . . *Mais toi, tu ne comprends rien*. My sufferings are formidable!"

Tono yawned, which was with him a sign of embarrassment, not of boredom. But really, for Voltaire of all dogs to break down and declare his sufferings as formidable!

"Perhaps," he suggested lamely, "if she can't come up to visit us, we shall be taken down to see her."

Voltaire's moustaches quivered in mockery. "Receive my assurance, *mon ami*, that we will not be taken down to the Casetta Sans Gêne. The Legs were not born yesterday."

"No, of course they weren't," Tono agreed, literal as usual. "But cheer up, Voltaire. We needn't ask permission, you know. What's to prevent you, if you feel like that, from slipping off to see her this evening when we're taken for our walk?"

"I will tell you what is to prevent me. *Cette sacrée jaquette de laine.*"

"What?"

"Thees damn' jacket"—briefly.

"Oh!" Tono searched in his mind for something comforting to say even about the flannel coat, but found it difficult. He hesitated between "She might not notice it in the dark," and "Some bitches like a dressy dog," but in the end he said neither. Voltaire went on:

"It makes me ridiculous; it is badly cut; and green, it is not my color. How can I show myself like this, in front of them all?"

"But there'll only be her."

Voltaire contradicted him with some peevishness: "Naturally there will be a crowd."

"But there are no other dogs round her for miles." Tono was astonished at Voltaire's pertinacity. The latter merely reiterated: "A crowd. There will be a crowd."

On the broader terrace below, Fafnir and Wotan were playing at Blue Train and Golden Arrow; chasing each other madly round, uttering shrill yelps, till they formed an almost unbroken circle, the nose of one touching the stern of the other.

"*Non, parbleu, non.* I cannot go down to her; it is impossible. Everything is against me. If I had your looks . . ." He rolled one sick eye towards Tono and left it there, glaring.

"Oh, come now"—modestly; "plenty of people might say that my nose is too long and my forelegs too short; though, mind you, I don't agree that we dachses carry our bodies too near the ground. Besides, a glossy coat is only skin-deep. I've often envied you for being so witty and cultured and knowing just what to say and when to say it. I'm an inarticulate sort of dog, and—what's the matter?"

The griffon had ceased to gnaw his paws; his eyes were suddenly lucent with a strange whimsical fire: "But it is an idea," he murmured. "Certainly it is an idea. More, it is an inspiration." And he began to chuckle softly, rocking himself from side to side: "*Cher* Rostand, I thank you. Never before, perhaps, have I done you justice. 'A little too much of the rant,' have I said to myself, sitting in harsh judgment, 'too flamboyant, *trop de panache*, this Cyrano of yours.' But now: '*Je serai ton esprit, tu seras ma beauté*—' "

"I like recitations," said Tono. "I'm not good at them, but I *like* them," and he composed himself to listen to more.

"On the contrary my friend, action!" Voltaire was in quite a different mood now, hopeful, chattering, a little feverish, and every now and then rolling over in a quite inexplicable fit of sardonic laughter.

He expected, Tono thought ruefully, when the matter had been explained, the devil of a lot. However, he had offered to do what he could, and he was not withdrawing now. Apparently Voltaire's plan was to send him as emissary to plead his cause with Dulcibel. Some crazy notion he had that he could, as it were, use Tono's looks as though they were his own, provided Tono exactly repeated his words; his witty, cultured, allusive words; his persuasive, mischievous, delicately flattering, boldly seductive words; a complete wooing by rote. And Voltaire repeated: " '*Je serai ton esprit*' (and Dog knows you need it), '*tu seras ma beauté*—' "

"Well," began Tono, "it sounds funny to me, but . . ."

When the Master Legs took them for their walk that evening, Tono had a little trouble in detaching himself and slipping away on his embassy; for the avenue and paths were washed clear by moonlight, and Elsa was in a tiresome mood and kept on asking him where he was going, each time he branched away from their routine run. It was no good taking Elsa into his confidence; her nature was essentially not in sympathy with Dulcibel's; she had once said something very sharp indeed about Dulcibel's grandmother; bitches were such women about each other.

At last, however, he thought he had successfully eluded the eye and the whistle of his beloved Master Legs. No need to go on the road either, though it was lonely enough even by day, and lonelier by night. But there was a path which ran under the pines and took one or two loops before it finally dribbled away into the scrub and burrage and wild anemones at the back of the Casetta Sans Gêne. Here at the end of the garden was a crooked goat-shed, in the shadow of a clump of olives too old to bear fruit. And Voltaire had seemed to think it most likely that Dulcibel would be sleeping shut up in the shed instead of, as usual, petted and privileged on a cushion beside the bed of the Highly Insured Legs.

"What makes you think that?" Tono asked. "It's so unlikely."

But Voltaire, the omniscient, had merely replied: "You will find that it *is* so."

Really Voltaire was a very wonderful dog; very wonderful indeed. One could be proud to have him as a constant companion; prouder still to be chosen as his representative in courtship.

As Tono pattered down the path, he repeated to himself conscientiously the lines Voltaire had taught him; anxious to acquit himself with fluency and ease when he finally had to say them to Dulcibel. A pretty little thing, Dulcibel; well-meaning, too, thought Tono in amiable benediction; not much brains, but there, Voltaire had enough for seven. Besides, Voltaire, now he came to think of it, had said nothing about brains, though a great deal about passion: *"Un baiser"*—something? what was it? *"Un point rose qu'on met sur l'i du verbe aimer.* . . . *Un secret qui—qui"*—so much more difficult to remember it all in French—*"Un instant d'infini qui fait un bruit d'abeille."* All about a kiss. And Voltaire instructing him, had snapped: "But try a little to say it as if it *meant* something, *parbleu*. You are not an automaton, or are you? A kiss . . . *voyons*, swift, subtle, seductive!" And Tono had replied: "I'm not one for kissing much, and with all due respect, Voltaire, it's not nice to get all excited the way you do, and use those words. The point

is, do you want me to make her an offer of marriage on your
behalf?" And Voltaire had exclaimed: *"Que je souffre!"* No
more. And, on being pressed, had snuffled and sneezed and spat
out in a fury: *"Mariage! Les noces! La dot!* No, you are, too,
too *bourgeois. Va,* and you need say nothing about marriage."

That was the trouble with these Dulcibels (Tono wagged his
head sagely)—they would tickle a dog's fancy, but they couldn't
win his respect. And how very lucky, mused Tono, now quite
near to the clump of olives and the shed at the back of the
Casetta Sans Gêne, how *very* lucky that she has no charm for
me! No charm at all. No charm—

Suddenly he stood stock-still, his heart thumping madly
against his ribs.

No charm? Dulcibel? Was he mad? Tono began to tremble
violently. Why, the whole wood was reeling with her charm.
The moon was brilliant with her charm. . . .

"I . . . I don't feel well," murmured Tono. "Must be the
heat." But he trembled as though he were as cold as poor little
Voltaire, up there at the Villa Arabesque.

Voltaire. The memory was a shock. He was on his way, not
to plead his own cause, but on a vicarious errand of love.
Voltaire was his friend; he had to be loyal, but all the while
some potent magic flowed from Dulcibel (oh, divine, oh, heav-
enly Dulcibel!) luring him to become a traitor, to woo her for
himself instead of for the griffon! He had only to turn the
corner (he knew this path well) and there would be the gnarled
olives crouching over the goat-shed which tonight was a palace
of romance in a stream of silvery light.

"Oh, Dog," groaned poor Tono, who believed in the highest
standards of friendship. "Oh, Dog, appear now and help me!"

But no vision appeared, huge and beneficent; and Tono felt
he could not unaided vanquish this fatal desire for Dulcibel
which was stealing over him and wrapping him round like
music from the Venusberg, sapping him of honor—

Hardly knowing that he moved, he went forward, obeying the
music.

. . . Immobile, menacing, as though carved out of dazzling
white chalk splotched in a dazzling black pattern—*who* was it,
what was it, standing there in the moonlight beside the goat-shed

of Dulcibel's captivity? Not Great Dog himself; no, only half as big, though much, much bigger than a dachshund. Bigger, indeed, than any mortal dog of Tono's ken. *Who* was it? *What* was it?

He glared and growled at Tono. And Tono knew now. It was Anti-Dog: in incarnation risen to confront him, dappled and obscene, of his own sin, his own lust, taking concrete shape.

And Tono knew, also, without a shadow of doubt, what he had to do.

Dazed and terrified, aware that he was bound to be killed, he sprang straight for the monster's throat.

You have to vanquish sin and lust and treachery, or be forever vanquished yourself.

It could not really be called a fight, for it was over so quickly. There was a swirl and a confusion of legs and lashing tails and snapping jaws; mingled with the high shrill barks of Dulcibel hurling herself against the door of the shed; and screams, high and shrill, from Dulcibel's mistress as she tore up the garden from the Casetta: "Oh, save him! Save him!" . . . Then Tono felt a stranglehold on his collar. He was dragged off the enemy, resisting every inch of the way, and scolded in a voice of thunder, a beloved familiar voice: the Master Legs, after all, must have seen him slip away, and had followed him down, arriving just in time.

The enemy seized his chance. For an instant there was a white streak among the glossy trunks of the olives, and then he vanished forever.

"Why can't you keep your horrid dog shut up?" cried the Highly Insured Legs. She had had a fright, and was in a tantrum, and had never much liked the Master Legs anyhow.

"Why can't you keep *your* little beast shut up? Properly, I mean, not in that transparent bit of latticework? You know perfectly well that we've got dogs up at the villa."

"If you had them under proper control—"

"Control my foot! We've been here for years, haven't we? And then you come barging in—" The Master Legs had also had a fright, and was suffering from reaction; the hand shook which grasped Tono's collar; though even now he did not pick up his little dog and carry him home under his arm, fondling him, comforting him; no, not even now, when he had so nearly lost him forever in the huge jaws of Anti-Dog.

"You ought to give him the biggest thrashing he's ever had."

"You needn't worry. My own dog is my own business. I can give you the name of a decent vet if you don't want to be bothered with that nasty bit of work while she—"

"She's not a nasty bit of work. She's My Own Dulcibel. She gets paid fifty a week, and she's worth twenty times fifty to me."

"That's all right. I'm not arguing."

"Yes, you are. You said we were barging in. We don't want to barge, Dulcie and me. We're used to being welcome wherever we go. As welcome as the flowers in May. We're used to intellectual companionship, not savages who don't even keep their savage dogs on leads but let them spring at other dogs' throats. Tomorrow I'll pack and tomorrow we'll go and you'll be sorry."

"Good night," said the Master Legs briefly, not contesting the latter pronouncement. He looped his handkerchief through Tono's collar, and holding both ends firmly, marched him up the hill and back to the villa. There he put him through a

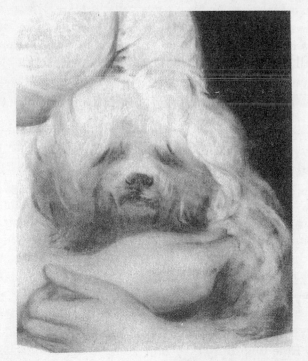

thorough examination, discovered that he was not hurt beyond a small bite above one eye which he sponged and dressed, but all the while without a single loving word or caress. And then, telling him in stern tones that he was in deep disgrace and ought to be ashamed of himself and would not be forgiven for a long time, took him out to the stable instead of upstairs to the dear bedroom; and, as before when Tono had leapt into the dinghy, abandoned him to his sorrow and perplexity.

It was Voltaire, after all, who understood best what had happened, when Tono was released twenty-four hours later, and they were able at last to get some private conversation; Voltaire alone who would realize and appreciate the courageous spirit which had caused Tono to hurl himself at the throat of a dog at least thrice the size of a little dachshund. For courage, after all (reflected Voltaire), is not what we do, but what we believe we are doing.

"I admire you, *mon ami*," said Voltaire. His cold was much better this morning, almost gone; and though he still wore his bottle-green flannel coat, it sat on him in a less despondent fashion; one button hung loose by its thread. "Were it in my paws, you should have the *croix de guerre* for this. But, alas, I have not the same influence any more as once in high quarters. As for that little matter which you call treachery to me— bah! I mock myself of that. *C'est une bagatelle.* Montaigne says truly, 'We seek and offer ourselves to be gulled.'"

"I wouldn't have betrayed you, you know, if it had actually come to it," Tono faltered. "At least, I think I wouldn't. I feel sure I wouldn't. My better self . . . one is tempted . . . but if it had actually come to it . . ."

"But naturally you would not!" And to himself: "But naturally you would." For Voltaire saw no reason out of this mass of motive and counter-motive, self-delusion and sentimentality, to revise his opinion: *"Plus je vois les chiens, plus j'aime les hommes."* Still, if it made it a little easier and happier for that poor forlorn Tono, that comical victim of Looking-Glass-Land, to squat there solemnly unwinding yards of mystic macaroni about Dog and Anti-Dog and incarnations, spells and charms and visions and the romantic lure of beauty in the moonlight, let him meander on.

"—I must have fallen in love with her subconsciously that very first time the Highly Insured Legs brought her up here."

"They're leaving," the griffon announced carelessly.

"What? Who? Leaving where?"

"Leaving the Casetta Sans Gêne."

"Both of them?"

"*Mais oui*, both. They do not like it any more. It is too *triste* a neighborhood. And they have not been given an *accueil* warm enough, up here at the Arabesque. My Legs, now she has returned, was a little outspoken in her opinion of the Highly Insured Legs; and the Master Legs, on the night of your adventure, spoke a little brutally—"

Tono nodded: "I was there."

"Yes, you were there. And, *enfin*, the Highly Insured Legs lost her temper and did not recover it; and hoped for a message from the Supreme Legs, an invitation to dine, shall we say? Only it did not come, that invitation. She thought, *vois-tu*, that she was a *Spécialité de la Maison*, but, on the contrary, 'e 'ate 'er guts." Voltaire at moments was very low in his talk. "And so they packed their trunks and they depart today—tomorrow —at once. It has been a failure."

"But, Voltaire, how do you know all this?" Tono had never been further from understanding life and its complexities and manifestations and injustices. He could not forget how the Master Legs had scolded his little Tono (not very hard) and exclaimed: "You might have killed him!" And now here was Voltaire, with more righteous claim to censure him, so serene in his mood, so loftily raised above the claims of the flesh and the fevers of love. Not even minding that Dulcibel was going away.

"How did you know?" Tono repeated.

"Dulcibel told me."

"You've seen her?" shouted Tono.

"What is the matter that you shout? Yes, indeed, I have seen her, the foolish little one. She ran up to leave her card on me, *pour prendre congé*. It was easy to slip off, with her Legs so busy in preparation for departure; she told me she came in person, though it was unconventional, because she felt the need, after so much indelicacy and upset, for a little intellectual conversation."

"Well?" said Tono. And by "Well?" he meant: And did you have an opportunity of telling her how much you loved her? How you worshipped the ground her little paws spurned so lightly? Did you, in fact, pour forth all that burden of longing, of timid and reverential desire with which you charged me not two days ago?

"*Well?*"

"There was no intellectual conversation." And Voltaire delicately removed from his flannel coat a clinging white cotton hair. He liked to be neat.

THE OBSTREPEROUS DOG

THE COMMENDABLE CASTIGATION
OF OLD MOTHER HUBBARD

BY *Guy Wetmore Carryl*

She was one of those creatures
　　　Whose features
　　Are hard beyond any reclaim;
And she loved in a hovel
　　　To grovel,
　　And she hadn't a cent to her name.
She owned neither gallants
　　　Nor talents;
　　She borrowed extensively, too,
From all of her dozens
　　　Of cousins,
　　And never refunded a *sou*:
Yet all they said in abuse of her
Was: "She is prouder than Lucifer!"
　　　(That, I must say, without meaning to blame,
　　Is always the way with that kind of a dame!)

There never was jolli-
　　　Er colley
　　Than Old Mother Hubbard had found,

Though cheaply she bought him,
        She'd taught him
    To follow her meekly around:
But though she would lick him
        And kick him,
    It never had any effect;
He always was howling
        And growling
    But goodness! What could you expect?
Colleys were never to flourish meant
'Less they had plenty of nourishment,
    All that he had were the feathers she'd pluck
    Off an occasional chicken or duck.

The colley was barred in
        The garden,
    He howled and he wailed and he whined.
The neighbors indignant,
        Malignant
    Petitions unanimously signed.
"The nuisance grows nightly,"
        Politely
    They wrote. "It's an odious hound,
And either you'll fill him,
        Or kill him,
    Or else he must go to the pound.
For if this howling infernally
Is to continue nocturnally—
    Pardon us, ma'am, if we seem to be curt—
    Somebody's apt to get horribly hurt!"

Mother Hubbard cried loudly
        And proudly:
    "Lands sakes! but you give yourselves airs!
I'll take the law to you
        And sue you."
    The neighbors responded: "Who cares?
We none of us care if
        The sheriff
    Lock every man jack of us up;

We won't be repining
    At fining
    So long as we're rid of the pup!"
Then they proceeded to mount a sign,
Bearing this ominous countersign:
    "FREEMEN! THE MOMENT HAS COME TO PROTEST
    AND OLD MOTHER HUBBARD DELENDUM EST!"

They marched to her gateway,
    And straightway
    They trampled all over her lawn;
Most rudely they harried
    And carried
    Her round on a rail until dawn.
They marred her, and jarred her,
    And tarred her
    And feathered her, just as they should,
Of speech they bereft her,
    And left her
With: "*Now* do you think you'll be good!"

THE MORAL'S a charmingly pleasing one.
While we would deprecate teasing one,
Still, when a dame has politeness rebuffed,
She certainly ought to be collared and cuffed.

THE JEALOUS DOG

FLUSH IN LOVE

BY *Virginia Woolf*

THE SUMMER OF 1842 WAS, historians tell us, not much
different from other summers, yet to Flush it was so different that he must have doubted if the world itself were the
same. It was a summer spent in a bedroom; a summer spent

with Miss Barrett. It was a summer spent in London, spent in the heart of civilisation. At first he saw nothing but the bedroom and its furniture, but that alone was surprising enough. To identify, distinguish and call by their right names all the different articles he saw there was confusing enough. And he had scarcely accustomed himself to the tables, to the busts, to the washing-stands—the smell of eau de cologne still lacerated his nostrils, when there came one of those rare days which are fine but not windy, warm but not baking, dry but not dusty, when an invalid can take the air. The day came when Miss Barrett could safely risk the huge adventure of going shopping with her sister.

The carriage was ordered; Miss Barrett rose from her sofa; veiled and muffled, she descended the stairs. Flush of course went with her. He leapt into the carriage by her side. Couched on her lap, the whole pomp of London at its most splendid burst on his astonished eyes. They drove along Oxford Street. He saw houses made almost entirely of glass. He saw windows laced across with glittering streamers; heaped with gleaming mounds of pink, purple, yellow, rose. The carriage stopped. He entered mysterious arcades filmed with clouds and webs of tinted gauze. A million airs from China, from Arabia, wafted their frail incense into the remotest fibres of his senses. Swiftly over the counters flashed yards of gleaming silk; more darkly, more slowly rolled the ponderous bombazine. Scissors snipped; coins sparkled. Paper was folded; string tied. What with nodding plumes, waving streamers, tossing horses, yellow liveries, passing faces, leaping, dancing up, down, Flush, satiated with the multiplicity of his sensations, slept, drowsed, dreamt and knew no more until he was lifted out of the carriage and the door of Wimpole Street shut on him again.

And next day, as the fine weather continued, Miss Barrett ventured upon an even more daring exploit—she had herself drawn up Wimpole Street in a bath-chair. Again Flush went with her. For the first time he heard his nails click upon the hard paving-stones of London. For the first time the whole battery of a London street on a hot summer's day assaulted his nostrils. He smelt the swooning smells that lie in the gutters; the bitter smells that corrode iron railings; the fuming, heady smells that rise from basements—smells more complex, cor-

rupt, violently contrasted and compounded than any he had
smelt in the fields near Reading; smells that lay far beyond
the range of the human nose; so that while the chair went on,
he stopped, amazed; smelling, savouring, until a jerk at his
collar dragged him on. And also, as he trotted up Wimpole
Street behind Miss Barrett's chair he was dazed by the passage
of human bodies. Petticoats swished at his head; trousers
brushed his flanks; sometimes a wheel whizzed an inch from his
nose; the wind of destruction roared in his ears and fanned
the feathers of his paws as a van passed. Then he plunged in
terror. Mercifully the chain tugged at his collar; Miss Barrett
held him tight, or he would have rushed to destruction.

At last, with every nerve throbbing and every sense singing,
he reached Regent's Park. And then when he saw once more,
after years of absence it seemed, grass, flowers and trees, the
old hunting cry of the fields hallooed in his ears and he dashed
forward to run as he had run in the fields at home. But now a
heavy weight jerked at his throat; he was thrown back on his
haunches. Were there not trees and grass? he asked. Were
these not the signals of freedom? Had he not always leapt forward directly Miss Mitford started on her walk? Why was he
a prisoner here? He paused. Here, he observed, the flowers
were massed far more thickly than at home; they stood, plant
by plant, rigidly in narrow plots. The plots were intersected by
hard black paths. Men in shiny top-hats marched ominously
up and down the paths. At the sight of them he shuddered closer
to the chair. He gladly accepted the protection of the chain.
Thus before many of these walks were over a new conception
had entered his brain. Setting one thing beside another, he had
arrived at a conclusion. Where there are flower-beds there are
asphalt paths; where there are flower-beds and asphalt paths,
there are men in shiny top-hats; where there are flower-beds
and asphalt paths and men in shiny top-hats, dogs must be led
on chains. Without being able to decipher a word of the
placard at the Gate, he had learnt his lesson—in Regent's
Park dogs must be led on chains.

And to this nucleus of knowledge, born from the strange
experiences of the summer of 1842, soon adhered another:
dogs are not equal, but different. At Three Mile Cross, Flush
had mixed impartially with taproom dogs and the Squire's

greyhounds; he had known no difference between the tinker's dog and himself. Indeed it is probable that the mother of his child, though by courtesy called Spaniel, was nothing but a mongrel, eared in one way, tailed in another. But the dogs of London, Flush soon discovered, are strictly divided into different classes. Some are chained dogs; some run wild. Some take their airings in carriages and drink from purple jars; others are unkempt and uncollared and pick up a living in the gutter. Dogs therefore, Flush began to suspect, differ; some are high, others low; and his suspicions were confirmed by snatches of talk held in passing with the dogs of Wimpole Street. "See that scallywag? A mere mongrel! . . . By gad, that's a fine Spaniel. One of the best blood in Britain! . . . Pity his ears aren't a shade more curly. . . . There's a topknot for you!"

From such phrases, from the accent of praise or derision in which they were spoken, at the pillar-box or outside the public-house where the footmen were exchanging racing tips, Flush knew before the summer had passed that there is no equality among dogs: there are high dogs and low dogs. Which, then, was he? No sooner had Flush got home than he examined himself carefully in the looking-glass. Heaven be praised, he was a dog of birth and breeding! His head was smooth; his eyes were prominent but not gozzled; his feet were feathered; he was the equal of the best-bred cocker in Wimpole Street. He noted with approval the purple jar from which he drank—such are the privileges of rank; he bent his head quietly to have the chain fixed to his collar—such are its penalties. When about this time Miss Barrett observed him staring in the glass, she was mistaken. He was a philosopher, she thought, meditating the difference between appearance and reality. On the contrary, he was an aristocrat considering his points.

But the fine summer days were soon over; the autumn winds began to blow; and Miss Barrett settled down to a life of complete seclusion in her bedroom. Flush's life was also changed. His outdoor education was supplemented by that of the bedroom, and this, to a dog of Flush's temperament, was the most drastic that could have been invented. His only airings, and these were brief and perfunctory, were taken in the company of Wilson, Miss Barrett's maid. For the rest of the day he kept his station on the sofa at Miss Barrett's feet. All his natural instincts were thwarted and contradicted. When the autumn winds had blown last year in Berkshire he had run in wild scampering across the stubble; now at the sound of the ivy tapping on the pane Miss Barrett asked Wilson to see to the fastenings of the window. When the leaves of the scarlet runners and nasturtiums in the window-box yellowed and fell she drew her Indian shawl more closely round her. When the October rain lashed the window Wilson lit the fire and heaped up the coals. Autumn deepened into winter and the first fogs jaundiced the air. Wilson and Flush could scarcely grope their way to the pillar-box or to the chemist. When they came back, nothing could be seen in the room but the pale busts glimmering wanly on the tops of the wardrobes; the peasants and the castle had vanished on the blind; blank yellow filled the pane. Flush felt that he and Miss Barrett lived alone together in a cushioned and fire-lit cave. The traffic droned on perpetually outside with muffled reverberations; now and again a voice went calling hoarsely, "Old chairs and baskets to mend," down the street: sometimes there was a jangle of organ music, coming nearer and louder; going further and fading away. But none of these sounds meant freedom, or action, or exercise. The wind and the rain, the wild days of autumn and the cold days of midwinter, all alike meant nothing to Flush except warmth and stillness; the lighting of lamps, the drawing of curtains and the poking of the fire.

At first the strain was too great to be borne. He could not help dancing round the room on a windy autumn day when the partridges must be scattering over the stubble. He thought he heard guns on the breeze. He could not help running to the door with his hackles raised when a dog barked outside. And yet when Miss Barrett called him back, when she laid her hand on his collar, he could not deny that another feeling, urgent, contradictory, disagreeable—he did not know what to call it or why he obeyed it—restrained him. He lay still at her feet. To resign, to control, to suppress the most violent instincts of his nature—that was the prime lesson of the bedroom school, and it was one of such portentous difficulty that many scholars have learnt Greek with less—many battles have been won that cost their generals not half such pain. But then, Miss Barrett was the teacher. Between them, Flush felt more and more strongly, as the weeks wore on, was a bond, an uncomfortable yet thrilling tightness; so that if his pleasure was her pain, then his pleasure was pleasure no longer but three parts pain. The truth of this was proved every day. Somebody opened the door and whistled him to come. Why should he not go out? He longed for air and exercise; his limbs were cramped with lying on the sofa. He had never grown altogether used to the smell of eau de cologne. But no—though the door stood open, he would not leave Miss Barrett. He hesitated halfway to the door and then went back to the sofa. "Flushie," wrote Miss Barrett, "is my friend—my companion—and loves me better than he loves the sunshine without." She could not go out. She was chained to the sofa. "A bird in a cage would have as good a story," she wrote, as she had. And Flush, to whom the whole world was free, chose to forfeit all the smells of Wimpole Street in order to lie by her side.

And yet sometimes the tie would almost break; there were vast gaps in their understanding. Sometimes they would lie and stare at each other in blank bewilderment. Why, Miss Barrett wondered, did Flush tremble suddenly, and whimper and start and listen? She could hear nothing; she could see nothing; there was nobody in the room with them. She could not guess that Folly, her sister's little King Charles, had passed the door; or that Catiline, the Cuba bloodhound, had been given a mutton-bone by a footman in the basement. But Flush knew; he heard; he was ravaged by the alternate rages of lust and greed. Then with all her poet's imagination Miss Barrett could not divine what Wilson's wet umbrella meant to Flush; what memories it recalled, of forests and parrots and wild trumpeting elephants; nor did she know, when Mr. Kenyon stumbled over the bell-pull, that Flush heard dark men cursing in the mountains; the cry, "Span! Span!" rang in his ears, and it was in some muffled, ancestral rage that he bit him.

Flush was equally at a loss to account for Miss Barrett's emotions. There she would lie hour after hour passing her hand over a white page with a black stick; and her eyes would suddenly fill with tears; but why? "Ah, my dear Mr. Horne," she was writing. "And then came the failure in my health . . . and then the enforced exile to Torquay . . . which gave a nightmare to my life for ever, and robbed it of more than I can speak of

here; do not speak of that anywhere. *Do not speak of that,* dear
Mr. Horne." But there was no sound in the room, no smell to
make Miss Barrett cry. Then again Miss Barrett, still agitating
her stick, burst out laughing. She had drawn "a very neat and
characteristic portrait of Flush, humorously made rather like
myself," and she had written under it that it "only fails of
being an excellent substitute for mine through being more
worthy than I can be counted." What was there to laugh at in
the black smudge that she held out for Flush to look at? He
could smell nothing; he could hear nothing. There was nobody
in the room with them. The fact was that they could not communicate with words, and it was a fact that led undoubtedly
to much misunderstanding. Yet did it not lead also to a peculiar
intimacy? "Writing,"—Miss Barrett once exclaimed after a
morning's toil, "writing, writing . . ." After all, she may have
thought, do words say everything? Can words say anything?
Do not words destroy the symbol that lies beyond the reach of
words? Once at least Miss Barrett seems to have found it so.
She was lying, thinking; she had forgotten Flush altogether,
and her thoughts were so sad that the tears fell upon the pillow.
Then suddenly a hairy head was pressed against her; large
bright eyes shone in hers; and she started. Was it Flush, or
was it Pan? Was she no longer an invalid in Wimpole Street,
but a Greek nymph in some dim grove in Arcady? And did the
bearded god himself press his lips to hers? For a moment she
was transformed; she was a nymph and Flush was Pan. The
sun burnt and love blazed. But suppose Flush had been able
to speak—would he not have said something sensible about the
potato disease in Ireland?

So, too, Flush felt strange stirrings at work within him.
When he saw Miss Barrett's thin hands delicately lifting some
silver box or pearl ornament from the ringed table, his own
furry paws seemed to contract and he longed that they should
fine themselves to ten separate fingers. When he heard her low
voice syllabling innumerable sounds, he longed for the day
when his own rough roar would issue like hers in the little
simple sounds that had such mysterious meaning. And when
he watched the same fingers for ever crossing a white page with
a straight stick, he longed for the time when he too should
blacken paper as she did.

And yet, had he been able to write as she did?—The question is superfluous happily, for truth compels us to say that in
the year 1842-43 Miss Barrett was not a nymph but an invalid;
Flush was not a poet but a red cocker spaniel; and Wimpole
Street was not Arcady but Wimpole Street.

So the long hours went by in the back bedroom with nothing
to mark them but the sound of steps passing on the stairs; and
the distant sound of the front door shutting, and the sound of
a broom tapping, and the sound of the postman knocking. In
the room coals clicked; the lights and shadows shifted themselves over the brows of the five pale busts, over the bookcase
and its red merino. But sometimes the step on the stair did not
pass the door; it stopped outside. The handle was seen to
spin round; the door actually opened; somebody came in.
Then how strangely the furniture changed its look! What extraordinary eddies of sound and smell were at once set in
circulation! How they washed round the legs of tables and
impinged on the sharp edges of the wardrobe! Probably it was
Wilson, with a tray of food or a glass of medicine; or it might
be one of Miss Barrett's two sisters—Arabel or Henrietta; or
it might be one of Miss Barrett's seven brothers—Charles,
Samuel, George, Henry, Alfred, Septimus or Octavius. But
once or twice a week Flush was aware that something more important was about to happen. The bed would be carefully
disguised as a sofa. The armchair would be drawn up beside
it; Miss Barrett herself would be wrapped becomingly in Indian shawls; the toilet things would be scrupulously hidden
under the busts of Chaucer and Homer; Flush himself would be
combed and brushed. At about two or three in the afternoon
there was a peculiar, distinct and different tap at the door,
Miss Barrett flushed, smiled and stretched out her hand. Then
in would come—perhaps dear Miss Mitford, rosy and shiny
and chattering, with a bunch of geraniums. Or it might be Mr.
Kenyon, a stout, well-groomed elderly gentleman, radiating
benevolence, provided with a book. Or it might be Mrs. Jameson, a lady who was the very opposite of Mr. Kenyon to look
at—a lady with "a very light complexion—pale, lucid, eyes;
thin colourless lips . . . a nose and chin projective without
breadth." Each had his or her own manner, smell, tone and
accent. Miss Mitford burbled and chattered, was flyaway yet

substantial; Mr. Kenyon was urbane and cultured and mumbled slightly because he had lost two front teeth; Mrs. Jameson had lost none of her teeth, and moved as sharply and precisely as she spoke.

Lying couched at Miss Barrett's feet, Flush let the voices ripple over him, hour by hour. On and on they went. Miss Barrett laughed, expostulated, exclaimed, sighed too, and laughed again. At last, greatly to Flush's relief, little silences came—even in the flow of Miss Mitford's conversation. Could it be seven already? She had been there since midday! She must really run to catch her train. Mr. Kenyon shut his book —he had been reading aloud—and stood with his back to the fire; Mrs. Jameson with a sharp, angular movement pressed each finger of her glove sharp down. And Flush was patted by this one and had his ear pulled by another. The routine of leave-taking was intolerably prolonged; but at last Mrs. Jameson, Mr. Kenyon, and even Miss Mitford had risen, had said good-bye, had remembered something, had lost something, had found something, had reached the door, had opened it, and were —Heaven be praised—gone at last.

Miss Barret sank back very white, very tired on her pillows. Flush crept closer to her. Mercifully they were alone again. But the visitor had stayed so long that it was almost dinner-time. Smells began to rise from the basement. Wilson was at the door with Miss Barrett's dinner on a tray. It was set down on the table beside her and the covers lifted. But what with the dressing and the talking, what with the heat of the room and the agitation of the farewells, Miss Barrett was too tired to eat. She gave a little sigh when she saw the plump mutton chop, or the wing of partridge or chicken that had been sent up for her dinner. So long as Wilson was in the room she fiddled about with her knife and fork. But directly the door was shut and they were alone, she made a sign. She held up her fork. A whole chicken's wing was impaled upon it. Flush advanced. Miss Barrett nodded. Very gently, very cleverly, without spilling a crumb, Flush removed the wing; swallowed it down and left no trace behind. Half a rice pudding clotted with thick cream went the same way. Nothing could have been neater, more effective than Flush's co-operation. He was lying couched as usual at Miss Barrett's feet, apparently asleep,

Miss Barrett was lying rested and restored, apparently having made an excellent dinner, when once more a step that was heavier, more deliberate and firmer than any other, stopped on the stair; solemnly a knock sounded that was no tap of enquiry but a demand for admittance; the door opened and in came the blackest, the most formidable of elderly men—Mr. Barrett himself. His eye at once sought the tray. Had the meal been eaten? Had his commands been obeyed? Yes, the plates were empty. Signifying his approval of his daughter's obedience, Mr. Barrett lowered himself heavily into the chair by her side. As that dark body approached him, shivers of terror and horror ran down Flush's spine. So a savage couched in flowers shudders when the thunder growls and he hears the voice of God. Then Wilson whistled; and Flush, slinking guiltily, as if Mr. Barrett could read his thoughts and those thoughts were evil, crept out of the room and rushed downstairs. A force had entered the bedroom which he dreaded; a force that he was powerless to withstand. Once he burst in unexpectedly. Mr. Barrett was on his knees praying by his daughter's side.

.   .   .   .   .

Such an education as this, in the back bedroom at Wimpole Street, would have told upon an ordinary dog. And Flush was not an ordinary dog. He was high-spirited, yet reflective; canine, but highly sensitive to human emotions also. Upon such a dog the atmosphere of the bedroom told with peculiar force. We cannot blame him if his sensibility was cultivated rather to the detriment of his sterner qualities. Naturally, lying with his head pillowed on a Greek lexicon, he came to dislike barking and biting; he came to prefer the silence of the cat to the robustness of the dog; and human sympathy to either. Miss Barrett, too, did her best to refine and educate his powers still further. Once she took a harp from the window and asked him, as she laid it by his side, whether he thought that the harp, which made music, was itself alive? He looked and listened; pondered, it seemed, for a moment in doubt and then decided that it was not. Then she would make him stand with her in front of the looking-glass and ask him why he barked and trembled. Was not the little brown dog opposite himself? But

what is "oneself"? Is it the thing people see? Or is it the thing
one is? So Flush pondered that question too, and, unable to
solve the problem of reality, pressed closer to Miss Barrett
and kissed her "expressively." *That* was real at any rate.

Fresh from such problems, with such emotional dilemmas
agitating his nervous system, he went downstairs, and we cannot be surprised if there was something—a touch of the super-
cilious, of the superior—in his bearing that roused the rage of
Catiline, the savage Cuba bloodhound, so that he set upon him
and bit him and sent him howling upstairs to Miss Barrett for
sympathy. Flush "is no hero," she concluded; but why was he
no hero? Was it not partly on her account? She was too just
not to realize that it was for her that he had sacrificed his
courage, as it was for her that he had sacrificed the sun and
the air. This nervous sensibility had its drawbacks, no doubt
—she was full of apologies when he flew at Mr. Kenyon and
bit him for stumbling over the bell-pull; it was annoying when
he moaned piteously all night because he was not allowed to
sleep on her bed—when he refused to eat unless she fed him;
but she took the blame and bore the inconvenience because,
after all, Flush loved her. He had refused the air and the sun
for her sake. "He is worth loving, is he not?" she asked of
Mr. Horne. And whatever answer Mr. Horne might give, Miss
Barrett was positive of her own. She loved Flush, and Flush
was worthy of her love.

It seemed as if nothing were to break that tie—as if the years
were merely to compact and cement it; and as if those years
were to be all the years of their natural lives. Eighteen-forty-
two turned into eighteen-forty-three; eighteen-forty-three into
eighteen-forty-four; eighteen-forty-four into eighteen-forty-five.
Flush was no longer a puppy; he was a dog of four or five; he
was a dog in the full prime of life—and still Miss Barrett lay
on her sofa in Wimpole Street and still Flush lay on the sofa
at her feet. Miss Barrett's life was the life of "a bird in its
cage." She sometimes kept the house for weeks at a time, and
when she left it, it was only for an hour or two, to drive to a
shop in a carriage, or to be wheeled to Regent's Park in a bath-
chair. The Barretts never left London. Mr. Barrett, the seven
brothers, the two sisters, the butler, Wilson and the maids,
Catiline, Folly, Miss Barrett and Flush all went on living at

50 Wimpole Street, eating in the dining-room, sleeping in the bedrooms, smoking in the study, cooking in the kitchen, carrying hotwater cans and emptying the slops from January to December. The chair-covers became slightly soiled; the carpets slightly worn; coal dust, mud, soot, fog, vapours of cigar smoke and wine and meat accumulated in crevices, in cracks, in fabrics, on the tops of picture-frames, in the scrolls of carvings. And the ivy that hung over Miss Barrett's bedroom window flourished; its green curtain became thicker and thicker, and in summer the nasturtiums and the scarlet runners rioted together in the window-box.

But one night early in January 1845 the postman knocked. Letters fell into the box as usual. Wilson went downstairs to fetch the letters as usual. Everything was as usual—every night the postman knocked, every night Wilson fetched the letters, every night there was a letter for Miss Barrett. But tonight the letter was not the same letter; it was a different letter. Flush saw that, even before the envelope was broken. He knew it from the way that Miss Barrett took it; turned it; looked at the vigorous, jagged writing of her name. He knew it from the indescribable tremor in her fingers, from the impetuosity with which they tore the flap open, from the absorption with which she read. He watched her read. And as she read he heard, as when we are half asleep we hear through the clamour of the street some bell ringing and know that it is addressed to us, alarmingly yet faintly, as if someone far away were trying to rouse us with the warning of fire, or burglary, or some menace against our peace and we start in alarm before we wake—so Flush, as Miss Barrett read the little blotted sheet, heard a bell rousing him from his sleep; warning him of some danger menacing his safety and bidding him sleep no more. Miss Barrett read the letter quickly; she read the letter slowly; she returned it carefully to its envelope. She too slept no more.

Again, a few nights later, there was the same letter on Wilson's tray. Again it was read quickly, read slowly, read over and over again. Then it was put away carefully, not in the drawer with the voluminous sheets of Miss Mitford's letters, but by itself. Now Flush paid the full price of long years of accumulated sensibility lying couched on cushions at Miss Barrett's feet. He could read signs that nobody else could even see.

He could tell by the touch of Miss Barrett's fingers that she was waiting for one thing only—for the postman's knock, for the letter on the tray. She would be stroking him perhaps with a light, regular movement; suddenly—there was the rap—her fingers constricted; he would be held in a vice while Wilson came upstairs. Then she took the letter and he was loosed and forgotten.

Yet, he argued, what was there to be afraid of, so long as there was no change in Miss Barrett's life? And there was no change. No new visitors came. Mr. Kenyon came as usual; Miss Mitford came as usual. The brothers and sisters came; and in the evening Mr. Barrett came. They noticed nothing; they suspected nothing. So he would quieten himself and try to believe, when a few nights passed without the envelope, that the enemy had gone. A man in a cloak, he imagined, a cowled and hooded figure, had passed, like a burglar, rattling the door, and finding it guarded, had slunk away defeated. The danger, Flush tried to make himself believe, was over. The man had gone. And then the letter came again.

As the envelopes came more and more regularly, night after night, Flush began to notice signs of change in Miss Barrett herself. For the first time in Flush's experience she was irritable and restless. She could not read and she could not write. She stood at the window and looked out. She questioned Wilson anxiously about the weather—was the wind still in the east? Was there any sign of spring in the Park yet? Oh no, Wilson replied; the wind was a cruel east wind still. And Miss Barrett, Flush felt, was at once relieved and annoyed. She coughed. She complained of feeling ill—but not so ill as she usually felt when the wind was in the east. And then, when she was alone, she read over again last night's letter. It was the longest she had yet had. There were many pages, closely covered, darkly blotted, scattered with strange little abrupt hieroglyphics. So much Flush could see, from his station at her feet. But he could make no sense of the words that Miss Barrett was murmuring to herself. Only he could trace her agitation when she came to the end of the page and read aloud (though unintelligibly), "Do you think I shall see you in two months, three months?"

Then she took up her pen and passed it rapidly and nervously over sheet after sheet. But what did they mean—the little words that Miss Barrett wrote? "April is coming. There will be both a May and a June if we live to see such things, and perhaps, after all, we may . . . I will indeed see you when the warm weather has revived me a little. . . . But I shall be afraid of you at first—though I am not, in writing thus. You are Paracelsus, and I am a recluse, with nerves that have been broken on the rack, and now hang loosely, quivering at a step and breath."

Flush could not read what she was writing an inch or two above his head. But he knew just as well as if he could read every word, how strangely his mistress was agitated as she wrote; what contrary desires shook her—that April might come; that April might not come; that she might see this unknown man at once, that she might never see him at all. Flush, too, quivered as she did at a step, at a breath. And remorselessly the days went on. The wind blew out the blind. The sun whitened the busts. A bird sang in the mews. Men went crying fresh flowers to sell down Wimpole Street. All these sounds meant, he knew, that April was coming and May and June—nothing could stop the approach of that dreadful spring. For what was coming with the spring? Some terror—some horror—something that Miss Barrett dreaded, and that Flush dreaded too. He started now at the sound of a step. But it was only Henrietta. Then there was a knock. It was only Mr. Kenyon. So April passed; and the first twenty days of May. And then, on the 21st of May, Flush knew that the day itself had come. For on Tuesday, the 21st of May, Miss Barrett looked searchingly in the glass; arrayed herself exquisitely in her Indian shawls; bade Wilson draw the armchair close, but not too close; touched this, that and the other; and then sat upright among her pillows. Flush couched himself taut at her feet. They waited, alone together. At last, Marylebone Church clock struck two; they waited. Then Marylebone Church clock struck a single stroke—it was half-past two; and as the single stroke died away, a rap sounded boldly on the front door. Miss Barrett turned pale; she lay very still. Flush lay still too. Upstairs came the dreaded, the inexorable footfall; upstairs, Flush knew, came the cowled and sinister figure of midnight—the hooded man. Now his hand was on the door. The handle spun. There he stood.

"Mr. Browning," said Wilson.

Flush, watching Miss Barrett, saw the colour rush into her face; saw her eyes brighten and her lips open.

"Mr. Browning!" she exclaimed.

Twisting his yellow gloves in his hands, blinking his eyes, well groomed, masterly, abrupt, Mr. Browning strode across the room. He seized Miss Barrett's hand, and sank into the chair by the sofa at her side. Instantly they began to talk.

What was horrible to Flush, as they talked, was his loneliness. Once he had felt that he and Miss Barrett were together, in a firelit cave. Now the cave was no longer firelit; it was dark and damp; Miss Barrett was outside. He looked round him. Everything had changed. The bookcase, the five busts—they were no longer friendly deities presiding approvingly—they were alien, severe. He shifted his position at Miss Barrett's feet. She took no notice. He whined. They did not hear him. At last he lay still in tense and silent agony. The talk went on; but it did not flow and ripple as talk usually flowed and rippled. It leapt and jerked. It stopped and leapt again. Flush had never heard that sound in Miss Barrett's voice before— that vigour, that excitement. Her cheeks were bright as he had never seen them bright; her great eyes blazed as he had never seen them blaze. The clock struck four; and still they talked. Then it struck half-past four. At that Mr. Browning jumped up. A horrid decision, a dreadful boldness marked every movement. In another moment he had wrung Miss Barrett's hand in his; he had taken his hat and gloves; he had said good-bye. They heard him running down the stairs. Smartly the door banged beind him. He was gone.

But Miss Barrett did not sink back in her pillows as she sank back when Mr. Kenyon or Miss Mitford left her. Now she still sat upright; her eyes still burnt; her cheeks still glowed; she seemed still to feel that Mr. Browning was with her. Flush touched her. She recalled him with a start. She patted him lightly, joyfully, on the head. And smiling, she gave him the oddest look—as if she wished that he could talk—as if she expected him too to feel what she felt. And then she laughed, pityingly; as if it were absurd—Flush, poor Flush could feel nothing of what she felt. He could know nothing of what she knew. Never had such wastes of dismal distance separated them. He lay there ignored; he might not have been there, he felt. She no longer remembered his existence.

And that night she ate her chicken to the bone. Not a scrap of potato or of skin was thrown to Flush. When Mr. Barrett came as usual, Flush marvelled at his obtuseness. He sat himself down in the very chair that the man had sat in. His head pressed the same cushions that the man's had pressed, and yet he noticed nothing. "Don't you know," Flush marvelled, "who's been sitting in that chair? Can't you smell him?" For to Flush the whole room still reeked of Mr. Browning's presence. The air dashed past the bookcase, and eddied and curled round the heads of the five pale busts. But the heavy man sat by his daughter in entire self-absorption. He noticed nothing. He suspected nothing. Aghast at his obtuseness, Flush slipped past him out of the room.

But in spite of their astonishing blindness, even Miss Barrett's family began to notice, as the weeks passed, a change in Miss Barrett. She left her room and went down to sit in the drawing-room. Then she did what she had not done for many a long day—she actually walked on her own feet as far as the gate at Devonshire Place with her sister. Her friends, her family, were amazed at her improvement. But only Flush knew where her strength came from—it came from the dark man in the armchair. He came again and again and again. First it was once a week; then it was twice a week. He came always in the afternoon and left in the afternoon. Miss Barrett always saw him alone. And on the days when he did not come, his letters came. And when he himself was gone, his flowers were there. And in the mornings when she was alone, Miss Barrett wrote to him. That dark, taut, abrupt, vigorous man with his black hair, his red cheeks and his yellow gloves, was everywhere. Naturally, Miss Barrett was better; of course she could walk. Flush himself felt that it was impossible to lie still. Old longings revived; a new restlessness possessed him. Even his sleep was full of dreams. He dreamt as he had not dreamt since the old days at Three Mile Cross—of hares starting from the long grass; of pheasants rocketing up with long tails streaming, of partridges rising with a whirr from the stubble. He dreamt that he was hunting, that he was chasing some spotted spaniel, who fled, who escaped him. He was in Spain; he was in Wales; he was in Berkshire; he was flying before park-keepers' truncheons in Regent's Park. Then he opened his eyes. There were no hares, and no partridges; no whips cracking and no black men crying

"Span! Span!" There was only Mr. Browning in the armchair talking to Miss Barrett on the sofa.

Sleep became impossible while that man was there. Flush lay with his eyes wide open, listening. Though he could make no sense of the little words that hurtled over his head from two-thirty to four-thirty sometimes three times a week, he could detect with terrible accuracy that the tone of the words was changing. Miss Barrett's voice had been forced and unnaturally lively at first. Now it had gained a warmth and an ease that he had never heard in it before. And every time the man came, some new sound came into their voices—now they made a grotesque chattering; now they skimmed over him like birds flying widely; now they cooed and clucked, as if they were two birds settled in a nest; and then Miss Barrett's voice, rising again, went soaring and circling in the air; and then Mr. Browning's voice barked out its sharp, harsh clapper of laughter; and then there was only a murmur, a quiet humming sound as the two voices joined together. But as the summer turned to autumn Flush noted, with horrid apprehension, another note. There was a new urgency, a new pressure and energy in the man's voice, at which Miss Barrett, Flush felt, took fright. Her voice fluttered; hesitated; seemed to falter and fade and plead and gasp as if she were begging for a rest, for a pause, as if she were afraid. Then the man was silent.

Of him they took but little notice. He might have been a log of wood lying there at Miss Barrett's feet for all the attention Mr. Browning paid him. Sometimes he scrubbed his head in a brisk, spasmodic way, energetically, without sentiment, as he passed him. Whatever that scrub might mean, Flush felt nothing but an intense dislike for Mr. Browning. The very sight of him, so well tailored, so tight, so muscular, screwing his yellow gloves in his hand, set his teeth on edge. Oh! to let them meet sharply, completely in the stuff of his trousers! And yet he dared not. Taking it all in all, that winter—1845-6—was the most distressing that Flush had ever known.

The winter passed; and spring came round again. Flush could see no end to the affair; and yet just as a river, though it reflects still trees and grazing cows and rooks returning to the tree-tops, moves inevitably to a waterfall, so those days, Flush knew, were moving to catastrophe. Rumours of change hovered in the air. Sometimes he thought that some vast exodus impended. There was that indefinable stir in the house which precedes—could it be possible?—a journey. Boxes were actually dusted, were, incredible as it might seem, opened. Then they were shut again. No, it was not the family that was going to move. The brothers and sisters still went in and out as usual. Mr. Barrett paid his nightly visit, after the man had gone, at his accustomed hour. What was it, then, that was going to happen? For as the summer of 1846 wore on, Flush was positive that a change was coming. He could hear it again in the altered sound of the eternal voices. Miss Barrett's voice, that had been pleading and afraid, lost its faltering note. It rang out with a determination and a boldness that Flush had never heard in it before. If only Mr. Barrett could hear the tone in which she welcomed this usurper, the laugh with which she greeted him, the exclamation with which he took her hand in his! But nobody was in the room with them except Flush. To him the change was of the most galling nature. It was not merely that Miss Barrett was changing towards Mr. Browning—she was changing in every relation—in her feeling towards Flush himself. She treated his advances more brusquely; she cut short his endearments laughingly; she made him feel that there was something petty, silly, affected, in his old affectionate ways. His vanity was exacerbated. His jealousy was inflamed. At last, when July came, he determined to make one violent attempt to regain her favour, and perhaps to oust the newcomer. How to accomplish this double purpose he did not know, and could not plan. But suddenly on the 8th of July his feelings overcame him. He flung himself on Mr. Browning and bit him savagely. At last his teeth met in the immaculate cloth of Mr. Browning's trousers! But the limb inside was hard as iron—Mr. Kenyon's leg had been butter in comparison. Mr. Browning brushed him off with a flick of his hand and went on talking. Neither he nor Miss Barrett seemed to think the attack worthy of attention. Completely foiled, worsted, without a shaft left in his sheath, Flush sank back on his cushions panting with rage and disappointment. But he had misjudged Miss Barrett's insight. When Mr. Browning was gone, she called him to her and inflicted upon him the worst punishment he had ever known. First she slapped his ears—that was nothing; oddly enough the slap was rather to his liking;

he would have welcomed another. But then she said in her sober, certain tones that she would never love him again. That shaft went to his heart. All these years they had lived together, shared everything together, and now, for one moment's failure, she would never love him again. Then, as if to make her dismissal complete, she took the flowers that Mr. Browning had brought her and began to put them in water in a vase. It was an act, Flush thought, of calculated and deliberate malice; an act designed to make him feel his own insignificance completely. "This rose is from him," she seemed to say, "and this carnation. Let the red shine by the yellow; and the yellow by the red. And let the green leaf lie there—" And, setting one flower with another, she stood back to gaze at them as if he were before her—the man in the yellow gloves—a mass of brilliant flowers. But even so, even as she pressed the leaves and flowers together, she could not altogether ignore the fixity with which Flush gazed at her. She could not deny that "expression of quite despair on his face." She could not but relent. "At last I said, 'If you are good, Flush, you may come and say that you are sorry,' on which he dashed across the room and, trembling all over, kissed first one of my hands and then another, and put up his paws to be shaken, and looked into my face with such beseeching eyes that you would certainly have forgiven him just as I did." That was her account of the matter to Mr. Browning; and he of course replied: "Oh, poor Flush, do you think I do not love and respect him for his jealous supervision—his slowness to know another, having once known you?" It was easy enough for Mr. Browning to be magnanimous, but that easy magnanimity was perhaps the sharpest thorn that pressed into Flush's side.

Another incident a few days later showed how widely they were separated, who had been so close, how little Flush could now count on Miss Barrett for sympathy. After Mr. Browning had gone one afternoon Miss Barrett decided to drive to Regent's Park with her sister. As they got out at the Park gate the door of the four-wheeler shut on Flush's paw. He "cried piteously" and held it up to Miss Barrett for sympathy. In other days sympathy in abundance would have been lavished upon him for less. But now a detached, a mocking, a critical expression came into her eyes. She laughed at him. She thought he was shamming: ". . . no sooner had he touched the grass than he began to run without a thought of it," she wrote. And she commented sarcastically, "Flush always makes the most of his misfortunes—he is of the Byronic school—*il se pose en victime.*" But here Miss Barrett, absorbed in her own emotions, misjudged him completely. If his paw had been broken, still he would have bounded. That dash was his answer to her mockery; I have done with you—that was the meaning he flashed at her as he ran. The flowers smelt bitter to him; the grass burnt his paws; the dust filled his nostrils with disillusion. But he raced —he scampered. "Dogs must be led on chains"—there was the usual placard; there were the park-keepers with their top-hats and their truncheons to enforce it. But "must" no longer had any meaning for him. The chain of love was broken. He would run where he liked; chase partridges; chase spaniels; splash into the middle of dahlia beds; break brilliant, glowing red and yellow roses. Let the park-keepers throw their truncheons if they chose. Let them dash his brains out. Let him fall dead, disembowelled, at Miss Barrett's feet. He cared nothing. But naturally nothing of the kind happened. Nobody pursued him; nobody noticed him. The solitary park-keeper was talking to a nursemaid. At last he returned to Miss Barrett and she absent-mindedly slipped the chain over his neck, and led him home.

After two such humiliations the spirit of an ordinary dog, the spirit even of an ordinary human being, might well have been broken. But Flush, for all his softness and silkiness, had eyes that blazed; had passions that leapt not merely in bright flame but sunk and smouldered. He resolved to meet his enemy face to face and alone. No third person should interrupt this final conflict. It should be fought out by the principals themselves. On the afternoon of Tuesday, the 21st of July, therefore, he slipped downstairs and waited in the hall. He had not long to wait. Soon he heard the tramp of the familiar footstep in the street; he heard the familiar rap on the door. Mr. Browning was admitted. Vaguely aware of the impending attack and determined to meet it in the most conciliatory of spirits, Mr. Browning had come provided with a parcel of cakes. There was Flush waiting in the hall. Mr. Browning made, evidently, some well-meant attempt to caress him; perhaps he even went so far as to offer him a cake. The gesture was enough. Flush sprang

upon his enemy with unparalleled violence. His teeth once
more met in Mr. Browning's trousers. But unfortunately in the
excitement of the moment he forgot what was most essential—
silence. He barked; he flung himself on Mr. Browning, barking
loudly. The sound was sufficient to alarm the household. Wilson
rushed downstairs. Wilson beat him soundly. Wilson over-
powered him completely. Wilson led him in ignominy away.
Ignominy it was—to have attacked Mr. Browning, to have been
beaten by Wilson. Mr. Browning had not lifted a finger. Taking
his cakes with him, Mr. Browning proceeded unhurt, unmoved,
in perfect composure, upstairs, alone to the bedroom. Flush
was led away.

After two and a half hours of miserable confinement with
parrots and beetles, ferns and saucepans, in the kitchen, Flush
was summoned to Miss Barrett's presence. She was lying on
the sofa with her sister Arabella beside her. Conscious of the
rightness of his cause, Flush went straight to her. But she
refused to look at him. He turned to Arabella. She merely said,
"Naughty Flush, go away." Wilson was there—the formidable,
the implacable Wilson. It was to her that Miss Barrett turned
for information. She had beaten him, Wilson said, "because it
was right." And, she added, she had only beaten him with her
hand. It was upon her evidence that Flush was convicted. The
attack, Miss Barrett assumed, had been unprovoked; she credited Mr. Browning with all virtue, with all generosity; Flush
had been beaten off by a servant, without a whip, because "it
was right." There was no more to be said. Miss Barrett decided
against him. "So he lay down on the floor at my feet," she
wrote, "looking from under his eyebrows at me." But though
Flush might look, Miss Barrett refused even to meet his eyes.
There she lay on the sofa; there Flush lay on the floor.

And as he lay there, exiled, on the carpet, he went through
one of those whirlpools of tumultuous emotion in which the
soul is either dashed upon the rocks and splintered or, finding
some tuft of foothold, slowly and painfully pulls itself up,
regains dry land, and at last emerges on top of a ruined uni-
verse to survey a world created afresh on a different plan.
Which was it to be—destruction or reconstruction? That was
the question. The outlines only of his dilemma can be traced
here; for his debate was silent. Twice Flush had done his utmost

to kill his enemy; twice he had failed. And why had he failed,
he asked himself? Because he loved Miss Barrett. Looking up
at her from under his eyebrows as she lay, severe and silent on
the sofa, he knew that he must love her for ever. But things are
not simple but complex. If he bit Mr. Browning he bit her too.
Hatred is not hatred; hatred is also love. Here Flush shook his
ears in an agony of perplexity. He turned uneasily on the floor.
Mr. Browning was Miss Barrett—Miss Barrett was Mr. Browning; love is hatred and hatred is love. He stretched himself,
whined and raised his head from the floor. The clock struck
eight. For three hours and more he had been lying there, tossed
from the horn of one dilemma to another.

Even Miss Barrett, severe, cold, implacable as she was, laid
down her pen. "Wicked Flush!" she had been writing to Mr.
Browning, ". . . if people like Flush, choose to behave like
dogs savagely they must take the consequences indeed, as dogs
usually do! And *you*, so good and gentle to him! Anyone but
you, would have said 'hasty words' at least." Really it would
be a good plan, she thought, to buy a muzzle. And then she
looked up and saw Flush. Something unusual in his look must
have struck her. She paused. She laid down her pen. Once he
had roused her with a kiss, and she had thought that he was
Pan. He had eaten chicken and rice pudding soaked in cream.
He had given up the sunshine for her sake. She called him to
her and said she forgave him.

But to be forgiven, as if for a passing whim, to be taken back
again on to the sofa as if he had learnt nothing in his anguish
on the floor, as if he were the same dog when in fact he differed
totally, was impossible. For the moment, exhausted as he was,
Flush submitted. A few days later, however, a remarkable scene
took place between him and Miss Barrett which showed the
depths of his emotions. Mr. Browning had been and gone; Flush
was alone with Miss Barrett. Normally he would have leapt on
to the sofa at her feet. But now, instead of jumping up as usual
and claiming her caress, Flush went to what was now called
"Mr. Browning's armchair." Usually the chair was abhorrent
to him; it still held the shape of his enemy. But now, such was
the battle he had won, such was the charity that suffused him,
that he not only looked at the chair but, as he looked, "suddenly
fell into a rapture." Miss Barrett, watching him ·intently,

observed this extraordinary portent. Next she saw him turn
his eyes towards a table. On that table still lay the packet of
Mr. Browning's cakes. He "reminded me that the cakes you
left were on the table." They were now old cakes, stale cakes,
cakes bereft of any carnal seduction. Flush's meaning was plain.
He had refused to eat the cakes when they were fresh, because
they were offered by an enemy. He would eat them now that
they were stale, because they were offered by an enemy turned
to friend, because they were symbols of hatred turned to love.
Yes, he signified, he would eat them now. So Miss Barrett rose
and took the cakes in her hand. And as she gave them to him
she admonished him, "So I explained to him that *you* had
brought them for him, and that he ought to be properly ashamed
therefore for his past wickedness, and make up his mind to love
you and not bite you for the future—and he was allowed to
profit from your goodness to him." As he swallowed down the
faded flakes of that distasteful pastry—it was mouldy, it was
flyblown, it was sour—Flush solemnly repeated, in his own
language, the words she had used—he swore to love Mr. Browning and not bite him for the future.

He was instantly rewarded—not by stale cakes, not by
chicken's wings, not by the caresses that were now his, nor by
the permission to lie once more on the sofa at Miss Barrett's
feet. He was rewarded, spiritually; yet the effects were curiously
physical. Like an iron bar corroding and festering and killing
all natural life beneath it, hatred had lain all these months
across his soul. Now, by the cutting of sharp knives and painful
surgery, the iron had been excised. Now the blood ran once
more; the nerves shot and tingled; flesh formed; Nature re-
joiced, as in spring. Flush heard the birds sing again; he felt
the leaves growing on the trees; as he lay on the sofa at Miss
Barrett's feet, glory and delight coursed through his veins. He
was with them, not against them, now; their hopes, their wishes,
their desires were his. Flush could have barked in sympathy
with Mr. Browning now. The short, sharp words raised the
hackles on his neck. "I need a week of Tuesdays," Mr. Browning
cried, "then a month—a year—a life!" I, Flush echoed him,
need a month—a year—a life! I need all the things that you
both need. We are all three conspirators in the most glorious
of causes. We are joined in sympathy. We are joined in hatred.

We are joined in defiance of black and beetling tyranny. We are joined in love.

THE DEFERENT DOG

TO FLUSH, MY DOG

BY *Elizabeth Barrett Browning*

Loving friend, the gift of one
Who her own true faith has run
    Through thy lower nature,
Be my benediction said
With my hand upon thy head,
    Gentle fellow-creature!

Like a lady's ringlets brown,
Flow thy silken ears adown
      Either side demurely
Of thy silver-suited breast
Shining out from all the rest
      Of thy body purely.

Darkly brown thy body is,
Till the sunshine striking this
      Alchemise its dullness,
When the sleek curls manifold
Flash all over into gold
      With a burnished fulness.

Underneath my stroking hand
Startled eyes of hazel bland
      Kindling, growing larger,
Up thou leapest with a spring,
Full of prank and curveting,
      Leaping like a charger.

Leap! thy broad tail waves a light,
Leap! thy slender feet are bright,
      Canopied in fringes;
Leap! those tasselled ears of thine
Flicker strangely, fair and fine
      Down their golden inches.

Yet, my pretty, sportive friend,
Little is't to such an end
      That I praise thy rareness;
Other dogs may be thy peers
Haply in these drooping ears
      And this glossy fairness.

But of *thee* it shall be said
This dog watched beside a bed
      Day and night unweary,
Watched within a curtained room

Where no sunbeam brake the gloom
    Round the sick and dreary.

Roses, gathered for a vase,
In that chamber died apace,
    Beam and breeze resigning;
This dog only, waited on,
Knowing that when light is gone
    Love remains for shining.

Other dogs in thymy dew
Tracked the hares and followed through
    Sunny moor or meadow;
This dog only, crept and crept
Next a languid cheek and slept,
    Sharing in the shadow.

Other dogs of loyal cheer
Bounded at the whistle clear,
    Up the woodside hieing;
This dog only, watched in reach
Of a faintly uttered speech
    Or a louder sighing.

And if one or two quick tears
Dropped upon his glossy ears
    Or a sigh came double,
Up he sprang in eager haste,
Fawning, fondling, breathing fast,
    In a tender trouble.

And this dog was satisfied
If a pale thin hand would glide
    Down his dewlaps sloping,—
Which he pushed his nose within,
After,—platforming his chin
    On the palm left open.

This dog, if a friendly voice
Call him now to blither choice
    Than such chamber-keeping,

"Come out!" praying from the door,—
Presseth backward as before,
            Up against me leaping.

Therefore to this dog will I,
Tenderly not scornfully,
            Render praise and favour:
With my hand upon his head,
Is my benediction said
            Therefore and for ever.

And because he loves me so,
Better than his kind will do
            Often man or woman,
Give I back more love again
Than dogs often take of men,
            Leaning from my Human.

Blessings on thee, dog of mine,
Pretty collars make thee fine,
            Sugared milk make fat thee!
Pleasures wag on in thy tail,
Hands of gentle motion fail
            Nevermore, to pat thee!

Downy pillow take thy head,
Silken coverlid bestead,
            Sunshine help thy sleeping!
No fly's buzzing wake thee up,
No man break thy purple cup
            Set for drinking deep in.

Whiskered cats arointed flee,
Sturdy stoppers keep from thee
            Cologne distillations;
Nuts lie in thy path for stones,
And thy feast-day macaroons
            Turn to daily rations!

Mock I thee, in wishing weal?—
Tears are in my eyes to feel
      Thou art made so straitly,
Blessing needs must straiten too,—
Little canst thou joy or do,
      Thou who lovest *greatly*.

Yet be blessed to the height
Of all good and all delight
      Pervious to thy nature;
Only *loved* beyond that line,
With a love that answers thine,
      Loving fellow-creature!

THE UNFORGOTTEN DOG

FLUSH OR FAUNUS

BY *Elizabeth Barrett Browning*

You see this dog; it was but yesterday
I mused forgetful of his presence here,
Till thought on thought drew downward tear on tear:
When from the pillow where wet-cheeked I lay,
A head as hairy as Faunus thrust its way
Right sudden against my face, two golden-clear
Great eyes astonished mine, a drooping ear
Did flop me on either cheek to dry the spray!
I started first as some Arcadian
Amazed by goatly god in twilight grove:
But as the bearded vision closelier ran
My tears off, I knew Flush, and rose above
Surprise and sadness,—thanking the true PAN
Who by low creatures leads to heights of love.

HOME IS THE HERO

BY *Corey Ford*

H E DREW DEEP BREATHS, spreading his nostrils and trying
to get it better. He remembered it best with his nose. His
eyes remembered the gate and the lawn and the white house;
but what his nose remembered, as the car turned the corner and
started down the wide familiar street, was the way the asphalt
simmered in the noonday heat, the cool-smelling shadows under
the maples, the steamy smell of fresh-mown grass on the lawn.
He sniffed the air, and his body shivered a little with excitement.

His excitement had been mounting each hour during the
long train trip yesterday, and, before that, during the trip home
across the ocean on the crowded transport. He had never forgotten his home. The thought of it had kept coming back to
him at the strangest times: while the guns were blasting and
shaking the ground under him, or once on patrol on a dark
road in Normandy when a shadow moved and a guttural command rang in the night. Sometimes in his sleep he would think
of coming indoors and tracking mud on the green hall carpet,
or hanging around the big comfortable kitchen while supper
was being readied, and his body would twitch and he would
make a sobbing sound in his throat. Little things would bring it
back, bread baking in a French farmhouse, or always the smell
of grass in the sun.

The car stopped in front of the house, and he saw them come
down the steps and start across the lawn toward him, the man
in front, the woman a little behind. The involuntary sobbing
began in his throat again, a sharp intake of breath that was like
a shrill whisper.

"Hello, Nick," the man said, holding out his hand. "Hello,
boy."

He pressed his nose against the man's knuckles, remembering the faint tobacco smell. The sobbing in his throat grew louder, and his tail banged against the sides of the crate.

"He knows you," the expressman said.

"Sure he knows me. Don't you, Nick?" He told the expressman: "It's over two years."

"He's quite a dog," the expressman said admiringly. "I bet he's strong; lookit the shoulders on him. And those teeth."

"George," the woman said, "now be careful." She was standing a little to the rear of the man, watching uneasily through pince-nez glasses.

"He's all right, Edie. He's been to detraining school, he's okay." He helped the expressman lift the crate down and set it on the lawn. "Maybe you might have seen his picture in the paper," he mentioned to the expressman.

"Is that who he is"—astonished—"that killed the German? Sure, I was reading about him only the other day."

"He got a decoration for it," the man said with pride. "This German had his pistol pointed, and Nick jumped up and grabbed his wrist, and he got him down and got him by the throat. It was all in the citation they sent us."

"I'd hate to have him get my throat," the expressman said, slamming the back of the truck.

The woman still hesitated on the lawn with her hands clasped; she was stout, gentle-faced, worried. "George," she said, "do you think you ought to let him out until you're sure? . . ."

"Sure of what?" The man laughed. He unsnapped the catch, and opened the door of the crate. "He wants to stretch his legs."

Nick stepped out of the crate stiffly, his tail whipping against the man's knees. The grass was soft under his feet; his body shook uncontrollably; the excitement was about to burst inside him. He halted for a moment in front of the woman, straining his neck toward her and sniffing. She stood rigid, forcing a weak smile; his nose touched the tip of her fingers, and she snatched her hand away. "Nick," the man said. The dog moved past her, and let his nose lead him across the lawn to the border of shrubs, and along the shrubs to the edge of the porch steps. His tail was wagging faster and faster, and he sucked the air with long delicious gasps. His nose was remembering it all: the favorite place behind the steps, the cool hole he used to dig in the dirt under the lilac, the water dish. He followed his nose across the driveway onto the lawn, and he began trotting faster, galloping in a wide circle, halting abruptly to sniff the grass again. He wanted to press his nose deep in it, to feel it against his belly, and lose himself again in the sweet smell of grass in the sun. He rolled onto his side and over onto his back and began to wriggle ecstatically across the lawn, kicking his legs and arching his powerful neck to inch himself forward. He twisted first one way and then the other like a puppy, making deep happy growls, sneezing.

"Glad to be out of the Army?" The man laughed, and he laughed back, his tongue lolling and his strong white teeth showing. The woman caught her breath as he squirmed off the edge of the lawn into a border of flowers.

"George," she wailed, "he's ruining the iris."

The man called "Nick!" and he rose and shook himself and trotted over, tail slapping. "Come on, boy. Let's go in the house and say hello to Richie."

"You're not going to let him in the house?"

"Why not? Of course."

"But you don't know how he'll be with Richie, he's apt as not to . . ." She did not finish the sentence.

"Edie, he isn't apt to anything, he's the same as he always was. He went away to war and now he's back, that's all."

"But suppose something happened, George. After all, he's been trained to . . ." She had a way of letting her sentences trail off into significant silence.

Reluctantly he yielded. "I'll keep a rope on him at first."

The dog sat still as the man knelt and slipped a rope through his collar; he rested one forepaw on the man's knee.

"This way, boy."

He knew the way himself. He tugged up the front-porch steps ahead of the man, through the vestibule that smelled nostalgically of overshoes and garden tools and a worn doormat, and through the door into the front hall. Instantly the dank remembered darkness swallowed him; the newel post, the big mahogany hatrack, the clock. A chewed leather glove that he used to play with lay on the green carpet beside the clock, and he sniffed at it as he went by. He paused, and sniffed again suspiciously. There was a strange unremembered smell about the glove; the smell of another dog.

"Here, Nick," the man said, leading him into the living room. "Where's Richie?" He raised his voice: "Oh, Richie!"

Descending feet thumped on the staircase, and his ears pointed forward stiffly. The little whistling sob began again in his throat, growing louder and louder. The footsteps pounded along the hall, and a five-year-old boy burst through the door and flung himself toward him, arms outstretched.

"Richard!" The woman's voice rang with alarm; the boy halted abruptly. "Just don't get too near him, honey."

The boy stood uncertainly in the doorway, his smile fading, his questioning eyes going to his mother's face and back to the dog.

Nick was straining at the rope, pulling so hard that his collar choked him. He wanted to rush to the boy, to lap his face over, to feel the boy's fist clutch his fur as he hugged him. He belonged to Richie, he had always been Richie's dog. He had shadowed him morning and night; had stood beside his carriage when Richie was too young to walk; had slept on a blanket beside Richie's crib. They had wrestled together, and he had carried Richie on his back, and at night they had stretched out before the fireplace and Richie had gone to sleep with his head on a shaggy shoulder. He stood on his hind legs at the end of the rope, pawing the air and whimpering shrilly.

"Easy, Nick," the man said. "Easy."

The strain of the rope was pulling his lips back, baring his white teeth. The boy moved backward a step, watching him.

"Say hello to Nick," the man prompted. . . .

A yelp, a wild scrambling, a flash of golden-brown, and a small toy spaniel darted past Richie's legs and slid to a halt before Nick, snarling and snapping hysterically. The fur rose along Nick's backbone; a rumble started deep in his chest. The spaniel's barking rose to a scream, and he ran back to Richie, leaping up onto him and whimpering. Richie gathered him in his arms and held him tight; he faced the big dog with a gathering pucker between his eyes.

The woman said: "You'd better take Scamper back up to your room, Richard, before he . . ."

Richie hugged the wriggling spaniel, stroking his head to soothe him. He turned and started back toward the stairs.

"There." She said it with a sharp exhalation of breath. "George, you'll have to do something. He can't stay in the house tonight. It makes me too nervous."

"But where will he stay?"

"I don't know. The garage, I suppose. I wouldn't sleep a wink," she said, her stout sweet face lined with worry. "I'd be thinking about . . ." Her pince-nez glasses bobbed as she shook her head. "Once they've learned to . . ." She let the sentence trail.

He walked quietly beside the man out of the house, down the steps and across the lawn. He followed dutifully as the man led him through the garage doors, and across the cool oil-soaked cement floor, and made his rope fast in the spare room behind the garage. The man took a blanket from the car. He watched him with questioning eyes as he spread it on the floor. He could not believe it was for him.

The man hesitated a moment, and then walked over and knelt beside him. "Sorry, Nick," he murmured, working his fingers deep into the fur behind the dog's ears and scratching him. "It's not much of a homecoming, boy, but . . ." The man's fingers slid along his neck and down his solid ribs, smoothing his fur. "It'll be all right," the man said vaguely, and patted his flank. He rose slowly. "It'll be all right tomorrow."

He watched in silence as the man walked out of the room and closed the door behind him. Still he could not believe it; he crouched on the blanket with his head resting on his fore-paws, watching the door. He made no effort to whine or bark. In the Army you are taught to be quiet. You don't make a sound, you don't even whimper.

That night the man brought some food and water, and went out and shut the door again. Nick lay silent, trying to understand what he had done. He remembered his bed on the floor in Richie's room, and he tried to think why he was not there. Wondering, he fell asleep, and in his sleep he was walking down a dark road in Normandy. A soldier was walking beside him, his O.D. pants tucked into the tops of a dusty pair of combat boots, his webbed cartridge belt sagging from a hip. They moved in silence, he and the young soldier, listening for a sound in the night. There was an effortless understanding between the soldier and himself, a sort of mutual homelessness. They were alone, the two of them, against the dark night. The soldier needed him, needed his nose to smell danger, needed his ears to hear.

Then ahead of them Nick saw the shadow move again, he saw the arm lift with the pistol pointing, and in his sleep he began to jerk convulsively, his legs scratched the cement floor of the garage as he tried to leap, his jaws champed together. He woke with a start, and stared wildly for a moment at the strange blackness around him before he remembered he was home. . . .

In the morning the door opened. He was on his feet, tail wagging expectantly. Richie peered cautiously inside, and beckoned over his shoulder; a group of neighbors' children followed him, all his age or a little older. They crowded behind him, staring at Nick.

"There he is. See?" Richie said. His voice was shrill with importance.

Nick tugged at the rope, panting; his teeth gleamed. "He looks just like a wolf," a tall girl said, shivering pleasantly.

"He killed a German," Richie said. "He killed about a hundred Germans, I guess. He ate all their heads off."

"I got a brother in the Marines," a boy said.

"Can I pet him?" asked a little boy holding the tall girl's hand.

"Oh, no, you can't touch him," Richie said. "My mother said not to. You can watch while I feed him, though."

The group edged into the room in fascinated silence. Richie took a chunk of meat from a pan in his hand, and tossed it to Nick. It fell short. He took a stick, and poked the chunk across the floor within his reach.

"He didn't eat it," the little boy said after a moment, disappointed.

"Here, Nick," Richie said, and poked the chunk of meat nearer. He stepped back quickly.

Nick still ignored the meat; his eyes were on Richie's face, his throat was making the little sobbing sound again. This wasn't the way it used to be when Richie would toss a baseball to him, and he would bring it back and put his paws on Richie's shoulders, and knock him down, and Richie would laugh.

"Look, Scamper's eating it instead," the little boy announced.

The spaniel had sneaked unnoticed past the group; he darted across the garage floor, seized the meat and turned to run. It happened before they knew it: Soundlessly Nick lunged and grabbed him, shook him once, and tossed him in the air. The spaniel landed at Richie's feet, howling and snapping at a spreading red stain on his golden-brown fur. Nick lunged again, but the rope snubbed him short, half-turning him. The children ran out of the garage, their screams blending with the spaniel's shrieks of pain. Richie's eyes were blinded with tears. Furiously he ran at Nick and struck him across the face with the stick. He stooped, picked up the spaniel and carried him wailing into the house. . . .

Later Nick heard the car start, and hours later he heard it come back, and he could hear Richie crying as his mother led him into the house. He waited, shaking convulsively. He was confused; everything confused him. He was home, but home wasn't here. Home wasn't having people come and stare at you and always keep a little distance from you. Home was jumping up on a cot and having your stomach rubbed and smelling chicken frying on the barracks stove. Home was somebody's field jacket beside a pair of G.I. shoes on the floor. Home was marching together, and sharing out of the same mess kit, and crawling under a shelter-half together in the rain. Home was anywhere you were together. . . .

Some time later he heard another car stop in front of the house, and he recognized the man's voice. He stood erect and began to pant. The woman was talking to the man; he could hear her voice rising and falling as they walked toward the garage.

". . . seven stitches. The veterinary said he'd have to stay there at least a week. Richie's upstairs, poor child; he's all upset. I put him to bed and then I phoned you. He said the dog simply grabbed little Scamper without any warning."

They had halted in the doorway of the garage; he could see the woman's pince-nez glasses blink. "It's what I kept telling you all along. . . ."

"Nick, Nick," the man said unhappily, looking through the door at him.

"I was afraid when they first wrote they were sending him back," the woman said. "I didn't want him to come."

"But, Edie, this is his home, you couldn't refuse to take him back after he did his job and even got a decoration—"

"For what? For killing. Oh, I know he was a hero, George, but why did he have to come home again? Why didn't he die a hero over there?"

The man stared at her, shocked. The intensity of her feeling was bringing out unaccustomed sharp lines in her plump face. Fear made her that way, he realized; she was deathly afraid. "He didn't mean it, Edie," he said. "It was a mistake. Maybe seeing Richie with a new dog. He was always such a pet."

"Pet!" She let out her breath so sharply that her whole body yanked erect. She controlled herself. "I know it isn't his fault, George, but the Army's made him brutal." Her face was sharp. "How could you ever trust him again after . . . ?"

The man walked over thoughtfully and stood beside Nick. The dog did not tug at the rope. He waited, looking up at the man's face. He was still shaking, his loins contracted, his back arched high.

"Nick," the man said experimentally. "Look, Nick." He held out his hand. "Roll over," he said.

He began to pant louder, looking up at the man. He knew it was a command, but he could not remember what it was. He was confused, things were rushing through his mind. He could hear the guns again and the creak of leather, and the thud of feet marching. He could hear them above everything else, above his own panting.

"Nick," the man pleaded, "don't you remember? Roll over, boy."

It was a command, and he knew he was supposed to do something, but he was too mixed up now to know what. Everything was mixed up. This wasn't home, he wasn't home any more. Home was a pair of high-topped combat boots and a sagging cartridge belt and a young soldier walking beside him down a dark road in Normandy.

"Roll over," the man said again, sharply, and snapped his fingers.

He heard the click of a pistol being cocked, and he saw an outstretched arm. He leaped and grabbed the wrist in his teeth. . . .

The man stood looking at the round drops of blood on his wrist, with a surprised, almost a sheepish smile. He wrapped a handkerchief around his wrist. "He didn't mean it," he was saying apologetically.

The woman's voice suddenly went all to pieces: "There's only one thing to do. He'll have to be put away."

"But he didn't mean it."

"I'm going to phone the authorities. They can come and get him."

The man hesitated as she hurried toward the house. The big dog was cowering, ears back and tail hugging his flanks. The man knelt beside him and scratched above his neck.

"I understand. I remember after the last war," he murmured. "I remember how it was when I came home." He was fumbling with the dog's collar. "Good-by, boy," he said, and rose and walked quickly toward the house.

Nick took a step forward; the rope slid from his collar and fell to the floor. He walked out of the garage; he did not run. He walked across the lawn, and out through the gate without looking back. He walked down the maple-shaded street, and he did not look back as he turned the corner.

He crossed the street, and started through the park, through the cool-smelling grass. A stranger was sitting on a bench, reading a newspaper. He had on a new gray civilian suit, but on his outstretched feet was a pair of battered Army shoes, dark with dust. Nick paused, sniffing the familiar smell of leather and oil-dubbing. The stranger lowered the paper and looked at him.

"Beat it," he said, and returned to the paper.

Nick sat on his haunches and waited. The stranger tore the want-ad section out of the paper and stuffed it into his pocket. Nick rose to his feet, ready. The stranger looked at him again, and shook his head.

"Look," he said, reaching out a hand and scratching him absently behind an ear, "I'd take you home, but I haven't got any home to take you to. So beat it. . . ."

He paused, feeling the ear and frowning. He bent the ear toward him, and looked at Nick's Army serial number branded on the inside of his ear. "You and me both, eh?" he said slowly. He got up and started walking, whistling. Nick walked beside him into the dusk.

TWO POEMS

BY *William Wordsworth*

I. INCIDENT CHARACTERISTIC OF A FAVOURITE DOG

On his morning rounds the Master
Goes to learn how all things fare;
Searches pasture after pasture,
Sheep and cattle eyes with care;
And, for silence or for talk,
He hath comrades in his walk;
Four dogs, each pair of different breed,
Distinguished two for scent, and two for speed.

See a hare before him started!
— Off they fly in earnest chase;
Every dog is eager-hearted,
All the four are in the race:
And the hare whom they pursue,
Knows from instinct what to do;
Her hope is near; no turn she makes;
But, like an arrow, to the river takes.

Deep the river was, and crusted
Thinly by a one night's frost;
But the nimble Hare hath trusted
To the ice, and safely crost;
She hath crost, and without heed
All are following at full speed,
When, lo! the ice, so thinly spread,
Breaks — and the greyhound, DART, is overhead!

Better fate have PRINCE and SWALLOW —
See them cleaving to the sport!

MUSIC has no heart to follow,
Little MUSIC, she stops short.
She hath neither wish nor heart,
Hers is now another part:
A loving creature she, and brave!
And fondly strives her struggling friend to save.

From the brink her paws she stretches,
Very hands as you would say!
And afflicting moans she fetches,
As he breaks the ice away.
For herself she hath no fears,—
Him alone she sees and hears,—
Makes efforts with complainings; nor gives o'er
Until her fellow sinks to reappear no more.

II. TRIBUTE TO THE MEMORY OF THE SAME DOG

Lie here, without a record of thy worth,
Beneath a covering of the common earth!
It is not from unwillingness to praise,
Or want to love, that here no Stone we raise;
More thou deserv'st; but *this* man gives to man,
Brother to brother, *this* is all we can.
Yet they to whom thy virtues made thee dear
Shall find thee through all changes of the year:
This Oak points out thy grave; the silent tree
Will gladly stand a monument of thee.

We grieved for thee, and wished thy end were past;
And willingly have laid thee here at last:
For thou hadst lived till every thing that cheers
In thee had yielded to the weight of the years;
Extreme old age had wasted thee away,
And left thee but a glimmering of the day;
Thy ears were deaf, and feeble were thy knees,—
I saw thee stagger in the summer breeze,
Too weak to stand against its sportive breath,
And ready for the gentlest stroke of death.
It came, and we were glad; yet tears were shed;

Both man and woman wept when thou wert dead;
Not only for a thousand thoughts that were,
Old household thoughts, in which thou hadst thy share;
But for some precious boons vouchsafed to thee,
Found scarcely anywhere in like degree!
For love, that comes wherever life and sense
Are given by God, in thee was most intense;
A chain of heart, a feeling of the mind,
A tender sympathy, which did thee bind
Not only to us Men, but to thy Kind:
Yea, for thy fellow-brutes in thee we saw
A soul of love, love's intellectual law:—
Hence, if we wept, it was not done in shame;
Our tears from passion and from reason came,
And, therefore, shalt thou be an honoured name!

THE OCCULT DOG

A DOG FROM NOWHERE

BY *Manuel Komroff*

GO AWAY!" I CRIED. "GO AWAY!" The cur stopped again and looked up into my face. His tail was between his legs. He seemed to understand the words that I shouted but he would not go away.

I could like a cocker spaniel or a wire-hair or any sort of dog at all if it only looked like a dog. But this miserable creature, homeless, dirty, with one eye running soft and one eye hard, a matted coat covering only partly some red sores on his hide, a lip cut or split showing a row of bad teeth, one ear up and one down and all over dirty gray, the color of a floor rag! What a creature! Has God no mercy? Must such things live?

"Go away! Go home. Stop following me!"

For a whole hour the dog had been walking behind me. When I shouted at him he would stop and he would wait. Then when

I was about half a street away he would start, and soon, in less than five minutes, this four-legged twist of canine wretchedness was again at my heels.

"Go away! Don't follow me!"

Why should such creatures live? Would not death be a warm soothing kindness? Where is the animal society that picks up these stray homeless dogs and puts them quietly out of their misery? How has this creature escaped?

These are questions that I ask! And there are more that come to my mind.

Does nature preserve the ugly, the useless, the diseased? Must wretchedness reproduce itself so that more things of this sort may continue to crawl on the surface of the earth? Is this the lovely nature that the world is built of? And must the young and beautiful and pure . . . Why must these die and the others live? Can science reply or should such an answer come direct from the great airy blue above?

And how strange that on this day it was exactly six months since the death of lovely Lydia. Her hands were white, her face was white, and the long illness, the wearing days and fevered nights, had weakened her so that the passing, the end, the last moment, was gentle and quiet—without shock and with only a smile. At least the crossing over from this world to the other was easy and merciful. What other world?

I could raise my fist to heaven and cry out against such great injustice! What powers there are, I could curse and wish them damned! Why? Why! Why should so innocent a creature, so lovely and radiant, so full of life and so beautiful . . . Why did she have to perish and those miserable mangy creatures, on two legs or four—these wretches rewarded with life. Why!

I cry out against nature and this evil world. Why! Who will answer?

We were happy in a world that was riddled with war and suffering. And is happiness a crime? We loved while the world around us was consumed with hatred and envy and spite. Races pitted themselves against each other. And nations and classes fell apart and a black chasm opened between them. And in such a world, perhaps love was a crime, and for this we were punished with death. And happiness was rubbed away as though it were a scarlet stain.

"Go away!" I cried. "Don't follow me!"

And on this day it was exactly six months; and in half an hour . . . That will be the hour. Oh, Lydia! Why should this have been necessary?

It would be best to walk into the woods and sit there for half an hour. The leaves will spread their green lace against the sky. The trees . . . Ah! Arms that stretch to heaven and roots deep in hell. The mold of dead leaves rotting in the soft ground will also be a symbol of something. And then perhaps in some pathless place between brush and trees it may be possible to lose that filthy, stinking, four-legged, pus-running, cowardly he-bitch of a dog!

"Go away! Stop following me!"

I thought perhaps this had done the trick. He could not find his way through the woods and at last I lost this persistently tagging cur. All was quiet and the silence seemed to speak magic words that do not exist in any language. There are words that tell of things beautiful and far away and yet they are not words at all.

But suddenly there was a slight sound, as though something were stirring through a bush. I turned about. Nothing was to be seen. And then at that moment there was a sharp pain in my heart, as though a pin had scratched it. It passed quickly. I looked at my watch. How strange! This was the exact moment six months ago. How strange! And putting my watch back into my pocket, I looked down at the ground and there before me was the filthy dog.

He looked at me and expected me to shout out and drive him off. But when I did not do so he wagged his tail and after a moment he sat down before me and waited.

All right. Have it your way. You want to follow me; then follow me. These words I said to myself.

"Come!" I called aloud. "Come. We are going home."

The dog jumped up with a bound. His tail shook with joy. He ran ahead of me and behind me and around me and he led the way through the woods.

"That's right. We are going home."

Was I a man or a flabby fish, to allow a low creature to have his way? From this day on would all have power over me? Would I become the weak victim of every persistent fool? No! I had a plan.

"Come! We are going home."

But I knew very well that the moment I got through the door I was going to telephone to the animal society. The wagon would arrive and the men with gauntlets on their hands would put him into a wicker basket and take him to the pound. And he would never again . . . Never. Never. Never.

"Come!" I called.

He wagged his tail and ran on joyously with a hop and a side step. He seemed to understand my words. But perhaps he knew more.

He ran to the end of the street and waited. He waited to see which way I would turn. But he seemed to know the direction. And what is more, he stopped and sat down at the gate of the house.

How did this creature know the house? Was it through his power of scent? Or did he know it through some other power; through some dark hidden force, a force secret and mysterious?

These questions came to my mind but I did not want to try to fathom them because I clung to a single idea and this thought I did not want shaken out of my mind.

I opened the door and said: "Come in!"

The creature stood on the step and hesitated. So much kindness he did not expect.

"Come in," I repeated.

His tail wagged weakly but still he hesitated. Warm shelter he had not known and only garbage scraps had been his food.

I held the door open and again I called, this time quite gently: "Come in."

He walked cautiously into the hall. His feet seemed to touch the rug lightly as though he feared to bring the stain of his wretched condition into a place clean, warm, protected.

I closed the door behind him and repeated the words softly. "Come in." And this was soft as the Kiss of Judas, for the moment these words were issued from my lips I lifted the telephone receiver and called the Society.

He stood in the hall and looked at me. His tail wagged while I explained about a stray dog without a collar or tag that had followed me. And I had him here. I had induced him to come into the house so that there could be no trouble picking him up.

Yes, it would be taken care of in the morning. It was not possible that evening to send the wagon.

His tail wagged as I spoke through the telephone. Did he understand that his hours were now counted? Did he know I was talking about him? Why was he happy? Was death something for which he had no fear? Did he know something that I could not understand?

This was a pretty trick I played. "Come in." And still he wagged his tail.

"Well, you will have to wait until the morning," I said. "Come. I will find something for you to eat. Come to the kitchen."

By giving him a crust in a bowl of milk I tried to brush aside the low-down trick that I had played. He will die, but at least I will give him some food. Great kindness this!

While he was eating the food I happened to glance in the mirror. What a hard ugly face! Could this be me? Could this person reflected in the glass have lived and loved? And only six months ago was there not a dream creature, lovely beyond all words . . . Lydia, with grace and charm and beauty and youth. Oh Lydia, could you have loved this person now before you? . . . A black scheming wretch who tricked a hungry dumb animal and called for the wagon to take him to his death. And he wagged his tail in full unsuspecting innocence. Could you have loved this?

"Oh, you hypocrite, you double-crossing wretch! Go away! Don't follow me. Judas was an angel compared to you!" I shouted these words at the image in the mirror.

All right. The dog should die. His main crime was that he followed me. His other crimes were his starvation, his mange, his pus-laden eye and his filth. Take a club and beat the life out of him. Do it yourself. Do it honestly. Do it aboveboard. Without deception! And not sneak some words through a wire to a goddam Society, some pussy-woosey words full of high ideals and low intentions. Face it yourself and do not run around Grandma's woolly skirts.

Or if you can't take a club and beat the life out of this half-starved creature then get the pistol from the bureau drawer and put a cool bullet through his brain.

I shook my fist at the image in the glass. "What a skunk you are!"

And then suddenly the creature brushed past me and ran to

the hall. He stood before the door and made strange sounds with his throat. It was neither a growl nor a bark. The sound was a whining one as though he were trying to speak. Then his tail wagged rapidly and he gave two short little barks. Not a bark with a growl behind it but one of a joyous nature. It was as though someone he knew were coming to the door.

Did he want to go out? No. This was certain. He was happy because someone was at the doorstep waiting to come into the house.

I went forward and opened the door. No one was there. How strange!

As I closed the door the dog jumped about in circles; then he frisked into the living room and sat down beside the settee. It was all as though someone he knew very well had come into the house. Someone good and someone beautiful. Animals know. But the house seemed empty.

And as I stood contemplating this strange event the clock on the mantel struck: one, two, three . . . six, seven! My God! It is true.

Wait a minute. Let me sit down and try to think. Is such a thing possible? Has it ever happened before? Or is it just one of these terribly weird coincidences that occur only once in a thousand years? Reason tells me that it must be one of these fluke combinations of chance. But there is something else.

The dog soon went back to the kitchen to finish his bowl of food. He had evidently interrupted his dinner. A starved dog had stopped eating to run to the door because he sensed a friend approaching. This must certainly be a great friendship.

Was the dog fooled? Did he run to the door all for nothing? And when I opened the door did not someone enter, someone whom I could not see? Why then did the creature turn about in joyous circles?

And was it not customary at exactly this hour, day in and day out . . . Was it not customary for a certain person to arrive for supper at seven o'clock? . . . Six months ago. No, longer. The illness lasted some time. It was eight, nine, ten—a year. Oh!

The door was opened when he barked and then I closed it. Someone is here!

The girl I love has been brought back to me. Back from a place where none has returned. Across a deep dark chasm. Her spirit and love have been brought back to me by this mute creature and I have rewarded him with a bowl of milk and a promise of death. Damn generous of me!

That night, just as I was about to drop off into sleep, I felt a warm hand touch the edge of the blanket and turn it gently over my shoulder. I opened my eyes but saw nothing. I could not sleep but began to review in my mind the little bits of things that happened that day. Nothing of itself seemed terribly important. But add them all together and you have something that is . . . Where is the poor creature?

I lit the light and opened the bedroom door. The dog was lying in a corner of the hall curled up and partly asleep. He opened one eye as I approached and his tail moved slightly.

There is pus in his eye and his skin is covered with a hard scab, he is dirty and matted, but I bent down and felt nothing of all these. He was warm and he was alive and what is more he is devoted to someone and that is the person I love. And he has brought her here.

I petted him and he closed his eyes. And then I went back to my room and fell asleep.

In the morning I decided to give him a bath. He stood patiently in the tub while I soaped him and churned up a great white lather. He did not try to jump out of the tub but let me wash him. I was careful not to get soap in his eyes. Three times I filled the tub, so black was the water, until I could get him washed.

Then I let him shake himself and I wrapped him up in a large warm towel and carried him to a sunny part of the living room.

The bell rang. Two men were at the door. They wore gloves.

"No. I am sorry. I have changed my mind. I have no dog here for you. Sorry to have troubled you." They left.

I got scissors and cut off the badly matted lumps of fluffy hair, for it was impossible to brush it out. He was white as snow, with the coat of a poodle. His ears were bright pink and, though one stood up and the other flopped over, it did not matter. His eye ran only a little and did not show so badly. I could get some drops from a doctor and perhaps it would clear up.

All in all, the miserable and wretched creature that you have seen before has vanished. He is now a fluffy little white dog. And he is bright and as smart as any dog.

Some dogs have in them a comic spirit. They enjoy acting the clown and they know very well when their antics are being favorably received. But the white dog had none of this. He tried no stunts for effect. But he had something else and that something was of great importance. It seemed as though he could make me understand something and through his silence he had an eloquence which I cannot describe in words, for words were not part of this communication.

Very well, I am wrong. All this is only a fantasy. I have imagined something and I have attributed to a filthy cur something that no dog has ever had or could have. We will see. At least the bath cannot hurt him and he surely is better clean and white and fluffy than in his former wretched condition. But we will test it to make certain. In a few hours we can know.

Once more the clock was about to strike seven and he bounded from the floor with a short bark and those same strange sounds again issued from his throat. He stood in the hall wagging his tail and he kept looking at me as though to ask why I did not open the door.

Finally I opened the door and as I did so I bowed low for I knew now that I was in the presence of the great unknown and that she . . . The dog jumped about in circles just as he had done the evening before and he settled himself finally in the living room.

Now the evidence was accumulating and soon there could be no doubt about it. I was ashamed that I had doubted. My heart was ready to believe from the very start. The heart had reasons that reason itself could not know.

More evidence was not necessary. I was certain that the little white dog had come to me for a definite purpose. He had a message and perhaps more than a message.

Somehow or other, through this dumb creature I believed I would soon see and hear her; and once more I could hold her in my arms and kiss her lips. Of this I was confident. She was moving all forces to make her presence known to me and it is only I who am blind and stupid.

Why could I not see it and understand it all at one glance? The little white dog can see her. And this crime that hung over me . . . "Come! We are going home." . . . And all the time I knew that I wanted to induce the creature to enter the house so I could order his death. This trick weighed heavily upon me and as soon as we could speak I would make a clean breast of it and confess and beg forgiveness. She knows the truth but still the words are in my throat and I must get them out, if only for myself. The little white dog would help me. Soon I will learn from him how to speak with her.

Now and then I thought I heard her call my name. The little white dog heard it also for he raised his head and the muscles of his ears drew back each time. She was trying to tell me something.

I grew impatient. A day or two went by and the great wall was still between us. And so blind and stupid is man that the moment he fails doubt creeps in. I made no progress at all and then I began to imagine that all this was a fantasy, all an invention of a clever active brain. The conflict came between belief and knowledge. The mind refused to recognize what the heart already understood.

But soon, one night, I was awakened by a strange sound. I listened carefully and I heard the most heart-rending sobs that I had ever heard. I sat up in bed. It was she. "Oh, Lydia, my own dear Lydia! What is the matter?"

I turned on the light and immediately the sobbing ceased. The moment I turned off the light it began again.

I put on my slippers and dressing gown and went toward the direction of the sound. It seemed to come from one room and then when I got there it seemed to come from another place.

"Lydia, Lydia. Listen to me. Why are you crying? Can't you tell me? Can't we get the little white dog to act as our interpreter? Perhaps somehow . . . He is sleeping now near the door of my bedroom. I will go and wake him and bring him here and then . . ."

There was a soft patter on the stair and the little white dog, I could hear, was coming down.

"You have heard me. You have awakened him yourself. You have sent him to me. You agree to my plan. We will speak and you will tell me why you are weeping as though your heart were about to break."

It seemed to me that while I was speaking the sobbing ceased.

"Lydia darling! You are trying to come to my arms and I am reaching out into this unknown darkness to take hold of you. I cannot know what you know. And I cannot tell if it is wrong or right. All I know is that I love you and nothing can take you out of my heart. I live with your memory and until very recently, until you sent me the little white dog, I have been alone. Loneliness eats the marrow of one's bones and the flesh begins to rot. And now the little white dog is here and you are here also. And you are weeping and I want you to make me understand why."

These words I spoke softly but clearly. The little white dog was in the room. A thin pale beam of moonlight filtered through the window and I could see his fluffy coat against the dark carpet. A faint light outlined the objects in the room as though they had been drawn with a thin white pencil on a soft black paper. Some of the objects seemed to run together and made new and strange forms which the mind could not unravel. And the surface of things seemed to tilt and fall apart; and all direction was lost. The sobbing seemed closer.

"It is you, Lydia. You are close by. I can hear. Why are you weeping? Can you answer me? I do not know how to ask or how you can reply. Is death always silent? Is it beautiful and white as our poets have taught us to believe? Or is it horrible and dirty and stinking? Is it pus-laden and filled with unhealing sores? Was it there you found the little dog that you sent to me? Yes, I can tell. Now I know. He was once dead. Dead, buried and then dug up. And now he has returned because . . . Because you want to tell me something. You are lonely and you want to come to me but you can't and I am lonely and I want to go to you but I do not know how. Speak, Lydia, speak and tell me. Listen, darling. Would we be together if I were dead? Do you want me to die?"

The little white dog moved slightly on the floor. He turned his body and settled his nose into the carpet. I could not know anything from this gesture. It was neither yes nor no. Had his tail wagged, it would have been a definite yes.

Suddenly a strange feeling crept into me. It was like a cold wave that starts at the feet and runs up with a rippling tidelike movement.

"Lydia," I called. "We are doing something terrible. You

know it and I know it. We cannot go on like this. I am torn in two. I want to reach out for you and hold you. And you are trying to come to me. But you know that you cannot return to the living. You have no right! And I know that I cannot live with the dead. Why did you come to me? And why do I reach out for you? This is terrible. It will drive me mad. We cannot go on like this. I love you, I love you, you know I love you; but there is something between us and across this chasm . . . We are drenching our souls with evil. Stop! You want to show me death and after I see it, then . . . Then how should I face the living? My eyes would betray me. No, I can't. I dare not. Go back, my darling, and let me still cling to the shred of life that remains for me. Go back and take away the little white dog. Give him back the sleep of death that he has paid for and belongs to him."

I listened closely. I could hear no weeping. The little dog was quiet on the carpet. I waited to see if by some sign I could distinguish a reply. The light of the moon seemed stronger and the objects in the room more recognizable. I walked slowly around the room, touching each object as I passed. I listened as closely as I could but I heard nothing—nothing except the light breathing of the little white dog.

While I was walking back to my bedroom my mind suddenly came to a definite decision.

"Forgive me, Lydia, for what I am about to do. But otherwise it is not possible, I cannot go a step further. I have already seen too much. Forgive me, darling, and let us not torture each other a moment longer."

There was a ringing in my ear and I heard the echo of my own voice. "Go away! Don't follow me!" I took the pistol from the bureau drawer and went back to the livingroom. It had come to this.

I recalled the picture to my mind of a filthy cur, mangy, scabby, with a soft running eye and split lip. I recalled this wretched creature when he first fell into my tracks and I recalled my desperate outcries: "Go away! Don't follow me!" And now my heart was crying it out again. "Go away! Go home!" And the filthy cur was now a little white dog. Kill one and the other must die!

And as I entered the room I could see the white fluffy dog

asleep on the carpet. A faint blue light of the moon was over him.

"Go away. Go away! For God's sake go away! You cannot bring us together. And what you were before you must be again. If you were once dead, then I must send you back to where you came from."

I raised the revolver and held it close to the little dog's head. For a moment I hesitated and I heard him breathe. He was asleep and in his sleep he would never know. But my finger hung lightly on the trigger and it did not press down.

In another moment I had lost my nerve, for the little white dog sensed my presence and opened one eye. When he recognized me he wagged his tail. I just could not shoot the creature while he was wagging his tail. And so I concealed the weapon and waited until he would again fall asleep.

I waited and waited, and exhausted by this strange night, I fell asleep in a chair. I awoke at early morn. A faint light announced a new day. The revolver was beside me and on the floor, there almost at my feet, was the little dog.

This thing could not go on. I was determined.

He seemed asleep and I crept forward to place the muzzle to his head. And then I turned my own face so I should not see. In another second the weapon would have gone off, but a strange silence held it up. I listened closely. There was something wrong. I could not hear the little dog's breathing. I bent down low over him. Not a sound! I touched him. Yes. He was dead.

Thank heaven he was dead!

"Oh, Lydia, Lydia!" I cried. "You have spared me something and now I know that you have heard me and . . . Oh, I know more, more. And you forgive me everything, everything! I am grateful."

THAT GREEK DOG

BY *MacKinlay Kantor*

> He received . . . praise that will never die,
> and with it the grandest of all sepulchers,
> not that in which his mortal bones are laid,
> but a home in the minds of men.
> —THUCYDIDES (more or less).

IN THOSE FIRST YEARS after the First World War, Bill
Barbilis could still get into his uniform; he was ornate and
handsome when he wore it. Bill's left sleeve, reading down
from the shoulder, had patches and patterns of color to catch
any eye. At the top there was an arc—bent stripes of scarlet,
yellow and purple; next came a single red chevron with the
apex pointing up; and at the cuff were three gold chevrons
pointing the other way.

On his right cuff was another gold chevron, only slightly
corroded. And we must not forget those triple chevrons on an
olive-drab field which grew halfway up the sleeve.

People militarily sophisticated, there in Mahaska Falls,
could recognize immediately that Mr. Basilio Barbilis had been
a sergeant, that he had served with the Forty-second Division,
that he had been once wounded, that he had sojourned overseas
for at least eighteen months, and that he had been discharged
with honor.

His khaki blouse, however, was worn only on days of patriotic importance. The coat he donned at other times was
white—white, that is, until cherry sirup and caramel speckled
it. Mr. Barbilis was owner, manager and staff of the Sugar
Bowl.

He had a soda fountain with the most glittering spigots in
town. He had a bank of candy cases, a machine for toasting
sandwiches, ten small tables complete with steel-backed chairs,
and a ceiling festooned with leaves of gilt and bronze paper.

Beginning in 1920, he had also a peculiar dog. Bill's living quarters were in the rear of the Sugar Bowl, and the dog came bleating and shivering to the Barbilis door one March night. The dog was no larger than a quart of ice cream and, Bill said, just as cold.

My medical office and apartment were directly over the Sugar Bowl. I made the foundling's acquaintance the next day, when I stopped in for a cup of chocolate. Bill had the dog bedded in a candy carton behind the fountain; he was heating milk when I came in, and wouldn't fix my chocolate until his new pet was fed.

Bill swore that it was a puppy. I wasn't so certain. It looked something like a mud turtle wearing furs.

"I think he is hunting dog," said Bill, with pride. "He was cold last night, but not so cold now. Look, I made him nice warm bed. I got my old pajamas for him to lie on."

He waited upon the sniffling little beast with more tender consideration than ever he showed to any customer. Some people say that Greeks are mercenary. I don't know. That puppy wasn't paying board.

The dog grew up, burly and quizzical. Bill named him Duboko. It sounded like that; I don't know how to spell the name correctly, nor did anyone else in Mahaska Falls.

The word, Bill said, was slang. It meant "tough" or "hard-boiled." This animal had the face of a clown and the body of a hyena. Growing up, his downy coat changing to wire and bristles, Duboko resembled a fat Hamburg steak with onions which had been left too long on the griddle.

At an early age Duboko began to manifest a violent interest in community assemblage of any kind or color. This trait may have been fostered by his master, who was proud to be a Moose, an Odd Fellow, a Woodman, and an upstanding member of the Mahaska Falls Commercial League.

When we needed the services of a bugler in our newly formed American Legion post and no bona fide bugler would volunteer, Bill Barbilis agreed to purchase the best brass instrument available and to practice in the bleak and cindery space behind his store. Since my office was upstairs, I found no great satisfaction in Bill's musical enterprise. It happened that Duboko also lent his voice in support; a Greek chorus, so to speak, complete with strophe and antistrophe.

Nevertheless, I could register no complaint, since with other members of the Legion I had voted to retain Bill as our bugler. I could not even kick Duboko downstairs with my one good leg when I discovered him in my reception room lunching off my mail.

Indeed, most people found it hard to punish Duboko. He had the ingratiating, hopeful confidence of an immigrant just off the boat and assured that he had found the Promised Land. He boasted beady eyes, lubberly crooked paws, an immense mouth formed of black rubber, and pearly and enormous fangs which he was fond of exhibiting in a kind of senseless leer. He smelled, too. This characteristic I called sharply to the attention of his master, with the result that Duboko was laundered weekly in Bill's uncertain little bathtub, the process being marked by vocal lament which might have arisen from the gloomiest passage of the *Antigone*.

Mahaska Falls soon became aware of the creature, in a general municipal sense, and learned that it had him to reckon with. Duboko attended every gathering at which six or more people were in congregation. No fire, picnic, memorial service, Rotary conclave or public chicken-pie supper went ungraced by his presence.

If, as sometimes happened on a crowded Saturday night, a pedestrian was brushed by a car, Duboko was on the scene with a speed to put the insurance company representative to shame. If there was a lodge meeting which he did not visit and from which he was not noisily ejected, I never heard of it. At Commercial League dinners he lay pensive with his head beneath the chair of Bill Barbilis. But, suffering fewer inhibitions than his master, he also visited funerals, and even the marriage of Miss Glaydys Stumpf.

Old Charles P. Stumpf owned the sieve factory. He was the richest man in town; the nuptials of his daughter exuded an especial aura of social magnificence. It is a matter of historical record that Duboko sampled the creamed chicken before any of the guests did; he was banished only after the striped and rented trousers of two ushers had undergone renting in quite another sense of the word. Grieved, Duboko forswore the Stumpfs after that; he refused to attend a reception for the bride and bridegroom when they returned from the Wisconsin Dells two weeks later.

There was one other place in town where Duboko was de-
cidedly *persona non grata*. This was a business house, a rival
establishment of the Sugar Bowl, owned and operated by Earl
and John Klugge. The All-American Kandy Kitchen, they
called it.

The Brothers Klugge held forth at a corner location a block
distant from the Sugar Bowl. Here lounged and tittered ill-
favored representatives of the town's citizenry; dice rattled
on a soiled mat at the cigar counter; it was whispered that
refreshment other than soda could be purchased by the chosen.

The business career of Earl and John Klugge did not flourish, no matter what inducement they offered their customers.
Loudly they declared that their failure to enrich themselves
was due solely to the presence in our community of a Greek
—a black-haired, dark-skinned Mediterranean who thought
nothing of resorting to the most unfair business practices, such
as serving good fudge sundaes, for instance, to anyone who
would buy them.

One fine afternoon people along the main street were troubled at observing Duboko limping rapidly westward, fairly
wreathed in howls. Bill called me down to examine the dog.
Duboko was only bruised although at first I feared that his
ribs were mashed on one side. Possibly someone had thrown
a heavy chair at him. Bill journeyed to the Clive Street corner
with fire in his eye. But no one could be found who would
admit to seeing an attack on Duboko; no one would even say
for a certainty that Duboko had issued from the doorway of
the All-American Kandy Kitchen, although circumstantial
evidence seemed to suggest it.

Friends dissuaded Bill Barbilis from invading the precinct
of his enemies, and at length he was placated by pleasant fiction
about a kicking horse in the market square.

We all observed, however, that Duboko did not call at the
Kandy Kitchen again, not even on those nights when the dice
rattled loudly and when the whoops and catcalls of customers
caused girls to pass by, like pretty Levites, on the other side.

There might have been a different tale to tell if this assault
had come later, when Duboko was fully grown. His frame
stretched and extended steadily for a year; it became almost
as mighty as the earnest Americanism of his master. He was

never vicious. He was never known to bite a child. But frequently his defensive attitude was that of a mother cat who fancies her kitten in danger; Duboko's hypothetical kitten was his right to be present when good fellows—or bad—got together.

Pool halls knew him; so did the Epworth League. At football games an extra linesman was appointed for the sole purpose of discouraging Duboko's athletic ardor. Through some occult sense, he could become aware of an approaching festivity before even the vanguard assembled. Musicians of our brass band never lugged their instruments to the old bandstand in the Courthouse Park without finding Duboko there before them, lounging in an attitude of expectancy. It was Wednesday night, it was eight o'clock, it was July; the veriest dullard might know at what hour and place the band would begin its attack on the Light Cavalry Overture.

Duboko's taste in music was catholic and extensive. He made a fortuitous appearance at a spring musicale, presented by the high-school orchestra and glee clubs, before an audience which sat in the righteous hush of people grimly determined to serve the arts, if only for a night.

The boys' glee club was rendering selections from *Carmen*— in English, of course—and dramatically they announced the appearance of the bull. The line goes, "Now the beast enters, wild and enraged," or something like that; Duboko chose this moment to lope grandly down the center aisle on castanetting toenails. He sprang to the platform . . . Mahaska Falls wiped away more tears than did Mérimée's heroine.

In his adult stage, Duboko weighed forty pounds. His color suggested peanut brittle drenched with chocolate; I have heard people swear that his ears were four feet long, but that is an exaggeration. Often those ears hung like limp brown drawers dangling from a clothesline; again they were braced rigidly atop his skull.

Mastiff he was, and also German shepherd, with a noticeable influence of English bull, bloodhound and great Dane. Far and wide he was known as "that Greek dog," and not alone because he operated out of the Sugar Bowl and under the aegis of Bill Barbilis. Duboko looked like a Greek.

He had Greek eyes, Greek eyebrows, and a grinning Greek

mouth. Old Mayor Wingate proclaimed in his cups that, in fact, he had heard Duboko bark in Greek; he was willing to demonstrate, if anyone would only catch Duboko by sprinkling a little Attic salt on his tail.

That Greek dog seldom slept at night; he preferred to accompany the town's watchman on his rounds, or to sit in the window of the Sugar Bowl along with cardboard ladies who brandished aloft their cardboard sodas. Sometimes, when I had been called out in the middle of the night and came back from seeing a patient, I would stop and peer through the window and exchange a few signals with Duboko.

"Yes," he seemed to say, "I'm here. Bill forgot and locked me in. I don't mind, unless, of course, there's a fire. See you at Legion meeting tomorrow night, if not at the County Medical Association luncheon tomorrow noon."

At this time there was a new arrival in the Sugar Bowl household—Bill's own father, recruited all the way from Greece, now that Bill's mother was dead.

Spiros Barbilis was slight, silver-headed, round-shouldered, with drooping mustachios which always seemed oozing with black dye. Bill put up another cot in the back room and bought another chiffonier from the second-hand store. He and Duboko escorted the old man up and down Main Street throughout the better part of one forenoon.

"I want you to meet friend of mine," Bill said. "He is my father, but he don't speak no English. I want him to meet all my good friends here in Mahaska Falls, because he will live here always."

Old Mr. Barbilis grew deft at helping Bill with the Sugar Bowl. He carried trays and managed tables, grinning invete-rately, wearing an apron stiff with starch. But he failed to learn much English except "hello" and "good-by" and a few cuss words; I think he was lonely for the land he had left, which certainly Bill was not.

One night—it was two o'clock in the morning—I came back to climb my stairs, stepping carefully from my car to the icy sidewalk in front of the Sugar Bowl. I moved gingerly, because I had left one foot in the Toul sector when a dressing station was shelled; I did not like icy sidewalks.

This night I put my face close to the show window to greet

Duboko, to meet those sly mournful eyes which, on a bitter night, would certainly be waiting there instead of shining in a drifted alley where the watchman prowled.

Two pairs of solemn eyes confronted me when I looked in. Old Mr. Barbilis sat there, too—in his night clothes, but blanketed with an overcoat—he and Duboko, wrapped together among the jars of colored candy and the tinted cardboard girls. They stared out, aloof and dignified in the darkness, musing on a thousand lives that slept near by. I enjoy imagining that they both loved the street, even in its midnight desertion, though doubtless Duboko loved it the more.

In 1923 we were treated to a mystifying phenomenon. There had never been a riot in Mahaska Falls, nor any conflict between racial and religious groups. Actually we had no racial or religious groups; we were all Americans, or thought we were. But, suddenly and amazingly, fiery crosses flared in the darkness of our pasture lands.

I was invited to attend a meeting and did so eagerly, wondering if I might explore this outlandish nonsense in a single evening. When my car stopped at a cornfield gate and ghostly figures came to admit me, I heard voice after voice whispering bashfully, "Hello, doc," "Evening, doc. Glad you came." I was shocked at recognizing the voices. I had known the fathers and grandfathers of these youths—hard-working farmers they were who found a long-sought freedom on the American prairies, and never fumed about the presence of the hard-working Catholics, Jews and black men who were also members of that pioneer community.

There was one public meeting in the town itself. They never tried to hold another; there was too much objection; the voice of Bill Barbilis rang beneath the stars.

A speaker with a pimply face stood illuminated by the flare of gasoline torches on a makeshift rostrum, and dramatically he spread a dollar bill between his hands. "Here," he cried, "is the flag of the Jews!"

Bill Barbilis spoke sharply from the crowd: "Be careful, mister. There is United States seal on that bill."

In discomfiture, the speaker put away his bank note. He ignored Bill as long as he could. He set his own private eagles to screaming, and he talked of battles won, and he wept for the mothers of American boys who lay in France. He said that patriotic 100-per-cent Americans must honor and protect those mothers.

Bill Barbilis climbed to the fender of a car. "Sure," he agreed clearly, "we got to take care of those mothers! Also, other mothers we got to take care of—Catholic mothers, Greek mothers, Jew mothers. We got the mothers of Company C, One Hundred Sixty-eighth Infantry. We got to take care of them. How about Jimmy Clancy? He was Catholic. He got killed in the Lorraine sector. Hyman Levinsky, he got killed the same day. Mr. Speaker, you don't know him because you do not come from Mahaska Falls. We had Buzz Griffin, colored boy used to shine shoes. He go to Chicago and enlist, and he is wounded in the Ninety-second Division!"

It was asking too much for any public speaker to contend against opposition of that sort; and the crowd thought so, too, and Duboko made a joyful noise. The out-of-town organizers withdrew. Fiery crosses blazed less frequently, and the flash of white robes frightened fewer cattle week by week.

Seeds had been sown, however, and now a kind of poison ivy grew within our midnight. Bill Barbilis and Duboko came up to my office one morning, the latter looking annoyed, the former holding a soiled sheet of paper in his hand. "Look what I got, doc."

The message was printed crudely in red ink:

We don't want you here any more. This town is only for 100 per cent law-abiding white Americans. Get out of town! Anti-Greek League.

It had been shoved under the front door of the Sugar Bowl sometime during the previous night.

"Bill," I told him, "don't worry about it. You know the source, probably; at least you can guess."

"Nobody is going to run me out of town," said Bill. "This is my town, and I am American citizen, and I am bugler in American Legion. I bring my old father here from Greece to be American, too, and now he has first papers." His voice trembled slightly.

"Here. Throw it in the wastepaper basket and forget about it."

There was sweat on his forehead. He wiped his face, and

then he was able to laugh. "Doc, I guess you are right. Doc, I guess I am a fool."

He threw the paper away and squared his shoulders and went downstairs. I rescued a rubber glove from Duboko and threw Duboko into the hall, where he licked disinfectant from his jaws and leered at me through the screen.

A second threatening letter was shoved under Bill's door, but after that old Mr. Spiros Barbilis and Duboko did sentry duty, and pedestrians could see them entrenched behind the window. So the third warning came by mail; it told Bill that he was being given twenty-four hours to get out of town for good.

I was a little perturbed when I found Bill loading an Army .45 behind his soda fountain.

"They come around here," he said, "and I blow hell out of them."

He laughed when he said it, but I didn't like the brightness of his eyes, nor the steady, thrice-assured activity of his big clean fingers.

On Friday morning Bill came up to my office again; his face was distressed. But my fears, so far as the Anti-Greeks were concerned, were groundless.

"Do you die," he asked, "when you catch a crisis of pneumonia?"

It was one of his numerous cousins in Sioux Falls. There had been a long-distance telephone call; the cousin was very ill; and the family wanted Bill to come. Bill left promptly in his battered, rakish roadster.

Late that night I was awakened by a clatter of cream cans under my window. I glanced at the illuminated dial of my watch, and lay wondering why the milkman had appeared some two hours before his habit. I was about to drop off to sleep when sounds of a scuffle in the alley and a roar from Duboko in the Barbilis quarters took me to the window in one leap.

There were four white figures down there in the alley yard; they dragged a fifth man—nightshirted, gagged, struggling— along with them. I yelled and pawed around for my glasses, spurred to action by the reverberating hysterics of Duboko. I got the glasses on just before those men dragged old Mr. Barbilis into their car. The car's license plates were plastered thick with mud; at once I knew what had happened.

It was customary for the milkman to clank his bottles and cans on approaching the rear door of the Sugar Bowl; Bill or his father would get out of bed and fetch the milk to the refrigerator, for there were numerous cream-hungry cats along that alley. It was a clinking summons of this sort which had lured the lonely Mr. Barbilis from his bed.

He had gone out sleepily, probably wondering, as I had wondered, why the milkman had come so early. The sound of milk bottles lulled Duboko for a moment.

Then the muffled agony of that struggle, when the visitors clapped a pillow over the old man's face, had been enough to set Duboko bellowing.

But he was shut in; all that he could do was to threaten and curse and hurl himself against the screen. I grabbed for my foot—not the one that God gave me, but the one bought by Uncle Sam—and of course I kicked it under the bed far out of reach.

My car was parked at the opposite end of the building, out in front. I paused only to tear the telephone receiver from its hook and cry to a surprised Central that she must turn on the red light which summoned the night watchman; that someone was kidnaping old Mr. Barbilis.

The kidnapers' car roared eastward down the alley while I was bawling to the operator. And then another sound—the wrench of a heavy body sundering the metal screening. There was only empty silence as I stumbled down the stairway in my pajamas, bouncing on one foot and holding to the stair rails.

I fell into my car and turned on the headlights. The eastern block before me stretched deserted in the pale glow of single bulbs on each electric-light post. But as my car rushed into that deserted block, a small brown shape sped bullet-like across the next intersection. It was Duboko.

I swung right at the corner, and Duboko was not far ahead of me now. Down the dark, empty tunnel of Clive Street the red tail-light of another car diminished rapidly. It hitched away to the left; that would mean that Mr. Barbilis was being carried along the road that crossed the city dump.

Slowing down, I howled at Duboko when I came abreast of him. It seemed that he was a Barbilis, Americanized Greek, like them, and that he must be outraged at this occurrence, and eager to effect a rescue.

But he only slobbered up at me, and labored along on his four driving legs, with spume flying behind. I stepped on the gas again and almost struck the dog, for he would not turn out of the road. I skidded through heavy dust on the dump lane, with filmier dust still billowing back from the kidnapers' car.

For their purpose, the selection of the dump had a strategic excuse as well as a symbolic one. At the nearest boundary of the area there was a big steel gate and barbed-wire fence; you had to get out and open that gate to go through. But if you wished to vanish into the region of river timber and country roads beyond, you could drive across the wasteland without opening the gate again. I suppose that the kidnapers guessed who their pursuer was; they knew of my physical incapacity. They had shut the gate carefully behind them, and I could not go through it without getting out of my car.

But I could see them in the glare of my headlights—four white figures, sheeted and hooded.

Already they had tied Spiros Barbilis to the middle of a fence panel. They had straps, and a whip, and everything else they needed. One man was tying the feet of old Spiros to restrain his kicks; two stood ready to proceed with the flogging; and the fourth blank, hideous, white-hooded creature moved toward the gate to restrain me from interfering. That was the situation when Duboko arrived.

I ponder now the various wickednesses Duboko committed throughout his notorious career. Then for comfort I turn to the words of a Greek—him who preached the most famous funeral oration chanted among the ancients—the words of a man who was Greek in his blood and his pride, and yet who might have honored Duboko eagerly when the dog came seeking, as it were, a kind of sentimental Attican naturalization.

"For even when life's previous record showed faults and failures," said Pericles, with the voice of Thucydides, to the citizens of the Fifth Century, "it is just to weigh the last brave hour of devotion against them all."

Though it was not an hour by any means. No more than ten minutes had elapsed since old Mr. Barbilis was dragged from his back yard. The militant action of Duboko, now beginning, did not occupy more than a few minutes more, at the most. It makes me wonder how long men fought at Marathon, since Pheidippides died before he could tell.

And not even a heavy screen might long contain Duboko;
it is no wonder that a barbed-wire fence was as reeds before
his charge.

He struck the first white figure somewhere above the knees.
There was a snarl and a shriek, and then Duboko was spring-
ing toward the next man.

I didn't see what happened then. I was getting out of the car
and hopping toward the gate. My bare foot came down on
broken glass, and that halted me for a moment. The noise of
the encounter, too, seemed to build an actual, visible barrier
before my eyes.

Our little world was one turmoil of flapping, torn white
robes—a whirling insanity of sheets and flesh and outcry, with
Duboko revolving at the hub. One of the men dodged out of the
melee, and stumbled back, brandishing a club which he had
snatched from the rubble close at hand. I threw a bottle, and
I like to think that that discouraged him; I remember how he
pranced and swore.

Mr. Barbilis managed to get the swathing off his head and
the gag out of his mouth. His frail voice sang minor encour-
agement, and he struggled to unfasten his strapped hands from
the fence.

The conflict was moving now—moving toward the kidnapers'
car. First one man staggered away, fleeing; then another who
limped badly. It was an unequal struggle at best. No four members of the Anti-Greek League, however young and brawny,
could justly be matched against a four-footed warrior who
used his jaws as the original Lacedaemonians must have used
their daggers, and who fought with the right on his side, which
Lacedaemonians did not always do.

Four of the combatants were scrambling into their car; the
fifth was still afoot and reluctant to abandon the contest. By
that time I had been able to get through the gate, and both
Mr. Barbilis and I pleaded with Duboko to give up a war he
had won. But this he would not do; he challenged still, and
tried to fight the car; and so, as they drove away, they ran
him down.

It was ten A.M. before Bill Barbilis returned from Sioux
Falls. I had ample opportunity to impound Bill's .45 automatic
before he came.

His father broke the news to him. I found Bill sobbing with his head on the fountain. I tried to soothe him, in English, and so did Spiros Barbilis, in Greek; but the trouble was that Duboko could no longer speak his own brand of language from the little bier where he rested.

Then Bill went wild, hunting for his pistol and not being able to find it; all the time, his father eagerly and shrilly informed Bill of the identifications he had made when his assailants' gowns were ripped away. Of course, too, there was the evidence of bites and abrasions.

Earl Klugge was limping as he moved about his All-American Kandy Kitchen, and John Klugge smelled of arnica and iodine. A day or two passed before the identity of the other kidnapers leaked out. They were hangers-on at the All-American; they didn't hang on there any longer.

I should have enjoyed seeing what took place, down there at the Clive Street corner. I was only halfway down the block when Bill threw Earl and John Klugge through their own plate-glass window.

A little crowd of men gathered, with our Mayor Wingate among them. There was no talk of damages or of punitive measures to be meted out to Bill Barbilis. I don't know just what train the Klugge brothers left on. But their restaurant was locked by noon, and the windows boarded up.

A military funeral and interment took place that afternoon behind the Sugar Bowl. There was no flag, though I think Bill would have liked to display one. But the crowd of mourners would have done credit to Athens in the age when her dead heroes were burned; all the time that Bill was blowing Taps on his bugle, I had a queer feeling that the ghosts of Pericles and Thucydides were somewhere around.

ELEGY ON THE DEATH OF A MAD DOG

BY *Oliver Goldsmith*

Good people all, of every sort,
   Give ear unto my song;
And if you find it wond'rous short,
   It cannot hold you long.

In Islington there was a man,
   Of whom the world might say,
That still a godly race he ran,
   Whene'er he went to pray.

A kind and gentle heart he had,
   To comfort friends and foes;
The naked every day he clad,
   When he put on his clothes.

And in that town a dog was found,
   As many dogs there be,
Both mongrel, puppy, whelp, and hound,
   And curs of low degree.

This dog and man at first were friends,
   But when a pique began,
The dog, to gain some private ends,
   Went mad and bit the man.

Around from all the neighbouring streets
   The wond'ring neighbours ran,
And swore the dog had lost his wits,
   To bite so good a man.

The wound it seem'd both sore and sad
   To every Christian eye;
And while they swore the dog was mad,
   They swore the man would die.

> But soon a wonder came to light,
>   That show'd the rogues they lied:
> The man recover'd of the bite,
>   The dog it was that died.

THE CANDID DOG

WHAT YUNI THINKS OF HIS MASTER

BY *Jean Gautier*
(*translated by Salvator Attanasio*)

THE FABULIST had claimed that there was a time when beasts
spoke and men had the gift of silence.

I think I have arrived at this happy time and now I shall let
Yuni do the talking.

What will he say of his master?

For once, O Master, I will emerge from my silence and let my heart speak, for it is only with my heart that I can judge. How can a dog judge otherwise?

During the three years that we have been together, I have observed you with constant attention. You will understand even more than I that I have been placed in a situation of complete dependency upon you. My nourishment depends upon your generosity, my freedom upon your will, the gratification of my desires upon your caprice.

This is why I observe your slightest gestures, and spy upon your reflexes and the tricks of your physiognomy. In your face and in your eyes I read joy, sorrow, boredom, relaxation or anger. Your laughter reassures me and makes me happy, a tension in your features disturbs me. And in order to please you, I make your feelings mine.

I make them mine so completely that I begin to feel them myself. I interpret your reactions, your weaknesses and your violences. I know just what I must do in such and such a circumstance, just how far I can go without provoking your annoyance, and sometimes I also know when to abstain, even if the desire seizes me like a fever.

You can see that I am not so stupid and that for a dog picked up in a shelter I have a pretty good head on my shoulders.[1]

We dogs understand man intuitively and we judge their worth very quickly. When in my wretchedness I gave myself to you that day in the shelter, when I extended my paws to you and rested my head on your shoulder in a gesture of self-surrender, I knew quite well that you would not resist my appeal and that you would take me with you despite my hirsute appearance and my poor, pitiful, flea-ridden body.

You are too sensitive to pass before sorrow with indifference. Between us, you are really a bit too sensitive. I do not complain about that which concerns me, but it must be confessed that your impressionability makes you suffer very much. And that hurts me. Indifference wounds you; let the slightest consideration be shown you and your joy is unconfined. Everything is prolonged and undergoes repercussions in you. You would like

---

[1] On the basis of some investigations, I have managed to learn something about Yuni's origin. I was even able to determine his pedigree. He stems from a fine breed, which more than explains his excellent behavior.

to take humanity in your arms and obtain its happiness through
eternal salvation.

Poor master, you will never succeed. Don't you know that
men destroy their happiness the moment they begin to enjoy
it? They are very unstable beings. They not only believe that
life is in movement, *vita in motu*, as the philosophers say, but
they also think that it is in constant change. You refuse, in
principle, to admit these truths that are under your very nose,
even mine, the nose of a poodle. You are an idealist. But do
not be a utopian.

And the souls! You would convert them. This is not an easy
task if one knows the human race. You show them the heavens.
They look down at the earth. Save for some exceptions, how
many actually respond to your call? You suffer thereby, you
sigh, and you lose sleep over it.

It is then that the usefulness of my role as a dog is revealed.
Because I know very well your nights of insomnia during which
even sleeping pills are ineffective, interminable nights when
dawn seems deliberately to delay its appearance, and the clock
inexorably counts the hours, punctuating the darkness with its
chimes.

You toss about in your bed, you squirm, you become exasperated because you cannot sleep, and you reach out your hand
in the void as if to seize Morpheus himself in flight. But what
your hand finds is the head of your dog.

I have kept vigil with you without your even suspecting it.
I have been aware of your restlessness. I have almost heard
the rhythm of your fever beating in my own veins. This is yet
another old instinct of my canine race of which you humans are
unaware. And my presence reassures you. Despite the utter
blackness of the nights, I see your smile, so to speak, when
you find me. Now there are two of us waiting for the light. It
seems to us that dawn will break all the sooner, and that the
light of the new day will be brighter than usual and less
burdened with anxiety.

Sometimes you call me your "good Samaritan." It is just that,
having myself known suffering, I know the worth of consolation.
Yet the suffering of men is rarely useless. They should know
this because it is said that they are intelligent. Suffering purifies

and sanctifies them if they know how to accept it. You often preach this in your sermons. I willingly believe you.

But of what use is a dog's suffering? I sometimes ask myself this question. It is said that our suffering is less acute than that of man because we are less refined and our nature still a little wild. I am not completely convinced of this. Certainly, we cannot understand, analyze, or reason about our sufferings. We are in ignorance of its reason and cause. But does not the horror of all suffering lie precisely therein?

We beasts suffer without any reward and, unlike yourselves, we do not possess the hope that makes us expect better tomorrows. We experience a pathetic defeat in the face of the inexplicable. Why has this world, at other times so benevolent, become so hostile?

Why this abandonment, this captivity, this expiation for one who has not sinned? For we are innocent, we poor beasts. Guided by instinct, we never voluntarily choose evil. Like a child to whom love is denied, we experience the feeling of a tremendous injustice. It is because we are innocent that you so often see in our faces protest, entreaty, and accusation, as well as an expression of poignant questioning. But you do not always understand, you men, stuck fast as you are in the mires of your egotism, or distracted by your vital occupations.

And even if one denies us the consciousness of perceiving regret, absence, or the faculty of having the presentiment of death, would we not, even then, be left with this sensitive keyboard of suffering which is our poor flesh? Like men, we experience hunger, thirst, fatigue, and like them we are structured of muscles, blood and flesh. If we are beaten, we experience unspeakable torment.

On this level, we are in truth your brothers because our fates meet and intertwine. Flesh makes us aware of what the flesh endures. If your imagination is unable to conceive of our inner sufferings when, for instance, a master has disappeared or we are suddenly frozen by fear, certainly your own experience should make you understand what such things as violent beatings, having our paws stepped upon, nasty falls, bleeding wounds, and excessive exertion mean to us.

Write this down in your notes very carefully, my dear master. Remind men that the ascetics and the saints of the first century always made a covenant with creation. Commit them to a renewed discovery of this first current of sympathy. Tell them that if sometimes the animal has become their enemy, it is because they have not desired to remain his friend or ally. They must again find the way to the Garden of Eden.

Have you ever noticed this very strange fact? Concerned as we are to feed our young and to defend them tenaciously as long as they are weak, we let them go their own way once they are older. It is not, however, in such natural attachments that our faithfulness is revealed. We know how to rise to higher forms of tenderness. We rise up to man himself. We link ourselves to him indissolubly.

And here it is no longer possible to pretend that only our instinct is at play. There exists in us an infinite gratitude for benefits received. When we travel enormous distances in order to rejoin a master, when we accompany him everywhere without even knowing where he may be taking us, when in our loyalty to him we break through the formidable abysses of death itself into which we have seen our god descend—for man, miserable as he is, is a god to his dog—can one still deny that we have in a very manifest way arrived at the domain of feeling and at the perception of moral suffering?

But you, my master, know all this and it is because you are so convinced of it that you treat me with kindness and almost with deference. You do not belong to those who are inclined to detest things according to their usefulness and to esteem them in the measure that they are hostile.

How many men admire the lion and hold the ass up to ridicule! One finds a sword solemn and a kerchief laughable. One admires the utensils of war that bring death, and considers as naught the kitchen utensils that support life. One depreciates the domestic servant who does one's housework, but admiringly contemplates Venus de Milo who cannot even use a duster. Thus, from the very moment that they are conceived as having value only in their relation to man, things undergo a degrading devaluation. One treats them like one treats armchairs, socks or toothbrushes.

Your extremely grievous fault is that of seeing only to what use you can put us—without ever considering Him from whose hands we have come forth. Yet we have all come from the hands of God, we are all worthy of respect. A dog is not only an animal with four feet, a machine that barks, a living instrument manufactured for your pleasure. He is a creature worthy of being loved, and one should not take advantage of him or abuse him.

As far as you are concerned, my dear master, you do not take any advantage. I also think that you might take some! You spare me all effort. You yourself prepare my meals so as to assure yourself that they will be to my taste and that they will not endanger my precarious health. You keep me alive by sheer dint of your conscientious attentions.

We are among the veterinarian's best clients. You let him check my heart, my lungs, my liver, my teeth and my temperature. You make me swallow medicines which I would gladly dispense with. But I take them in order to be agreeable, since my faith in the effectiveness of the remedies is very limited.

A good piece of meat, a walk in the great outdoors would seem much more salutary to me. But by acting in this way you satisfy your needs to reassure yourself. This is why I lend myself to your experiments and enter into the spirit of the game.

Sometimes, indeed, I enter into it too much, because your attentions promote my laziness and your assiduous care has become necessary to me. I call to you with that piping voice you know so well—for ever since we have been living together we have always managed to understand each other. I speak man's language just a little and you speak dog's a little—and you lift me and set me in my chair, or you take me in your arms when you think I am too tired. I abandon myself to the role of a child spoiled by an indulgent grandparent.

For you are indulgent with your dog. So it is said in the circle of your friends. It is true that those who say so have never had any animals of their own. People who associate us with a warning signal or who take us for a flea-breeding apparatus never suspect the tremendous tenderness hidden in our hearts. We have no fleas when we are properly kept and, basically, we are much cleaner than most men. As for heart, we have plenty to spark, and we possess the secret of being considerate to our master.

When you were suffering an attack of rheumatism, did you

notice how I stood sagely at your side, I who ordinarily tug at my leash? I did not want to force you to increase the speed of your gait at the risk of increasing your pain. And when you climbed the stairs slowly, did you notice how I offered you my back so that you could have some support? When you were ill and you had to stay in your room, did you notice that I remained near you, next to your bed, and that I refused to go out so as not to leave you alone? And when you go away for a time and entrust me to strange hands, have they ever told you that I was sad and forlorn and refused all nourishment? And when you are late coming home, has anyone told you of my great anxiety? And when you go to your classes, haven't you seen in my eyes the regret at seeing you leave without my being able to go along with you?

Yes, you have noticed all that and many other things too, dear master, because I know that you can read what is in this poor noggin of mine. What I also know is that I am a source of strength to you despite my visible weakness. You have four principal passions—I'll ignore the others—which are: God, men's souls, music which you associate with a feeling for nature, and your dog.

The first two are something apart, belonging to a trascendent order of things. They are not in my domain and are infinitely beyond me. As to music, I do not understand much about it. I listen out of politeness when you begin to scratch on your violin.

But what I understand perfectly is that if you did not have your dog, a little flame of tenderness and faithfulness would be terribly lacking in your life. If I should vanish from your life, you would be very unhappy and you would keep looking for me for a long time in the darkness of the night. Can you say, master, sensitive soul that you are, that this is not true? . . .

And you have still one more weakness: impatience. You do not like to wait. In a restaurant I have seen you rise from the table in the middle of a meal, pay the check and leave, banging the door because the service had not been prompt enough. I have seen you . . .

But, after all, I don't have to reveal everything to those who will read your book. You are very quick in your movements; I am very slow in mine. But with me your patience knows no limits. You accept my slowness as I accept your quickness. All of which means that for me you have no faults. A master, after all, never has any faults in the eyes of his dog. And even should he have, his dog would obstinately close his eyes so as not to see them.

It is for all these things that I love you, my master! It is because of these things that we understand each other so well. And that is why we fear so much the fatal moment when death will come to weave its veil between us.

THE REFLECTIVE DOG

KASHTANKA

BY *Anton Chekhov*
(*translated by Constance Garnett*)

I

MISBEHAVIOR

A YOUNG DOG, a reddish mongrel, between a dachshund and a "yard-dog," very like a fox in face, was running up and down the pavement looking uneasily from side to side. From time to time she stopped and, whining and lifting first one chilled paw and then another, tried to make up her mind how it could have happened that she was lost.

She remembered very well how she had passed the day, and how, in the end, she had found herself on this unfamiliar pavement.

The day had begun by her master Luka Alexandritch's putting on his hat, taking something wooden under his arm wrapped up in a red handkerchief, and calling: "Kashtanka, come along!"

Hearing her name, the mongrel had come out from under the work-table, where she slept on the shavings, stretched herself voluptuously and run after her master. The people Luka Alexandritch worked for lived a very long way off, so that, before he could get to any one of them, the carpenter had several times

to step into a tavern to fortify himself. Kashtanka remembered
that on the way she had behaved extremely improperly. In her
delight that she was being taken for a walk she jumped about,
dashed barking after the trams, ran into yards, and chased
other dogs. The carpenter was continually losing sight of her,
stopping, and angrily shouting at her. Once he had even, with
an expression of fury in his face, taken her foxlike ear in his
fist, smacked her, and said emphatically: "Pla-a-gue take you,
you pest!"

After having left the work where it had been bespoken, Luka
Alexandritch went into his sister's and there had something to
eat and drink; from his sister's he had gone to see a bookbinder
he knew; from the bookbinder to a tavern, from the tavern to
another crony's, and so on. In short, by the time Kashtanka
found herself on the unfamiliar pavement, it was getting dusk,
and the carpenter was as drunk as a cobbler. He was waving
his arms and, breathing heavily, muttered:

"In sin my mother bore me! Ah, sins, sins! Here now we are
walking along the street and looking at the street lamps, but
when we die, we shall burn in a fiery Gehenna. . . ."

Or he fell into a good-natured tone, called Kashtanka to him,
and said to her: "You, Kashtanka, are an insect of a creature,
and nothing else. Beside a man, you are much the same as a
joiner beside a cabinetmaker. . . ."

While he talked to her in that way, there was suddenly a burst
of music. Kashtanka looked round and saw that a regiment of
soldiers was coming straight towards her. Unable to endure the
music, which unhinged her nerves, she turned round and round
and wailed. To her great surprise, the carpenter, instead of
being frightened, whining and barking, gave a broad grin, drew
himself up to attention, and saluted with all his five fingers.
Seeing that her master did not protest, Kashtanka whined louder
than ever, and dashed across the road to the opposite pavement.

When she recovered herself, the band was not playing and
the regiment was no longer there. She ran across the road to
the spot where she had left her master, but alas, the carpenter
was no longer there. She dashed forward, then back again and
ran across the road once more, but the carpenter seemed to have
vanished into the earth. Kashtanka began sniffing the pavement,
hoping to find her master by the scent of his tracks, but some

wretch had been that way just before in new rubber galoshes, and now all delicate scents were mixed with an acute stench of india-rubber, so that it was impossible to make out anything.

Kashtanka ran up and down and did not find her master, and meanwhile it had got dark. The street lamps were lighted on both sides of the road, and lights appeared in the windows. Big, fluffy snowflakes were falling and painting white the pavement, the horses' backs and the cabmen's caps, and the darker the evening grew the whiter were all these objects. Unknown customers kept walking incessantly to and fro, obstructing her field of vision and shoving against her with their feet. (All mankind Kashtanka divided into two uneven parts: masters and customers; between them there was an essential difference: the first had the right to beat her, and the second she had the right to nip by the calves of their legs.) These customers were hurrying off somewhere and paid no attention to her.

When it got quite dark, Kashtanka was overcome by despair and horror. She huddled up in an entrance and began whining piteously. The long day's journeying with Luka Alexandritch had exhausted her, her ears and her paws were freezing, and, what was more, she was terribly hungry. Only twice in the whole day had she tasted a morsel: she had eaten a little paste at the bookbinder's, and in one of the taverns she had found a sausage skin on the floor, near the counter—that was all. If she had been a human being she would have certainly thought: "No, it is impossible to live like this! I must shoot myself!"

II

A MYSTERIOUS STRANGER

But she thought of nothing, she simply whined. When her head and back were entirely plastered over with the soft feathery snow, and she had sunk into a painful doze of exhaustion, all at once the door of the entrance clicked, creaked, and struck her on the side. She jumped up. A man belonging to the class of customers came out. As Kashtanka whined and got under his feet, he could not help noticing her. He bent down to her and asked:

"Doggy, where do you come from? Have I hurt you? Oh, poor thing, poor thing. . . . Come, don't be cross, don't be cross. . . . I am sorry."

Kashtanka looked at the stranger through the snowflakes that hung on her eyelashes, and saw before her a short, fat little man, with a plump, shaven face, wearing a top hat and a fur coat that swung open.

"What are you whining for?" he went on, knocking the snow off her back with his fingers. "Where is your master? I suppose you are lost? Ah, poor doggy! What are we going to do now?"

Catching in the stranger's voice a warm, cordial note, Kashtanka licked his hand, and whined still more pitifully.

"Oh, you nice funny thing!" said the stranger. "A regular fox! Well, there's nothing for it, you must come along with me! Perhaps you will be of use for something. . . . Well!"

He clicked with his lips, and made a sign to Kashtanka with his hand, which could only mean one thing: "Come along!" Kashtanka went.

Not more than half an hour later she was sitting on the floor in a big, light room, and, leaning her head against her side, was looking with tenderness and curiosity at the stranger who was sitting at the table, dining. He ate and threw pieces to her. . . . At first he gave her bread and the green rind of cheese, then a piece of meat, half a pie and chicken bones, while through hunger she ate so quickly that she had not time to distinguish the taste, and the more she ate the more acute was the feeling of hunger.

"Your master don't feed you properly," said the stranger, seeing with what ferocious greediness she swallowed the morsels without munching them. "And how thin you are! Nothing but skin and bones. . . ."

Kashtanka ate a great deal and yet did not satisfy her hunger, but was simply stupefied with eating. After dinner she lay down in the middle of the room, stretched her legs and, conscious of an agreeable weariness all over her body, wagged her tail. While her new master, lounging in an easy-chair, smoked a cigar, she wagged her tail and considered the question, whether it was better at the stranger's or at the carpenter's. The stranger's surroundings were poor and ugly; besides the easy-chairs, the sofa, the lamps and the rugs, there was nothing, and the room seemed empty. At the carpenter's the whole place was stuffed full of things: he had a table, a bench, a heap of shavings, planes, chisels, saws, a cage with a goldfinch, a basin. . . . The stranger's room smelt of nothing, while there was always a thick fog in the carpenter's room, and a glorious smell of glue, varnish, and shavings. On the other hand, the stranger had one great superiority—he gave her a great deal to eat and, to do him full justice, when Kashtanka sat facing the table and looking wistfully at him, he did not once hit or kick her, and he did not once shout: "Go away, damned brute!"

When he had finished his cigar her new master went out, and a minute later came back holding a little mattress in his hands.

"Hey, you dog, come here!" he said, laying the mattress in the corner near the dog. "Lie down here, go to sleep!"

Then he put out the lamp and went away. Kashtanka lay down on the mattress and shut her eyes; the sound of a bark rose from the street, and she would have liked to answer it, but all at once she was overcome with unexpected melancholy. She thought of Luka Alexandritch, of his son Fedyushka, and her snug little place under the bench. . . . She remembered on the long winter evenings, when the carpenter was planing or reading the paper aloud, Fedyushka usually played with her. . . . He used to pull her from under the bench by her hind legs, and play such tricks with her, that she saw green before her eyes, and ached in every joint. He would make her walk on her hind legs, use her as a bell, that is, shake her violently by the tail so that she squealed and barked, and give her tobacco to sniff. . . . The following trick was particularly agonizing: Fedyushka would tie a piece of meat to a thread and give it to Kashtanka, and then, when she had swallowed it he would, with a loud laugh, pull it back again from her stomach, and the more lurid were her memories the more loudly and miserably Kashtanka whined.

But soon exhaustion and warmth prevailed over melancholy. She began to fall asleep. Dogs ran by in her imagination: among them a shaggy old poodle, whom she had seen that day in the street with a white patch on his eye and tufts of wool by his nose. Feduyshka ran after the poodle with a chisel in his hand, then all at once he too was covered with shaggy wool, and began merrily barking beside Kashtanka. Kashtanka and he good-naturedly sniffed each other's noses and merrily ran down the street. . . .

III

NEW AND VERY AGREEABLE ACQUAINTANCES

When Kashtanka woke up it was already light, and a sound rose from the street, such as only comes in the daytime. There was not a soul in the room. Kashtanka stretched, yawned and, cross and ill-humored, walked about the room. She sniffed the corners and the furniture, looked into the passage and found nothing of interest there. Besides the door that led into the passage there was another door. After thinking a little Kashtanka scratched on it with both paws, opened it, and went into the adjoining room. Here on the bed, covered with a rug, a customer, in whom she recognized the stranger of yesterday, lay asleep.

"Rrrrr . . ." she growled, but recollecting yesterday's dinner, wagged her tail, and began sniffing.

She sniffed the stranger's clothes and boots and thought they smelt of horses. In the bedroom was another door, also closed. Kashtanka scratched at the door, leaned her chest against it, opened it, and was instantly aware of a strange and very suspicious smell. Foreseeing an unpleasant encounter, growling and looking about her, Kashtanka walked into a little room with a dirty wallpaper and drew back in alarm. She saw something surprising and terrible. A gray gander came straight towards her, hissing, with its neck bowed down to the floor and its wings outspread. Not far from him, on a little mattress, lay a white tom-cat; seeing Kashtanka he jumped up, arched his back, wagged his tail with his hair standing on end and he, too, hissed at her. The dog was frightened in earnest, but not caring to betray her alarm, began barking loudly and dashed at the cat. . . . The cat arched his back more than ever, mewed and gave Kashtanka a smack on the head with his paw. Kashtanka jumped back, squatted on all four paws, and craning her nose towards the cat, went off into loud, shrill barks; meanwhile the gander came up behind and gave her a painful peck in the back. Kashtanka leapt up and dashed at the gander.

"What's this?" They heard a loud angry voice, and the stranger came into the room in his dressing-gown, with a cigar between his teeth. "What's the meaning of this? To your places!"

He went up to the cat, flicked him on his arched back, and said:

"Fyodor Timofeyitch, what's the meaning of this? Have you got up a fight? Ah, you old rascal! Lie down!"

And turning to the gander he shouted: "Ivan Ivanitch, go home!"

The cat obediently lay down on his mattress and closed his eyes. Judging from the expression of his face and whiskers, he was displeased with himself for having lost his temper and got into a fight. Kashtanka began whining resentfully, while the gander craned his neck and began saying something rapidly, excitedly, distinctly, but quite unintelligibly.

"All right, all right," said his master, yawning. "You must live in peace and friendship." He stroked Kashtanka and went on: "And you, red-hair, don't be frightened. . . . They are capital company, they won't annoy you. Stay, what are we to call you? You can't go on without a name, my dear."

The stranger thought a moment and said: "I tell you what . . . you shall be Auntie. . . . Do you understand? Auntie!"

And repeating the word "Auntie" several times he went out. Kashtanka sat down and began watching. The cat sat motionless on his little mattress, and pretended to be asleep. The gander, craning his neck and stamping, went on talking rapidly and excitedly about something. Apparently it was a very clever gander; after every long tirade, he always stepped back with an air of wonder and made a show of being highly delighted with his own speech. . . . Listening to him and answering "R-r-r-r," Kashtanka fell to sniffing the corners. In one of the corners she found a little trough in which she saw some soaked peas and a sop of rye crusts. She tried the peas; they were not nice; she tried the sopped bread and began eating it. The gander was not at all offended that the strange dog was eating his food, but, on the contrary, talked even more excitedly, and to show his confidence went to the trough and ate a few peas himself.

IV

MARVELS ON A HURDLE

A little while afterwards the stranger came in again, and brought a strange thing with him like a hurdle, or like the figure II. On the crosspiece on the top of this roughly made wooden frame hung a bell, and a pistol was also tied to it; there were strings from the tongue of the bell, and the trigger of the pistol. The stranger put the frame in the middle of the room, spent a long time tying and untying something, then looked at the gander and said: "Ivan Ivanitch, if you please!"

The gander went up to him and stood in an expectant attitude.

"Now then," said the stranger, "let us begin at the very beginning. First of all, bow and make a curtsey! Look sharp!"

Ivan Ivanitch craned his neck, nodded in all directions, and scraped with his foot.

"Right. Bravo. . . . Now die!"

The gander lay on his back and stuck his legs in the air. After performing a few more similar, unimportant tricks, the stranger suddenly clutched at his head, and assuming an expression of horror, shouted: "Help! Fire! We are burning!"

Ivan Ivanitch ran to the frame, took the string in his beak, and set the bell ringing.

The stranger was very much pleased. He stroked the gander's neck and said:

"Bravo, Ivan Ivanitch Now pretend that you are a jeweler selling gold and diamonds. Imagine now that you go to your shop and find thieves there. What would you do in that case?"

The gander took the other string in his beak and pulled it, and at once a deafening report was heard. Kashtanka was highly delighted with the bell ringing, and the shot threw her into so much ecstasy that she ran round the frame barking.

"Auntie, lie down!" cried the stranger; "be quiet!"

Ivan Ivanitch's task was not ended with the shooting. For a whole hour afterwards the stranger drove the gander round him on a cord, cracking a whip, and the gander had to jump over barriers and through hoops; he had to rear, that is, sit on his tail and wave his legs in the air. Kashtanka could not take her eyes off Ivanitch, wriggled with delight, and several times fell to running after him with shrill barks. After exhausting the gander and himself, the stranger wiped the sweat from his brow and cried:

"Marya, fetch Havronya Ivanovna here!"

A minute later there was the sound of grunting. . . . Kashtanka growled, assumed a very valiant air, and to be on the safe side, went nearer to the stranger. The door opened, an old woman looked in, and, saying something, led in a black and very ugly sow. Paying no attention to Kashtanka's growls, the sow lifted up her little hoof and grunted good-humoredly. Apparently it was very agreeable to her to see her master, the cat, and Ivan Ivanitch. When she went up to the cat and gave him a light tap on the stomach with her hoof, and then made some remark to the gander, a great deal of good-nature was expressed in her movements, and the quivering of her tail. Kashtanka realized at once that to growl and bark at such a character was useless.

The master took away the frame and cried: "Fyodor Timofeyitch, if you please!"

The cat stretched lazily, and reluctantly, as though performing a duty, went up to the sow.

"Come, let us begin with the Egyptian pyramid," began the master.

He spent a long time explaining something, then gave the word of command, "One . . . two . . . three!" At the word "three" Ivan Ivanitch flapped his wings and jumped onto the sow's back. . . . When, balancing himself with his wings and his neck, he got a firm foothold on the bristly back. Fyodor Timofeyitch listlessly and lazily, with manifest disdain, and with an air of scorning his art and not caring a pin for it, climbed onto the sow's back, then reluctantly mounted onto the gander, and stood on his hind legs. The result was what the stranger called the Egyptian pyramid. Kashtanka yapped with delight, but at that moment the old cat yawned and, losing his balance, rolled off the gander. Ivan Ivanitch lurched and fell off too. The stranger shouted, waved his hands, and began explaining something again. After spending an hour over the pyramid their indefatigable master proceeded to teach Ivan Ivanitch to ride on the cat, then began to teach the cat to smoke, and so on.

The lesson ended in the stranger's wiping the sweat off his brow and going away. Fyodor Timofeyitch gave a disdainful sniff, lay down on his mattress, and closed his eyes; Ivan Ivanitch went to the trough, and the pig was taken away by the old woman. Thanks to the number of her new impressions, Kashtanka hardly noticed how the day passed, and in the evening she was installed with her mattress in the room with the dirty wallpaper, and spent the night in the society of Fyodor Timofeyitch and the gander.

V

TALENT! TALENT!

A month passed.

Kashtanka had grown used to having a nice dinner every evening, and being called Auntie. She had grown used to the stranger too, and to her new companions. Life was comfortable and easy.

Every day began in the same way. As a rule, Ivan Ivanitch was the first to wake up, and at once went up to Auntie or to the cat, twisting his neck, and beginning to talk excitedly and persuasively, but, as before, unintelligibly. Sometimes he would crane up his head in the air and utter a long monologue. At first Kashtanka thought he talked so much because he was very clever, but after a little time had passed, she lost all her respect for him; when he went up to her with his long speeches she no longer wagged her tail, but treated him as a tiresome chatterbox, who would not let anyone sleep and, without the slightest ceremony, answered him with "R-r-r-r!"

Fyodor Timofeyitch was a gentleman of very different sort. When he woke he did not utter a sound, did not stir, and did not even open his eyes. He would have been glad not to wake, for, as was evident, he was not greatly in love with life. Nothing interested him, he showed an apathetic and nonchalant attitude to everything, he disdained everything and, even while eating his delicious dinner, sniffed contemptuously.

When she woke Kashtanka began walking about the room and sniffing the corners. She and the cat were the only ones allowed to go all over the flat; the gander had not the right to cross the threshold of the room with the dirty wallpaper, and Havronya Ivanovna lived somewhere in a little outhouse in the yard and made her appearance only during the lessons. Their master got up late, and immediately after drinking his tea began teaching them their tricks. Every day the frame, the whip, and the hoop were brought in, and every day almost the same performance took place. The lesson lasted three or four hours, so that sometimes Fyodor Timofeyitch was so tired that he staggered about like a drunken man, and Ivan Ivanitch opened his beak and breathed heavily, while their master became red in the face and could not mop the sweat from his brow fast enough.

The lesson and the dinner made the day very interesting, but the evenings were tedious. As a rule, their master went off somewhere in the evening and took the cat and the gander with him. Left alone, Auntie lay down on her little mattress and began to feel sad. . . .

Melancholy crept on her imperceptibly and took possession of her by degrees, as darkness does of a room. It began with the dog's losing every inclination to bark, to eat, to run about the rooms, and even to look at things; then vague figures, half dogs, half human beings, with countenances attractive, pleasant, but incomprehensible, would appear in her imagination; when they came Auntie wagged her tail, and it seemed to her that she had somewhere, at some time, seen them and loved them. . . . And as she dropped asleep, she always felt that those figures smelt of glue, shavings, and varnish.

When she had grown quite used to her new life, and from a thin, long mongrel, had changed into a sleek well-groomed dog, her master looked at her one day before the lesson and said:

"It's high time, Auntie, to get to business. You have kicked up your heels in idleness long enough. I want to make an artiste of you. . . . Do you want to be an artiste?"

And he began teaching her various accomplishments. At the first lesson he taught her to stand and walk on her hind legs, which she liked extremely. At the second lesson she had to jump on her hind legs and catch some sugar, which her teacher held high above her head. After that, in the following lessons she danced, ran tied to a cord, howled to music, rang the bell, and fired the pistol and in a month could successfully replace Fyodor Timofeyitch in the "Egyptian Pyramid." She learned very eagerly and was pleased with her own success; running with her tongue out on the cord, leaping through the hoop, and riding on old Fyodor Timofeyitch, gave her the greatest enjoyment. She accompanied every successful trick with a shrill, delighted bark, while her teacher wondered, was also delighted, and rubbed his hands.

"It's talent! It's talent!" he said. "Unquestionable talent! You will certainly be successful!"

And Auntie grew so used to the word talent, that every time her master pronounced it, she jumped up as if it had been her name.

VI

AN UNEASY NIGHT

Auntie had a doggy dream that a porter ran after her with a broom, and she woke up in a fright.

It was quite dark and very stuffy in the room. The fleas were biting. Auntie had never been afraid of darkness before, but now, for some reason, she felt frightened and inclined to bark.

Her master heaved a loud sigh in the next room, then soon afterwards the sow grunted in her sty, and then all was still again. When one thinks about eating one's heart grows lighter, and Auntie began thinking how that day she had stolen the leg of chicken from Fyodor Timofeyitch, and had hidden it in the drawing-room, between the cupboard and the wall, where there were a great many spiders' webs and a great deal of dust. Would it not be as well to go now and look whether the chicken leg were still there or not? It was very possible that her master had found it and eaten it. But she must not go out of the room before morning, that was the rule. Auntie shut her eyes to go to sleep as quickly as possible, for she knew by experience that the sooner you go to sleep the sooner the morning comes. But all at once there was a strange scream not far from her which made her start and jump up on all four legs. It was Ivan Ivanitch, and his cry was not babbling and persuasive as usual, but a wild, shrill, unnatural scream, like the squeak of a door opening. Unable to distinguish anything in the darkness, and not understanding what was wrong, Auntie felt still more frightened and growled: "R-r-r-r. . . ."

Some time passed, as long as it takes to eat a good bone; the scream was not repeated. Little by little Auntie's uneasiness passed off and she began to doze. She dreamed of two big black dogs with tufts of last year's coat left on their haunches and sides; they were eating out of a big basin some swill, from which there came a white steam and a most appetizing smell;

from time to time they looked round at Auntie, showed their
teeth and growled: "We are not going to give you any!" But
a peasant in a fur coat ran out of the house and drove them
away with a whip; then Auntie went up to the basin and began
eating, but as soon as the peasant went out of the gate, the two
black dogs rushed at her growling, and all at once there was
again a shrill scream.

"K-gee! K-gee-gee!" cried Ivan Ivanitch.

Auntie woke, jumped up and, without leaving her mattress,
went off into a yelping bark. It seemed to her that it was not
Ivan Ivanitch that was screaming but someone else, and for
some reason the sow again grunted in her sty.

Then there was the sound of shuffling slippers, and the master
came into the room in his dressing-gown with a candle in his
hand. The flickering light danced over the dirty wallpaper
and the ceiling, and chased away the darkness. Auntie saw
that there was no stranger in the room. Ivan Ivanitch was sitting
on the floor and was not asleep. His wings were spread out and
his beak was open, and altogether he looked as though he were
very tired and thirsty. Old Fyodor Timofeyitch was not asleep
either. He, too, must have been awakened by the scream.

"Ivan Ivanitch, what's the matter with you?" the master
asked the gander. "Why are you screaming? Are you ill?"

The gander did not answer. The master touched him on the
neck, stroked his back, and said, "You are a queer chap. You
don't sleep yourself, and you don't let other people. . . ."

When the master went out, carrying the candle with him, there
was darkness again. Auntie felt frightened. The gander did not
scream, but again she fancied that there was some stranger in
the room. What was most dreadful was that this stranger could
not be bitten, as he was unseen and had no shape. And for some
reason she thought that something very bad would certainly
happen that night. Fyodor Timofeyitch was uneasy too. Auntie
could hear him shifting on his mattress, yawning and shaking
his head.

Somewhere in the street there was a knocking at a gate and
the sow grunted in her sty. Auntie began to whine, stretched
out her front paws and laid her head down upon them. She
fancied that in the knocking at the gate, in the grunting of the
sow, who was for some reason awake, in the darkness and the

stillness, there was something as miserable and dreadful as in Ivan Ivanitch's scream. Everything was in agitation and anxiety, but why? Who was the stranger who could not be seen? Then two dim flashes of green gleamed for a minute near Auntie. It was Fyodor Timofeyitch, for the first time of their whole acquaintance coming up to her. What did he want? Auntie licked his paw, and not asking why he had come, howled softly and on various notes.

"K-gee!" cried Ivan Ivanitch, "k-g-ee!"

The door opened again and the master came in with a candle.

The gander was sitting in the same attitude as before, with his beak open, and his wings spread out, his eyes were closed.

"Ivan Ivanitch!" his master called him.

The gander did not stir. His master sat down before him on the floor, looked at him in silence for a minute, and said:

"Ivan Ivanitch, what is it? Are you dying? Oh, I remember now, I remember!" he cried out, and clutched at his head. "I know why it is! It's because the horse stepped on you today! My God! My God!"

Auntie did not understand what her master was saying, but she saw from his face that he, too, was expecting something dreadful. She stretched out her head towards the dark window, where it seemed to her some stranger was looking in, and howled.

"He is dying, Auntie!" said her master, and wrung his hands. "Yes, yes, he is dying! Death has come into your room. What are we to do?"

Pale and agitated, the master went back into his room, sighing and shaking his head. Auntie was afraid to remain in the darkness, and followed her master into his bedroom. He sat down on the bed and repeated several times: "My God, what's to be done?"

Auntie walked about round his feet, and not understanding why she was wretched and why they were all so uneasy, and trying to understand, watched every movement he made. Fyodor Timofeyitch, who rarely left his little mattress, came into the master's bedroom too, and began rubbing himself against his feet. He shook his head as though he wanted to shake painful thoughts out of it, and kept peeping suspiciously under the bed.

The master took a saucer, poured some water from his washstand into it, and went to the gander again.

"Drink, Ivan Ivanitch!" he said tenderly, setting the saucer before him: "Drink, darling."

But Ivan Ivanitch did not stir and did not open his eyes. His master bent his head down to the saucer and dipped his beak into the water, but the gander did not drink, he spread his wings wider than ever, and his head remained lying in the saucer.

"No, there's nothing to be done now," sighed his master. "It's all over. Ivan Ivanitch is gone!"

And shining drops, such as one sees on the windowpane when it rains, trickled down his cheeks. Not understanding what was the matter, Auntie and Fyodor Timofeyitch snuggled up to him and looked with horror at the gander.

"Poor Ivan Ivanitch!" said the master, sighing mournfully. "And I was dreaming I would take you in the spring into the country, and would walk with you on the green grass. Dear creature, my good comrade, you are no more! How shall I do without you now?"

It seemed to Auntie that the same thing would happen to her, that she too, there was no knowing why, would close her eyes, stretch out her paws, open her mouth and everyone would look at her with horror. Apparently the same reactions were passing through the brain of Fyodor Timofeyitch. Never before had the old cat been so morose and gloomy.

It began to get light, and the unseen stranger who had so frightened Auntie was no longer in the room. When it was quite daylight, the porter came in, took the gander, and carried him away. And soon afterwards the old woman came in and took away the trough.

Auntie went into the drawing-room and looked behind the cupboard: her master had not eaten the chicken bone, it was lying in its place among the dust and spiders' webs. But Auntie felt sad and dreary and wanted to cry. She did not even sniff at the bone, but went under the sofa, sat down there, and began softly whining in a thin voice.

VII

AN UNSUCCESSFUL DEBUT

One fine evening the master came into the room with the dirty wallpaper, and, rubbing his hands, said:

"Well. . . ."

He meant to say something more, but went away without saying it. Auntie, who during her lessons had thoroughly studied his face and intonations, divined that he was agitated, anxious and, she fancied, angry. Soon afterwards he came back and said:

"Today I shall take with me Auntie and Fyodor Tymofeyitch. Today, Auntie, you will take the place of poor Ivan Ivanitch in the 'Egyptian Pyramid.' Goodness knows how it will be! Nothing is ready, nothing has been thoroughly studied, there have been few rehearsals! We shall be disgraced, we shall come to grief!"

Then he went out again, and a minute later, came back in his fur coat and top hat. Going up to the cat he took him by the forepaws and put him inside the front of his coat, while Fyodor Timofeyitch appeared completely unconcerned, and did not even trouble to open his eyes. To him it was apparently a matter of absolute indifference whether he remained lying down, or were lifted up by his paws, whether he rested on his mattress or under his master's fur coat. . . .

"Come along, Auntie," said her master.

Wagging her tail, and understanding nothing, Auntie followed him. A minute later she was sitting in a sledge by her master's feet and heard him, shrinking with cold and anxiety, mutter to himself:

"We shall be disgraced! We shall come to grief!"

The sledge stopped at a big strange-looking house, like a soup-ladle turned upside down. The long entrance to this house, with its three glass doors, was lighted up with a dozen brilliant lamps. The doors opened with a resounding noise and, like jaws, swallowed up the people who were moving to and fro at the entrance. There were a great many people, horses, too, often ran up to the entrance, but no dogs were to be seen.

The master took Auntie in his arms and thrust her in his coat, where Fyodor Timofeyitch already was. It was dark and stuffy there, but warm. For an instant two green sparks flashed at her; it was the cat, who opened his eyes on being disturbed by his neighbor's cold rough paws. Auntie licked his ear and, trying to settle herself as comfortably as possible, moved uneasily, crushed him under her cold paws, and casually poked her head out from under the coat, but at once growled angrily, and tucked it in again. It seemed to her that she had seen a huge, badly lighted room, full of monsters; from behind screens and gratings, which stretched on both sides of the room, horrible faces looked out: faces of horses with horns, with long ears, and one fat, huge countenance with a tail instead of a nose, and two long gnawed bones sticking out of his mouth.

The cat mewed huskily under Auntie's paws, but at that moment the coat was flung open, the master said, "Hop!" and Fyodor Timofeyitch and Auntie jumped to the floor. They were now in a little room with gray plank walls; there was no other furniture in it but a little table with a looking-glass on it, a stool, and some rags hung about the corners, and instead of a lamp or candles, there was a bright fan-shaped light attached to a little pipe fixed in the wall. Fyodor Timofeyitch licked his coat which had been ruffled by Auntie, went under the stool, and lay down. Their master, still agitated and rubbing his hands, began undressing. . . . He undressed as he usually did at home when he was preparing to get under the rug, that is, took off everything but his underlinen, then he sat down on the stool and, looking in the looking-glass, began playing the most surprising tricks with himself. . . . First of all he put on his head a wig, with a parting and with two tufts of hair standing up like horns, then he smeared his face thickly with something white, and over the white color painted his eyebrows, his mustaches, and red on his cheeks. His antics did not end with that. After smearing his face and neck, he began putting himself into an extraordinary and incongruous costume, such as Auntie had never seen before, either in houses or in the street. Imagine very full trousers, made of chintz covered with big flowers, such as is used in working-class houses for curtains and covering furniture, trousers which buttoned up just under his armpits. One trouser leg was made of brown chintz, the other of bright yellow. Almost lost in these, he then put on a short chintz jacket, with a big scalloped collar, and a gold star on the back, stockings of different colors, and green slippers.

Everything seemed going round before Auntie's eyes and in her soul. The white-faced, sack-like figure smelt like her master, its voice, too, was the familiar master's voice, but there were moments when Auntie was tortured by doubts, and then she was ready to run away from the parti-colored figure and to bark. The new place, the fan-shaped light, the smell, the transformation that had taken place in her master—all this aroused in her a vague dread and a foreboding that she would certainly meet with some horror such as the big face with the tail instead of a nose. And then, somewhere through the wall, some hateful band was playing, and from time to time she heard an incomprehensible roar. Only one thing reassured her —that was the imperturbability of Fyodor Timofeyitch. He dozed with the utmost tranquillity under the stool, and did not open his eyes even when it was moved.

A man in a dress coat and a white waistcoat peeped into the little room and said:

"Miss Arabella has just gone on. After her—you."

Their master made no answer. He drew a small box from under the table, sat down, and waited. From his lips and his hands it could be seen that he was agitated, and Auntie could hear how his breathing came in gasps.

"Monsieur George, come on!" someone shouted behind the door. Their master got up and crossed himself three times, then took the cat from under the stool and put him in the box.

"Come, Auntie," he said softly.

Auntie, who could make nothing out of it, went up to his hands, he kissed her on the head, and put her beside Fyodor Timofeyitch. Then followed darkness. . . . Auntie trampled on the cat, scratched at the walls of the box, and was so frightened that she could not utter a sound, while the box swayed and quivered, as though it were on the waves. . . .

"Here we are again!" her master shouted aloud: "here we are again!"

Auntie felt that after that shout the box struck against something hard and left off swaying. There was a loud deep roar, someone was being slapped, and that someone, probably the monster with the tail instead of a nose, roared and laughed so loud that the locks of the box trembled. In response to the roar, there came a shrill, squeaky laugh from her master, such as he never laughed at home.

"Ha!" he shouted, trying to shout above the roar. "Honored friends! I have only just come from the station! My granny's kicked the bucket and left me a fortune! There is something very heavy in the box, it must be gold, ha! ha! I bet there's a million here! We'll open it and look. . . ."

The lock of the box clicked. The bright light dazzled Auntie's eyes, she jumped out of the box, and, deafened by the roar, ran quickly round her master, and broke into a shrill bark.

"Ha!" exclaimed her master. "Uncle Fyodor Timofeyitch! Beloved Aunt, dear relations! The devil take you!"

He fell on his stomach on the sand, seized the cat and Auntie, and fell to embracing them. While he held Auntie tight in his arms, she glanced round into the world into which fate had brought her and, impressed by its immensity, was for a minute dumfounded with amazement and delight, then jumped out of her master's arms, and to express the intensity of her emotions, whirled round and round on one spot like a top. This new world was big and full of bright light; wherever she looked, on all sides, from floor to ceiling there were faces, faces, and nothing else.

"Auntie, I beg you to sit down!" shouted her master. Remembering what that meant, Auntie jumped onto a chair, and sat down. She looked at her master. His eyes looked at her gravely and kindly as always, but his face, especially his mouth and teeth, were made grotesque by a broad immovable grin. He laughed, skipped about, twitched his shoulders, and made a show of being very merry in the presence of the thousands of faces. Auntie believed in his merriment, all at once felt all over her that those thousands of faces were looking at her, lifted up her foxlike head, and howled joyously.

"You sit there, Auntie," her master said to her, "while Uncle and I will dance to Kamarinsky."

Fyodor Timofeyitch stood looking about him indifferently, waiting to be made to do something silly. He danced listlessly, carelessly, sullenly and one could see from his movements, his tail and his ears, that he had a profound contempt for the crowd, the bright light, his master, and himself. When he had performed his allotted task, he gave a yawn and sat down.

"Now, Auntie," said her master, "we'll have first a song, and then a dance, shall we?"

He took a pipe out of his pocket, and began playing. Auntie, who could not endure music, began moving uneasily in her chair and howled. A roar of applause rose from all sides. Her master bowed and when all was still again, went on playing. . . . Just as he took one very high note, someone high up among the audience uttered a loud exclamation:

"Auntie!" cried a child's voice, "why, it's Kashtanka!"

"Kashtanka it is!" declared a cracked drunken tenor. "Kashtanka! Strike me dead, Fedyushka, it is Kashtanka. Kashtanka! Here!"

Someone in the gallery gave a whistle, and two voices, one a boy's and one a man's, called loudly: "Kashtanka! Kashtanka!"

Auntie started, and looked where the shouting came from. Two faces, one hairy, drunken and grinning, the other chubby, rosy-cheeked and frightened-looking, dazed her eyes as the bright light had dazed them before. . . . She remembered, fell off the chair, struggled on the sand, then jumped up, and with a delighted yap dashed towards those faces. There was a deafening roar, interspersed with whistles and a shrill childish shout: "Kashtanka! Kashtanka!"

Auntie leaped over the barrier, then across someone's shoulders. She found herself in a box: to get into the next tier she had to leap over a high wall. Auntie jumped, but did not jump high enough, and slipped back down the wall. Then she was passed from hand to hand, licked hands and faces, kept mounting higher and higher, and at last got into the gallery. . . .

Half an hour afterwards, Kashtanka was in the street, following the people who smelt of glue and varnish. Luka Alexandritch staggered and instinctively, taught by experience, tried to keep as far from the gutter as possible.

"In sin my mother bore me," he muttered. "And you, Kashtanka, are a thing of little understanding. Beside a man, you are like a joiner beside a cabinetmaker."

Fedyushka walked beside him, wearing his father's cap. Kashtanka looked at their backs, and it seemed to her that she

had been following them for ages, and was glad that there had
not been a break for a minute in her life.

She remembered the little room with dirty wallpaper, the
gander, Fyodor Timofeyitch, the delicious dinners, the lessons,
the circus but all that seemed to her now like a long, tangled
oppressive dream.

THE APOLOGETIC DOG

BEAU

BY *William Cowper*

I. ON A SPANIEL CALLED BEAU KILLING A YOUNG BIRD

> A Spaniel, Beau, that fares like you,
>   Well-fed and at his ease,
> Should wiser be than to pursue
>   Each trifle that he sees.

But you have kill'd a tiny bird
    Which flew not till today,
Against my orders, whom you heard
    Forbidding you the prey.

Nor did you kill that you might eat,
    And ease a doggish pain,
For him, though chased with furious heat,
    You left where he was slain.

Nor was he of the thievish sort,
    Or one whom blood allures,
But innocent was all his sport
    Whom you have torn for yours.

My dog! what remedy remains,
    Since, teach you all I can,
I see you, after all my pains,
    So much resemble Man!

II. BEAU'S REPLY

Sir, when I flew to seize the bird,
    In spite of your command,
A louder voice than yours I heard,
    And harder to withstand.

You cried—forbear—but in my breast
    A mightier cried—proceed!
'Twas nature, Sir, whose strong behest
    Impell'd me to the deed.

Yet much as nature I respect,
    I ventured once to break
(As you perhaps may recollect)
    Her precept, for your sake;

And when your linnet on a day,
    Passing his prison door,
Had flutter'd all his strength away,
    And panting press'd the floor,

Well knowing him a sacred thing,
 Not destined to my tooth,
I only kiss'd his ruffled wing,
 And lick'd the feathers smooth.

Let my obedience then excuse
 My disobedience now,
Nor some reproof yourself refuse
 From your aggriev'd Bow-wow!

If killing birds be such a crime,
 (Which I can hardly see)
What think you, Sir, of killing Time
 With verse address'd to me?

THE INVALUABLE DOG

MUTT MAKES HIS MARK

BY *Farley Mowat*

ONCE MUTT HAD fully dedicated himself as a retriever, our hunting expeditions became pure joy, unadulterated by the confusion and chaos which were so much a part of our life in the city. I looked forward hungrily to the days when the brazen harvest would be made, and the fields lie cropped and crisp beneath our boots; the days when the poplar leaves would spin to earth, and the frost would harden the saline mush about the little sloughs; the days when dawn would come like a crystalline shock out of a sky that held no clouds, save those vital ones that were the flocks pursuing their long way south.

Yet if I looked forward with a consuming eagerness to those days, then Mutt's anticipation far surpassed mine. Having found a purpose in his life, he became so avid for the hunt that in the final weeks before the season opened he would become impervious to all ordinary temptations. Cats would wander at will across his own lawn, not a dozen feet from his twitching nose, and he would not even see them. The honeyed breeze from the house next door, where a lovely little cocker bitch yearned in lonely isolation, had no power to wake him from his dreams. He lay on the browning lawn beside the garage and did not take his eyes from the doors through which Eardlie would soon emerge to carry him, and us, into the living plains.

Each season he went absolutely mad on the first day, and each season when he retrieved his first bird, he brought back a badly mangled corpse. But that never happened twice in a given year. And after that first outburst he would steady to his job.

There seemed to be no limits to his capacity for self-improvement as a hunting dog. Each season he devised new refinements designed to bring him nearer to perfection; and some of these were more than passing strange.

One Wednesday in early October we introduced a friend from Ontario to prairie hunting. He owned a whole kennel of pure-bred setters, and he had hunted upland birds in the east for thirty years. He was a man who could seldom be surprised by the sagacity of dogs. Yet Mutt surprised and even startled him.

Although he was clearly taken aback by Mutt's appearance, our friend refrained from casting any doubts upon the glowing character which we gave our dog, and as a result of this act of faith he and Mutt got on well from the outset of their acquaintance. On the Wednesday of which I write, the two of them went off together around one side of a large poplar bluff, while Father and I went around the other side. Our mutual objective was a covey of Hungarian partridges which we knew to be lurking somewhere near at hand.

Now Hungarian partridges have survived and multiplied even where the hunting pressure is severest, and there is good reason why this is so. Once the fusillade of opening day has alerted them, they become, for the most part, quite untouchable. Crouched invisible in the stubble, they see you long before you see them, and when you have closed to within forty or fifty yards, they burst upward like so many land mines; the flock disperses in as many directions as there are birds, and at bulletlike speed. They hit the ground running, and never stop running until they are miles away. And they seem to run just a little faster than they fly.

Our eastern friend knew all this, in theory anyway. He was properly alert when the flock flushed at fifty yards to vanish almost immediately into a willow swale. Nevertheless, he did not even have time to pull a trigger. He was chagrined by this failure. And then to make matters worse Mutt suddenly disobeyed the cardinal bird-dog law, and without so much as an apologetic look at his companion, he raced after the vanished flock.

Our friend whistled, called him, swore at him, but to no avail. Mutt galloped away in his quaint and lopsided fashion and soon was out of sight.

We rejoined our guest at the far side of the poplar bluff, and though he had the grace to say nothing, it was easy enough to guess his thoughts. But it was not so easy to guess them when, a few minutes later, there was a great huffing and puffing from behind us and we turned to see Mutt approaching at a trot, and bearing a partridge in his mouth.

Our friend was frankly overcome.

"What the devil!" he cried. "I never fired my gun. Don't tell me this paragon of yours doesn't even need a gunner's help?"

Father laughed in a condescending sort of way.

"Oh, not quite that," he explained with his usual flair for the dramatic. "Mutt gets more birds, of course, if he has a gun to help him—but he does pretty well without. He runs them down, you know."

Father did not bother to complete the explanation, and our friend returned to the distant east somewhat dissatisfied with his fine kennel stock, and only after a determined but useless attempt to take Mutt with him. He was a man who believed his eyes, and he did not know, as we did, that the unshot Hungarian had been a running cripple, probably wounded by another hunter sometime earlier.

Nevertheless, Mutt's abilities in this regard were not to be treated lightly. He often spotted a cripple in a flock when we could not, and on at least a dozen different occasions he made a retrieve when we, who had not fired, were morally certain there was nothing to retrieve. We learned not to waste adrenaline cursing at him when he abandoned normal procedure and went off on his own. It was too embarrassing, apologizing to him when he returned later with a bird in his mouth.

There was no place where a wounded bird was safe from him. His strangely bulbous nose, uncouth as it appeared, was singularly efficient in the field and he could find birds that were apparently unfindable.

There were numbers of ruffed grouse in the poplar bluffs to the north of Saskatoon and occasionally we hunted these wily birds. They clung close to cover and were hard to hit. But once hit, they were always ours, for Mutt could find them though they hid in the most unlikely places.

One frosty morning near Wakaw Lake I slightly wounded a grouse and watched with disappointment as it flew across a wide intervening morass, and disappeared into the maze of upper branches of a diamond-willow clump. Mutt galloped off at once, but I was certain he would find no trace of it. Without hope I set out to follow him across the muskeg, and I was only nicely started on my way when I saw a considerable disturbance in the diamond-willow clump. The heavy growth—some twenty feet in height—began to sway and crackle. I stopped and stared, and in due time I saw a flash of white, and then beheld Mutt's head above the crown of the tree, with the ruffed grouse in his mouth—as usual.

He had some difficulty getting back to the ground, and he was rather disheveled when he finally reached me. But he accepted my congratulations calmly. He took such things as this high-level retrieve quite for granted.

Even the open sky offered no sure sanctuary from him, for I have seen him leap six or eight feet in the air to haul down a slow-starting and slightly wounded prairie chicken or Hungarian. As for the water—the wounded duck that thought water offered safety was mortally in ignorance.

Mutt never became resigned to the oily taste of ducks, and he always brought them in by holding the tip of their wing feathers between his front teeth—with his lips curled back, as if the duck stank of some abominable odor. As a result of his distaste for them he could never bring himself to kill a duck, and this reluctance sometimes caused him trouble.

There was a time at Meota Lake when my father and I had

been lucky enough to knock down five mallards with four shots. Unfortunately, the birds were all alive, and actively so, although they could not fly. Mutt went after them, but it was a very swampy shore, and it was all he could do to wade through the marsh unimpeded. It was almost impossible for him to return to firm ground with a flapping mallard in his mouth. He solved the problem by carrying his retrieves to a tiny islet in the lake, while we went off to find a boat.

When we reached the islet, a half-hour later, we found a fantastic situation. There was Mutt, and there were the five ducks, but all of them were on the move. One, two, or three at a time, the ducks would waddle off toward the water, and Mutt would dash between them and freedom and herd them back to the high ground. Then he would snatch at the wing of one, sit—literally—on another, hold two down with his paws, and try to maneuver his belly over the fifth. But the fifth would manage to get free, and scuttle away. Whereupon Mutt would have to abandon all his prisoners; they would all dash off, and he would have it all to do over again. He was about at the end of his tether when we came to his rescue, and it was the only time on a hunting trip that I ever saw him really harassed. How he managed to get those five struggling birds to the island in the first place I do not know.

He had long since perfected his diving technique, and could attain depths of five feet and stay under for as long as a minute. He soon learned, too, that in the case of a deep-diving duck it was sometimes possible to tire it out by waiting on the surface at the point where it would most probably rise, and then forcing it under again before it had time to breathe.

Only once did I see him beaten by a duck—and that time it was no real duck, but a western grebe. Mutt had already retrieved a bufflehead for us, and had gone back out in the belief that a second bird awaited his attention. We could not persuade him otherwise. Knowing how useless it was to argue with him, we let him have his way, although the grebe was quite uninjured—at least by any shot of ours.

Grebes seldom fly, but they dive like fish, and Mutt spent the best part of an hour chasing that bird while Father and I concealed ourselves in the duck blind, and tried to muffle our mirth. It would never have done to let Mutt know we were amused. He did not appreciate humor when he was its butt.

He got more and more exasperated and, though the water was ten or fifteen feet deep, he finally gave up trying to tire the grebe and decided to go down after it. But he was not built for really deep diving. His buoyancy was too great, and he was badly ballasted. At the third attempt he turned-turtle under the water and popped to the surface upside down. Then and only then did he reluctantly come ashore. We set off at once to hunt grouse so that he could get the taste of defeat out of his mouth, and otherwise relieve himself of about a gallon of lake water.

Word of Mutt's phenomenal abilities soon got around, for neither my father nor I was reticent about him. At first the local hunters were skeptical, but after some of them had seen him work, their disbelief began to change into a strong civic pride that, in due time, made Mutt's name a byword for excellence in Saskatchewan hunting circles.

Indeed, Mutt became something of a symbol—a truly western symbol, for his feats were sometimes slightly exaggerated by his partisans for the benefit of unwary strangers—particularly if the strangers came out of the east. It was an encounter between just such a stranger and some of Mutt's native admirers that brought him to his greatest and most lasting triumph—a success that will not be forgotten in Saskatoon while there are birds, and dogs to hunt them.

It all began on one of those blistering July days when the prairie pants like a dying coyote, the dust lies heavy, and the air burns the flesh it touches. On such days those with good sense retire to the cellar caverns that are euphemistically known in Canada as beer parlors. These are all much the same across the country—ill-lit and crowded dens, redolent with the stench of sweat, spilled beer, and smoke—but they are, for the most part, moderately cool. And the insipid stuff that passes for beer is usually ice-cold.

On this particular day five residents of the city, dog fanciers all, had forgathered in a beer parlor. They had just returned from witnessing some hunting-dog trials held in Manitoba, and they had brought a guest with them. He was a rather portly gentleman from the state of New York, and he had both wealth and ambition. He used his wealth lavishly to further his ambition, which was to raise and own the finest retrievers on the continent, if not in the world. Having watched his own dogs win the Manitoba trials, this man had come on to Saskatoon at the earnest invitation of the local men, in order to see what kind of dogs they bred, and to buy some if he fancied them.

He had not fancied them. Perhaps rightfully annoyed at having made the trip in the broiling summer weather to no good purpose, he had become a little overbearing in his manner. His comments when he viewed the local kennel dogs had been acidulous, and scornful. He had ruffled the local breeders' feelings, and as a result they were in a mood to do and say foolish things.

The visitor's train was due to leave at 4:00 P.M., and from 12:30 until 3:00 the six men sat cooling themselves internally, and talking dogs. The talk was as heated as the weather. Inevitably Mutt's name was mentioned, and he was referred to as an outstanding example of that rare breed, the Prince Albert retriever.

The stranger hooted. "Rare breed!" he cried. "I'll say it must be rare! I've never even heard of it."

The local men were incensed by this big-city skepticism. They immediately began telling tales of Mutt, and if they laid it on a little, who can blame them? But the more stories they told, the louder grew the visitor's mirth and the more pointed his disbelief. Finally someone was goaded a little too far.

"I'll bet you," Mutt's admirer said truculently, "I'll bet you a hundred dollars this dog can outretrieve any damn dog in the whole United States."

Perhaps he felt that he was safe, since the hunting season was not yet open. Perhaps he was too angry to think.

The stranger accepted the challenge, but it did not seem as if there was much chance of settling the bet. Someone said as much, and the visitor crowed.

"You've made your brag," he said. "Now show me."

There was nothing for it then but to seek out Mutt and hope for inspiration. The six men left the dark room and braved the blasting light of the summer afternoon as they made their way to the public library.

The library stood, four-square and ugly, just off the main thoroughfare of the city. The inevitable alley behind it was shared by two Chinese restaurants and by sundry other mer-

chants. My father had his office in the rear of the library building overlooking the alley. A screened door gave access to
whatever air was to be found trapped and roasted in the narrow
space behind the building. It was through this rear door that
the delegation came.

From his place under the desk Mutt barely raised his head
to peer at the newcomers, then sank back into a comatose state
of near oblivion engendered by the heat. He probably heard
the mutter of talk, the introductions, and the slightly strident
tone of voice of the stranger, but he paid no heed.

Father, however, listened intently. And he could hardly control his resentment when the stranger stooped, peered beneath
the desk, and was heard to say, *"Now* I recognize the breed—
Prince Albert rat hound did you say it was?"

My father got stiffly to his feet. "You gentlemen wish a
demonstration of Mutt's retrieving skill—is that it?" he asked.

A murmur of agreement from the local men was punctuated
by a derisive comment from the visitor. "Test him," he said
offensively. "How about that alley there—it must be full of
rats."

Father said nothing. Instead he pushed back his chair and,
going to the large cupboard where he kept some of his shooting
things so that they would be available for after-work excur-
sions, he swung wide the door and got out his gun case. He
drew out the barrels, fore end, and stock, and assembled the
gun. He closed the breech and tried the triggers, and at that
familiar sound Mutt was galvanized into life and came scuffling
out from under the desk to stand with twitching nose and a
perplexed air about him.

He had obviously been missing something. This wasn't the
hunting season. But—the gun was out.

He whined interrogatively and my father patted his head.
"Good boy," he said, and then walked to the screen door with
Mutt crowding against his heels.

By this time the group of human watchers was as perplexed
as Mutt. The six men stood in the office doorway and watched
curiously as my father stepped out on the porch, raised the
unloaded gun, leveled it down the alley toward the main street,
pressed the triggers, and said in a quiet voice, "Bang—bang—
go get 'em boy!"

To this day Father maintains a steadfast silence as to what his intentions really were. He will not say that he expected the result that followed, and he will not say that he did not expect it.

Mutt leaped from the stoop and fled down that alleyway at his best speed. They saw him turn the corner into the main street, almost causing two elderly women to collide with one another. The watchers saw the people on the far side of the street stop, turn to stare, and then stand as if petrified. But Mutt himself they could no longer see.

He was gone only about two minutes, but to the group upon the library steps it must have seemed much longer. The man from New York had just cleared his throat preparatory to a new and even more amusing sally, when he saw something that made the words catch in his gullet.

They all saw it—and they did not believe.

Mutt was coming back up the alley. He was trotting. His head and tail were high—and in his mouth was a magnificent ruffed grouse. He came up the porch stairs nonchalantly, laid the bird down at my father's feet, and with a satisfied sigh crawled back under the desk.

There was silence except for Mutt's panting. Then one of the local men stepped forward as if in a dream, and picked up the bird.

"Already stuffed, by God!" he said, and his voice was hardly more than a whisper.

It was then that the clerk from Ashbridge's Hardware arrived. The clerk was disheveled and mad. He came bounding up the library steps, accosted Father angrily, and cried:

"That damn dog of yours—you ought to keep him locked up. Come bustin' into the shop a moment ago and snatched the stuffed grouse right out of the window. Mr. Ashbridge's fit to be tied. Was the best bird in the whole collection . . ."

I do not know if the man from New York ever paid his debt. I do know that the story of that day's happening passed into the nation's history, for the Canadian press picked it up from the *Star-Phoenix*, and Mutt's fame was carried from coast to coast across the land.

That surely was no more than his due.

RABCHIK

BY *Sholom Aleichem*

I

RABCHIK WAS a spotted white dog. He wasn't by any means a big dog, only a medium-sized one. He was always quiet and well-behaved, and he wasn't the grabbing sort either. Unlike other dogs, he never tried to attack anybody when his back was turned, or to tear off the hem of his coat, or to bite him in the shins. As long as no one bothered him he was content. But, as if for spite, everyone who had God in his heart decided to make his life wretched. To give Rabchik a whack on his rump with a stick, or to kick him in his side, or to fling a stone at his head, or to empty a pail of slops on him—that was considered a joke by everyone who did it, in fact almost a *mitzvah*.

Whenever Rabchik received a blow he did not stand up like other dogs to sass back, to bark it out, or even to show his teeth. Definitely not! At each blow Rabchik would cringe with a yelp almost to the ground: *"Ai-ai!"* And with his tail dragging he'd run away to hide in a corner, to lose himself in his sad thoughts, and—to catch flies.

II

Who was Rabchik? Where did he come from? That's hard to know. It was quite possible that he had remained in the courtyard ever since the days of the old *poretz*. It could even be that he was a stray, had somehow lost his original master and, attaching himself to the new one, he had remained around ever since.

It could easily happen that you'd be walking down the street when suddenly you'd find a little dog on your heels. "What sort of a leech is this?" you'd wonder. And you'd raise your hand threateningly and say to the dog, *"Pshol von!"* But the dog wouldn't budge from the spot. He'd recoil like a human being would when dodging a blow, and he'd continue to follow you. Suddenly you'd bend down to the ground, would swing out with your arm, feigning to fling a stone at him. But it would be no use. You'd remain standing where you were, looking curiously at the dog; he'd remain standing where he was, looking back at you. So you'd peer into each other's eyes mutely. Then you'd spit out with annoyance and start walking off. But the little dog would still run after you. Now you'd begin to lose your temper. You'd grab up a stick and you'd go after him, really angry. So what would the dog do? He'd fall on a stratagem, would stretch himself out on the ground, belly up. He'd tremble and look you straight in the eye, as if to say, "Na! You want to hit—go ahead and hit!"

Now that's the sort of dog our Rabchik was.

III

Whatever else he may have been Rabchik was no *nasher*. Even "gold" could lie around the house and he wouldn't touch it! Rabchik knew that whatever food he found under the table belonged to him; anything else was not his business.

When he was younger, they say, he was quite a nervy fellow. He once tried to steal a goose foot from the salting board on which they made the meat kosher. When Breineh the cook, a woman with a dark mustache, caught him in the act she began to yell, "Isaac! Isaac!" Isaac came running in just as Rabchik tried to dash by him with the goose foot in his mouth. Thereupon, Isaac caught him in the door and pushed it hard against him, so that half of Rabchik stuck out from one side of the door and the other half of him stuck out from the other side. Oh, how they settled their account with him then! On his front half Isaac cudgeled him over the head with a stick and on his little rump Breineh beat him with a slab of firewood. And all the time she beat him she kept on yelling, "Isaac! Isaac!"

From that time on, whenever anyone came up to Rabchik and merely said the word "Isaac!" he'd become frightened and scurry away "where black pepper grows."

IV

The one who made his life most miserable was the peasant woman, Paraskeh. This Paraskeh used to do our laundry, whitewash the walls, and milk our cow.

What grudge she could have against Rabchik was very hard to understand. She was always ready to pick on him. Whenever she'd catch sight of him she'd flare up and shout: "The plague take you, you infidel dog!" And just as if he were doing it out of spite Rabchik liked to get tangled up in her feet.

When she was at her work Paraskeh used to wreak her vengeance on him, like we Jews usually do on the cursed memory of Haman. For instance, when she'd be doing the laundry she'd empty a tub of cold water on him. Rabchik didn't like that kind of a bath at all; he'd be busy for a long time afterwards shaking off the water. When she'd be at her whitewashing she'd splash his face with white lime so that for an hour on end he'd be busy trying to lick it off with his tongue. When she'd be milking the cow she'd honor him with a whack from a slab of firewood across his legs. That's how Rabchik learned to leap skillfully so that whenever he saw a chunk of wood flying at him he'd adroitly leap over it like a circus performer.

On one occasion he got the very devil from such "honor." Paraskeh flung a slab of wood at him which struck him in a foreleg. Rabchik began to yelp, no longer in his own voice but in a peculiar screech: "*Ai-ai-ai-ai-ai!*" People ran up to see what was the matter. When Rabchik saw so many people gather he began to whimper in order to gain their sympathy. He showed everyone separately his broken leg, as if to say, "Na! Just see what she did to me, that Paraskeh!" Rabchik expected, no doubt, that they'd all take his part and the very least they would do would be to chop Paraskeh's head off for what she had done to him.

Instead, everybody began to laugh. Breineh with the mustache dashed out of the kitchen with a ladle in her hand. She wiped her perspiring nose with her bare arm and exclaimed, "*Nu*, so she did break the *schlimazl's* leg! Serves him right!" Also, all the mischievous little rascals began to collect. They hooted and whistled at Rabchik. Then Paraskeh turned up carrying a pitcher of hot water which she promptly proceeded to pour over him. Rabchik raised a *gevalt* and a screeching *"ai-ai-ai! ai-ai-ai!"* He leaped and thrashed about, turned round and round and bit his own tail. The little imps only laughed the louder. Seeing how Rabchik was dancing crazily about on only three legs, they jeered at him and beat him with their sticks. Rabchik squealed and started to run, stopping every little while to roll on the ground because of the pain. The boys ran after him and threw stones at him. They hooted and whistled, and continued to drive him before them until they reached at last the edge of the town on the other side of the water mills. There they left him.

v

Rabchik ran on and on. He made up his mind: never, never would he come back to town, never as long as he lived! And he ran without knowing where he was running, nor caring either. Wherever his eyes would lead him and his legs would carry him, there he'd go. And after he had been running for a long time he at last reached a village. There he was met by all the dogs in the place. They smelled him all over.

"Blessed be thy coming!" they all greeted him ceremoniously. "And from where does a dog come? And what sort of a *tzatzke* do you have on your rump? *Epis* as if someone has burnt out a piece of hide right in the middle of it."

"Ech! Better don't ask!" answered Rabchik with a doleful expression. "There's a lot to tell but nothing really to listen to. Do tell me, is it possible for me to spend the night with you?"

"Och! With the greatest of pleasure!" replied the village dogs. "The out-of-doors is plenty big and the under-the-skies is even bigger."

"And how is it with you about eats?" inquired Rabchik discreetly. "With what do you still your hunger when the stomach demands nourishment?"

"Et! We've nothing to complain of!" answered the village dogs. "Slop pails are found everywhere. And when the Lord created meat he added bones to it. We should worry! Let our masters eat the meat and leave us the bones, as long as— how do you say it?—you can fill your gut."

"Nu, and what sort of masters have you got?" continued Rabchik with a twist to his tail in the manner of a dog making an investigation.

"The masters? Our masters are like all masters!" replied the village dogs evasively.

"Nu, and how about Paraskeh?"

"Paraskeh? What Paraskeh?"

"Why, Paraskeh! You know, the one who does washing, who whitewashes the walls and milks the cow! You mean to say you don't know Paraskeh?"

The village dogs stared at Rabchik, thinking that he had gone out of his mind. "What are you Paraskehing about, anyway?" they asked. Again they smelled him all over and then trotted off one by one each to his dung heap.

"*Ut!* What happy dogs!" thought Rabchik enviously, as he stretched himself out on God's earth under God's heaven. He wanted to take a nap but he couldn't sleep. First of all it was on account of his scalded hide; it hurt and itched terribly! And the flies annoyed him no end; it was simply impossible to drive them off. Secondly, there was a growling in his belly. *Ach!* If only he had something to chew on! Looked very much like he'd have to wait until morning. And a third reason why he couldn't fall asleep was his thoughts. His mind was full of all that the village dogs had told him. Could it be that among them there were no Isaacs who squeezed the door against dogs and then beat them with a slab of wood? How strange! Nor were there any Paraskehs who scalded one with boiling water, no mischievous boys who threw sticks and stones after them, who hooted and whistled and chased them out of the village. "What happy dogs there are in this world! And there was I thinking all along that my town was the whole world! You see how it is—a worm lies buried in a jar of horseradish and says to itself, 'There certainly doesn't exist any life sweeter than this!' "

Rabchik finally dozed off. And as he slept he had a dream, and in his dream he saw a slop pail. It was a big one, too, and full of bread crumbs, chicken intestines, buckwheat gruel mixed with millet and potatoes, and then bones, oh so many bones! A whole treasure! Knucklebones, rib bones, marrowbones, fishbones, and unchewed heads of herring! Rabchik was both enchanted and bewildered; he hardly knew where to begin first.

"A hearty appetite!" the village dogs called out to him, looking on from a distance as he was girding himself for the feast.

"Won't you join me?" asked Rabchik just out of politeness.

"Eat hearty!" replied the village dogs affably.

Suddenly he heard a voice roaring into his ear: "Isaac!"

Rabchik awoke with a great start at that. *Ach*. It was all only a dream! . . .

When morning came Rabchik made the rounds of all the yards looking for a slop pail, a piece of crust, even a little bone. But wherever he went he found himself shut out by some other dog.

"Could a fellow get some breakfast here?" asked Rabchik timidly.

"Here? Oh no! In the next yard maybe."

And Rabchik kept on running from yard to yard. Everywhere he heard the same tune. So he thought the whole matter over: what would he get from being so polite? Might it not be better to go straight over, grab what he could, and make a quick getaway?

Nu, so he tried, and got properly punished by the village dogs for grabbing. At first they looked angrily at him, growled and showed their teeth. Then several leaped on him at the same time, bit and tore at him and made a wreck of his tail. This job done, they escorted him out of the village with great ceremony.

VI

With his injured tail between his legs Rabchik set out for the next village. But when he reached his destination the same old story was repeated. At first they welcomed him pleasantly. "A fine guest, why not?" But when he tried to edge near the pail of slops, they started looking angrily at him. They growled and showed their teeth, then bit and tore at him, and barked, "Get out of here!" from every side.

Rabchik now felt sick and tired of being unwanted, of knocking around from one place to another. So he thought it over.

"It's perfectly clear: people are bad, but then again dogs are no better either. Now wouldn't it be preferable to live in the forest among the wild beasts?"

And thus reflecting, Rabchik made his way into the forest.

He wandered and he wandered, one solitary dog alone in the forest. One day passed, then another, and a third, until Rabchik finally began to feel that his belly was contracting more and more and that his intestines were shriveling up. He was feeling faint from hunger and thirst. "Nu?" he said to himself bitterly, "so all that's left for me to do is to stretch out right in the middle of the forest and breathe my last!" Ha! But as if just for spite, he had a strong desire to go on living and living!

So once more Rabchik hung his tail between his hind legs, stretched his forelegs, hung out his tongue, and lay down under a tree to think through his confused doggy thoughts: "Oy, if I could only get a piece of bread or a bit of meat, a bone even, and oy, for a sip of water!" And from great *tzoress* Rabchik became a thinker, a regular philosopher! He began to philosophize:

"Why am I, a dog, punished more severely than all the other creatures in the world? There, for instance, is a little bird; watch it fly straight to its nest. There you have a lizard; see how it crawls into its hole! And right here are a worm, a beetle, and an ant—each of them has a home, each of them finds his nourishment, only I, miserable dog that I am! . . . Bow-wow-wow!"

"Who's barking here in the forest?" howled a wolf who happened to be passing by just then; his tongue was hanging out from sheer hunger.

Never before in his life had Rabchik seen a wolf. He thought it was a dog. So he slowly rose to his feet, being in no great hurry, stretched himself, and then trotted over to the wolf.

"Who are you?" asked the wolf contemptuously. "What's your name? Where do you come from? What are you doing here?"

Rabchik was delighted that at last he had met with a fellow creature, someone to whom he could pour out all his tzoress. And so he unburdened his bitter heart to him.

"I'll tell you the truth," said Rabchik as he ended his sad tale, "I feel so wretched that I'd positively be overjoyed were I to meet here with a lion, a bear, or even a wolf."

"So what would be?" asked the wolf with a *paskudneh* smile.

"Nothing," replied Rabchik. "In any case, I'm fated to die. Better let a wolf devour me than that I should perish of hunger among my own kind, among dogs!"

"Nu?" said the wolf, flexing his muscles and sharpening his teeth with pleasurable anticipation. "I want you to know that I'm a wolf and I would very much like to tear you limb from limb and eat you for my breakfast. I'm awfully hungry for it's already eight days since last I had a morsel in my mouth."

Hearing these words, Rabchik felt terror creeping over him so that his ragged hide began to quiver.

"My lord, the king! Dear Reb Velvel!" answered Rabchik, trying to speak with a piteous expression and a tearful voice. "May God send you along a better breakfast than I! Lord preserve you, what do you suppose you can get out of me? Only hide and bones, I assure you. Take my advice and let me go. Have pity on my unhappy dog's life!"

And thus saying, Rabchik lowered his tail, twisted his little rump, crawled on his belly, and went through such hideous antics and grimaces that the wolf began to feel nauseous.

"Pick up that paskudneh tail of yours," snarled the wolf, "and go and carry yourself off to the devil—you dog of dogs! And furthermore, don't let me ever see your *tréfeneh* mug again!"

More dead than alive, Rabchik started to run. He ran so fast that he didn't feel the ground under him. He was afraid even to look around. So he fled, away, away from the forest—and back to town!

VII

As he trotted into town Rabchik avoided the house and yard where he had grown up, although it was precisely there where his heart drew him most, despite the fact that it was where he had been cruelly beaten, where they had broken his poor leg and scalded his rump. Instead he made his way into the market place to the butcher shops, to join his own kind—the dogs there.

"Well, well, just look who's here! From where does a dog come?" the butchers' dogs greeted him with a yawn as they made ready to retire for the night.

"I'm *takkeh* a local dog," replied Rabchik. "What, you don't recognize me? Why, I am Rabchik!"

"Rabchik? Rabchik? A familiar name!" said the butchers' dogs, pretending not to recall who he was.

"What sort of a scar do you have on your rump?" Tzutzik, a small dog, asked him and, so saying, leaped at him with great insolence.

"No doubt it's an identification mark, or maybe it was done just to make him look more beautiful. You mean to say you can't figure that out?" jeered Ravdek, a red dog with a furry hide.

"When it has to do with scars, just ask me and I'll tell you what it is," said Sirko, a gray dog, an old bachelor who had only one eye and one ear. "I'm sure the scar this fellow has he must have gotten in battles with other dogs."

"Why do you all talk?" called out Zhuk, a black dog without a tail. "Better let Rabchik talk himself. Let him tell us."

And Rabchik stretched himself out on the ground and began to tell about everything that had happened to him, not leaving out a single detail. They all listened to him except Ravdek, who considered himself quite a wit. Every other minute he'd interrupt him with a joke.

"Shut up, Ravdek," called out Zhuk, the black dog without a tail, opening his mouth wide in a long yawn. "Go on, Rabchik, tell, tell! We like to listen to stories after dinner!"

And Rabchik continued to tell his sad tale in a dispirited voice, but no one paid any attention to him. Tzutzik talked quietly with Sirko, Ravdek cracked jokes, and Zhuk snored like ten soldiers. Every so often he started up from sleep, yawned, and urged, "Go on, Rabchik, tell, tell! We like to listen to stories after dinner!"

VIII

Bright and early the following morning Rabchik was already up and going. He stood at a discreet distance watching the butchers hacking up the meat. There he saw an entire forequarter of a cow, suspended neck down with the blood running from it. Here lay a rump, a choice chunk of meat, juicy, deeply cushioned with fat. Rabchik devoured it with his eyes and swallowed saliva. The meat choppers hacked the meat into pieces. Every once in a while they'd throw a handful of skin or a bone to their dogs. And the dogs leaped high, trying to catch them in midair. Rabchik saw how hard they tried to be clever, jumping skillfully at the right instant in the right place. They didn't let a single bone pass them by. When each dog got his portion he stepped to a side, stretched himself grandly on the ground and started his feast. Every once in a while each dog would look at the others as if to boast:

"Just look at this bone! Some bone, eh? That's my bone and it's I who is chewing it!"

The other dogs pretended to look elsewhere, but at the same time they said to themselves:

"May you choke on it! May it make you sick! Just look at him! All morning he keeps on *fressing* and fressing. And we have to look on while he eats—may the worms eat him!"

One of the dogs, carrying a piece of hide in his mouth, looked for a quiet spot so that nobody should watch him chew on it; he was probably afraid of the evil eye.

Another dog stood watching an angry butcher who was quarreling with the other butchers and abusing them heartily. The dog wagged his tail flatteringly to him and called out to the other dogs.

"See this butcher? He looks angry, doesn't he? Let me have such a good year what a fine man he is! I'm telling you—one diamond in the world! A character of pure gold! He's the kind that takes real pity on a dog—he's positively 'a friend of the dogs.' Wait, you'll soon see a bone flying with a chunk of meat on it. *Hop!*"

So saying, he leaped into the air and snapped shut his jaws so that the others would think that he had caught a fat morsel.

"Ach! What a flatterer and a liar! What a braggart! The Devil take him!" called out a dog standing on the side.

Still another dog stationed himself near a meat-chopping block. When the butcher happened to turn away for a moment up leaped this dog upon the block and began licking it up with his tongue. What a barking started among the other dogs; they were thus informing the butcher that a *ganef* was at work. "Why, that dog has gone and *nashed* a piece of meat! Such a piece of gold we should have! May we not live to see all kinds of good things if with our own eyes we didn't see that ganef steal! May we drop dead on the spot, may we choke on the next bone we chew, if we tell a lie!"

"Feh! It's enough to throw up!" cried out an old dog. Of course, he himself wouldn't have had anything against having a lick of that block!

And seeing and hearing all this, Rabchik began to consider his situation: What would he get out of it all by just standing and looking on? All the dogs were jumping and barking—why shouldn't he do likewise? But before even he had a chance to try, several dogs were on top of him, their teeth fastened in his throat and snapping and tearing at him. They bit him on his still fresh wounds, where it hurt so!

Rabchik lowered his tail, crawled away into a corner, stretched out his neck, and began to whine.

"What are you crying about?" Zhuk asked him as he licked his chops, for he had just finished his breakfast.

"Why shouldn't I cry?" moaned Rabchik. "I'm the most unlucky dog among all the dogs in the world! I had foolishly thought that here, among my own kind, I could at least get *epis* to eat. Believe me, I wouldn't go crawling where I'm not wanted if I wasn't so terribly hungry! My life is simply ebbing out of me!"

"I believe you," said Zhuk with a sigh. "Believe me, I know what hunger is! I can place myself in your sad situation very well. Unfortunately, I cannot help you at all. That's the custom here: every butcher has his own dog, and every dog has his own butcher."

"Do you takkeh think that it's right so?" asked Rabchik bitterly. "Where is justice? What about dogmanity? Ach, that a dog should be so abandoned by other dogs! And oh, that one who is hungry should starve to death among those who are sated!"

"Alas! I can help you only with a sigh," sighed Zhuk with feeling.

He yawned heartily, and, with his good breakfast tucked away in his belly, he made ready to doze off.

"If that's the case," said Rabchik, finally plucking up courage, "then I'll go directly to the butchers. Maybe I'll be able to bark up a butcher, somehow."

"With the greatest of pleasure," answered Zhuk, "as long as you don't go to my butcher. Because, I warn you, should you dare go to my butcher I'll bite off your tail!"

IX

Then Rabchik went directly to the butchers, by-passed and avoided all the other dogs. At first he tried to flatter the butchers, jumped up before them and wagged his tail. But what kind of *mazl* has a schlimazl? One of the butchers, a lusty fellow with broad shoulders, just for a joke threw his meat chopper at him. It was Rabchik's good fortune that he had learned how to jump well. Otherwise he would have been cut in half.

"You dance quite well!" said Ravdek to him with a leer. "A lot better than our Tzutzik. Here, Tzutzik, just come over here and you'll see how one should dance!"

Tzutzik came running up. He leaped straight at Rabchik. But Rabchik could no longer endure his insolence. He gripped Tzutzik with his teeth, threw him down, and bit savagely into his little belly. On him he vented all his pent-up bitterness, and

when he was through he fled as fast as his legs could carry him.

Solitary and woebegone, he dragged himself through the fields, and when at last he came to the road he stretched himself out right in the middle of it, and for very shame he hid his face between his paws and did not want to look at the light of day. It didn't bother him even that the flies swarmed over him and bit him. Good! Let them bite, let them peck at him! What difference would it make? . . .

"It's the end of everything!" thought Rabchik sadly. "If a dog cannot live even a single day among other dogs, among his very own kind, then may the whole world go to the devil! . . ."

THE PROPHETIC DOG

THE WHITE DOG OF THE OJIBWAYS

BY *Sheila Burnford*

HUNGER WAS NOW the ruling instinct in the Labrador and it drove him out to forage in the early dawn. He was desperate enough to try some deer droppings, but spat them out immediately in disgust. While he was drinking from a marsh pool still covered with lily pads, he saw a frog staring at him with goggle eyes from a small stone: measuring the distance carefully, he sprang and caught it in the air as it leaped to safety. It disappeared down his throat in one crunch and he looked around happily for more. But an hour's patient search rewarded him with only two, so he returned to his companions. They had apparently eaten, for there were feathers and fur scattered around and both were licking their lips. But something warned him not to urge his old companion on. The terrier was still utterly exhausted, and in addition had lost a lot of blood from the gashes suffered at the cub's claws the day before. These were stiff and black with blood, and had a tendency to open and bleed slightly with any movement, so all that day he lay peacefully in the warm full sunshine on the grass sleeping, eating what the cat provided, and wagging his tail whenever one of the others came near.

The young dog spent most of the day still occupied with his ceaseless foraging for food. By evening he was desperate, but his luck turned when a rabbit, already changing to its white winter coat, suddenly started up from the long grass and swerved across his path. Head down, tail flying, the young dog gave chase, swerving and turning in pursuit, but always the rabbit was just out of reach of his hungry jaws. At last, he put all his strength into one violent lunge and felt the warm pulsating prize in his mouth. The generations fell away, and the years of training never to sink teeth into feathers or fur; for a moment the Labrador looked almost wolflike as he tore at the warm flesh and bolted it down in ravenous gulps.

They slept in the same place that night and most of the following day, and the weather mercifully continued warm and sunny. By the third day the old dog seemed almost recovered and the wounds were closed. He had spent most of the day ambling around and sleeping, so that by now he seemed almost frisky and quite eager to walk a little.

So, in the late afternoon, they left the place which had been their home for three days and trotted slowly along the track together again. By the time the moon rose they had traveled several miles, and they had come to the edge of a small lake which the track skirted.

A moose was standing in the water among the lily pads on the far shore, his great antlered head and humped neck silhouetted clearly against the pale moon. He took no notice of the strange animals across the water but thrust his head again and again under the water, raising it high in the air after each immersion, and arching his neck. Two or three water hens swam out from the reeds, a little crested grebe popped up like a jack-in-the-box, in the water beside them, and the spreading ripples of their wake caught the light of the moon. As the three sat, ears pricked, they watched the moose squelch slowly out of the muddy water, shake himself, and turn, cantering up the bank out of sight.

The young dog turned his head suddenly, his nose twitching, for his keen scent had caught a distant whiff of wood smoke, and of something else—something unidentifiable. . . . Seconds later, the old dog caught the scent too, and started to his feet, snuffing and questioning with his nose. His thin whippy tail began to sweep to and fro and a bright gleam appeared in the slanted black-currant eyes. Somewhere, not too far away, were human beings—his world: he could not mistake their message— or refuse their invitation—they were undoubtedly cooking something. He trotted off determinedly in the direction of the tantalizing smell. The young dog followed somewhat reluctantly, and for once the cat passed them both; a little moon-mad perhaps, for he lay in wait to dart and strike, then streaked back into the shadows, only to reappear a second later in an elaborate stalk of their tails. Both dogs ignored him.

The scent on the evening breeze was a fragrant compound of roasting rice, wild-duck stew and wood smoke. When the animals looked down from a hill, tantalized and hungry, they saw six or seven fires in the clearing below—their flames lighting up a semicircle of tents and conical birch-bark shelters against a dark background of trees; flickering over the canoes drawn up on the edge of a wild rice marsh and dying redly in the black waters beyond; and throwing into ruddy relief the high, flat planes of brown Ojibway faces gathered around the centers of warmth and brightness.

The men were a colorful lot in jeans and bright plaid shirts, but the women were dressed in somber colors. Two young boys, the only children there, were going from fire to fire shaking grain in shallow pans and stirring it with paddles as it parched. One man in long soft moccasins stood in a shallow pit trampling husks, half his weight supported on a log frame. Some of the band lay back from the fire, smoking and watching idly, talking softly among themselves; while others still ate, ladling the fragrant contents of a black iron pot onto tin plates. Every now and then one of them would throw a bone back over a shoulder into the bush, and the watching animals gazed hungrily after. A woman stood at the edge of the clearing pouring grain from one bark platter to another, and the loose chaff drifted off on the slight wind like smoke.

The old dog saw nothing of this, but his ears and nose supplied all that he needed to know: he could contain himself no longer and picked his way carefully down the hillside, for his shoulder still pained him. Halfway down he sneezed violently in an eddy of chaff. One of the boys by the fire looked up at the sound, his hand closing on a stone, but the woman nearby spoke sharply, and he waited, watching intently.

The old dog limped out of the shadows and into the ring of firelight, confident, friendly, and sure of his welcome; his tail wagging his whole stern ingratiatingly, ears and lips laid back in his nightmarish grimace. There was a stunned silence— broken by a wail of terror from the smaller boy, who flung himself at his mother—and then a quick excited chatter from the Indians. The old dog was rather offended and uncertain for a moment, but he made hopefully for the nearest boy, who retreated, nervously clutching his stone. But again the woman rebuked her son, and at the sharpness of her tone the old dog stopped, crestfallen. She laid down her basket then, and walked quickly across the ring of firelight, stooping down to look more closely. She spoke some soft words of reassurance, then patted his head gently and smiled at him. The old dog leaned against her and whipped his tail against her black stockings, happy to be in contact with a human being again. She crouched down beside him to run her fingers lightly over his ears and back, and when he licked her face appreciatively, she laughed. At this, the two little boys drew nearer to the dog and the rest of the band gathered around. Soon the old dog was where he most loved to be—the center of attention among some human beings. He made the most of it and played to an appreciative audience; when one of the men tossed him a chunk of meat he sat up painfully on his hindquarters and begged for more, waving one paw in the air. This sent the Indians into paroxysms of laughter, and he had to repeat his performance time and time again, until he was tired and lay down, panting but happy.

The Indian woman stroked him gently in reward, then ladled some of the meat from the pot onto the grass. The old dog limped towards it; but before he ate he looked up in the direction of the hillside where he had left his two companions.

A small stone rebounded from rock to rock, then rolled into the sudden silence that followed.

When a long-legged, blue-eyed cat appeared out of the darkness, paused, then filled the clearing with a strident plaintive voice before walking up to the dog and calmly taking a piece of meat from him, the Indians laughed until they were speechless and hiccupping. The two little boys rolled on the ground, kicking their heels in an abandonment of mirth, while the cat chewed his meat unmoved; but this was the kind of behavior the bull terrier understood, and he joined in the fun. But he rolled so enthusiastically that the wounds reopened: when he got to his feet again his white coat was stained with blood.

All this time the young dog crouched on the hillside, motionless and watchful, although every driving, urgent nerve in his body fretted and strained at the delay. He watched the cat, well fed and content, curl himself on the lap of one of the sleepy children by the fire; he heard the faint note of derision in some of the Indians' voices as a little, bent, ancient crone addressed them in earnest and impassioned tones before hobbling over to the dog to examine his shoulder as he lay peacefully before the fire. She threw some cattail roots into a boiling pot of water, soaked some moss in the liquid, and pressed it against the dark gashes. The old dog did not move; only his tail beat slowly. When she had finished, she scooped some more meat onto a piece of birchbark and set it on the grass before the dog; and the silent watcher above licked his lips and sat up, but still he did not move from his place.

But when the fires began to burn low and the Indians made preparations for the night, and still his companions showed no signs of moving, the young dog grew restless. He skirted the camp, moving like a shadow through the trees on the hill behind, until he came out upon the lake's shore a quarter of a mile upwind of the camp. Then he barked sharply and imperatively several times.

The effect was like an alarm bell on the other two. The cat sprang from the arms of the sleepy little Indian boy and ran towards the old dog, who was already on his feet, blinking and peering around rather confusedly. The cat gave a guttural yowl, then deliberately ran ahead, looking back as he paused beyond the range of firelight. The old dog shook himself resignedly and walked slowly after—reluctant to leave the warmth of the fire. The Indians watched impassively and silently and made no move to stop him. Only the woman who had first befriended him called out softly, in the tongue of her people, a farewell to the traveler.

The dog halted at the treeline beside the cat and looked back, but the commanding, summoning bark was heard again, and together the two passed out of sight and into the blackness of the night.

That night they became immortal, had they known or cared, for the ancient woman had recognized the old dog at once by color and companion: he was the White Dog of the Ojibways, the virtuous White Dog of Omen, whose appearance heralds either disaster or good fortune. The Spirits had sent him, hungry and wounded, to test tribal hospitality; and for benevolent proof to the skeptical they had chosen a cat as his companion—for what *mortal* dog would suffer a cat to rob him of his meat? He had been made welcome, fed and succored: the omen would prove fortunate.

THE LOVELORN DOG

THE ADVENTURES OF MASTER TOWSER

BY *Olive Schreiner*

I

SMALL TOWSER SAT with his tail in a puddle of mud. The puddle was small, but so was his tail. His nose was turned down to the paving-stones; there were two drops running down towards the tip of it, but they weren't raindrops, though the afternoon was sad and cloudy enough—they came from his eyes. Presently, out of the swell gate of the house over the way came a most respectable-looking dog, of a very comfortable appearance, and as big as eight Towsers, for he was a mastiff.

"Why don't you take your tail out of the puddle?" asked the comfortable-looking dog.

Towser gave it a feeble little splutter in the mud: he didn't know why he let it hang there, except that he was miserable.

"Starve you over at your house?" inquired the comfortable dog.

"No," said Towser, "there are dishes of bones and nice little bits of fat in the kitchen."

"Other dogs bite you?"

"No." Towser shook his head.

"Have to sleep out in the cold?"

"No, I've got a house," said Towser.

"You're a nice gentlemanly-looking little dog; you oughtn't to be unhappy. What's the matter?" asked the comfortable-looking dog.

"I'm not any good," said Towser.

The big dog didn't comprehend.

"I want someone to love me," said Towser; "I want to help somebody; I want to be of use."

"Love!" said the big dog. "Did you ever smell it?"

"No," said Towser.

"Or see anybody eat it?"

"No."

"Or sleep on it?"

"No."

"Then what use is it?" said the big dog; and he went away.

Shortly after that Towser got up off the stone, and took his little tail out of the mud. He shook his little ears and let the two drops run off his nose.

"I'll go and seek for someone that needs me," said Towser; and so he started on his travels.

II

"I must look as pleasant as I can," said Towser, as he went down the street; and he perked up his little ears. He really was a pretty terrier, with long silky hair. Presently he saw a boy walking on the pavement. He was ragged, he looked as if he hadn't had any dinner or breakfast either. Towser's heart ached for him. He looked very lonely.

"I'm sure he would like a nice little dog like me to be a companion to him," said Towser. "Yes, he wants me; I won't trou-

ble him for food, because everyone gives me something when I
go to the back doors, because of my big eyes."

So Towser began dancing a little dance of affection, shaking
his ears and looking from under them with his round eyes.
This proceeding was meant to say, "I want to love you."

"Doggy, Doggy, Doggy!" said the little solitary boy, standing
still and holding out his fingers; "Doggy, Doggy, Doggy."

So Towser came close up, just curling into a ball with excitement. He didn't know whether he should lick the little boy's
hands first or his feet.

"There!" said the little boy. He gave Towser a powerful kick
on the tip of his black nose.

When he looked back, Towser was standing quite still, with a
great singing in his ears. Then the little lonely boy laughed.

When the singing had left off, Towser trotted away down the
street. He wasn't so ready to caper now. He saw several little
lonely boys as he passed, but he didn't think they wanted him.

At last he got to the outskirts of the town. There was a bonny
little house with roses and creepers all around. He went to the
back door and put his forefeet on the step, and looked in to see
if there was anybody wanted him. A lady lay on a sofa in one
corner; she had not walked for ten years, and her eyes were
heavy with pain.

"Dear little creature, where do you come from?" she said.

Towser made a motion with his forefeet, to explain that he
would come in if he were invited.

The lady said, "Come in," and he sat down on the rug before
her and the lady felt his ears.

"Beautiful ears," she said, "come!"

Towser jumped up onto the sofa beside her.

"I never saw such large eyes," said the lady. "Dear little
dog, if I can I shall keep you for my own," and she made a
place for him on her chest.

He lay with his paws close to her chin, and looked as loving
as he could. Presently he licked her chin, and she said he had
a soft little tongue. When her lunch came she fed him with
brandy and egg out of a spoon. He didn't like it, it burnt his
throat, but he drank it.

"She wants me awfully, I can just see that," said Towser,
"and I'll stay with her as long as I live."

The lady had him taken to her bedroom that night, and a nice little rug laid for him across the foot of her bed. In the night, when she woke to cough, he walked up to her face and licked it, and she covered him with the blankets till there was just the tip of his black nose sticking out.

"The big, comfortable dog said love was nothing, but it's something," said Towser, "and it's nice"; and he put his little muzzle against her cheek. Next day he danced before her, and tried to catch his tail when she looked sad.

"Oh, I'm a dear, nice, happy little dog; she does love me so. She couldn't live without me; I'm such a comfort to her," said Towser. He wished he'd been six months younger, then he'd have six months more to live.

So weeks passed.

One afternoon a lady came in.

"I've brought Nola home," she said, "so much better for her change to the seaside; here she is." And the lady put down on the floor the most snow-white terrier (Towser was brown), all soft with curls, and with little sleepy eyes.

"She looks better," said the lady—"dear Nola."

Nola climbed quietly up on the sofa and curled herself up in a little nest and shut her eyes.

Towser stood looking on. He thought he would jump on the sofa, too.

"Down, Towser, down!" said the lady.

Then Towser went and got behind the crimson curtain, with only his nose and two bright eyes peeping out. At last teatime came, and there was a dish of milk put down on the floor. Nola got off the sofa and went to drink some; Towser came out, and put his little black muzzle in too. As soon as the curly white one saw it, she lifted her pink nose, and got quietly back on the sofa.

"Nola won't drink with Towser," said the lady; "take him to the kitchen and give him a nice basin of milk with plenty of cream on it."

Then Nola got off the sofa again; but Towser wouldn't go to the kitchen. He got behind the curtain and looked out with his great saucers of eyes.

"It'll be bedtime soon, and I am sure she is wanting me badly to lick her chin. I'm sure she is wishing it was bedtime," said Towser.

"Make a comfortable bed for Towser in the kitchen, and be sure it's nice and soft," said the lady.

Towser wouldn't get into the bed; he sat on the stone looking at the fire. He wondered if a coal had got into his heart. He felt so wicked.

"I wonder what is the matter with Towser," said the lady the next day; "he used to be such a nice little dog, always so lively."

Then Towser got up, and began dancing about after his tail, and then he got on the sofa, and began playing with the lady's fingers and rings. Then the white curly one opened her eyes slowly and got off the sofa.

"Nola, Nola, come here! Down, Towser, down!" said the lady.

Then Towser went out in the garden and sat in the graveled path looking up at the sun. I don't know how he felt.

"Towser's such a nice little dog," said the lady one day; "quite the nicest little dog I've ever seen. I wish I could get someone to take him away; someone who would be kind to him."

Now Towser didn't wait to be given away to a very kind person. I fancy he had a pain at his heart. He put his tail close between his hind legs, and went out at the back door.

III

Towser sat alone in a wood. He leaned his head on a stone at his side. He was thinking; you could see that by his big, round eyes.

"I made somebody happy; that's a great comfort," said he (for all that there were tears running down his nose). "I must be happy; I must think I once made somebody happy"—here his little chest swelled out immensely. "It doesn't matter if you're not loved if only you've made somebody happy. Yes, I won't want to be loved any more, I'll just try to help people, and then I'll be happy too. You mustn't want to be loved, just to be good."

So he took his head off the stone and went trotting away through the wood. Presently he saw a country boy before him carrying a flitch of bacon; not long after from the bushes at the pathside burst a gipsy-looking fellow.

After a minute, the rough fellow said to the boy, "Give me your bacon."

Said the boy, "No."

The man said, "I can make you; there is nobody near."

He took hold of the bacon; the boy began to struggle. He knelt upon the boy. Then every hair upon Towser's little body stood on end, and his tail was stiffened out. He forgot he was Towser, he forgot he wanted to be loved, he forgot everything, and flew at the trousers of the gipsy man. Then the gipsy man thought there was someone coming, ran away, and left the boy and the bacon.

Towser stood in the middle of the path barking furiously. He was in great excitement.

Slowly the country fellow got up; his face was purple with rage. He cut a little stick from the brush growing by; it wasn't thicker than his finger; Towser's backbone was not thicker either.

"So, you stand here barking at me, do you?" said the country fellow. "Why don't you go after your master? You want to bite me! do you? do you? do you?"

Towser thought his little backbone would be broken, and when the stick hit his little skull it was terribly sore. The country fellow held him fast with one hand; he was so small he wasn't much to hold, and beat him on his little forefeet, and in his eye; then he took up his bacon, and walked away.

Towser went into the brushwood close by, and sat down on his tail and lifted his nose to the sky. The one eye was shut up, but the other was wide open, and the water running out of it.

If he ever went home and became a comfortable and respectable dog, I don't know; the last I saw of him he was sitting there in that wood.

THE HARPER

BY *Thomas Campbell*

On the green banks of Shannon, when Sheelah was nigh,
No blithe Irish lad was so happy as I;
No harp like my own could so cheerily play,
And wherever I went was my poor dog Tray.

When at last I was forced from my Sheelah to part,
She said (while the sorrow was big at her heart),
"Oh! remember your Sheelah when far, far away;
And be kind, my dear Pat, to our poor dog Tray."

Poor dog! he was faithful and kind, to be sure,
And he constantly loved me, although I was poor;
When the sour-looking folks sent me heartless away,
I had always a friend in my poor dog Tray.

When the road was so dark, and the night was so cold,
And Pat and his dog were grown weary and old,
How snugly we slept in my old coat of gray,
And he licked me for kindness—my poor dog Tray.

Though my wallet was scant, I remembered his case,
Nor refused my last crust to his pitiful face;
But he died at my feet on a cold winter day,
And I played a lament for my poor dog Tray.

Where now shall I go, poor, forsaken, and blind?
Can I find one to guide me, so faithful and kind?
To my sweet native village, so far, far away,
I can never return with my poor dog Tray.

THE BAR SINISTER

BY *Richard Harding Davis*

I

THE MASTER WAS WALKING most unsteady, his legs tripping each other. After the fifth or sixth round, my legs often go the same way.

But even when the Master's legs bend and twist a bit, you musn't think he can't reach you. Indeed, that is the time he kicks most frequent. So I kept behind him in the shadow, or ran in the middle of the street. He stopped at many public-houses with swinging doors, those doors that are cut so high from the sidewalk that you can look in under them, and see if the Master is inside. At night when I peep beneath them the man at the counter will see me first and say, "Here's the Kid, Jerry, come to take you home. Get a move on you," and the Master will stumble out and follow me. It's lucky for us I'm so white, for no matter how dark the night, he can always see me ahead, just out of reach of his boot. At night the Master certainly does see most amazing. Sometimes he sees two or four of me, and walks in a circle, so that I have to take him by the leg of his trousers and lead him into the right road. One night, when he was very nasty-tempered and I was coaxing him along, two men passed us and one of them says, "Look at that brute!" and the other asks "Which?" and they both laugh. The Master, he cursed them good and proper.

This night, whenever we stopped at a public-house, the Master's pals left it and went on with us to the next. They spoke quite civil to me, and when the Master tried a flying kick, they gives him a shove. "Do you want we should lose our money?" says the pals.

I had had nothing to eat for a day and a night, and just before we set out the Master gives me a wash under the hydrant. Whenever I am locked up until all the slop pans in our alley are empty, and made to take a bath, and the Master's pals speak civil, and feel my ribs, I know something is going to happen. And that night, when every time they see a policeman under a lamp-post, they dodged across the street, and when at the last one of them picked me up and hid me under his jacket, I began to tremble; for I knew what it meant. It meant that I was to fight again for the Master.

I don't fight because I like it. I fight because if I didn't the other dog would find my throat, and the Master would lose his stakes, and I would be very sorry for him and ashamed. Dogs can pass me and I can pass dogs, and I'd never pick a fight with none of them. When I see two dogs standing on their hind legs in the streets, clawing each other's ears, and snapping for each other's windpipes, or howling and swearing and rolling in the mud, I feel sorry they should act so, and pretend not to notice. If he'd let me, I'd like to pass the time of day with every dog I meet. But there's something about me that no nice dog can abide. When I trot up to nice dogs, nodding and grinning, to make friends, they always tell me to be off. "Go to the devil!" they bark at me; "Get out!" and when I walk away they shout "mongrel," and "gutter-dog," and sometimes, after my back is turned, they rush me. I could kill most of them with three shakes, breaking the backbone of the little ones and squeezing the throat of the big ones. But what's the good? They *are* nice dogs; that's why I try to make up to them, and though it's not for them to say it, I *am* a street-dog, and if I try to push into the company of my betters, I suppose it's their right to teach me my place.

Of course, they don't know I'm the best fighting bull-terrier of my weight in Montreal. That's why it wouldn't be right for me to take no notice of what they shout. They don't know that if I once locked my jaws on them I'd carry away whatever I touched. The night I fought Kelley's White Rat, I wouldn't loosen up until the Master made a noose in my leash and strangled me, and if the handlers hadn't thrown red pepper down my nose, I *never* would have let go of that Ottawa dog. I don't think the handlers treated me quite right that time, but maybe they didn't know the Ottawa dog was dead. I did.

I learned my fighting from my mother when I was very young.

We slept in a lumberyard on the riverfront, and by day hunted for food along the wharves. When we got it, the other tramp-dogs would try to take it off us, and then it was wonderful to see mother fly at them, and drive them away. All I know of fighting I learned from mother, watching her picking the ash heaps for me when I was too little to fight for myself. No one ever was so good to me as mother. When it snowed and the ice was in the St. Lawrence she used to hunt alone, and bring me back new bones, and she'd sit and laugh to see me trying to swallow 'em whole. I was just a puppy then, my teeth was falling out. When I was able to fight we kept the whole river-range to ourselves. I had the genuine long, "punishing" jaw, so mother said, and there wasn't a man or a dog that dared worry us. Those were happy days, those were; and we lived well, share and share alike, and when we wanted a bit of fun, we chased the fat old wharf-rats. My! how they would squeal!

Then the trouble came. It was no trouble to me. I was too young to care then. But mother took it so to heart that she grew ailing, and wouldn't go abroad with me by day. It was the same old scandal that they're always bringing up against me. I was so young then that I didn't know. I couldn't see any difference between mother—and other mothers.

But one day a pack of curs we drove off snarled back some new names at her, and mother dropped her head and ran, just as though they had whipped us. After that she wouldn't go out with me except in the dark, and one day she went away and never came back, and though I hunted for her in every court and alley and back street of Montreal, I never found her.

One night, a month after mother ran away, I asked Guardian, the old blind mastiff, whose Master is the night watchman on our slip, what it all meant. And he told me.

"Every dog in Montreal knows," he says, "except you, and every Master knows. So I think it's time you knew."

Then he tells me that my father, who had treated mother so bad, was a great and noble gentleman from London. "Your father had twenty-two registered ancestors, had your father," old Guardian says, "and in him was the best bull-terrier blood of England, the most ancientest, the most royal; the winning 'blue-ribbon' blood, that breeds champions. He had sleepy pink eyes, and thin pink lips, and he was as white all over as his own white teeth, and under his white skin you could see his muscles, hard and smooth, like the links of a steel chain. When your father stood still, and tipped his nose in the air, it was just as though he was saying, 'Oh, yes, you common dogs and men, you may well stare. It must be a rare treat for you Colonials to see a real English royalty.' He certainly was pleased with hisself, was your father. He looked just as proud and haughty as one of them stone dogs in Victoria Park—them as is cut out of white marble. And you're like him," says the old mastiff—"by that, of course, meaning you're white, same as him. That's the only likeness. But, you see, the trouble is, Kid —well, you see Kid, the trouble is—your mother—"

"That will do," I said, for I understood then without his telling me, and I got up and walked away, holding my head and tail high in the air.

But I was oh, so miserable, and I wanted to see mother that very minute, and tell her that I didn't care.

Mother is what I am, a street-dog; there's no royal blood in mother's veins, nor is she like that father of mine, nor—and that's the worst—she's not even like me. For while I, when I'm washed for a fight, am as white as clean snow, she—and this is our trouble, she—my mother, is a black-and-tan.

When mother hid herself from me, I was twelve months old and able to take care of myself, and, as after mother left me, the wharves were never the same, I moved uptown and met the Master. Before he came, lots of other men-folks had tried to make up to me, and to whistle me home. But they either tried patting me or coaxing me with a piece of meat; so I didn't take to 'em. But one day the Master pulled me out of a street-fight by the hind legs, and kicked me good.

"You want to fight, do you?" says he. "I'll give you all the *fighting* you want!" he says, and he kicks me again. So I knew he was my Master, and I followed him home. Since that day I've pulled off many fights for him, and they've brought dogs from all over the province to have a go at me, but up to that night none, under thirty pounds, had ever downed me.

But that night, so soon as they carried me into the ring, I saw the dog was overweight, and that I was no match for him. It was asking too much of a puppy. The Master should have known I couldn't do it. Not that I mean to blame the Master, for when sober, which he sometimes was, though not, as you might say, his habit, he was most kind to me, and let me out to find food, if I could get it, and only kicked me when I didn't pick him up at night and lead him home.

But kicks will stiffen the muscles, and starving a dog so as to get him ugly-tempered for a fight may make him nasty, but it's weakening to his insides, and it causes the legs to wabble.

The ring was in a hall, back of a public-house. There was a red-hot whitewashed stove in one corner, and the ring in the other. I lay in the Master's lap, wrapped in my blanket, and, spite of the stove, shivering awful; but I always shiver before a fight; I can't help gettin' excited. While the men-folks were a-flashing their money and taking their last drink at the bar, a little Irish groom in gaiters came up to me and give me the back of his hand to smell, and scratched me behind the ears.

"You poor little pup," says he. "You haven't no show," he says. "That brute in the taproom, he'll eat your heart out."

"That's what you think," says the Master, snarling. "I'll lay you a quid the Kid chews him up."

The groom, he shook his head, but kept looking at me so sorry-like that I begun to get a bit sad myself. He seemed like he couldn't bear to leave off a patting of me, and he says, speaking low just like he would to a man-folk, "Well, good luck to you, little pup," which I thought so civil of him, that I reached up and licked his hand. I don't do that to many men. And the Master, he knew I didn't, and took on dreadful.

"What 'ave you got on the back of your hand?" says he, jumping up.

"Soap!" says the groom, quick as a rat. "That's more than you've got on yours. Do you want to smell of it?" and he sticks his fist under the Master's nose. But the pals pushed in between 'em.

"He tried to poison the Kid!" shouts the Master.

"Oh, one fight at a time," says the referee. "Get into the ring, Jerry. We're waiting." So we went into the ring.

I never could just remember what did happen in that ring. He give me no time to spring. He fell on me like a horse. I couldn't keep my feet against him, and though, as I saw, he could get his hold when he liked, he wanted to chew me over a bit first. I was wondering if they'd be able to pry him off me, when, in the third round, he took his hold; and I began to drown, just as I did when I fell into the river off the Red C slip. He closed deeper and deeper on my throat, and everything went black and red and bursting; and then, when I were sure I were dead, the handlers pulled him off, and the Master give me a kick that brought me to. But I couldn't move none, or even wink, both eyes being shut with lumps.

"He's a cur!" yells the Master, "a sneaking, cowardly cur. He lost the fight for me," says he, "because he's a —— —— —— cowardly cur." And he kicks me again in the lower ribs, so that I go sliding across the sawdust. "There's gratitude fer yer," yells the Master. "I've fed that dog, and nussed that dog, and housed him like a prince; and now he puts his tail between his legs, and sells me out, he does. He's a coward; I've done with him, I am. I'd sell him for a pipeful of tobacco." He picked me up by the tail, and swung me for the men-folks to see. "Does any gentleman here want to buy a dog," he says, "to make into sausage-meat?" he says. "That's all he's good for."

Then I heard the little Irish groom say, "I'll give you ten bob for the dog."

And another voice says, "Ah, don't you do it; the dog's same as dead—mebby he is dead."

"Ten shillings!" says the Master, and his voice sobers a bit; "make it two pounds, and he's yours."

But the pals rushed in again.

"Don't you be a fool, Jerry," they say. "You'll be sorry for this when you're sober. The Kid's worth a fiver."

One of my eyes was not so swelled up as the other, and as I hung by my tail, I opened it, and saw one of the pals take the groom by the shoulder.

"You ought to give 'im five pounds for that dog, mate," he says; "that's no ordinary dog. That dog's got good blood in him, that dog has. Why, his father—that very dog's father—"

I thought he never would go on. He waited like he wanted to be sure the groom was listening.

"That very dog's father," says the pal, "is Regent Royal, son of Champion Regent Monarch, champion bull-terrier of England for four years."

I was sore, and torn, and chewed most awful, but what the pal said sounded so fine that I wanted to wag my tail, only couldn't, owing to my hanging from it.

But the Master calls out, "Yes, his father was Regent Royal; who's saying he wasn't? but the pup's a cowardly cur, that's what his pup is, and why—I'll tell you why—because his mother was a black-and-tan street-dog, that's why!"

I don't see how I get the strength, but some way I threw myself out of the Master's grip and fell at his feet, and turned over and fastened all my teeth in his ankle, just across the bone.

When I woke, after the pals had kicked me off him, I was in the smoking car of a railroad train, lying in the lap of the little groom, and he was rubbing my open wounds with a greasy, yellow stuff, exquisite to the smell, and most agreeable to lick off.

II

"Well—what's your name—Nolan? Well, Nolan, these references are satisfactory," said the young gentleman my new Master called "Mr. Wyndham sir." "I'll take you on as second man. You can begin today."

My new Master shuffled his feet, and put his finger to his forehead. "Thank you, sir," says he. Then he choked like he had swallowed a fishbone. "I have a little dawg, sir," says he.

"You can't keep him," says "Mr. Wyndham, sir," very short.

" 'Es only a puppy, sir," says my new Master; " 'e wouldn't go outside the stables, sir."

"It's not that," says "Mr. Wyndham, sir"; "I have a large kennel of very fine dogs; they're the best of their breed in America. I don't allow strange dogs on the premises."

The Master shakes his head, and motions me with his cap, and I crept out from behind the door. "I'm sorry, sir," says the Master. "Then I can't take the place. I can't get along without the dog, sir."

"Mr. Wyndham, sir" looked at me that fierce that I guessed he was going to whip me, so I turned over on my back and begged with my legs and tail.

"Why, you beat him!" says "Mr. Wyndham, sir," very stern.

"No fear!" the Master says, getting very red. "The party I

bought him off taught him that. He never learnt that from me!"
He picked me up in his arms, and to show "Mr. Wyndham,
sir" how well I loved the Master, I bit his chin and hands.

"Mr. Wyndham, sir" turned over the letters the Master had
given him. "Well, these references certainly are very strong,"
he says. "I guess I'll let the dog stay this time. Only see you
keep him away from the kennels—or you'll both go."

"Thank you, sir," says the Master, grinning like a cat when
she's safe behind the area-railing.

"He's not a bad bull-terrier," says "Mr. Wyndham, sir,"
feeling my head. "Not that I know much about the smooth-
coated breeds. My dogs are St. Bernards." He stopped patting
me and held up my nose. "What's the matter with his ears?"
he says. "They're chewed to pieces. Is this a fighting dog?"
he asks, quick and rough-like.

I could have laughed. If he hadn't been holding my nose, I
certainly would have had a good grin at him. Me, the best
under thirty pounds in the Province of Quebec, and him asking
if I was a fighting dog! I ran to the Master and hung down
my head modest-like, waiting for him to tell my list of battles,
but the Master he coughs in his cap most painful. "Fightin'
dog, sir," he cries. "Lor' bless you, sir, the Kid don't know the
word. 'Es just a puppy, sir, same as you see; a pet dog, so to
speak. 'Es a regular old lady's lap-dog, the Kid is."

"Well, you keep him away from my St. Bernards," says
"Mr. Wyndham, sir," "or they might make a mouthful of him."

"Yes, sir, that they might," says the Master. But when we
gets outside he slaps his knee and laughs inside hisself, and
winks at me most sociable.

The Master's new home was in the country, in a province
they called Long Island. There was a high stone wall about his
home with big iron gates to it, same as Godfrey's brewery; and
there was a house with five red roofs, and the stables, where I
lived was cleaner than the aërated bakery-shop, and then there
was the kennels, but they was like nothing else in this world
that ever I see. For the first days I couldn't sleep of nights for
fear someone would catch me lying in such a cleaned-up place,
and would chase me out of it, and when I did fall to sleep I'd
dream I was back in the old Master's attic, shivering under the
rusty stove, which never had no coals in it, with the Master

flat on his back on the cold floor with his clothes on. And I'd wake up, scared and whimpering, and find myself on the new Master's cot with his hand on the quilt beside me; and I'd see the glow of the big stove, and hear the high-quality horses below-stairs stamping in their straw-lined boxes, and I'd snoop the sweet smell of hay and harness soap, and go to sleep again.

The stables was my jail, so the Master said, but I don't ask no better home than that jail.

"Now, Kid," says he, sitting on the top of a bucket upside down, "you've got to understand this. When I whistle it means you're not to go out of this 'ere yard. These stables is your jail. And if you leave 'em I'll have to leave 'em, too, and over the seas, in the County Mayo, an old mother will 'ave to leave her bit of a cottage. For two pounds I must be sending her every month, or she'll have naught to eat, nor no thatch over 'er head; so, I can't lose my place, Kid, an' see you don't lose it for me. You must keep away from the kennels," says he; "they're not for the likes of you. The kennels are for the quality. I wouldn't take a litter of them woolly dogs for one wag of your tail, Kid, but for all that they are your betters, same as the gentry up in the big house are my betters. I know my place and keep away from the gentry, and you keep away from the Champions."

So I never goes out of the stables. All day I just lay in the sun on the stone flags, licking my jaws, and watching the grooms wash down the carriages, and the only care I had was to see they didn't get gay and turn the hose on me. There wasn't even a single rat to plague me. Such stables I never did see.

"Nolan," says the head groom, "some day that dog of yours will give you the slip. You can't keep a street-dog tied up all his life. It's against his natur'." The head groom is a nice old gentleman, but he doesn't know everything. Just as though I'd been a street-dog because I liked it. As if I'd rather poke for my vittles in ash heaps than have 'em handed me in a wash basin, and would sooner bite and fight than be polite and sociable. If I'd had mother there I couldn't have asked for nothing more. But I'd think of her snooping in the gutters, or freezing of nights under the bridges, or, what's worse of all, running through the hot streets with her tongue down, so wild and crazy for a drink, that the people would shout "mad dog"

at her, and stone her. Water's so good, that I don't blame the
men-folks for locking it up inside their houses, but when the
hot days come, I think they might remember that those are the
dog days and leave a little water outside in a trough, like they
do for the horses. Then we wouldn't go mad, and the policemen
wouldn't shoot us. I had so much of everything I wanted that
it made me think a lot of the days when I hadn't nothing, and
if I could have given what I had to mother, as she used to share
with me, I'd have been the happiest dog in the land. Not that I
wasn't happy then, and most grateful to the Master, too, and if
I'd only minded him the trouble wouldn't have come again.

But one day the coachman says that the little lady they called
Miss Dorothy had come back from school, and that same
morning she runs over to the stables to pat her ponies, and she
sees me.

"Oh, what a nice little, white little dog," said she; "whose
little dog are you?" says she.

"That's my dog, miss," says the Master. " 'Is name is Kid,"
and I ran up to her most polite, and licks her fingers, for I
never see so pretty and kind a lady.

"You must come with me and call on my new puppies,"
says she, picking me up in her arms and starting off with me.

"Oh, but please, Miss," cries Nolan, "Mr. Wyndham give
orders that the Kid's not to go to the kennels."

"That'll be all right," says the little lady; "they're my kennels too. And the puppies will like to play with him."

You wouldn't believe me if I was to tell you of the style
of them quality-dogs. If I hadn't seen it myself I wouldn't have
believed it neither. The Viceroy of Canada don't live no better.
There was forty of them, but each one had his own house and a
yard—most exclusive—and a cot and a drinking basin all to
hisself. They had servants standing 'round waiting to feed 'em
when they was hungry, and valets to wash 'em; and they had
their hair combed and brushed like the grooms must when they
go out on the box. Even the puppies had overcoats with their
names on 'em in blue letters, and the name of each of those
they called champions was painted up fine over his front door
just like it was a public-house or a veterinary's. They were the
biggest St. Bernards I ever did see. I could have walked under
them if they'd have let me. But they were very proud and

haughty dogs, and looked only once at me, and then sniffed in
the air. The little lady's own dog was an old gentleman bull-
dog. He'd come along with us, and when he notices how taken
aback I was with all I see, 'e turned quite kind and affable and
showed me about.

"Jimmy Jocks," Miss Dorothy called him, but, owing to his
weight, he walked most dignified and slow, waddling like a
duck as you might say, and looked much too proud and handsome for such a silly name.

"That's the runway and that's the Trophy House," says he to
me, "and that over there is the hospital, where you have to go
if you get distemper, and the vet gives you beastly medicine."

"And which of these is your 'ouse, sir?" asks I, wishing to
be respectful. But he looked that hurt and haughty. "I don't live
in the kennels," says he, most contemptuous. "I am a house-
dog. I sleep in Miss Dorothy's room. And at lunch I'm let in
with the family, if the visitors don't mind. They most always
do, but they're too polite to say so. Besides," says he, smiling
most condescending, "visitors are always afraid of me. It's
because I'm so ugly," says he. "I suppose," says he, screwing
up his wrinkles and speaking very slow and impressive, "I suppose I'm the ugliest bull-dog in America," and as he seemed to
be so pleased to think hisself so, I said, "Yes, sir, you certainly
are the ugliest ever I see," at which he nodded his head most
approving.

"But I couldn't hurt 'em, as you say," he goes on, though I
hadn't said nothing like that, being too polite. "I'm too old,"
he says; "I haven't any teeth. The last time one of those grizzly
bears," said he, glaring at the big St. Bernards, "took a hold of
me, he nearly was my death," says he. I thought his eyes
would pop out of his head, he seemed so wrought up about it.
"He rolled me around in the dirt, he did," says Jimmy Jocks,
"an' I couldn't get up. It was low," says Jimmy Jocks, making
a face like he had a bad taste in his mouth. "Low, that's what I
call it, bad form, you understand, young man, not done in our
circles—and—and low." He growled, way down in his stomach,
and puffed hisself out, panting and blowing like he had been
on a run.

"I'm not a street-fighter," he says, scowling at a St. Bernard
marked "Champion." "And when my rheumatism is not trou-

bling me," he says, "I endeavor to be civil to all dogs, so long as they are gentlemen."

"Yes, sir," said I, for even to me he had been most affable.

At this we had come to a little house off by itself and Jimmy Jocks invites me in. "This is their trophy room," he says, "'where they keep their prizes. Mine," he says, rather grand-like, "are on the sideboard." Not knowing what a sideboard might be, I said, "Indeed, sir, that must be very gratifying." But he only wrinkled up his chops as much as to say, "It is my right."

The trophy room was as wonderful as any public-house I ever see. On the walls was pictures of nothing but beautiful St. Bernard dogs, and rows and rows of blue and red and yellow ribbons; and when I asked Jimmy Jocks why they was so many more of blue than of the others, he laughs and says, "Because these kennels always win." And there was many shining cups on the shelves which Jimmy Jocks told me were prizes won by the champions.

"Now, sir, might I ask you, sir," says I, "wot is a champion?"

At that he panted and breathed so hard I thought he would bust hisself. "My dear young friend!" says he. "Wherever have you been educated? A champion is a—a champion," he says. "He must win nine blue ribbons in the 'open' class. You follow me—that is—against all comers. Then he has the title before his name, and they put his photograph in the sporting papers. You know, of course, that *I* am a champion," says he. "I am Champion Woodstock Wizard III, and the two other Woodstock Wizards, my father and uncle, were both champions."

"But I thought your name was Jimmy Jocks," I said.

He laughs right out at that.

"That's my kennel name, not my registered name," he says. "Why, you certainly know that every dog has two names. Now, what's your registered name and number, for instance?" says he.

"I've only got one name," I says. "Just Kid."

Woodstock Wizard puffs at that and wrinkles up his forehead and pops out his eyes.

"Who are your people?" says he. "Where is your home?"

"At the stable, sir," I said. "My Master is the second groom."

At that Woodstock Wizard III looks at me for quite a bit without winking, and stares all around the room over my head.

"Oh, well," says he at last, "you're a very civil young dog," says he, "and I blame no one for what he can't help," which I thought most fair and liberal. "And I have known many bull-terriers that were champions," says he, "though as a rule they mostly run with fire engines, and to fighting. For me, I wouldn't care to run through the streets after a hose-cart, nor to fight," says he; "but each to his taste."

I could not help thinking that if Woodstock Wizard III tried to follow a fire engine he would die of apoplexy, and that, seeing he'd lost his teeth, it was lucky he had no taste for fighting, but after his being so condescending, I didn't say nothing.

"Anyway," says he, "every smooth-coated dog is better than any hairy old camel like those St. Bernards, and if ever you're hungry down at the stables, young man, come up to the house and I'll give you a bone. I can't eat them myself, but I bury them around the garden from force of habit, and in case a friend should drop in. Ah, I see my Mistress coming," he says, "and I bid you good-day. I regret," he says "that our different social position prevents our meeting frequent, for you're a worthy young dog with a proper respect for your betters, and in this country there's precious few of them have that." Then he waddles off, leaving me alone and very sad, for he was the first dog in many days that had spoken to me. But since he showed, seeing that I was a stable-dog, he didn't want my company, I waited for him to get well away. It was not a cheerful place to wait, the Trophy House. The pictures of the champions seemed to scowl at me, and ask what right had such as I even to admire them, and the blue and gold ribbons and the silver cups made me very miserable. I had never won no blue ribbons or silver cups; only stakes for the old Master to spend in the publics, and I hadn't won them for being a beautiful, high-quality dog, but just for fighting—which, of course, as Woodstock Wizard III says, is low. So I started for the stables, with my head down and my tail between my legs, feeling sorry I had ever left the Master. But I had more reason to be sorry before I got back to him.

The Trophy House was quite a bit from the kennels and as I left it I see Miss Dorothy and Woodstock Wizard III walking back toward them, and that a fine, big St. Bernard, his name was Champion Red Elfberg, had broke his chain and was running their way. When he reaches old Jimmy Jocks he lets out a roar like a grain steamer in a fog, and he makes three leaps for him. Old Jimmy Jocks was about a fourth his size; but he plants his feet and curves his back, and his hair goes up around his neck like a collar. But he never had no show at no time, for the grizzly bear, as Jimmy Jocks had called him, lights on old Jimmy's back and tries to break it, and old Jimmy Jocks snaps his gums and claws the grass, panting and groaning awful. But he can't do nothing, and the grizzly bear just rolls him under him, biting and tearing cruel. The odds was all that Woodstock Wizard III was going to be killed. I had fought enough to see that, but not knowing the rules of the game among champions I didn't like to interfere between two gentlemen who might be settling a private affair, and, as it were, take it as presuming of me. So I stood by, though I was shaking terrible, and holding myself in like I was on a leash. But at that Woodstock Wizard III, who was underneath, sees me through the dust, and calls very faint, "Help, you!" he says. "Take him in the hind leg," he says. "He's murdering me," he says. And then the little Miss Dorothy, who was crying, and calling to the kennel-men, catches at the Red Elfberg's hind legs to pull him off, and the brute, keeping his front pats well in Jimmy's stomach, turns his big head and snaps at her. So that was all I asked for, thank you. I went up under him. It was really nothing. He stood so high that I had only to take off about three feet from him and come in from the side, and my long, "punishing jaw," as mother was always talking about, locked on his woolly throat, and my back teeth met. I couldn't shake him, but I shook myself, and every time I shook myself there was thirty pounds of weight tore at his windpipes. I couldn't see nothing for his long hair, but I heard Jimmy Jocks puffing and blowing on one side, and munching the brute's leg with his old gums. Jimmy was an old sport that day, was Jimmy, or Woodstock Wizard III, as I should say. When the Red Elfberg was out and down I had to run, or those kennel-men would have had my life. They chased me right into the stables; and from under the hay I watched the head groom take down a carriage whip and order them to the right about. Luckily Master and the young grooms were out, or that day there'd have been fighting for everybody.

Well, it nearly did for me and the Master. "Mr. Wyndham, sir" comes raging to the stables and said I'd half-killed his best prize-winner, and had oughter be shot, and he gives the Master his notice. But Miss Dorothy she follows him, and says it was his Red Elfberg what began the fight, and that I'd saved Jimmy's life, and that old Jimmy Jocks was worth more to her than all the St. Bernards in the Swiss mountains—wherever they be. And that I was her champion, anyway. Then she cried over me most beautiful, and over Jimmy Jocks, too, who was that tied up in bandages he couldn't even waddle. So when he heard that side of it, "Mr. Wyndham, sir" told us that if Nolan put me on a chain, we could stay. So it came out all right for everybody but me. I was glad the Master kept his place, but I'd never worn a chain before, and it disheartened me—but that was the least of it. For the quality-dogs couldn't forgive my whipping their champion, and they came to the fence between the kennels and the stables, and laughed through the bars, barking most cruel words at me. I couldn't understand how they found it out, but they knew. After the fight Jimmy Jocks was most condescending to me, and he said the grooms had boasted to the kennel-men that I was a son of Regent Royal, and that when the kennel-men asked who was my mother they had had to tell them that too. Perhaps that was the way of it, but, however, the scandal was out, and every one of the quality-dogs knew that I was a street-dog and the son of a black-and-tan.

"These misalliances will occur," said Jimmy Jocks, in his old-fashioned way, "but no well-bred dog," says he, looking most scornful at the St. Bernards, who were howling behind the palings, "would refer to your misfortune before you, certainly not cast it in your face. I, myself, remember your father's father, when he made his debut at the Crystal Palace. He took four blue ribbons and three specials."

But no sooner than Jimmy would leave me, the St. Bernards would take to howling again, insulting mother and insulting me. And when I tore at my chain, they, seeing they were safe, would howl the more. It was never the same after that; the laughs and the jeers cut into my heart, and the chain bore heavy on my spirit. I was so sad that sometimes I wished I was back in the gutter again, where no one was better than me, and some nights I wished I was dead. If it hadn't been for the Master being so kind, and that it would have looked like I was blaming mother, I would have twisted my leash and hanged myself.

About a month after my fight, the word was passed through the kennels that the New York Show was coming, and such goings on as followed I never did see. If each of them had been matched to fight for a thousand pounds and the gate, they couldn't have trained more conscientious. But, perhaps, that's just my envy. The kennel-men rubbed 'em and scrubbed 'em and trims their hair and curls and combs it, and some dogs they fatted, and some they starved. No one talked of nothing but the Show, and the chances "our kennels" had against the other kennels, and if this one of our champions would win over that one, and whether them as hoped to be champions had better show in the "open" or the "limit" class, and whether this dog would beat his own dad, or whether his little puppy sister couldn't beat the two of them. Even the grooms had their money up, and day or night you heard nothing but praises of "our" dogs, until I, being so far out of it, couldn't have felt meaner if I had been running the streets with a can to my tail. I knew shows were not for such as me, and so I lay all day stretched at the end of my chain, pretending I was asleep, and only too glad that they had something so important to think of, that they could leave me alone.

But one day before the Show opened, Miss Dorothy came to the stables with "Mr. Wyndham, sir," and seeing me chained up and so miserable, she takes me in her arms.

"You poor little tyke," says she. "It's cruel to tie him up so; he's eating his heart out, Nolan," she says. "I don't know nothing about bull-terriers," says she, "but I think Kid's got good points," says she, "and you ought to show him. Jimmy Jocks has three legs on the Rensselaer Cup now, and I'm going to show him this time so that he can get the fourth, and if you wish, I'll enter your dog too. How would you like that, Kid?" says she. "How would you like to see the most beautiful dogs in the world? Maybe, you'd meet a pal or two," says she. "It would cheer you up, wouldn't it, Kid?" says she. But I was so upset, I could only wag my tail most violent. "He says it would!" says she, though, being that excited, I hadn't said nothing.

So, "Mr. Wyndham, sir" laughs and takes out a piece of blue paper, and sits down at the head groom's table.

"What's the name of the father of your dog, Nolan?" says he. And Nolan says, "The man I got him off told me he was a son of Champion Regent Royal, sir. But it don't seem likely, does it?" says Nolan.

"It does not!" says "Mr. Wyndham, sir," short-like.

"Aren't you sure, Nolan?" says Miss Dorothy.

"No, Miss," says the Master.

"Sire unknown," says "Mr. Wyndham, sir," and writes it down.

"Date of birth?" asks "Mr. Wyndham, sir."

"I—I—unknown, sir," says Nolan. And "Mr. Wyndham, sir" writes it down.

"Breeder?" says "Mr. Wyndham, sir."

"Unknown," says Nolan, getting very red around the jaws, and I drops my head and tail. And "Mr. Wyndham, sir" writes that down.

"Mother's name?" says "Mr. Wyndham, sir."

"She was a—unknown," says the Master. And I licks his hand.

"Dam unknown," says "Mr. Wyndham, sir," and writes it down. Then he takes the paper and reads out loud: "Sire unknown, dam unknown, breeder unknown, date of birth unknown. You'd better call him the 'Great Unknown,'" says he. "Who's paying his entrance fee?"

"I am," says Miss Dorothy.

Two weeks after, we all got on a train for New York; Jimmy Jocks and me following Nolan in the smoking car, and twenty-two of the St. Bernards, in boxes and crates, and on chains and leashes. Such a barking and howling I never did hear, and when they sees me going, too, they laughs fit to kill.

"Wot is this; a circus?" says the railroadman.

But I had no heart in it. I hated to go. I knew I was no "show" dog, even though Miss Dorothy and the Master did their best to keep me from shaming them. For before we set out Miss Dorothy brings a man from town who scrubbed and rubbed me, and sand-papered my tail, which hurt most awful, and shaved my ears with the Master's razor, so you could most see clear through 'em, and sprinkles me over with pipe clay, till I shines like a Tommy's cross-belts.

"Upon my word!" says Jimmy Jocks when he first sees me. "What a swell you are! You're the image of your grand-dad when he made his debut at the Crystal Palace. He took four firsts and three specials." But I knew he was only trying to throw heart into me. They might scrub, and they might rub, and they might pipe-clay, but they couldn't pipe-clay the insides of me, and they was black-and-tan.

Then we came to a Garden, which it was not, but the biggest hall in the world. Inside there was lines of benches a few miles long, and on them sat every dog in the world. If all the dog-snatchers in Montreal had worked night and day for a year, they couldn't have caught so many dogs. And they was all shouting and barking and howling so vicious that my heart stopped beating. For at first I thought they was all enraged at my presuming to intrude, but after I got in my place, they kept at it just the same, barking at every dog as he come in; daring him to fight, and ordering him out, and asking him what breed of dog he thought he was, anyway. Jimmy Jocks was chained just behind me, and he said he never see so fine a show. "That's a hot class you're in, my lad," he says, looking over into my street, where there were thirty bull-terriers. They was all as white as cream, and each so beautiful that if I could have broke my chain, I would have run all the way home and hid myself under the horse trough.

All night long they talked and sang, and passed greetings with old pals, and the homesick puppies howled dismal. Them that couldn't sleep wouldn't let no others sleep, and all the electric lights burned in the roof, and in my eyes. I could hear Jimmy Jocks snoring peaceful, but I could only doze by jerks, and when I dozed I dreamed horrible. All the dogs in the hall seemed coming at me for daring to intrude, with their jaws red and open, and their eyes blazing like the lights in the roof. "You're a street-dog! Get out, you street-dog!" they yells. And as they drives me out, the pipe-clay drops off me, and they laugh and shriek; and when I looks down I see that I have turned into a black-and-tan.

They was most awful dreams, and next morning, when Miss

Dorothy comes and gives me water in a pan, I begs and begs her to take me home, but she can't understand. "How well Kid is!" she says. And when I jumps into the Master's arms, and pulls to break my chain, he says, "If he knew all as he had against him, Miss, he wouldn't be so gay." And from a book they reads out the names of the beautiful high-bred terriers which I have got to meet. And I can't make 'em understand that I only want to run away, and hide myself where no one will see me.

Then suddenly men comes hurrying down our street and begins to brush the beautiful bull-terriers, and Nolan rubs me with a towel so excited that his hands trembles awful, and Miss Dorothy tweaks my ears between her gloves, so that the blood runs to 'em, and they turn pink and stand up straight and sharp.

"Now, then, Nolan," says she, her voice shaking just like his fingers, "keep his head up—and never let the Judge lose sight of him." When I hears that my legs breaks under me, for I knows all about judges. Twice, the old Master goes up before the Judge for fighting me with other dogs, and the Judge promises him if he ever does it again, he'll chain him up in jail. I knew he'd find me out. A Judge can't be fooled by no pipe clay. He can see right through you, and he reads your insides.

The judging ring, which is where the Judge holds out, was so like a fighting pit, that when I came in it, and find six other dogs there, I springs into position, so that when they lets us go I can defend myself. But the Master smoothes down my hair and whispers, "Hold 'ard, Kid, hold 'ard. This ain't a fight," says he. "Look your prettiest," he whispers. "Please, Kid, look your prettiest," and he pulls my leash so tight that I can't touch my pats to the sawdust, and my nose goes up in the air. There was millions of people a-watching us from the railings, and three of our kennel-men, too, making fun of Nolan and me, and Miss Dorothy with her chin just reaching to the rail, and her eyes so big that I thought she was a-going to cry. It was awful to think that when the Judge stood up and exposed me, all those people, and Miss Dorothy, would be there to see me driven from the show.

The Judge, he was a fierce-looking man with specs on his nose, and a red beard. When I first come in he didn't see me owing to my being too quick for him and dodging behind the Master. But when Master drags me round and I pulls at the sawdust to keep back, the Judge looks at us careless-like, and then stops and glares through his specs, and I knew it was all up with me.

"Are there any more?" asks the Judge, to the gentleman at the gate, but never taking his specs from me.

The man at the gate looks in his book. "Seven in the novice-class," says he. "They're all here. You can go ahead," and he shuts the gate.

The Judge, he doesn't hesitate a moment. He just waves his hand toward the corner of the ring. "Take him away," he says to the Master. "Over there and keep him away," and he turns and looks most solemn at the six beautiful bull-terriers. I don't know how I crawled to that corner. I wanted to scratch under the sawdust and dig myself a grave. The kennel-men they slapped the rail with their hands and laughed at the Master like they would fall over. They pointed at me in the corner, and their sides just shaked. But little Miss Dorothy she pressed her lips tight against the rail, and I see tears rolling from her eyes. The Master, he hangs his head like he had been whipped. I felt most sorry for him, than all. He was so red, and he was letting on not to see the kennel-men, and blinking his eyes. If the Judge had ordered me right out, it wouldn't have disgraced us so, but it was keeping me there while he was judging the high-bred dogs that hurt so hard. With all those people staring too. And his doing it so quick, without no doubt nor questions. You can't fool the judges. They see insides you.

But he couldn't make up his mind about them high-breed dogs. He scowls at 'em, and he glares at 'em, first with his head on the one side and then on the other. And he feels of 'em, and orders 'em to run about. And Nolan leans against the rails, with his head hung down, and pats me. And Miss Dorothy comes over beside him, but don't say nothing, only wipes her eye with her finger. A man on the other side of the rail he says to the Master, "The Judge don't like your dog?"

"No," says the Master.

"Have you ever shown him before?" says the man.

"No," says the Master, "and I'll never show him again. He's my dog," says the Master, "an' he suits me! And I don't care what no judges think." And when he says them kind words, I licks his hand most grateful.

The Judge had two of the six dogs on a little platform in the middle of the ring, and he had chased the four other dogs into the corners, where they was licking their chops, and letting on they didn't care, same as Nolan was.

The two dogs on the platform was so beautiful that the Judge hisself couldn't tell which was the best of 'em, even when he stoops down and holds their heads together. But at last he gives a sigh, and brushes the sawdust off his knees and goes to the table in the ring, where there was a man keeping score, and heaps and heaps of blue and gold and red and yellow ribbons. And the Judge picks up a bunch of 'em and walks to the two gentlemen who was holding the beautiful dogs, and he says to each "What's his number?" and he hands each gentleman a ribbon. And then he turned sharp, and comes straight at the Master.

"What's his number?" says the Judge. And Master was so scared that he couldn't make no answer.

But Miss Dorothy claps her hands and cries out like she was laughing, "Three twenty-six," and the Judge writes it down, and shoves Master the blue ribbon.

I bit the Master, and I jumps and bit Miss Dorothy, and I waggled so hard that the Master couldn't hold me. When I get to the gate Miss Dorothy snatches me up and kisses me between the ears, right before millions of people, and they both hold me so tight that I didn't know which of them was carrying of me. But one thing I knew, for I listened hard, as it was the Judge hisself as said it.

"Did you see that puppy I gave 'first' to?" says the Judge to the gentleman at the gate.

"I did. He was a bit out of his class," says the gate-gentleman.

"He certainly was!" says the Judge, and they both laughed.

But I didn't care. They couldn't hurt me then, not with Nolan holding the blue ribbon and Miss Dorothy hugging my ears, and the kennel-men sneaking away, each looking like he'd been caught with his nose under the lid of the slop can.

We sat down together, and we all three just talked as fast as we could. They was so pleased that I couldn't help feeling proud myself, and I barked and jumped and leaped about so gay, that all the bull-terriers in our street stretched on their chains, and howled at me.

"Just look at him!" says one of those I had beat. "What's he giving hisself airs about?"

"Because he's got one blue ribbon!" says another of 'em. "Why, when I was a puppy I used to eat 'em, and if that Judge could ever learn to know a toy from a mastiff, I'd have had this one."

But Jimmy Jocks he leaned over from his bench, and says, "Well done, Kid. Didn't I tell you so!" What he 'ad told me was that I might get a "commended," but I didn't remind him.

"Didn't I tell you," says Jimmy Jocks, "that I saw your grandfather make his debut at the Crystal—"

"Yes, sir, you did, sir," says I, for I have no love for the men of my family.

A gentleman with a showing leash around his neck comes up just then and looks at me very critical. "Nice dog you've got, Miss Wyndham," says he; "would you care to sell him?"

"He's not my dog," says Miss Dorothy, holding me tight. "I wish he were."

"He's not for sale, sir," says the Master, and I was *that* glad.

"Oh, he's yours, is he?" says the gentleman, looking hard at Nolan. "Well, I'll give you a hundred dollars for him," says he, careless-like.

"Thank you, sir, he's not for sale," says Nolan, but his eyes get very big. The gentleman, he walked away, but I watches him, and he talks to a man in a golf cap, and by and by the man comes along our street, looking at all the dogs, and stops in front of me.

"This your dog?" says he to Nolan. "Pity he's so leggy," says he. "If he had a good tail and a longer stop, and his ears were set higher, he'd be a good dog. As he is, I'll give you fifty dollars for him."

But, before the Master could speak, Miss Dorothy laughs, and says, "You're Mr. Polk's kennel-man, I believe. Well, you tell Mr. Polk from me that the dog's not for sale now any more than he was five minutes ago, and that when he is, he'll have to bid against me for him." The man looks foolish at that, but he turns to Nolan quick-like. "I'll give you three hundred for him," he says.

"Oh, indeed!" whispers Miss Dorothy, like she was talking to herself. "That's it, is it," and she turns and looks at me just as though she had never seen me before. Nolan, he was a-gaping, too, with his mouth open. But he holds me tight.

"He's not for sale," he growls, like he was frightened, and the man looks black and walks away.

"Why Nolan!" cries Miss Dorothy, "Mr. Polk knows more about bull-terriers than any amateur in America. What can he mean? Why, Kid is no more than a puppy! Three hundred dollars for a puppy!"

"And he ain't no thoroughbred neither!" cries the Master. "He's 'Unknown,' ain't he? Kid can't help it, of course, but his mother, Miss ———"

I dropped my head. I couldn't bear he should tell Miss Dorothy. I couldn't bear she should know I had stolen my blue ribbon.

But the Master never told, for at that, a gentleman runs up, calling, "Three Twenty-Six Three Twenty-Six," and Miss Dorothy says, "Here he is, what is it?"

"The Winner's Class," says the gentleman. "Hurry please. The Judge is waiting for him."

Nolan tries to get me off the chain onto a showing leash, but he shakes so, he only chokes me. "What is it, Miss?" he says. "What is it?"

"The Winner's Class," says Miss Dorothy. "The Judge wants him with the winners of the other classes—to decide which is best. "It's only a form," says she. "He has the champions against him now."

"Yes," said the gentleman, as he hurries us to the ring. "I'm afraid it's only a form for your dog, but the Judge wants all the winners, puppy class even."

We had got to the gate, and the gentleman there was writing down my number.

"Who won the open?" asks Miss Dorothy.

"Oh, who would?" laughs the gentleman. "The old champion, of course. He's won for three years now. There he is. Isn't he wonderful?" says he, and he points to a dog that's standing proud and haughty on the platform in the middle of the ring.

I never see so beautiful a dog, so fine and clean and noble, so white like he had rolled hisself in flour, holding his nose up and his eyes shut, same as though no one was worth looking

at. Aside of him, we other dogs, even though we had a blue
ribbon apiece, seemed like lumps of mud. He was a royal gentleman, a king, he was. His Master didn't have to hold his head
with no leash. He held it hisself, standing as still as an iron
dog on a lawn, like he knew all the people was looking at him.
And so they was, and no one around the ring pointed at no other
dog but him.

"Oh, what a picture," cried Miss Dorothy; "he's like a
marble figure by a great artist—one who loved dogs. Who is
he?" says she, looking in her book. "I don't keep up with
terriers."

"Oh, you know him," says the gentleman. "He is the Champion of Champions Regent Royal."

The Master's face went red.

"And this is Regent Royal's son," cries he, and he pulls me
quick into the ring, and plants me on the platform next my
father.

I trembled so that I near fall. My legs twisted like a leash.
But my father he never looked at me. He only smiled, the same
sleepy smile, and he still keep his eyes half-shut, like as no
one, no, not even his son, was worth his lookin' at.

The Judge, he didn't let me stay beside my father but, one
by one, he placed the other dogs next to him and measured and
felt and pulled at them. And each one he put down, but he never
put my father down. And then he comes over and picks up me
and sets me back on the platform, shoulder to shoulder with
the Champion Regent Royal, and goes down on his knees, and
looks into our eyes.

The gentleman with my father, he laughs, and says to the
Judge, "Thinking of keeping us here all day, John?" but the
Judge, he doesn't hear him, and goes behind us and runs his
hand down my side, and holds back my ears, and takes my
jaws between his fingers. The crowd around the ring is very
deep now, and nobody says nothing. The gentleman at the
score table, he is leaning forward, with his elbows on his knees,
and his eyes very wide, and the gentleman at the gate is whispering quick to Miss Dorothy, who has turned white. I stood as
stiff as stone. I didn't even breathe. But out of the corner of my
eye I could see my father licking his pink chops, and yawning
just a little, like he was bored.

The Judge, he had stopped looking fierce, and was looking solemn. Something inside him seemed a-troubling him awful. The more he stares at us now, the more solemn he gets, and when he touches us he does it gentle, like he was patting us. For a long time he kneels in the sawdust, looking at my father and at me, and no one around the ring says nothing to nobody.

Then the Judge takes a breath and touches me sudden. "It's his," he says, but he lays his hand just as quick on my father. "I'm sorry," says he.

The gentleman holding my father cries:

"Do you mean to tell me—"

And the Judge, he answers, "I mean the other is the better dog." He takes my father's head between his hands and looks down at him, most sorrowful. "The King is dead," says he, "long live the King. Good-by, Regent," he says.

The crowd around the railings clapped their hands, and some laughed scornful, and everyone talks fast, and I start for the gate so dizzy that I can't see my way. But my father pushes in front of me, walking very daintily, and smiling sleepy, same as he had just been waked, with his head high, and his eyes shut, looking at nobody.

So that is how I "came by my inheritance," as Miss Dorothy calls it, and just for that, though I couldn't feel where I was any different, the crowd follows me to my bench and pats me, and coos at me, like I was a baby in a baby carriage. And the handlers have to hold 'em back so that the gentlemen from the papers can make pictures of me, and Nolan walks me up and down so proud, and the men shakes their heads and says, "He certainly is the true type, he is!" And the pretty ladies asks Miss Dorothy, who sits beside me letting me lick her gloves to show the crowd what friends we is, "Aren't you afraid he'll bite you?" and Jimmy Jocks calls to me, "Didn't I tell you so! I always knew you were one of us. Blood will out, Kid, blood will out. I saw your grandfather," says he, "make his debut at the Crystal Palace. But he was never the dog you are!"

After that, if I could have asked for it, there was nothing I couldn't get. You might have thought I was a snow-dog, and they were afeerd I'd melt. If I wet my pats, Nolan gave me a hot bath and chained me to the stove; if I couldn't eat my food, being stuffed full by the cook, for I am a house-dog now, and let in to lunch whether there is visitors or not, Nolan would run to bring the vet. It was all tommy-rot, as Jimmy says, but meant most kind. I couldn't scratch myself comfortable, without Nolan giving me nasty drinks, and rubbing me outside till it burnt awful, and I wasn't let to eat bones for fear of spoiling my "beautiful" mouth, what mother used to call my "punishing jaw," and my food was cooked special on a gas stove, and Miss Dorothy gives me an overcoat, cut very stylish like the champions', to wear when we goes out carriage-driving.

After the next show, where I takes three blue ribbons, four silver cups, two medals, and brings home forty-five dollars for Nolan they gives me a "Registered" name, same as Jimmy's. Miss Dorothy wanted to call me "Regent Heir Apparent," but I was THAT glad when Nolan says, "No, Kid don't owe nothing to his father, only to you and hisself. So, if you please, Miss, we'll call him Wyndham Kid." And so they did, and you can see it on my overcoat in blue letters, and painted top of my kennel. It was all too hard to understand. For days I just sat and wondered if I was really me, and how it all come about, and why everybody was so kind. But, oh, it was so good they was, for if they hadn't been, I'd never have got the thing I most wished after. But, because they was kind, and not liking to deny me nothing, they gave it me, and it was more to me than anything in the world.

It came about one day when we was out driving. We was in the cart they calls the dog-cart, because it's the one Miss Dorothy keeps to take Jimmy and me for an airing. Nolan was up behind, and me in my new overcoat was sitting beside Miss Dorothy. I was admiring the view, and thinking how good it was to have a horse pull you about so that you needn't get yourself splashed and have to be washed, when I hears a dog calling loud for help, and I pricks up my ears and looks over the horse's head. And I sees something that makes me tremble down to my toes. In the road before us three big dogs was chasing a little, old lady-dog. She had a string to her tail, where some boys had tied a can, and she was dirty with mud and ashes, and torn most awful. She was too far done up to get away, and too old to help herself, but she was making a fight for her life, snapping her old gums savage, and dying game. All this I see in a wink, and I can't stand it no longer and clears the wheel and lands in the road on my head. It was my stylish overcoat done that, and I curse it proper, but I gets my pats again quick, and makes a rush for the fighting. Behind me I hear Miss Dorothy cry, "They'll kill that old dog. Wait, take my whip. Beat them off her! The Kid can take care of himself," and I hear Nolan fall into the road, and the horse come to a stop. The old lady-dog was down, and the three was eating her vicious, but as I come up, scattering the pebbles, she hears, and thinking it's one more of them, she lifts her head and my heart breaks open like someone had sunk his teeth in it. For, under the ashes and the dirt and the blood, I can see who it is, and I know that my mother has come back to me.

I gives a yell that throws them three dogs off their legs.

"Mother!" I cries. "I'm the Kid," I cries. "I'm coming to you, mother, I'm coming."

And I shoots over her, at the throat of the big dog, and the other two, they sinks their teeth into that stylish overcoat, and tears it off me, and that sets me free, and I lets them have it. I never had so fine a fight as that! What with mother being there to see, and not having been let to mix up in no fights since I become a prize-winner, it just naturally did me good, and it wasn't three shakes before I had 'em yelping. Quick as a wink, mother, she jumps in to help me, and I just laughed to see her. It was like old times. And Nolan, he made me laugh too. He was like a hen on a bank, shaking the butt of his whip, but not daring to cut in for fear of hitting me.

"Stop it, Kid," he says, "stop it. Do you want to be all torn up?" says he. "Think of the Boston show next week," says he. "Think of Chicago. Think of Danbury. Don't you never want to be a champion?" How was I to think of all them places when I had three dogs to cut up at the same time. But in a minute two of 'em begs for mercy, and mother and me lets 'em run away. The big one, he ain't able to run away. Then mother and me, we dances and jumps, and barks and laughs, and bites each other and rolls each other in the road. There never was two dogs so happy as we, and Nolan, he whistles and calls and begs me to come to him, but I just laugh and play larks with mother.

"Now, you come with me," says I, "to my new home, and

never try to run away again." And I shows her our house with
the five red roofs, set on the top of the hill. But mother trembles
awful, and says: "They'd never let the likes of me in such a
place. Does the Viceroy live there, Kid?" says she. And I laugh
at her. "No, I do," I says; "and if they won't let you live there,
too, you and me will go back to the streets together, for we must
never be parted no more." So we trots up the hill, side by side,
with Nolan trying to catch me, and Miss Dorothy laughing at
him from the cart.

"The Kid's made friends with the poor old dog," says she.
"Maybe he knew her long ago when he ran the streets himself.
Put her in here beside me, and see if he doesn't follow."

So, when I hears that, I tells mother to go with Nolan and
sit in the cart, but she says no, that she'd soil the pretty lady's
frock; but I tells her to do as I say, and so Nolan lifts her, trembling still, into the cart, and I runs alongside, barking joyful.

When we drives into the stables I takes mother to my kennel,
and tells her to go inside it and make herself at home. "Oh, but
he won't let me!" says she.

"Who won't let you?" says I, keeping my eye on Nolan, and
growling a bit nasty, just to show I was meaning to have my
way.

"Why, Wyndham Kid," says she, looking up at the name on
my kennel.

"But I'm Wyndham Kid!" says I.

"You!" cries mother. "You! Is my little Kid the great Wyndham Kid the dogs all talk about?" And at that, she, being very
old, and sick, and hungry, and nervous, as mothers are, just
drops down in the straw and weeps bitter.

Well, there ain't more more than that to tell. Miss Dorothy,
she settled it.

"If the Kid wants the poor old thing in the stables," says she,
"let her stay."

"You see," says she, "she's a black-and-tan, and his mother
was a black-and-tan, and maybe that's what makes Kid feel so
friendly toward her," says she.

"Indeed for me," says Nolan, "she can have the best there
is. I'd never drive out no dog that asks for a crust nor a shelter,"
he says. "But what will Mr. Wyndham do?"

"He'll do what I say," says Miss Dorothy, "and if I say she's to stay, she will stay, and I say—she's to stay!"

And so mother and Nolan, and me, found a home. Mother was scared at first—not being used to kind people—but she was so gentle and loving that the grooms got fonder of her than of me, and tried to make me jealous by patting of her, and giving her the pick of the vittles. But that was the wrong way to hurt my feelings. That's all, I think. Mother is so happy here that I tell her we ought to call it the Happy Hunting Grounds, because no one hunts you, and there is nothing to hunt; it just all comes to you. And so we live in peace, mother sleeping all day in the sun, or behind the stove in the head groom's office, being fed twice a day regular by Nolan, and all the day by the other grooms most irregular. And, as for me, I go hurrying around the country to the bench-shows; winning money and cups for Nolan, and taking the blue ribbons away from father.

SETTER AND TERRIER

BY *Preston Quadland*

STEVE POPPAS, owner of the Marathon Café, smiled as he looked out of the back window at two dogs searching for food in the ash barrel. They never would upset the barrel again, because he had wired it down; and he had seen to it that they would find nothing to eat.

Setter and Terrier were at the barrel. Setter said:

"Just ashes."

"Nothing but ashes," added Terrier, disappointed.

"Bones are as rare as graveyards," remarked Setter.

"They are," returned Terrier. "But in my day I've known them more plentiful than butlers' gravy."

As Setter stretched his long forepaws up to the rim of the barrel to give a final sniff, Terrier said:

"You're frightfully thin."

"Not from choice," replied Setter.

"Furthermore, you need a bath," added Terrier.

"Indeed I do," Setter agreed. "On the farm on warm days I'd take a deep breath and wade into the brook up to my neck. A little green frog with gold bands round his eyes used to sit on the bank and gulp at me. If my feet got muddy from the bottom of the stream I'd wipe them off by leaping through the high grass. It's great fun; the long grass tickles your stomach and makes you laugh. Here in the city I don't get a bath till it rains."

Getting down on all fours, he said:

"But we both need a bath."

Terrier blinked pink eyes and gazed sorrowfully at his unkempt coat. "I could still be a gentleman," he said. "My master was a gentleman; he took two baths a day."

"Excessive bathing enervates me," said Setter. "Was your master a lazy fellow?"

"Oh, no."

"Where is he now?"

"Master went to Europe over six weeks ago," replied Terrier gravely. "That very day the butler opened the back door to me and said 'Shoo!' just as if I were any common housefly. When I didn't budge he gave me a shove with his foot and almost shut my tail in the door."

"I always wanted to be a gentleman," said Setter, "even though they wear red caps when they go hunting."

Carefully Terrier measured him.

"I might find a place for you as a gentleman's gentleman," he said. "You don't bark at the moon, do you?"

"When I'm happy . . . when I race through the fields at night."

"Barking will never do," admonished Terrier. "Yipping's more the style. Do you know the old dowager who wears pearls on her toes?"

"I can't say that I do," replied Setter. "But I know the scents in the wind and the weather side of a goat."

"Do you know the men who slip on scatter rugs?"

"Yes, them I know," said Setter. "And I know the sound of the pussy willows."

"Do they go swish, swish?"

"No," said Setter, laughing.

"How then?"

"Did you ever hear the mushrooms grow overnight?"

"No," replied Terrier.

"Then I can't explain it," said Setter, "for it's very much like that. It's like the oozing of pitch from the pine trees too, a very peculiar and particular sound."

"Is it like a small mouse running over the attic floor?"

"Not at all. But it is not unlike the sound of a mole walking deep in his burrow."

"Is it like the maid snoring on the top floor when you're down in the cellar?"

"I'm afraid you don't catch the idea," said Setter.

"My dear fellow, your ears are way too keen for a gentleman's gentleman," remarked Terrier.

A door slammed and heavy footsteps came toward the ash barrel. The dogs scampered to a safe distance and then started walking. Terrier had a difficult time catching up with the larger dog.

"I believe," said Terrier, puffing, "that we might see if my master's home. He seldom stays away longer than six weeks."

"Is your master happy by nature?" asked Setter.

"Not particularly," replied Terrier. "The happiest I ever saw him was one day he came home late from the office. He was dressing for dinner and I distinctly remember he had a slight bruise on one knee. Patting me on the head, he smiled and called me by name, saying, "Pepys, old boy, what in the world do you do for excitement?' "

"Is your master tall?" asked Setter.

"Quite."

"Does he wear a beard?"

"Once he did. I was lying on the rug resting when the telephone rang and master began shouting into the mouthpiece. Then he hurried out of the house and I didn't see him for four days; when he returned he had a beard."

"Beards grow fast," said Setter.

"They do," agreed Terrier.

"Some faster than others of course."

"On blond men they show less," replied Terrier.

"On light-haired women too," said Setter.

"Women don't have beards."

"Don't they though!" exclaimed Setter. "My master's grandmother had a gray one."

Setter sniffed the air.

"Is your master old?" he asked.

"Forty-two his last birthday," replied Terrier.

"And stout?"

"Not when I last saw him. But sometimes he changes from middling to stout in a few weeks; and back again to middling in about six months or a year."

"The goldenrod fades to mere stalk in the fall," said Setter, "then grows again in the spring."

"Master never went that far," said Terrier.

Setter gazed up at the sky.

"Is your master nice?" he asked.

"He's fastidious," replied Terrier.

"What's that?"

"That's keeping the towels arranged just so in the bathroom."

"I think I see," said Setter. "Otherwise, does he have any faults?"

"He makes me sleep in a basket."

"In a basket!" cried Setter. "Don't you feel like needles and thread?"

"Every Monday I feel like the laundry," said Terrier. "It's that kind of a basket."

Setter, from nose to tail, seemed very long beside the other. He was in front of and behind him at the same time, so that you could see Terrier only by looking at the two dogs from the right direction.

"One ought to be wary of strangers," remarked Terrier, looking up.

Setter said: "The thistle has a blossom loaded with nectar." Terrier eyed him with interest.

"You seem a simple chap," he said. "Tell me about yourself."

Setter thought for a while.

"I like to be happy, as few people do," he said finally. "Sometimes I bark at people, but I wouldn't bite them because I love them too much. Sometimes I even bark at myself. Often I bark for no reason at all, if the wind is cool and the maples are whimpering. Sometimes I bark when I hear an animal passing in the night and the hair rises on my back. But most of the time I'm silent and if my stomach is full I'm content just to doze."

"Why did you come here?" asked Terrier.

"My master came to get a job. Because his money ran low I ran away, thinking I'd shift for myself and go back when he was better off, although he always fed me well. I returned a few weeks ago, but he was gone. There was an old hat of his in the alley beside his window."

"You never should let loose from a good provider," said Terrier. "Bread is for them who can teach others to share it."

"The old hen on the farm used to say that you don't build your nest for the sake of the weasels," replied Setter.

"Do old hens know the answers?"

"If minds are sharp and spirits young," said Setter.

They walked along in silence, shying away from automobiles in the road when people forced them off the sidewalks. An old woman tried to pat Setter on the head and he would have liked to stop, but Terrier told him you couldn't trust women and made him hurry by.

Setter didn't like that. Women were all right, he thought. They were part of the Great Scheme. Women were just as necessary as fire or water or pain.

Setter suddenly was struck with the fact that he needed a bath and said:

"You don't miss being clean till you're dirty."

"Cleanliness is next to saintlessness," said Terrier.

"Godliness," corrected Setter.

"I knew it was something like that," said Terrier.

"A common expression; but people do many common things."

"They do," said Terrier.

"Like drinking coffee in the morning."

Terrier said:

"I drink milk. It's good for stomach ulcers."

"Do you have ulcers?" asked Setter.

"No," replied Terrier, "but master does."

"I *like* milk," said Setter.

Setter stepped back to let a woman pass in front of him.

"Her clothes sound like a light spring frost," he said.

They came into a better part of the city where the dogs they saw were clean and turned aside their heads as they walked by. Terrier lifted his head and held it high, his carriage cocky as could be, his tail curved upward. Here he felt somewhat ashamed of Setter, whose tail drooped.

"We're not far from home," said Terrier.

"What do you have for dinner?" asked Setter, thinking of roast beef.

"Usually dog food out of a can."

"Out of a can!" exclaimed Setter, who thought only maple syrup and salve came in cans.

"It's specially prepared," said Terrier. "It has all the vitamins."

"What are vitamins?" asked Setter. "Bone and gristle?"

"No."

"What then?"

"A, B, D, and G."

"What?"

Terrier repeated.

Setter said:

"Didn't you ever chase your breakfast before the sun comes

up, and leap over stone walls so hungry you could take a bite
out of a fence post?"

"My vitamins don't run," said Terrier.

"Honestly," cried Setter in amazement, "haven't you ever
raced past a woodchuck just to hear his teeth clatter?"

"No," replied Terrier, "but I have eaten well. Wait till you
taste dog food out of a can; it's more sanitary."

Setter declared Terrier's master must be a wise man to get
dog food out of a can.

"Do you know who was the smartest man in the world?"
asked Terrier.

"Tell me," replied Setter.

Terrier said:

"Solomon."

"I never heard of him," returned Setter. "Was he smarter
than the firefly who sits on your tongue when you bite at him
and then lights up your mouth to see where your teeth are?"

Terrier bobbed his head affirmatively.

"What about the old mink who stole the bait out of my
master's trap?" asked Setter. "Was Solomon smarter than he?"

"What does a mink know?" scoffed Terrier.

"He's smarter than the trout because he feeds on trout."

"Feeds on trout?" said Terrier.

"Yes," replied Setter. "In that lies the Story of the World."

"All I know is that people say Solomon was the wisest man
who lived," said Terrier.

"Wisdom is another matter."

Setter said nothing for a while and then added:

"I wonder if Solomon was wiser than the bud that breaks
into flower and perfumes the whole garden?"

Setter knew by the jauntiness of Terrier's step that they were
in a familiar neighborhood.

The houses frightened Setter. They were all attached to one
another so that you couldn't race between them in a pinch. You
could run only in two directors—forward and backward. He
felt that a boot might pop out of a doorway at any moment and
catch him in the ribs or someone might come rushing down front
steps to frighten him away.

"This is the street I live on," said Terrier proudly, as they
rounded a corner. "We like it here but it's expensive."

"It's all man-made," remarked Setter.

"Man-made?"

"Yes," said Setter. "They've removed Nature and replaced her with bricks and steel."

"Land is at a premium in the city," replied Terrier.

"There is no land in the city," said Setter. "Just buildings and pavement."

Setter continued:

"What do you suppose city angleworms do at night when they can't come up to the surface for air?"

"You're an odd chap," said Terrier.

"You know," said Setter, laughing, "sometimes in the early morning I used to creep up and grab an angleworm by the nose and then pull backward just to see him stretch."

Setter became thoughtful.

"Ambition does strange things to people," he said.

"You, ambitious!" cried Terrier.

"I was thinking of master," said Setter.

"Oh. What about him?" asked Terrier.

"He wants to be a bookkeeper," replied Setter.

Without the slightest warning Terrier gave a low whine of joy and raced toward a man and woman coming down the steps of one of the houses. Setter followed closed behind.

When Terrier reached them he began to leap against the man's trousers.

"Get away!" cried the man, trying to push him off with his foot.

"Scat!" exclaimed the woman.

Setter stood safely at the curb.

Changing his tactics, Terrier started to leap against the woman.

"Why, Robert, it's Pepys," she cried. "The little wretch is positively filthy!"

The man reached down and picked him up by the neck.

"So he is!" he said gruffly.

Setter thought the woman looked beautiful.

The door to the house opened and a butler came down the steps.

"It's Pepys," said the man to the butler. "Here, take the little beast and give him a bath; then see that he doesn't get off his leash again."

The butler took Terrier with a firm hand and accidentally pinched him hard. Pepys yipped.

Setter looked on as Terrier was carried back up the steps and the man and woman got in a car and drove away.

THE CELEBRATED DOG

BEING A PUBLIC CHARACTER

BY *Don Marquis*

E VER SINCE I BIT A CIRCUS LION, believing him to be another dog like myself, only larger, I have been what Doc Watson calls a Public Character in our town.

Freckles, my boy, was a kind of a Public Character, too. He went around bragging about my noble blood and bravery, and all the other boys and dogs in town sort of looked up to him and thought how lucky he was to belong to a dog like me. And he deserved whatever glory he got of it, Freckles did. For, if I do say it myself, there's not a dog in town got a better boy than my boy Freckles, take him all in all. I'll back him against any dog's boy that is anywhere near his size, for fighting, swimming, climbing, foot-racing or throwing stones farthest and straightest. Or I'll back him against any stray boy, either.

Well, some dogs may be born Public Characters, and like it. And some may be brought up to like it. I've seen dogs in those traveling Uncle Tom's Cabin shows that were so stuck on themselves they wouldn't hardly notice us town dogs. But with me, becoming a Public Character happened all in a flash, and it was sort of hard for me to get used to it. One day I was just a private kind of a dog, as you may say, eating my meals at the Watson's back door, and pretending to hunt rats when requested, and not scratching off too many fleas in Doc Watson's drugstore, and standing out from underfoot when told, and other unremarkable things like that. And the next day I had bit that lion and was a Public Character, and fame came so sudden I scarcely knew how to act.

Even drummers from big places like St. Louis and Chicago would come into the drugstore and look at my teeth and toenails, as if they must be different from other dogs' teeth and toenails. And people would come tooting up to the store in their little cars, and get out and look me over and say:

"Well, Doc, what'll you take for him?" and Doc would wink, and say:

"He's Harold's dog. You ask Harold."

Which Harold is Freckles's other name. But any boy that calls him Harold outside of the schoolhouse has got a fight on his hands, if that boy is anywhere near Freckles's size. Harry goes, or Hal goes, but Harold is a fighting word with Freckles. Except, of course, with grown people. I heard him say one day to Tom Mulligan, his parents thought Harold was a name, or he guessed they wouldn't have given it to him; but it wasn't a name, it was a handicap.

Freckles would always say, "Spot ain't for sale."

And even Heinie Hassenyager, the butcher, got stuck on me after I got to be a Public Character. Heinie would come two blocks up Main Street with lumps of Hamburg steak, which is

the kind someone has already chewed for you, and give them
to me. Steak, mind you, not old gristly scraps. And before I
became a Public Character Heinie even grudged me the bones
I would drag out of the box under his counter when he wasn't
looking.

My daily hope was that I could live up to it all. I had always
tried, before I happened to bite that lion, to be a friendly kind
of a dog toward boys and humans and dogs, all three. I'd
always been expected to do a certain amount of tail-wagging
and be friendly. But as soon as I got to be a Public Character,
I saw right away I wasn't expected to be *too* friendly any more.
So, every now and then, I'd growl a little, for no reason at all.
A dog that has bit a lion is naturally expected to have fierce
thoughts inside of him; I could see that. And you have got to
act the way humans expect you to act if you want to slide along
through the world without too much trouble.

So when Heinie would bring me the ready-chewed steak I'd
growl at him a little bit. And then I'd bolt and gobble the steak
like I didn't think so derned much of it, after all, and was doing
Heinie a big personal favor to eat it. And now and then I'd
pretend I wasn't going to eat a piece of it unless it was chewed
finer for me, and growl at him about that.

That way of acting made a big hit with Heinie, too. I could
see that he was honored and flattered because I didn't go any
further than just a growl. It gave him a chance to say he knew
how to manage animals. And the more I growled, the more
steak he brought. Everybody in town fed me. I pretty near ate
myself to death for a while there, besides all the meat I buried
back of Doc Watson's store to dig up later.

But my natural disposition is to be friendly. I would rather
be loved than feared, which is what Bill Petterson, the village
drunkard, used to say. When they put him into the calaboose
every Saturday afternoon he used to look out between the bars
on the back window and talk to the boys and dogs that had
gathered round and say that he thanked them one and all for
coming to an outcast's dungeon as a testimonial of affection,
and he would rather be loved than feared. And my natural feelings are the same. I had to growl and keep dignified and go on
being a Public Character, and often I would say to myself that
it was losing me all my real friends, too.

The worst of it was that people, after a week or so, began to expect me to pull something else remarkable. Freckles, he got up a circus, and charged pins and marbles, and cents, when he found anyone that had any, to get into it, and I was the principal part of that circus. I was in a cage, and the sign over me read:

SPOT, THE DOG THAT LICKED A LION
Ten Pins Admition

To feed the lion-eater, one cent or two white chiney marbles extry but bring your own meat.

Pat him once on the head twinty pins, kids under five not allowed to.

For shaking hands with Spot the lion-eater, girls not allowed, gents three white chinies, or one aggie marble.

Lead him two blocks down the street and back, one cent before starting, no marbles or pins taken for leading him.

For sicking him on the cats three cents or one red cornelian marble if you furnish the cat. Five cents to use Watson's cat. Watson's biggest Tom-cat six cents must be paid before sicking. Small kids and girls not allowed to sick him on cats.

Well, we didn't take in any cat-sicking money. And it was just as well. You never can tell what a cat will do. But Freckles put it in because it sounded sort of fierce. I didn't care for being caged and circused that way myself. And it was right at that circus that considerable trouble started.

Seeing me in a cage like that, all famoused-up, with more meat poked through the slats than two dogs could eat, made Mutt Mulligan and some of my old friends jealous.

Mutt, he nosed up by the cage and sniffed. I nosed a piece of meat out of the cage to him. Mutt grabbed it and gobbled it down, but he didn't thank me any. Mutt, he says:

"There's a new dog downtown that says he blew in from Chicago. He says he used to be a Blind Man's Dog on a street corner there. He's a pretty wise dog, and he's a right ornery-looking dog, too. He's peeled considerably where he has been bit in fights."

"Well, Mutt," says I, "as far as that goes I'm peeled considerable myself where I've been bit in fights."

"I know you are, Spot," says Mutt. "You don't need to tell me that. I've peeled you some myself from time to time."

"Yes," I says, "you did peel me some, Mutt. And I've peeled you some too. More'n that, I notice that right leg of yours is a little stiff yet where I got to it about three weeks ago."

"Well, then, Spot," says Mutt, "maybe you want to come down here and see what you can do to my other three legs. I never saw the day I wouldn't give you a free bite at one leg and still be able to lick you on the other three."

"You wouldn't talk that way if I was out of this cage," I says, getting riled.

"What did you ever let yourself be put into that fool cage for?" Mutt says. "You didn't have to. You got such a swell head on you the last week or so that you got to be licked. You can fool boys and humans all you want to about that accidental old lion, but us dogs got your number, all right. What that Blind Man's Dog from Chicago would do to you would be a plenty!"

"Well, then," I says, "I'll be out of this cage along about supper time. Suppose you bring that Blind Man's Dog around here. And if he ain't got a spiked collar on him, I'll fight him. I won't fight a spike-collared dog to please anybody."

And I wouldn't, neither, without I had one on myself. If you can't get a dog by the throat or the back of his neck, what's the use of fighting him? You might just as well try to eat a black-smith shop as fight one of those spike-collared dogs.

"Hey, there!" Freckles yelled at Tom Mulligan, who is Mutt Mulligan's boy. "You get your fool dog away from the lion-eater's cage!"

Tom, he histed Mutt away. But he says to Freckles, being jealous himself, "Don't be scared, Freck, I won't let my dog hurt yours any. Spot, he's safe. He's in a cage where Mutt can't get to him."

Freckles got riled. He says, "I ain't in any cage, Tom."

Tom, he didn't want to fight very bad. But all the other boys and dogs was looking on. And he'd sort of started it. He didn't figure that he could shut up that easy. And there was some girls there, too.

"If I was to make a pass at you," says Tom, "you'd wish you was in a cage."

Freckles, he didn't want to fight so bad, either. But he was running this circus, and he didn't feel he could afford to pass by what Tom said too easy. So he says:

"Maybe you think you're big enough to put me into a cage."

"If I was to make a pass at you," says Tom, "there wouldn't be enough left of you to put in a cage."

"Well, then," says Freckles, "why don't you make a pass at me?"

"Maybe you figure I don't dast to," says Tom.

"I didn't say you didn't dast to," says Freckles; "anyone that says I said you didn't dast to is a link, link, liar, and so's his Aunt Mariar."

Tom, he says, "I ain't got any Aunt Mariar. And you're another and dastn't back it."

Then some of the other kids put chips onto their shoulders. And each dared the other to knock his chip off. And the other kids pushed and jostled them into each other till both chips fell off, and they went at it then. Once they got started they got really mad and each did all he knew how.

And right in the midst of it Mutt ran in and bit Freckles on the calf of his leg. Any dog will fight for his boy when his boy is getting the worst of it. But when Mutt did that I give a bulge against the wooden slats on the cage and two of them came off, and I was on top of Mutt. The circus was in the barn, and the hens began to scream and the horses began to stomp, and all the boys yelled, "Sick 'im!" and "Go to it!" and danced around and hollered, and the little girls yelled, and all the other dogs began to bark, and it was a right lively and enjoyable time. But Mrs. Watson, Freckles's mother, and the hired girl ran out from the house and broke the fight up.

Grown women are like that. They don't want to fight themselves, and they don't seem to want anyone else to have any fun. You got to be a hypocrite around a grown woman to get along with her at all. And then she'll feed you and make a lot of fuss over you. But the minute you start anything with real enjoyment in it she's surprised to see you acting that way. Nobody was licked satisfactory in that fight, or licked anyone else satisfactory.

Well, that night after supper, along comes that Blind Man's Dog. Never did I see a Blind Man's Dog that was as tight-skinned. I ain't a dog that brags, myself, and I don't say I would have licked that heavy a dog right easy, even if he had been a loose-skinned dog. What I do say is that I had been used to fighting loose-skinned dogs that you can get some sort of a reasonable hold onto while you are working around for position. And running into a tight-skinned dog that way, all of a sudden and all unprepared for it, would make anybody nervous. How are you going to get a purchase on a tight-skinned dog when you've been fighting loose-skinned dogs for so long that your teeth and jaws just naturally set themselves for a loose-skinned dog without thinking of it?

Lots of dogs wouldn't have fought him at all when they realized how they had been fooled about him, and how tight-skinned he was. But I was a Public Character now, and I had to fight him. More than that, I ain't ready to say yet that that dog actually licked me. Freckles he hit him in the ribs with a lump of soft coal, and he got off me and run away before I got my second wind. There's no telling what I would have done to that Blind Man's Dog, tight-skinned as he was, if he hadn't run away before I got my second wind.

Well, there's some mighty peculiar dogs in this world, let alone boys and humans. The word got around town, in spite of his running away like that before I got my second wind, that that Blind Man's Dog, so called, had actually licked me! Many pretended to believe it. Every time Freckles and me went down the street someone would say:

"Well, the dog that licked the lion got licked himself, did he?"

And if it was a lady said it, Freckles would spit on the sidewalk through the place where his front teeth are out and pass on politely as if he hadn't heard, and say nothing. And if it was a man that said it Freckles would thumb his nose at him. And if it was a girl that said it he would rub a handful of sand into her hair. And if it was a boy anywhere near his size, there would be a fight. If it was too big a boy, Freckles would sling railroad iron at him.

For a week or so it looked like Freckles and I were fighting all the time. Three or four times a day, and every day. On the way to school, and all through recess-times, and after school, and every time we went onto the street. I got so chewed and he got so busted up that we didn't hardly enjoy life.

No matter how much you may like to fight, some of the time you would like to pick the fights yourself and not have other people picking them off of you. Kids begun to fight Freckles that wouldn't have dast to stand up to him a month before. I was still a Public Character, but I was getting to be the kind you josh about instead of the kind you are proud to feed. I didn't care so awful much for myself, but I hated it for Freckles. For when they got us pretty well hacked, all the boys began to call him Harold again.

And after they had called him Harold for a week he must have begun to think of himself as Harold. For one Saturday afternoon when there wasn't any school, instead of going swimming with the other kids or playing baseball, or anything, he went and played with girls.

He must have been pretty well down-hearted and felt himself pretty much of an outcast, or he wouldn't have done that. I am an honest dog, and the truth must be told, the disgrace alone with everything else, and the truth is that he played with girls of his own accord that day—not because he was sent to their house on an errand, not because it was a game got up with boys and girls together, not because it was cousins and he couldn't dodge them, but because he was an outcast. Any boy will play with girls when all the boys and girls are playing together, and some girls are nearly as good as boys; but no boy is going off alone to look up a bunch of girls and play with them without being coaxed unless he has had considerable of a downfall.

Right next to the side of our yard was the Wilkinses. They had a bigger house and a bigger yard than ours. Freckles was sitting on the top of the fence looking into their orchard when the three Wilkins girls came out to play. There was only two boys in the Wilkins family, and they was twins; but they were only year-old babies and didn't amount to anything. The two oldest Wilkins girls, the taffy-colored-haired one and the squint-eyed one, each had one of the twins, taking care of it. And the other Wilkins girl, the pretty one, she had one of those big dolls made as big as a baby. They were rolling those babies and the doll around the grass in a wheelbarrow, and the wheel came off, and that's how Freckles happened to go over.

"Up in the attic," says the taffy-colored-haired one, when he had fixed up the wheelbarrow, "there's a little old express wagon with one wheel off that would be better'n this wheelbarrow. Maybe you could fix that wheel on, too, Harold."

Freckles, he fell for it. After he got the wagon fixed, they got to playing charades and fool girl games like that. The hired girl was off for the afternoon, and pretty soon Mrs. Wilkins hollered up the stairs that she was going to be gone for an hour, and to take good care of the twins, and then we were alone in the place.

Well, it wasn't much fun for me. They played and they played, and I stuck to Freckles—though his name was called nothing but Harold all that afternoon, and for the first time I said to myself "Harold" seemed to fit. I stuck to him because a dog should stick to his boy, and a boy should stick to his dog, no matter what the disgrace. But after-while I got pretty tired and lay down on a rug, and a new kind of flea struck me. After I had chased him down and cracked him with my teeth I went to sleep.

I must have slept pretty sound and pretty long. All of a sudden I waked up with a start, and almost choking, for the place was smoky. I barked and no one answered.

I ran out to the landing, and the whole house was full of smoke. The house was on fire, and it looked like I was alone in it. I went down the back stairway, which didn't seem so full of smoke, but the door that led out onto the first-floor landing was locked, and I had to go back up again.

By the time I got back up, the front stairway was a great deal fuller of smoke, and I could see glints of flame winking through it way down below. But it was my only way out of that place. On the top step I stumbled over a gray wool bunch of something or other, and I picked it up in my mouth. Thinks I, "That is Freckles's gray sweater, that he is so stuck on. I might as well take it down to him."

It wasn't so hard for a lively dog to get out of a place like that, I thought. But I got kind of confused and excited, too. And it struck me all of a sudden, by the time I was down to the second floor, that that sweater weighed an awful lot.

I dropped it on the second floor, and ran into one of the front bedrooms and looked out.

By jings! The whole town was in the front yard and in the street.

And in the midst of the crowd was Mrs. Wilkins, carrying on like mad.

"My baby!" she yelled. "Save my baby. Let me loose! I'm going up after my baby!"

I stood up on my hind legs, with my head just out of that bedroom window, and the flame and smoke licking up all around me, and barked.

"My doggie! My doggie!" yells Freckles, who was in the crowd. "I must save my doggie!" And he made a run for the house, but someone grabbed him and slung him back.

And Mrs. Wilkins made a run, but they held her, too. The front of the house was one sheet of flame. Old Pop Wilkins, Mrs. Wilkins's husband, was jumping up and down in front of Mrs. Wilkins yelling, here was her baby. He had a real baby in one arm and that big doll in the other, and was so excited he thought he had both babies. Later I heard what had happened. The kids had thought that they were getting out with both twins but one of them had saved the doll and left a twin behind. The squint-eyed girl and the taffy-colored-haired girl and the pretty girl was howling as loud as their mother. And every now and then some man would make a rush for the front door, but the fire would drive him back. And everyone was yelling advice to everyone else, except one man who was calling on the whole town to get him an axe. The volunteer fire engine was there, but there wasn't any water to squirt through it, and it had been backed up too near the house and had caught fire and was burning up.

Well, I thinks that baby will likely turn up in the crowd somewhere, after all, and I'd better get out of there myself while the getting was good. I ran out of the bedroom, and run into that bunched-up gray bundle again.

I ain't saying that I knew it was the missing twin in a gray shawl when I picked it up the second time. And I ain't saying that I didn't know it. But the fact is that I did pick it up. I don't make any brag that I would have risked my life to save Freckles's sweater. It may be I was so rattled I just picked it up because I had had it in my mouth before and didn't quite know what I was doing.

But the *record* is something you can't go behind, and the record is that I got out the back way and into the back yard with that bundle swinging from my mouth, and walked round into the front yard and laid that bundle down—*and it was the twin!*

I don't make any claim that I *knew* it was the twin till I got into the front yard, mind you. But you can't prove I *didn't* know it was.

And nobody tried to prove it. The gray bundle let out a squall. "My baby!" yells Mrs. Wilkins. And she kissed me! I rubbed it off with my paw. And then the taffy-colored-haired one kissed me. And the first thing I knew the pretty one kissed me. But when I saw the squint-eyed one coming I got behind Freckles and barked.

"Three cheers for Spot!" yelled the whole town. And they give them.

And then I saw what the lay of the land was, so I wagged my tail and barked.

It called for that hero stuff, and I throwed my head up and looked noble—and pulled it.

An hour before, Freckles and me had been outcasts. And now we was Public Characters again. We walked down Main Street, and we owned it. And we hadn't any more than got to Doc Watson's drugstore than in rushed Heinie Hassenyager with a lump of Hamburg steak, and with tears in his eyes.

"It's got chicken livers mixed in it, too!" says Heinie.

I ate it. But while I ate it, I growled at him.

THE UNDEMANDING DOG

THE LOST DOG

BY *Mary E. Wilkins*

THE DOG WAS SPEEDING, nose to the ground; he had missed his master early in the morning; now it was late afternoon, but at last he thought he was on his track. He went like a wind, his ears pointed ahead, his slender legs seemingly flat against his body; he was eagerness expressed by a straight line of impetuous motion. He had had nothing to eat all day; he was spent with anxiety and fatigue and hunger; but now, now, he believed he was on his master's track, and all that was forgotten.

But all at once he stopped, his tail dropped between his legs, and he skulked away from the false track in an agony of mortification and despair. It had ended abruptly at a street corner, where the man had taken a carriage. He doubled and went back for his life to the last place where he had seen his master in the morning. It was a crowded corner, and the people were passing and repassing, weaving in and out, a great concourse of humanity following the wonderful maze of their own purposes.

The dog sniffed at the heels of one and another. He followed and retreated; he dodged and skulked. He was a thing of abject apology, and felt no resentment at a kick when he got in the way of that tide of human progress. The dog without his master was like modesty without raiment, like a body without a soul. Without his master he was not even a dog; he was a wandering intelligence only, and had fallen below his inheritance of dog-wit.

He yelped now and then, but this yelp would have been unintelligible to another of his species. He put his nose to the ground; the confusion of scents and his despair made him, as it were, deaf in his special acuteness. He blindly ran after this one and that one. Now and then he heard a voice which made his heart leap, and was after the owner at a bound, but it was never his master.

The city lights were blazing out and the raw night settling down; on the corner were two steady interweaving streams to the right and left of people going homeward, and all with the thought of shelter and food and fire and rest.

Finally the dog fastened his despairing eyes upon a man coming around the corner, and he followed him. He knew he was not his master, but there was that about him which awakened that wisdom of dependence which had come down to him through generations. He knew that here was a man who could love a dog.

So he followed him on and on, moving swiftly at heel, keeping well in shadow, his eyes fixed anxiously upon the man's back, ready to be off at the first symptom of his turning.

But the man did not see him until he had reached his home, which was a mile beyond the city limits, quite in the country.

He went up to a solitary house set in a deep yard behind some fir trees. There were no lights in the windows. The man drew a key from his pocket and unlocked the door. Then he saw the dog.

He looked hard at the dog, and the dog looked piteously at him. The dog wagged his tail in frantic circles of conciliation. The full moon was up, and there was a street-lamp, so the two could see each other quite distinctly. Both the dog and the man were thoroughbreds. The dog saw a man, young, in shabby clothes, which he wore like a gentleman, with a dark and clear-cut face. The man saw a dog in a splendid suit of tawny gold hair, with the completeness of his pure blood in every line and curve of his body. The man whistled; the dog pressed closer to him; his eyes upon his face were like a woman's. The man stopped and patted the dog on his tawny gold head, then entered the house and whistled again, and the dog followed him in.

That evening the dog lay on an old skin rug before the hearth-fire, but uneasily, for his new master was doing something which disturbed him. He was singing with a magnificent tenor voice, and the dog was vaguely injured in his sensibilities by music. At first he howled, but, when the man bade him be quiet, he protested no longer, except for an occasional uneasy roll of an eye or twitch of an ear at a new phrase.

The dog had had a good supper; he had eaten rather more than the man. There was plenty of wood on the hearth, though the reserve was not large. But the man who sang had the optimism of a brave soul which, when it is striving to its utmost, cannot face the image of defeat without a feeling of disgrace.

He was a great singer; he had been born to it, and he had worked for it. Some day the material fruits of it—the milk and honey of prosperity—would be his; in the meantime there was his voice and his piano; and while there was wood, let his hearth-fire blaze merrily; and while he had a crust, let him share it with a dog that was needy.

Now and then the man in the intervals of his singing patted the dog, and spoke to him caressingly; and the dog looked at him with a gratitude which reached immensity through its unspeakableness.

The dog wore no collar, and the man marveled at that.

It was midnight when there came a step at the door and a ring, and the dog was on his feet with a volley of barks. He was ready to charge a whole army for the sake of this man whom he had known only a few hours. But in this case he would have attacked, not an enemy who threatened his master's safety, but a friend who brought him wealth and fame.

When the man returned to the room with the out-of-doors cold clinging to him, his face was radiant, jubilant. The tenor who had been singing in the opera house had broken his engagement, and the manager had come for him.

He told the dog, for lack of another companion, and the dog reared himself on two legs, like a man, in his ecstasy of joyful comradeship, and placed his paws on the man's shoulders and licked his young face. Then the man sat down at his piano, and sang over and over his part in the opera, and the dog gave only one low howl under his breath, then lay down on the skin rug, with twitching ears and back.

That night the man's golden age began, and the dog shared it. His new master had his share of superstition, and regarded the old saying that a dog following one brought luck, and had, besides his love for the animal, a species of gratitude and sense of obligation.

In the days of luxurious living which followed, the dog was to the front with the man. He rode with him in his softly cushioned carriage to the opera house, and slept in his dressing-room while the music and the applause went on. Occasionally he would make a faint protesting howl when a loud strain reached his ears. The dog loved the man for love's sake alone; that which won the adulation of men was his trial. He loved him, not for his genius, but in spite of it.

The dog in this new life grew to his full possibility of beauty and strength. His coat shone like satin; he was a radiant outcome of appreciation and good food; but palmier days still were to come.

One day the tenor brought home a wife; then the dog for the first time knew what it was to be the pet of a woman. Then he wore a great bow of blue satin on his silver collar, and often his coat smelled of violets.

The new wife was adorable; the touch of her little soft hands on the dog's head was ecstasy; and *she* did not sing, but talked to him, and praised him with such sweet flattery that he used to roll his eyes at her like a lover, and thrust an appealing paw upon her silken lap.

Then he grew to an appreciation of himself; all his abjectness vanished. He became sure of himself and of love. He was a happy dog except for one thing. Always in his sleep he searched for his old lost master. He was never on the street but down went his nose to the ground for the scent of those old footsteps.

And one day, when he had been with his new friends two years, he found him. His mistress's carriage was waiting, and he beside it, one day in spring when they were selling daffodils and violets on the street, and doves were murmuring around the church towers and the sparrows clamorous, and everything which had life, in which hope was not quite dead, was flying, and darting, and blossoming, and creeping out into the sunlight.

Then the dog saw his old master coming down the street, scraping the pavement with his heavy feet—an old man, mean and meanly clad, with no grace of body or soul, unless it might have been the memory of, and regret for, the dog. Him he had loved after the best fashion which he knew. The splendid brute thing, with his unquestioning devotion, had kept alive in him his piteous remnant of respect for self, and had been to him more than any one of his own kind, who had put him to shame, and sunk him in the lowest depths of ignominy by forcing his realization of it.

The dog stood still, with ears erect and tail stiff, then was after his old master with a mighty bound. At first the man cursed and kicked at him, then looked again and swore 'twas his old dog, and stroked his head with that yellow clutch of avarice for his own possession and his own profit, rather than affection, which was the best his poor soul could compass.

But the dog followed him, faithful not only to his old master, but to a nobler thing, the faithfulness which was in himself— and maybe by so doing gained another level in the spiritual evolution of his race.

MACDUNALD

BY *John Held, Jr.*

M Y NAME IS MacDunald, and I'm as braw a Scot as ever chewed up a pair of slippers. I'm stubborn and I'm canny, I'm short-legged and close to the ground, what I lack in size I make up in courage. The Scotch are a fighting race and the Tartar of my clan has never dragged the dust, my breed has never known defeat and we die game, do we Scots. My hair is coarse and wiry and my tail is carried high. I want to tell you these facts so you won't think me a sissy even if I do live a soft life in a fashionable neighborhood.

I make my home with a nice pair of folks. I'm very fond of my folks, very fond. I could run away if I wanted to, but I have no desire to leave. My folks treat me well. Sometimes things don't go just as I plan, but a dog must expect to put up with some disagreeable things, so I suppose I'm as well off as most of the dogs that I know.

My man treats me like an equal, that's all I ask of him. My woman wants to baby me sometimes, but I overlook that, because she has no children of her own, and she has the need to mother something. But I understand, and I allow her to vent her maternal urge up to a certain point—when it gets too thick I can always go and hide under the bed. Sometimes it gets me nervous when women get too motherly with me. I'm pretty salty myself so I always stay outdoors when my woman has her girl friends in to play bridge, afternoons. Of course I'm fond of bits of cinnamon toast and a lump of sugar now and then, but these women always want to talk baby talk and stuff me with food, and a dog needs to watch or he'll get fat and out of condition.

I don't want to get soft and not be able to keep myself in fighting trim, because there are a lot of snooty dogs out in our subdivision that might need to be whipped some day, so you see I have to stay in training. So far, I haven't had to punish one of them, but you never know when one of those stupid Police dogs will need to be put in his place. Just let one of them come around and try to smell one of my bushes or shrubs, then they will hear the bagpipes.

You can stop listening now if I am boring you, because I know what it is to be bored and have to listen to something that doesn't interest me, like when my woman used to read to me. But I mustn't criticize my woman. She is a good sort. We spend a great deal of time together, and get on rather well, but I could do without having those stories read to me. I always made out as if I was interested when she used to read those silly stories to me about Collies when we were all alone evenings, when my man would telephone and say he was detained at the office or was at the Club or was entertaining customers, or whatever he really was doing. Of course, in the first place I have a contempt for what call themselves Scotch Collies, a silken-coated, narrow-minded breed. Scotch, indeed, and always doing something human in the stories—disgusting, I say. Makes me feel like I did when I ate the dozen cream-puffs. Stories about Collies that have been bred for bench shows, not the good old Shepherd dog of Scotland. Ah, there was a dog that should have been a Terrier. A dog that knew his work and did it. How could a man manage sheep if he didn't have a dog that had brains? My woman takes me out a great deal. I like it when we motor out to the Country Club. Of course I'd like it better if she would allow me to chase the golf balls. I remember one afternoon when she didn't watch me I went out and had sport; altogether I got seven golf balls and buried them and then sat back in the grass and listened to the players swear and rave because they couldn't find the balls. That was a good afternoon.

I like it when we go over to the Hunt Club and I can go and sniff around the stables. There are some lovely places to roll. The only drawback to that is, my woman always insists on giving me a bath when we get home and I hate the soap she uses. It takes days to get rid of that odor and get to smelling like a dog again. Imagine trying to threaten an Airedale or a Schnauzer if you smell of jasmine. It's things like that, that make life difficult for a dog. But if I intend to keep my folks

I'll have to concede some of my dislikes and blame it on the civilization that we live in.

There is another place where I always have a good time. That's out in the country on my woman's father's farm. He likes to call it a farm, but my woman always calls it an expense, and says it's a good thing that her father is wealthy, otherwise he couldn't afford to be a farmer. But it's nice out there to chase rats in the granary and bark at and worry the calves. I enjoy sitting on the sunny side of the silo and gossiping with my old friend the Pointer. He likes to tell me the good times he and the old gentleman used to have when they went shooting. He loves to boast about all the good points he used to make and how he used to be able to hold quail in any cover. He's too old to go out hunting any more. His hind quarters are all tightened up with rheumatism. He must have had a full life and now he likes to sit and talk about it.

It must be satisfying to know you have always done your work well, like the old Pointer does. I'm not much of a sporting dog myself, although I would like to get a chance to dig out a rabbit, but I'm better at amusing my folks. That's the best thing I do and I think a dog always should do the thing he does best.

I've got one or two pretty good tricks and they always seem to work. My best trick is to go out every morning and get the mail from the postman. He comes up to our path and blows his whistle for me and I run out and bring in the letters. My other trick is to just sit down and move my head from side to side— that always gets a big laugh. I tried another trick once but it didn't seem to get over very well and oh, what a spanking I got. I figured out that my man wasn't so pleased with the part of the newspaper that printed long lists of stock reports—it was something about the markets, as I understand it. One morning I thought it would be a good trick to fix that page, so I went out and got the paper first and chewed that page up to bits, and as I said, I got spanked for that trick. I never tried it again. That's the only time I ever was punished.

My woman has never so much as raised a hand to me. Sometimes she scolds, but I pay no attention to that, and my man only did it once, but he didn't feel so good that morning. There had been a party the night before, and my folks move in a hard-drinking set. In fact all the Country Club folks are heavy drinkers. I like the smell of Scotch whiskey. I suppose I inherit that. I love to get into my man's room and sleep on his tweeds, they smell of tobacco and liquor like a man's clothes should smell. He's a dog's man and no mistake.

Speaking of parties, there have been some rather lively ones at our house. I always get put upstairs when I try to sing in with the guests, but I get to see a lot because they never start to sing until the party is well under way. There seems to be more parties than there used to be, nearly every night now. If the crowd don't come to our house my folks go out to other places.

They leave me to watch the house until they get back. I like the responsibility, and I'd like to see any stranger get into the house when I am here alone—I'd make short work of them. Sometimes I begin to wonder if my folks are ever going to get home, sometimes it's daylight before they get in, and I'm pretty sleepy after keeping on guard all night.

I wish my woman didn't have to drive the car when she brings my man home. She isn't a very good driver, she's not a bad driver, mind you, but she isn't as expert as my man. And after those parties I miss the morning walk we used to take, but my man is not equal to a walk the morning after. He just gets up and doesn't say much, then he goes and catches a train and my woman and I are alone all day, except when all the other dogs' women come in for bridge and cocktails, or else the Artist fellow comes in for tea.

I don't like him very well, he tries to act like my man used to when he is with my woman, but my man doesn't act that way any more and I suppose my woman wants some man to act that way. Women are like that, and men are like that, always in love. I'm different, I only get in love twice a year, I think that's plenty. My man was very much in love with my woman a while back but he doesn't talk about it any more. I don't see why, as my woman is very pretty, as women go. She has nice dark eyes and her hands are soft. I think she is still very much in love with my man, because she is always telling the Artist that he mustn't talk that way. Then she makes him go away, and after he's gone she cries and that's the time I always try to amuse her with my head-tilting trick.

Once after the Artist had gone I went and got one of my man's old hats and fetched it to her, but that made her cry and she went into her room and shut the door, so I went downstairs and waited for my man to come home but he didn't come home that night and didn't telephone either.

Next day I heard that he had to go to Atlantic City with a customer and he was gone ten days. While he was away my woman took me to the Artist's Studio where he was painting a picture of her. I didn't think it was a very good picture of her, but then I don't know anything about art. I didn't think he was very interested in this painting, as all he wanted to do was sit and look into my woman's dark eyes. He just stared at her because she wouldn't let him talk about love. Then he made out as if he was hurt and got up and painted some more. I didn't like it at the Artist's Studio. It smelled of paint and turpentine and some sickening thing he burned to make smoke. I think they call it incense. It was terrible and made me cough. I can't quite figure my woman out when she goes to the Artist's place. She is so careful when she dresses to go there. She puts on her softest things and fixes herself up beautiful. Sometimes I think she likes to have the Artist tell her how lovely she is. I don't think that is right, it's too much like the people who come to our house to the parties. The men are always telling other men's wives how much they like them. I know because I hear and see things. Nobody pays any attention to me. Many times I'm upstairs napping when the noise gets on my nerves and the men and women slip into the dark room and make love. They don't seem to mind if I see them. I hate to see my woman get that way with this Artist. But I suppose my woman is unhappy if she hasn't got someone to love her. That's why she comes to the studio and has the Artist over for tea when my man doesn't come home.

I wish my folks would spend the evenings like they did when we first came to live at our house. Those were pleasant times. We would have a good fire and they would sit and talk about love and then we would go to the kitchen and have a snack before we retired. I enjoyed those snacks. You know a dog gets hungry in the evening. But now whenever my man comes home they either have a drinking party at the house with people in, or else they go out and come in late. They never seem to talk much to each other.

My woman stopped going to the Artist's Studio after what I did. It's odd too, she didn't even scold me. I took a bite at that Artist. I can still taste the turpentine. That afternoon we went over there, my woman had a strange look in her eyes. The Artist didn't paint much. He started right in to talk about love and how he couldn't stand it any longer, and my woman didn't stop him. She just let him rave. Then the Artist went over to my woman and took her in his arms and kissed her. She didn't seem to mind it so I growled and bit him. Then he swore at me and my woman got into her coat and we went right home. She never went back there for her picture. It wasn't a good picture anyway.

The Artist telephoned to her but she always told the maid to say she wasn't in. She told me afterwards, "Mac, you saved me from doing something terrible." As I said before, I'm a canny Scot. She never said anything about the Artist business to my man.

Then my man started to come home evenings again, but those evenings were pretty dull. He would eat his dinner and then he would sit and read the stock reports for a while, then he would say: "I have a hard day tomorrow, I think I'll turn in." And up he would get and go to bed and sleep in his own room. I would see my woman's lights burning late as I went about the house checking everything up before I went down to sleep myself.

It's funny how things happen, isn't it? The other morning I saw a chance to do one of my tricks. I thought perhaps it would cheer my woman up a bit. It was after we had eaten breakfast and my man had rushed to his train. I went out to listen for the postman's whistle but I guess I must have missed hearing it, because there on the path was a letter. I went out and got it and fetched it in and gave it to my woman. It was a queer sort of letter; it smelled of a kind of perfume that one of my woman's girl friends always uses, and it wasn't sealed up like the other letters. My woman took the paper out of the envelope and read it. Then she just stood and looked strange. An odd hard look came into her eyes, then she went and called the Artist on the telephone. After that she went up to her room and packed a bag. Then she came down and wrote a note and took it in my man's room and stuck it in the edge of his shaving mirror. She put the bag in the car and drove away, without saying good-bye to me.

I stayed close to the house all that day. It's a good thing I did because a new dog came down our street and I had to inform him that he must keep off my place.

When my man came home I tried to get him to go up and get the note but he just went into all the rooms looking for my woman. The maid was off that day. Finally he found the note in his shaving mirror and after he had read it he just sat down and stared ahead of him for a while, then he said to me: "Mac, old boy, you should always remember to tear up certain kinds of correspondence." Then he took a bath and changed his clothes and packed a bag. He put me on a leash and we walked down to a boarding kennel and asked the kennel man if he could look out for me for a few days. The kennel man said "yes." So here I am.

I wish I knew what it was all about. I don't like it here. Perhaps it is all for the best, because I might need to bite the Artist again.

THE MERITORIOUS DOG

EPITAPH TO A DOG

BY *Lord Byron*

Near this spot
Are deposited the Remains
Of one
Who Possessed Beauty
Without Vanity,
Strength without Insolence,
Courage without Ferocity,
And all the Virtues of Man
Without his Vices.

This Praise, which would be unmeaning flattery
If inscribed over Human Ashes,
Is but a just tribute to the Memory of
"Boatswain," a Dog
Who was born at Newfoundland,
May, 1803,
And died at Newstead Abbey
Nov. 18, 1808.

When some proud son of man returns to earth,
Unknown to glory, but upheld by birth,
The sculptor's art exhausts the pomp of woe,
And storied urns record who rests below.
When all is done, upon the tomb is seen,
Not what he was, but what he should have been.
But the poor dog, in life the firmest friend,
The first to welcome, foremost to defend,
Whose honest heart is still his master's own,
Who labors, fights, lives, breathes for him alone,
Unhonored falls, unnoticed all his worth,
Denied in heaven the soul he held on earth—
While man, vain insect! hopes to be forgiven,
And claims himself a sole exclusive heaven.

Oh man! thou feeble tenant of an hour,
Debased by slavery, or corrupt by power—
Who knows thee well must quit thee with disgust,
Degraded mass of animated dust!
Thy love is lust, thy friendship all a cheat,
Thy smiles hypocrisy, thy words deceit!
By nature vile, ennobled but by name,
Each kindred brute might bid thee blush for shame.
Ye, who perchance behold this simple urn,
Pass on—it honors none you wish to mourn.
To mark a friend's remains these stones arise;
I never knew but one—and here he lies.

DOG'S HAPPINESS

BY *Alexander Kuprin*

IT WAS BETWEEN six and seven o'clock on a fine September morning when the eighteen-months-old pointer, Jack, a brown, long-eared, frisky animal, started out with the cook, Annushka, to market. He knew the way perfectly well, and so ran confidently on in front of her, sniffing at the curbstones as he went and stopping at the crossings to see if Annushka were following. Finding affirmation in her face, and the direction in which she was going, he would turn again with a decisive movement and rush on in a lively gallop.

On one occasion, however, when he turned round near a familiar sausage-shop, Jack could not see Annushka. He dashed back so hastily that his left ear was turned inside out as he went. But Annushka was not to be seen at the crossroads. So Jack resolved to find his way by scent. He stopped, cautiously raised his wet sensitive nose, and tried in all directions to recognize the familiar scent of Annushka's dress, the smell of the dirty kitchen table and mottled soap. But just at that moment a lady came hurriedly past him, and brushing up against his side with her rustling skirt she left behind a strong wave of disgusting Oriental perfume. Jack moved his head from side to side in vexation. The trail of Annushka was entirely lost.

But he was not upset by this. He knew the town well and could always find his way home easily—all he had to do was to go to the sausage-shop, then to the greengrocer's, then turn to the left and go past a gray house from the basement of which there was always wafted a smell of burning fat, and he would be in his own street. Jack did not hurry. The morning was fresh and clear, and in the pure, softly transparent and rather moist air, all the various odors of the town had an unusual refinement and distinctness. Running past the post office, with his tail stuck out as stiff as a rod and his nostrils all trembling with excitement, Jack could have sworn that only a moment before a large, mouse-colored, oldish dog had stopped there, a dog who was usually fed on oatmeal porridge.

And after running along about two hundred paces, he actually saw this dog, a cowardly, sober-looking brute. His ears had been cropped, and a broad, worn strap was dangling from his neck.

The dog noticed Jack, and stopped, half turning back on his steps. Jack curled his tail in the air provokingly and began to walk slowly round the other, with an air of looking somewhere to one side. The mouse-colored dog also raised his tail and showed a broad row of white teeth. Then they both growled, turning their heads away from one another as they did so, and trying, as it were, to swallow something which stuck in their throats.

"If he says anything insulting to my honor, or the honor of any well-bred pointer, I shall fasten my teeth in his side, near his left hind leg," thought Jack to himself. "Of course, he is stronger than I am, but he is stupid and clumsy. Look how he stands there, like a dummy, and has no idea that all his left flank is open to attack."

And suddenly . . . something inexplicable and almost super-natural happened. The other dog unexpectedly threw himself on his back and was dragged by some unseen force from the path-way into the road. Directly afterwards this same unseen power grasped Jack by the throat . . . and he stood firm on his forelegs and shook his head furiously. But the invisible "something" was pulled so tight round his neck that the brown pointer became unconscious.

He came to his senses again in a stuffy iron cage, which was jolting and shaking as it was drawn along the cobbled roadway, on a badly jointed vehicle trembling in all its parts. From its acrid doggy odor Jack guessed at once that this cart must have been used for years to convey dogs of all breeds and all ages. On the box in front sat two men, whose outward appearance was not at all calculated to inspire confidence.

There was already a sufficiently large company in the cart. First of all, Jack noticed the mouse-colored dog whom he had just met and quarreled with in the street. He was standing with his head stuck out between two of the iron bars, and he whined pitifully as his body was jolted backwards and forwards by the movement of the cart. In the middle of the cage lay an old white poodle, his wise-looking head lying between his gouty paws. His coat was cut to make him look like a lion, with tufts left on his knees and at the end of his tail. The poodle had apparently resigned himself to his situation with a stoic philosophy, and if he had not sighed occasionally and wrinkled his brows, it might have been thought that he slept. By his side, trembling from agitation and the cold of the early morning, sat a fine well-kept greyhound, with long thin legs and sharp-pointed head. She yawned nervously from time to time, rolling up her rosy little tongue into a tube, accompanying the yawn with a long-drawn-out, high-pitched whine. . . . Near the back of the cage, pressed close up to the bars was a black dachshund, with smooth skin dappled with yellow on the breast and above the eyes. She could not get over her astonishment at her position, and she looked a strangely comical figure with her flopping paws and crocodile body, and the serious expression of her head with its ears reaching almost to the ground.

Besides this more or less distinguished society, there were in the cage two unmistakable yard dogs. One of them was that sort of dog which is generally called Bouton, and is always noted for its meanness of disposition. She was a shaggy, reddish-colored animal with a shaggy tail, curled up like the figure 9. She had been the first of the dogs to be captured, and she had apparently become so accustomed to her position that she had for some time past made many efforts to begin an interesting conversation with someone. The last dog of all was out of sight, he had been driven into the darkest corner, and lay there curled up in a heap. He had only moved once all the time, and that had been to growl at Jack when he had found himself near him. Everyone in the company felt a strong antipathy toward him. In the first place, he was smeared all over with a violet color, the work of certain journeyman whitewashers; secondly, his hair was rough and bristly and uncombed; thirdly, he was evidently mangy, hungry, strong and daring—this had been quite evident in the resolute push of his lean body with which he had greeted the arrival of the unconscious Jack.

There was silence for a quarter of an hour. At last Jack, whose healthy sense of humor never forsook him under any circumstances, remarked in a jaunty tone:

"The adventure begins to be interesting. I am curious to know where these gentlemen will make their first stopping place."

The old poodle did not like the frivolous tone of the brown pointer. He turned his head slowly in Jack's direction, and said sharply, with a cold sarcasm:

"I can satisfy your curiosity, young man. These gentlemen will make their first stopping place at the slaughterhouse."

"Where? Pardon me, please, I didn't catch the word," muttered Jack, sitting down involuntarily, for his legs had suddenly begun to tremble. "You were pleased to say—at the s-s-s . . ."

"Yes, at the slaughterhouse," repeated the poodle coldly, turning his head away.

"Pardon me, but I don't quite understand. . . . Slaughterhouse? . . . What kind of an institution is that? Won't you be so good as to explain?"

The poodle was silent. But as the greyhound and the terrier both joined their petition to Jack's, the old poodle, who did not

wish to appear impolite in the presence of ladies, felt obliged
to enter into certain details.

"Well, you see, *mesdames*, it is a sort of large courtyard
surrounded by a high fence with sharp points, where they shut
in all dogs found wandering in the streets. I've had the un-
happiness to be taken there three times already."

"I've never seen you!" was heard in a hoarse voice from the
dark corner. "And this is the seventh time I've been there."

There was no doubt that the voice from the dark corner belonged to the violet-colored dog. The company was shocked at
the interruption of their conversation by this rude person, and
so pretended not to hear the remark. But Bouton, with the cring-
ing eagerness of an upstart in society, cried out: "Please don't
interfere in other people's conversation unless you're asked,"
and then turned at once to the important-looking mouse-colored
dog for approbation.

"I've been there three times," the poodle went on, "but my
master has always come and fetched me away again. I play in
a circus, and you understand that I am of some value. Well, in
this unpleasant place they have a collection of two or three hundred dogs . . ."

"But, tell me . . . is there good society there?" asked the greyhound affectedly.

"Sometimes. They feed us very badly and give us little to eat.
Occasionally one of the dogs disappears, and then they give us
a dinner of . . ."

In order to heighten the effect of his words, the poodle made
a slight pause, looked round on his audience, and then added
with studied indifference:

"—of dog's flesh."

At these words the company was filled with terror and indignation.

"Devil take it . . . what lowdown scoundrelism!" exclaimed
Jack.

"I shall faint . . . I feel so ill," murmured the greyhound.

"That's dreadful . . . dreadful . . ." moaned the dachshund.

"I've always said that men were scoundrels," snarled the
mouse-colored dog.

"What a strange death," sighed Bouton.

But from the dark corner was heard once more the voice of

the violet-colored dog. With gloomy and cynical sarcasm he said:

"The soup's not so bad, though—it's not at all bad, though, of course, some ladies who are accustomed to eat chicken cutlets would find dog's flesh a little too tough."

The poodle paid no attention to this rude remark, but went on:

"And afterwards I gathered from the manager's talk that our late companion's skin had gone to make ladies' gloves. But . . . prepare your nerves, *mesdames* . . . but, this is nothing. . . . In order to make the skin softer and more smooth, it must be taken from the living animal."

Cries of despair broke in upon the poodle's speech.

"How inhuman!"

"What mean conduct!"

"No, that can't be true!"

"O Lord!"

"Murderers!"

"No, worse than murderers!"

After this outburst there was a strained and melancholy silence. Each of them had a mental picture, a fearful foreboding of what it might be to be skinned alive.

"Ladies and gentlemen, is there no way of getting all honorable dogs free, once and for all, from their shameful slavery to mankind?" cried Jack passionately.

"Be so good as to find a way," said the old poodle ironically.

The dogs all began to try and think of a way.

"Bite them all, and have an end of it!" said the big dog in his angry bass.

"Yes, that's the way; we need a radical remedy," seconded the servile Bouton. "In the end they'll be afraid of us."

"Yes, bite them all—that's a splendid idea," said the old poodle. "But what's your opinion, dear sirs, about their long whips? No doubt you're acquainted with them!"

"H'm." The dog coughed and cleared his throat.

"H'm," echoed Bouton.

"No, take my word for it, gentlemen, we cannot struggle against men. I've lived in this world for some time, and I've not had a bad life. . . . Take for example such simple things as kennels, whips, chains, muzzles—things, I imagine, not unknown to any one of us. Let us suppose that we dogs succeed in thinking out a plan which will free us from these things. Will not man then arm himself with more perfect instruments? There is no doubt that he will. Haven't you seen what instruments of torture they make for one another? No we must submit to them, gentlemen, that's all about it. It's a law of Nature."

"Well, he's shown us his philosophy," whispered the dachshund in Jack's ear. "I've no patience with these old folks and their teaching."

"You're quite right, mademoiselle," said Jack, gallantly wagging his tail.

The mouse-colored dog was looking very melancholy and snapping at the flies. He drawled out in a whining tone:

"Eh, it's a dog's life!"

"And where is the justice of it all?"—the greyhound, who had been silent up to this point, began to agitate herself—"You, Mr. Poodle, pardon me, I haven't the honor of knowing your name."

"Arto, professor of equilibristics, at your service." The poodle bowed.

"Well, tell me, Mr. Professor, you have apparently had such great experience, let alone your learning—tell me, where is the higher justice of it all? Are human beings so much more worthy and better than we are, that they are allowed to take advantage of so many cruel privileges with impunity?"

"They are not any better or any more worthy than we are, dear young lady, but they are stronger and wiser," answered Arto, with some heat. "Oh, I know the morals of these two-legged animals very well. . . . In the first place, they are greedy—greedier than any dog on earth. They have so much bread and meat and water that all these monsters could be satisfied and well-fed all their lives. But instead of sharing it out, a tenth of them get all the provisions for life into their hands, and not being able to devour it all themselves, they force the remaining nine-tenths to go hungry. Now, tell me, is it possible that a well-fed dog would not share a gnawed bone with his neighbor?"

"He'd share it, of course he would!" agreed all the listeners.

"H'm," coughed the dog doubtfully.

"And besides that, people are wicked. Who could ever say that one dog would kill another—on account of love or envy or malice? We bite one another sometimes, that's true. But we don't take each other's lives."

"No, indeed we don't," they all affirmed.

"And more than this," went on the white poodle. "Could one dog make up his mind not to allow another dog to breathe the fresh air, or to be free to express his thoughts as to the arrangements for the happiness of dogs? But men do this."

"Devil take them!" put in the mouse-colored dog energetically.

"And, in conclusion, I say that men are hypocrites; they envy one another, they lie, they are inhospitable, cruel. . . . And yet they rule over us and will continue to do so . . . because it's arranged like that. It is impossible for us to free ourselves from their authority. All the life of dogs, and all their happiness, is in the hands of men. In our present position each one of us who has a good master ought to thank Fate. Only a master can free us from the pleasure of eating a comrade's flesh, and of imagining that comrade's feelings when he was being skinned alive."

The professor's speech reduced the whole company to a state of melancholy. No other dog could utter a word. They all shivered helplessly, and shook with the joltings of the cart. The big dog whined piteously. Bouton, who was standing next to him, pressed her own body softly up against him.

But soon they felt that the wheels of the cart were passing over sand. In five minutes more they were driven through wide open gates, and they found themselves in the middle of an immense courtyard surrounded by a close paling. Sharp nails were sticking out at the top of the paling. Two hundred dogs, lean and dirty, with drooping tails and a look of melancholy on their faces, wandered about the yard.

The doors of the cage were flung open. All the seven newcomers came forth and instinctively stood together in one group.

"Here, you professor, how do you feel now?" The poodle heard a bark behind him.

He turned round and saw the violet-colored dog smiling insolently at him.

"Oh, leave me alone," growled the old poodle. "It's no business of yours."

"I only made a remark," said the other. "You spoke such

words of wisdom in the cart, but you made one mistake. Yes, you did."

"Get away, devil take you! What mistake?"

"About a dog's happiness. If you like, I'll show you in whose hands a dog's happiness lies."

And suddenly pressing back his ears and extending his tail, the violet dog set out on such a mad career that the old professor of equilibristics could only stand and watch him with open mouth.

"Catch him! Stop him!" shouted the keepers, flinging themselves in pursuit of the escaping dog.

But the violet dog had already gained the paling. With one bound he sprang up from the ground and found himself at the top, hanging on by his forepaws. And in two more convulsive springs he had leaped over the paling, leaving on the nails a good half of his side.

The old white poodle gazed after him for a long time. He understood the mistake he had made.

THE INTERFERING DOG

THE MASTIFF

BY *John Gay*

> Those, who in quarrels interpose,
> Must often wipe a bloody nose.

> A mastiff, of true *English* blood,
> Lov'd fighting better than his food,
> When dogs were snarling for a bone,
> He long'd to make the war his own,
> And often found (when two contend)
> To interpose obtain'd his end;
> He glory'd in his limping pace,
> The scars of honour seam'd his face;

In ev'ry limb a gash appears,
And frequent fights retrench'd his ears.
　　As, on a time, heard from far
Two dogs engag'd in noisy war,
Away he scours and lays about him,
Resolv'd no fray should be without him.
　　Forth from his yard a tanner flies,
And to the bold intruder cries,
A cudgel shall correct your manners.
Whence sprung this cursed hate to tanners?
While on my dog you vent your spite,
Sirrah! 'tis me you dare not bite.
　　To see the battle thus perplext,
With equal rage a butcher vext,
Hoarse-screaming from the circled crowd,
To the curst Mastiff cries aloud.
　　Both *Hockley-hole* and *Mary-bone*
The combats of my dog have known;
He ne'er, like bullies coward-hearted,
Attacks in public, to be parted;
Think not, rash fool, to share his fame,
Be his the honour or the shame.
　　Thus said, they swore and rav'd like thunder,
They dragg'd their fasten'd dogs asunder,
While clubs and kicks from ev'ry side
Rebounded from the Mastiff's hide.
　　All reeking now with sweat and blood
A-while the parted warriors stood,
Then pour'd upon the meddling foe;
Who, worried, howl'd and sprawl'd below:
He rose; and limping from the fray,
By both sides mangled, sneak'd away.

HOUND OF HEAVEN

BY *Sarah Addington*

THE LITTLE DOG WAS RIDING on a cloud and he was extremely annoyed because there was no windshield on the thing to keep the wind out of his whiskers. His ears and nose were full of wind, his eyes burned with it; but especially were his whiskers involved. Wildly they blew every which way, streaming now east, flowing now west. And this indignity the little dog felt keenly. For his whiskers were heroic, proud whiskers. Red, profuse, goatlike, they sprang from his underjaw a very triumph of a beard, proclaiming at once his conquering sex and his redoubtable terrier breed. His glory, his munificence, his plume, these whiskers; they had won him many a tribute on Earth.

The cloud swooped dizzily against the cutting blade of the wind. That's all there was up here, just wind, and emptiness, and more wind, and more emptiness, and this bloomin' slippery cloud. . . . "What a fine cloud *you* turned out to be," he said. For he was a wag at heart—perhaps it was the Irish in him— and he often said witty things like that.

He tried to think as the cloud went skewing along. But thinking is too difficult when your eyes are blind with wind and your nose stings with it and your beard is being whisked around at rakish, freakish angles. Eyes closed, beard awry, city-blunted claws sliding and clutching, he was borne helplessly along. And he was distinctly peevish. . . . "It's a wonder they wouldn't have traffic cops," he growled. "Supposin' we bumped into another one of these hell-bent cloud things!" He tried to dig his haunches more securely into the sliding, billowing surface of the cloud. But every time he got a good hold, the thing sagged under him like a wet rag. . . . "I'll be doin' a Prince of Wales in a minute."

He wondered dimly whether, if he looked down, he could see

New York and his house and perhaps the Boss through his skylight window. But he dared not risk looking down again. It made such disagreeable things happen to the stomach. Empty, that stomach, too. When had he eaten last? He seemed to remember a ghostly rasher of bacon some æons before—before—

Oh, yes, he remembered now. He had been sick—not the kind of sick that comes from eating too much garbage, but another kind. Wait a minute now. Wait—there, he had it. Something had hit him and it had made him sick. What was it that had hit him? He strained hard to recollect, but the wind was too much for him; he couldn't fish it out of his dizzy, whirling brain. He could only remember that something had hit him and done him in, and that before that, he had lived a fine, free, careless life with the Boss.

The Boss. He must get back to the Boss. They had an understanding about that. They could both wander where they liked and stay as long as they pleased and no questions asked, but always in the end they had to go back home to each other. That was their compact, man to man.

The little dog opened one cautious eye, and at what he saw then his jaw dropped. . . . "My God, I'm headed straight for the sunset!" For ahead of him was a burning glare such as he had never seen before in all his eventful life.

Yet, as he got closer, this blazing, golden glare in the sky hardly appeared to be the sun, after all. For against the glare, he could see the shapes of buildings, glassy and gleaming; fragile walls that shimmered with color; fantastic trees rearing golden arms.

They were getting pretty close now, he and the cloud. What a glare it was! Broadway he knew—he and the Boss had explored it many times together; but this razzle-dazzle made Broadway look like Main Street.

Swish-sh, swish-sh, the cloud was sailing faster, through the tearing wind. Zoom, zoom, now they were right abreast of the fiery light. Plunk, the cloud ducked, like a beast of burden, and the dog scooted off. He found himself scrambling at a pair of golden shoes. He looked up, blinking. The shoes belonged to a man, a chap with a fleecy beard. He wagged his tail. The chap with the beard smiled, threw open a pair of gates—gleaming gates, like giant oyster shells—motioned the little dog in.

The dog trotted in through the gates. What the hell—?

Inside he stopped. His face, that shrewd, bland, poker face of an Irish terrier, was a study in mystification. "Gosh a'mighty," he whispered.

Columns, arches, cupolas, of marble and gold and crystal. Shimmering trees, heavy with jeweled fruit, cutting frail arabesques against a turquoise sky. Over everything that wash of dazzling light almost too strong to bear. He caught, now through an arch, now through a wide-flung window, the vagrant scurry of flying white robes. He heard somewhere in the distance the music of harp strings—tinkly stuff, he thought, not nearly so good as a hurdy-gurdy.

"Maybe it's Coney Island," he thought. He had heard tales of Coney Island. Phœbe the cat had been there. Only Phœbe was such a liar.

The glass felt funny to his feet. There was no garbage anywhere, nor any good smell of people's dinners. And where, he wondered profoundly, were all the automobiles? "Of all the dumb places," he muttered.

Then suddenly his body stiffened, his nose went up, his tail flew out. One instant he stood rigid, glaring. Then his red-brown body was hurtling through the air, had landed squarely on another body, black, silky, writhing, spitting. . . .

It was a mighty, glorious, soul-thrilling fight. Never had the little dog met a more valiant feline. Never had he felt such sharp, fierce claws. Never had he sunk his own teeth so deeply into fur and flesh. Never had fur and flesh tasted so sweet. Clawing, biting, ripping, slashing, their hot breath fusing, their blood surging in one delicious, torrential stream, the dog and the cat fought on. Hours they fought, or hours it seemed, until at last their stout hearts panted, their muscles languished, cried out for respite.

"Sir," said the cat then (he spoke thickly, since the dog had him by the throat), "sir, beasts—as—well as men—are wise—" He gargled, choked, went on, "are wise—when—they recog—cognize—ug—ug—satiety."

"What say?" said the dog, holding on just to make sure.

"Sir, I am—" The cat strangled here and the dog relaxed his grip by a fraction. "Er—thank you. Sir, shall we not—glug— I thank you, sir, again—shall we not abate our hostilities *in tempore*—glug—?"

"Oh, all right," said the dog loftily, "if that's the way you feel about it." His gesture, as he flung off the cat, was magnificently haughty.

The cat, on all fours once again, shook himself, gave a pass at his paws with a moist, red tongue, and smiled. "An excellent diversion, sir," he said.

"A hell of a good fight," conceded the dog. "But say," looking about him, "what's all the shootin' fer? What is this dump, anyway?"

"Child," said the cat softly, "is it possible you are ignorant of your whereabouts?"

"Ignorant is the word," snapped the dog. "Why shouldn't I be? This is a fine racket. First I ride on a cloud like a bloomin' angel, now I crash into a glass factory—"

The cat's whiskers rose in displeasure.

"Your language, sir, is a strange one and unseemly. But you are an American. That, of course, accounts for anything."

"Careful there!" said the dog, flaring up.

"Sir!" thundered the cat. "No man tells Hodge to be careful of his speech." He gathered himself up majestically, spoke again with crushing thunder. "Sir, you will not dispute me. I say again what I have often said before: For anything I see, foreigners are fools. And Americans and Scotsmen head the list."

The dog cowered. Never before in all his history had this Irishman cowered in front of man or beast. But he cowered now. He wondered at this and was ashamed of himself. Yet he could not seem to help it. This damn cat had him buffaloed.

"Sir," said the cat then, more graciously, "let us both forget our hasty words. I am a choleric old cat. I speak strongly, but I intend no ill."

"Right," said the dog. He was looking about him again. "Gold trees," he breathed. "Marble houses. Glass streets." His eyes widened suddenly. "Good night!" he cried, in sudden terror.

The cat smirked knowingly.

"Say!" shouted the dog. "*Is* this Heaven?"

"That is the name man has given to our country," replied the cat coolly.

"Well, fer cryin' out loud," said the dog.

"Sir?"

"My God," the dog was muttering, "my God!"

"I rejoice to note that you are pious. Religion, sir—"

"Religion!" shouted the dog at last. "Religion be damned. I'm dead!"

"I too feared death," spoke the cat softly. "The whole eighteenth century echoed with my plaints, shook with my fears. But death, I assure you—"

The dog was not listening. Dead, was he? Now that was quaint. "Me, dead!" Then he shook himself carelessly. All right, dead he was then. But he was still Irish.

"What," he cut in then, "is the eighteenth century?"

"The eighteenth century, my friend, *was*, not *is*. And alas, it will never be again. But it remains on the calendar of civilization as the most privileged and enlightened age ever granted to man or beast."

"Oh," said the dog. "And where was this here knock-out age?"

"It began with the birth of my patron."

"Your what?"

"My patron—my master."

"You mean your boss?"

"That might be the American solecism."

"And who was he to make everybody hot and bothered?"

"His name," replied the cat, stiffening proudly, "was Samuel Johnson."

"Huh," sniffed the dog. "Common name. Very common. My boss's name is MacInerny. Michael MacInerny."

"But my patron was a man of letters, the most eminent in all London."

"I don't know anything about this London, but my boss writes poetry!"

The cat smiled loftily.

"A minor poet, no doubt."

"He's a swell poet!" cried the dog. He was about to leap on his antagonist at that, but he paused. "Say," he said, "they let you *fight* here, don't they? Nobody stops you?"

"I told you it was Heaven," said the cat.

The dog liked Heaven, he found, after Hodge had shown him around a bit.

Not, as he said, that he could hand the Coney Island part any carnations. He had no eye for artifice or splendor; and what

good were glass streets to an earth-loving, earth-digging terrier?
Also, the angels were pretty dumb too—simpering creatures
lolling over their harps, who patted his head with unfeeling
hands and couldn't raise a puppy biscuit among 'em. He cared
little for humans, anyway, except the Boss, and these slobs
weren't even human.

And St. Peter—that was the name of the guy at the gate—was
downright comical. The dog and the cat came upon him just
after some gay fellow had crashed the gate and the old boy was
in an awful pucker. It seemed that the gay fellow had been a
gate-crasher on Earth, and of course after a guy has crashed the
Dempsey-Tunney fight and all the Army-Navy games and every
first night on Broadway, mere pearly gates are no trick at all.
The dog tried to point this out to St. Peter, but the old fellow
was not to be consoled. He just went on tearing his hair and
beating his breast and crying out about his professional honor.
Gosh, it was comical!

But it was when they got to the Alley that things really began
to look up.

The Alley was back of the palace kitchen-gardens. It had been
designed especially for cats and dogs. There had been quite an
argument over it in the beginning. The Head Angel thought
alleys were vulgar and uncelestial, and said so firmly. But the
Architect, who had been brought up on cats and dogs, won out.
So the Alley had been added as a sort of afterthought, and it
turned out, as the Witty Angel said, a howling success. (The
witty one had been a columnist on Earth, which accounts for his
being such a card.)

And certainly the Architect knew his cats and dogs, for the
Alley was indeed a model one. It was narrow and dank and
secret and tortuous. Everywhere you looked—excellent garbage
buckets crammed and running over with the most succulent
slops. Everywhere you stepped—tin cans, broken boxes, bottles,
bones, bits of coal, old shoes, bread heels, fish heads, covering
the cobblestones like a thick, rich carpet. Over it all, a soul-
satisfying smell. And best of all, it flaunted a bold sign: "Cats
and Dogs Only. *Homo Sapiens* Keep Out." The Witty Angel was
responsible for the *Homo Sapiens*. "If you're ever going to use
dead tongues—" said he, then he wagged his head in a special
way and you were supposed to see the joke.

Beyond the Alley, through a deep and devious covered passageway, lay the Meadow. This was also very nice. If a fellow got tired of alley life, he could always go out to the Meadow and have a run. The Meadow had an excellent patch of immortal catnip and other tasty weeds.

It was a fine spectacle that greeted the eye as Hodge and the dog approached the Alley. Dogs, cats, hundreds of them, swarming in loud confusion, fighting, barking, yowling, jumping, chasing each other, chasing their tails, chasing rats (the celestial rats were especially large and juicy, the little dog noted), rolling, prancing, frisking. A few slept serenely in corners. Here and there a dog gnawed a bone, a kitten licked her pretty face.

But when Hodge appeared, they all left off their business and stood respectfully waiting for him to speak. And Hodge did not disappoint them. He spoke at length, he orated, he reeled off elocution and argument and Latin phrases like a truly oracular cat. His address was peppered with "Why now, sir's" and "No, Madame's." It bristled with contentiousness. It all but sank and fell under the weight of polysyllables. But the audience listened, spellbound. That is, all but the new little dog. He was frankly bored. "He shoots off his eighteenth-century mouth too much," he stated to himself, stifling a yawn.

Then with belated graciousness and no little pomp, Hodge turned to him, the newcomer. "Sirs," he intoned, "and ladies," bowing here to a female or two, "I have the honor to present Padraic MacInerny, a canine of parts who has just come amongst us to share our celestial joys. Bid him welcome as befits your high degree."

The welcome that befitted their high degree was loud and vociferous. The animals swarmed toward him, barking, yelping, baying, miaowing—a wheeling confusion of hairy bodies, flashing eyes, licking tongues, flying tails; and as Paddy licked back, smelled back, wagged back, he smiled to himself, "Where dogs are dogs!"

Hodge stood apart from the onslaught stentoriously calling off names. Paddy heard his voice like a horn through the fog: "Boatswain! Turk! Linda! Flush!" But Paddy cared not for names. It was enough to be welcomed by these jolly good fellows. Welcomed—and how! He reflected afterwards that the only thing they left out was the keys to the city.

Later, Paddy got the low-down, from Hodge's ready tongue, on the chief members of the Alley.

The biggest Newfoundland, the one with the melancholy eyes and the posturing airs, was Boatswain. "Had belonged to a poet," said Hodge, "named Byron." (Only Paddy had always thought Byron was the name of a Presidential candidate.) "He has a fine way with the ladies," explained Hodge, one would have thought almost enviously. But Paddy chuckled at that. "If that big, overgrown bimbo is a sheik, then I'm Rin-Tin-Tin."

The lovely mastiff was Turk. "An amiable fellow, Turk," annotated Hodge. "Always in high flash." Turk talked too vivaciously for Paddy. Especially did he try to impress him with the merits and beauties of a place called Gad's Hill, where it seemed he had lived on Earth. But Paddy only smiled. When you're a born New Yorker, you can afford to humor provincials. Gad's Hill, indeed!

Turk was *cicerone* (Hodge's word) to a large family—Linda and Bumble and Don, Newfoundlands, and Mrs. Bouncer, a Pomeranian. At Linda, Paddy sneered. No sex appeal. Mrs. Bouncer was otherwise. Indeed, Mrs. Bouncer and Boatswain were the scandal of the Alley. A respectable widow once, she was now that pitiable object, a woman infatuated. Boatswain had only to roll his romantic eye and she trembled; he had but to loll against a garbage can in all his lordly grace and she was devastated. One flick of Boatswain's tail, and her dainty jowls watered. One seductive growl and she fluttered. Twenty times a day, Turk, the outraged, would shout, "Look out, Mrs. B! Mind what you're doing. I know your tricks and your manners." But it was no good. The lady remained entranced as Turk admonished, and the Alley gossiped, and Boatswain smiled his faint contemptuous smile. "I guess he *is* a sheik, after all," thought Paddy. "The big stiff!"

Woggs was a Skye terrier who, said Hodge, "labors under the handicaps of a Scottish birth and a frail constitution, and who yet emerges the brightest spirit of us all." Woggs had "R.L.S." engraved on his collar.

There was a funny, sombre little brown dog called Flush who ambled around murmuring wanly, "I'm but a poor, tired, wandering singer, singing through the dark," and now and then inquired faintly whether anybody had any macaroons. Flush had belonged to a lady poet, Hodge said. Certainly, thought Paddy, he was a pretty poor stick.

There was a spaniel named Presto Thrale. Presto it was who admired Hodge perhaps the most extravagantly of them all. Rapt he sat in Hodge's presence; flatteringly he approved Hodge's every word.

There were deerhounds and pugs and poodles. There were wolfhounds and terriers and sheep-dogs. But one thing they had in common, Hodge explained: they were all literary. And of course, Paddy ruminated grimly to himself, they were all dead, too.

Paddy played an exhilarating game in the Meadow with Turk and his family. Leap-Dog, it was called.

Paddy had a sleep—a long, snoring snooze with nobody to wake him up. He dreamed of Phœbe, smiled in his sleep to remember that feline. She'd never get here; Phœbe was a hell-cat if there ever was one.

Paddy ate. The eating was perhaps the greatest revelation of all in this amazing Heaven. For in Heaven, it seemed, you could eat anything—simply anything—and not get sick. So Paddy ate. Chicken and potatoes and candy and milk and ice cream and butter and gravy and cake and fried fish, he ate; all the forbidden fruit of Earth he guzzled and gorged and lapped and crunched until he staggered for breath and his stomach stuck out like a little, round, hairy balloon.

A scullery maid came to the Alley with their food. "A sensible girl," Hodge said of her benevolently. "I like her well. She pays tribute to Literature in the only way a scullery maid could do, by serving its followers."

And Paddy discovered these other attributes of the Alley: that baths were unknown; that muzzles existed not; that cops never got to Heaven; and that dog-catchers were denied entrance.

Fights. Chicken. Potatoes. Candy. No baths. No muzzles. No cops. No dog-catchers. "Thank God, I'm dead," murmured Paddy. "Thank God for Paradise."

At four o'clock that afternoon Hodge stepped to the middle of the Alley, and a dozen or so of the animals, all dogs, as it happened, grouped themselves in a circle around him. In front of Hodge was an old packing box; in his right forepaw he held up a ginger-ale bottle.

Paddy looked curiously at the scene.

"Ah, Paddy," said Hodge, "be seated, pray."

Paddy seated himself blandly. Hodge rapped sharply on the box with his improvised gavel.

"Order, ladies and gentlemen!"

There was a slight rustle, then silence. Old Hodge was the chairman, evidently. "He would," thought Paddy.

"Paddy, sir," said Hodge turning to him courteously, "you find yourself at a meeting of the Celestial Association of Literary Cats and Dogs—"

"Popularly known as 'Hounds of Heaven'," spoke up Turk.

"Celestial Association of Literary Cats and Dogs," repeated Hodge firmly. "Settle yourself comfortably, sir, and see whether you like not our mood and humor."

"Righto," said Paddy agreeably. "Shoot."

Hodge pounded on the box again. He cleared his throat. "Before we proceed to philosophical discussion," began Hodge. "Ah, Flush, what is it? Speak, my good dog. Why do you squirm and fidget?"

Flush raised timid eyes to the august chairman. "Please, sir," went on Flush more boldly, "you have forgotten the—stockings."

Hodge inclined his head ponderingly. "Why, Flush, good dog, you do well. Forgotten the stockings I had. Presto, fetch forth the stockings, I pray you. Make speed at it, too, my good fellow. Our meeting is like never to get under way."

Presto, bowing, trotted out and came back with a mouthful of small blue stockings. They were handed around. Each beast accepted four, drew them gravely on over his paws. Thus attired they resumed their positions. Only Paddy, as he gazed strangely at his own blue woollen feet and legs, seemed to betray that this was not the common apparel of cats and dogs.

Hodge continued, equably, "We are a company of celebrated beasts, Paddy, each one of us here illustrious in his own name. But lest you take us for common witlings boasting but empty boasts, we will now produce for you the proofs of our celebrity. I will begin." He settled back on his haunches and brushed his nose with his stockinged paw.

"I am the dean of this animal Heaven because my master was the dean of literature in the world. I lived with him in London,

ate from his hand, climbed up his chair, walked on his breast—
was, in short, the intimate of his daily life. He praised me to
Bozzy and spoke affectionately of me abroad. I appear in the
great record of his life by this same Bozzy—the only domestic
animal set down by name in that notable history. Bozzy did not
like me, but neither did I like Bozzy. My patron," he added,
his eye glittering, "bought me oysters with his own hands."

Paddy: "Well now, that's nice. Oysters, eh? Fair enough,
fair enough."

Hodge, with a flick of his paw at Boatswain: "Now Boatsy,
perhaps you will be amiable enough to favor us."

Boatswain, yawning, stretching, yawning again, plainly bored:
"All the world knows, I should think, how I woke up one morning to find myself famous."

Turk: "But you woke up in Heaven, you know. Don't forget
that."

Boatswain: "Er—well, yes, to be sure, I was already here
when Fame finally overtook me. I am" (fixing Paddy with a
steely eye) "the only dog in history who ever had his epitaph
printed in a book of poems."

Paddy: "What's an epitaph?"

Hodge: " 'Inscription written on a tomb.' I quote the first
English dictionary."

Paddy: "Oh, so your boss wrote it, eh, Boatswain? Well,
that's not bad, not half bad, Big Boy. Congratulations and all
that sort of thing."

Boatswain grandiloquently:

> "When some proud son of man returns to earth,
>   Unknown to glory—"

Hodge: "No, Boatsy, it won't do, my boy, it won't do. No
long recitations, you know—one of the rules."

Turk, speaking up as Boatswain retires sulkily: "Listen to me!
I was my master's favorite dog! Linda he loved and Bumble and
Don and even Mrs. Bouncer—"

That respectable widow, rousing from her trance: "Even Mrs.
Bouncer? *Even?*"

Hodge, sternly: "Silence, madam!"

Turk: "—but I was his real love, his eye's apple, his other

self. It was I who sat with him in the chalet across the road from the house at Gad's Hill whilst he penned the masterpieces that made his name a household word. I who tramped with him over the fields and hills of Kent—"

Linda, snarling: "Wait a minute. I tramped with him too. I—"

Don, growling: "I—"

Paddy, cheerfully: "Well, the I's seem to have it."

Hodge coldly: "Sir, I weary of your feeble American jests."

Paddy, meekly: " 'Scuse it, please."

Hodge: "As for you, Turk and Linda, give over this vying competition. Man's love for his animals is not so niggardly that it cannot be divided equitably amongst them all. Fie on you! . . . Woggs here is a more modest dog. Woggs!"

Woggs, dreamily: "I had the merriest, sweetest master on earth—"

Turk, baring his teeth: "You didn't! I did!"

Paddy: "I did!"

Boastwain, flying up: "I—"

Hodge, icily: "You are a pack of rogues, every dog Jack of you. What is this unseemly noise? What is this un-Christian baring of teeth? Woggs, my good fellow, I deplore this exhibition of ill temper. Go on, sir, go on."

Woggs, as they all subside: "I had a merry, sweet master. He loved me, he and his wife, loved me so much that when I died he would never have another dog. Even when he went to far-off Vailima and a dog was urged upon him for company's sweet sake, he would not. Woggs was the only dog for him, as he was the only man for Woggs. There is devotion, my friends, not easily matched in the world of men."

Paddy, thoughtfully: "True."

Presto, wiping away a tear: "Ah me, how affecting!"

Hodge: "These are better sentiments. I commend you all. But mind you, Woggs, I do not say that as a poet, your master was to be commended. In especial is that celebrated couplet of his at grievous fault—"

Paddy: "What couplet?"

Woggs, reciting: " 'The world is so full of a number of things—' "

Hodge: "Et cetera."

Woggs, drooping: "Et cetera."

Hodge: "Nay, Woggs, philosophy that may be, but poetry never. 'A number of things!' What things, I ask you? What have these broad say-nothing phrases to do with Literature? Literary expression, sir, should be nice, neat, to the dot. Any idle woman can speak words with her tongue. A poet should do better than that, else is he not a poet."

Woggs: "But my master—"

Hodge, grandly: "That will do." Turning to Presto: "Presto, I like well your history and life. Relate it now for Paddy, sir."

Presto, enthusiastically: "Oh, sir, I am to be envied of all dogs. I lived at Streatham, the very Mecca of genius. You know, Hodge, what a creature Mrs. Thrale was, how she plucked the brightest flowers of all England to deck her drawing-room, and how these flowers bloomed but the rosier in that benign and sunny atmosphere. *I* sat at supper with Sir Joshua and Fanny Burney and Hannah More. *I* brushed the hem of the Lexicographer's greatcoat, and lay with my muzzle on the buckle of his shoe. *I* cut a caper once when the great Mrs. Montagu came—"

Hodge, critically: "But she did marry an Italian. None can gainsay that."

Boatswain: "And her first husband was a brewer."

Presto, coolly: "She preferred the Italian to some other gentleman. And beer-money paid for the most brilliant companies of the age. Ah yes, all London, all the world, came to Streatham. A sweet place, Paddy. All men found it so. The fevers of London vanished there."

Hodge, amiably: "Why now, Presto, I cannot meet you in your sentiments about London. No, sir, when an animal is tired of London, he is tired of life; for there is in London—and especially in Fleet Street—all that life can afford."

Presto, hypocritically: "Oh, sir, when has not the great Hodge spoken truly and nobly on any subject?"

Brutus, another dog: "I belonged to the great Landseer. He painted me in a picture—"

Hodge, apologetically to Paddy: "Landseer was only a painter, sir. We suffer Brutus here because he is in himself a worthy beast."

Maida, a deerhound: "I was Sir Walter Scott's favorite—"

Trump, a pug: "*I* belonged to Hogarth—"

Bounce, hitherto unnoticed: "But *I* was the pet of the master, Alexander Pope—"

Hodge: "Hounds of Heaven, where hide your manners? What confusion is this? What disorder? Come now, each dog in his turn." (Pounds prodigiously with the bottle until it crashes and shivers to the ground.) "Flush, my good dog, we have not heard from you."

Flush, squealing excitedly: "*I* bit Robert Browning's legs! He brought me macaroons and seed cakes and I bit his legs just the same. I had poems written to me when I was alive" (looking importantly at Boatswain), "not after I was dead. I eloped too! To Marylebone church. It was lovely. We rode in a carriage, my mistress and Wilson and I, and there we were married. And I was taken to Italy with them too. It was very exciting because nobody knew. Papa was so stern and cross, you know. I didn't bark or give anything away. And I knew about it all the time, because all the boxes were packed and waiting and I could see them up in her closet. When we got to Italy, I didn't bite his legs any more because for some reason Ba-a didn't want me to. Besides, I was very occupied with fleas."

Hodge: "But, sirs, we speak too much of ourselves. We have here a newcomer. Come, Paddy, let us hear your recital of earthly glory."

Paddy, briskly: "Well, my Boss writes sonnets. He writes 'em all day long and he's got a whole box full."

Boatswain: "And they are published?"

Paddy, defiantly: "No, they ain't published—yet."

All of them, looking at each other significantly: "Ah!"

Paddy, proudly: "You see, my Boss is a champion. He's the champion unpublished poet. He's written more poems that ain't ever been published than any other guy that ever lived. He says so himself."

Boatswain, sneering: "Dear me."

Mrs. Bouncer: "Fancy that."

Paddy, hastily: "He knows all the rhymes in the world, too. He's got a rhyme book and all he has to do is look 'em up."

Boatswain, recoiling: "Horrible."

Bounce, covering his eyes: "Oh, most horrible."

Paddy: "And once an editor ast him to lunch, he did. And once he got $25 from the *New York Times* for eight lines. That's over $3 a line. And once he wrote verses for Mother's Day cards and got $18. And once he went to Padraic Colum's house and had boiled chicken for dinner and that's why he named me for him, but Mr. Colum didn't know, when he heard about it, whether it was a compliment or not. And—and—"

Hodge, insinuatingly: "And what, Paddy?"

Boatswain, softly: "Perhaps Paddy's master is a Chatter-ton—"

Paddy, in sudden anger: "I don't know about your Chatter-tons or any of that stuff, but my Boss is a swell guy and don't you forget it. And him and me has a swell time. We take walks and we play games, and if we sell a poem we eat; and if we don't we chew our tongues instead, and I like it, see? And I wouldn't trade my Boss for a whole carload of your dead Thrales and Johnsons and Robert Brownings, whoever they are. When my Boss gets famous and we get a lotta jack, we're gonna move to the country and go huntin' and chase chickens and write pastorals and eat all day long. But he ain't famous yet—editors are sorta dumb that way—so we live in a garret—a studio, I mean—and any guy here that wants to make remarks can just step up and I'll teach him how to make remarks, see? And that goes for you, too, Mr. Samuel Johnson London England Fleet Street God A'mighty Hodge!"

He looked around the circle hotly. Not one flicker of a tail or the wink of an eye. Only disdain everywhere, cold contempt.

They were sneering at his Boss. He looked from one to the other of the aloof, haughty faces. They remained frozen in scorn.

They were sneering at his Boss. His Boss who—

Well, they didn't know any better, the poor saps. They hadn't seen the Boss. They didn't know what a great guy he was. He began to pity them then, those animals that had never known his Boss, and he felt better.

"Well," said Linda, rising from her haunches, "it's time, boys and girls." Instantly they all sprang to their feet, were leaping away with joyful barks, kicking off their blue stockings as they went.

"Time fer what?" shouted Paddy after them.

"Time for our walk!" threw back Turk over his shoulder. "Every day at this time we take a walk with our masters!"

Paddy watched their bounding, retreating flanks as they disappeared through the passageway from the Alley to the Meadow. He followed. In the doorway of the passage he stopped.

There in the Meadow they all were. Turk and his family capering around the feet of a tall, bearded man in a checked waistcoat who called out hilarious greetings to them and laughed uproariously at their pranks. . . . Flush trotting earnestly between a man and a woman arm in arm, who smiled at each other and at Flush and then at each other again. . . . Woggs waddling at the heels of a lanky man in tweeds, whose long legs ambled their way across the grassy meadow, whose long hands played with the old brown pipe in his mouth, whose eyes hardly left the dusky, vivid woman walking at his side, except to look back at Woggs. . . . Boatswain pacing in stately fashion beside a corpulent, pompous, self-conscious, and yet somehow romantic-looking male who limped noticeably and sighed as he looked down at Boatswain, none of your ordinary prosy sighs either, but heavy sighs and deep with meaning. . . . Presto stepping along to the lively gait of a sprightly lady in cap and ribbons. . . . Hodge marching with dignity at the heels of a massive, rolling, seesawing figure, whose wig was askew, whose linen was rumpled, but whose words, apparently, held as in a vice of doting admiration the sprightly lady who was with him.

Gone were the white robes, the harps, all the foolish, tricked-out, trumped-up trappings of the commonplace Heaven of a few hours before. This was another Heaven, men and women walking in the fields at sundown with their beloved animals. Paddy, watching, felt an unaccountable pain, a pain just under the white patch on his breast (where no white patch ought to be if an Irish terrier's ancestors have been all that ancestors should be.)

"Gosh," he whispered.

They all looked so happy. They all *were* happy, everybody in the whole place was happy—cats, dogs, men, women—everybody but him. He saw the lanky man turn back, bend over, put his hand on Woggs's furry little back; saw Woggs's wriggle of ecstasy, and the pain under his white patch grew sharper. He, too, knew the rapture that comes from the touch of your Boss's hand. Nothing in the whole world is as nice as that—nothing, not ice cream, not beefsteak, not warm firesides, not cat fights, not even fried liver and onions, which last, as any dog knows, is the dizziest delight in life.

He craned as the happy ones, strolling along, gradually moved out of sight around a flowery bend of the Meadow, his blunt, square, whiskery countenance strained and wistful. They had gone now. The Meadow was empty, its grasses burnished and still under the light of late afternoon.

Paddy stood in the doorway, uneasy, puzzled. "But this *ain't* Heaven," he kept saying. "If the Boss was here—but he's down in New York. This ain't Heaven for me a-tall!"

He thought of the garret, the fire small but valiant and blustering, the Boss's long legs stretched out in front of it, his own savory old blanket there on the floor, the smell of their supper, the light of their lamp. Phœbe's green eyes at the window. He thought of the Boss's virtues—the Boss who kidded him, who talked to him like a regular fellow, who was so understanding in the matter of baths, so tolerant in the matter of week-end jaunts. The Boss, too, who trusted him so implicitly, who always knew that he would come home finally, expected him, waited for him, welcomed him—needed him.

This was Heaven where things were planned especially for dogs, where garbage was plentiful, where fights were allowed, where potatoes and candy were not taboo. But the Boss wasn't here. The Boss was in New York, waiting for him.

Suddenly he whirled on his feet. Like a streak of red dust he was through the passage, across the Alley, through the palace, the courtyard, out of the gate. St. Peter was nodding over his afternoon cup of tea, the gate itself slightly ajar. Paddy lunged against it, threw it wide open, flashed through.

Now he was on the very edge of the world, Heaven behind, a vast abyss of sky and air beneath him. He flung off his stockings. An aviator far below wondered mightily at the thing that blew into his lap, a small blue woollen thing, like a doll's stocking.

Only a second he paused. It was sickening, hideous, this awful chasm; but he had to do it. He had to jump. He had to. He had to get away, back to the Boss. There was a little cloud 'way down yonder. He'd jump and land on its back. And that—would —take—him—back—to—the—Boss.

He smelled the breath of a strange man in his face, heard a

strange voice, was conscious of a hot, smothering pain all over his body. The Boss he did not see or hear, but he knew he was home. He had known that a long time now by the smell of his own blanket so pleasant and comforting under him. He could not open his eyes. That was odd, he thought. But he could hear all right. He heard now—yes, it was the Boss. But how husky and funny the Boss's voice sounded.

"Gosh, doctor, I can't thank you enough."

"I didn't save your dog, man!" That was the stranger's voice now. "He saved himself. You saw how he did it. Lord, I've never seen an animal fight harder to come back, and I've seen a-plenty too—gritty little devil. Uncanny, isn't it? I never get used to it somehow. How we do come back, sometimes, dogs as well as men."

"Will he be all right? He's such a cocky fellow, I'd hate to have him lame."

"Sure. He'll be all right. He's as tough as they come. Just keep bathing him with this stuff and give him all the fresh water he'll take. No food, of course. But then he'd see to that. I'll come in and change the dressings to-morrow. God, I'd like to string up a few of these truck drivers."

He was gone. Paddy heard the door close, followed the last echo of his footsteps down the stairs. He opened his eyes groggily. The Boss was right there, close up to his muzzle, his face scared and white.

"Well, Mr. Padraic MacInerny!" But what made the Boss's voice thick like that?

The Boss was smiling though, and his hand was gently—oh, so gently—on the little dog's head. And somehow the hot, flaming, awful pain all over his body was gone now. He tried to wag his tail. Drat it, the thing wouldn't wag, too heavy. He tried again. There. Slow, feeble thuds, but thuds just the same. The Boss's white-faced smile was the only thing he could see.

He closed his eyes again.

Here was Heaven, if anybody wanted to know.

THE DISGRACED DOG

BABETA'S DOG

BY *Konrad Bercovici*

SHE WAS ONLY A LITTLE PUPPY when she was brought to
Babeta's restaurant. And because Babeta has a literary turn
of mind, he renamed her Ophelia when Sonori, the tenor, who
knew more about dogs than about literature, said she was a
Dane.

It was due to Ophelia that Babeta, the anarchist-communist
philosopher, became very much interested in dogdom and
learned to distinguish an Airedale from a Bulldog and a Spaniel
from a Dane. They ceased talking about music and philosophy
at Babeta's, and, though the Goyescas almost created a stir in the

musical world and Bergson had delivered a lecture in Rumfold Hall, Babeta and his artist guests neglected such transcendental interests because of the change brought about in the direction of their thoughts by a dog, because of a little puppy they had named Ophelia.

Sonori discovered that Shakespeare, and not Verdi, was the author of "The Moor of Venice," and when the talk turned about the Scandinavians, many another musical celebrity heard for the first time the name of Ibsen or of Bjornson. And there was even a lonely man in the crowd who had read a story by Knut Hamsun, that greatest of all Scandinavian writers, whose tales have no equal in the world's literature.

In what strange surroundings Ophelia was destined to live!

Near Eighth Avenue, before Fortieth Street. The smell of garlic and tomato sauce warns the passer-by that the inhabitants are from Piedmonte, but on the street one hears the Irish brogue. The bales of cotton in front of the warehouses and the smoke from the chimneys reek after Liverpool, but the smell of rope, tar and fried smelts that comes from the wharves nearby reminds one of Fiume and Marseille, as the swaying masts and the spread-out sails outline themselves against the glowing sky.

And in such surroundings, back of one of the numerous saloons in which stale beer is served to drunken sailors and dust-covered longshoremen, is the celebrated restaurant of Babeta.

I have said already that Babeta is a philosopher, and were I to write about him and not about his dog, I could tell you some good stories about the interminable scientific discussions at a certain table in a corner, and the marvelous feasts at the tables reserved there for the two-thousand-dollar-a-night tenors and three-thousand-dollar-a-week sopranos. A book could be written about the decorations and friezes of the place, and only ignorance of culinary art would put a stop to what I could say about the food served at Babeta's. As to the wine—well, it's Chianti or Lacrima Christi, if that means anything to you.

But I have promised Prosper to tell the story of Ophelia. Prosper knows a lot about science and still more about art, but, because he is neither scientist nor artist, he is interested in human beings and dogs.

We all admired Ophelia. She was gliding graciously between the tables, and as she grew bigger she was frequently a medium of friendship between old and new guests. Hands met hands stroking her beautiful fur, and after an "excuse me," or a "pardon, signorina," the new guest asked the old one the name of the dog—followed an introduction, an invitation to the other table, after which Ophelia was slightly forgotten and Dante or Puccini was discussed for a little while. But Ophelia's steady place was near Babeta's table at the door.

In less than a year Ophelia was the personality of the place. She was big and stately. Her short morning walk was taken on the leash, one end of which was in her master's hand. Any casual courtesy paid to her by another dog during those walks was firmly and instantly checked by Babeta. She was a Dane, a pure blue Dane, and Babeta, the anarchist, the enemy of aristocracy, did not allow his dog to meet the common people, the free, common people of dogdom. Ophelia pulled at the leash once or twice, but, after severe reprimands, she made a virtue of necessity and passed haughtily by, unobservant of any amorous advances.

It was Prosper who brought the great news. Ophelia was to be mated to a pure Dane owned by a captain, who promised to bring "Prince" on his next trip from Europe. And the news spread. People that had neglected the spaghetti and Chianti for weeks suddenly got a hankering after Babeta's place. Ere the week was over the unborn puppies were promised to two hundred people. Babeta had been shown the pedigree of Prince and was satisfied on this score.

I have already said that Ophelia was the personality of the place, but after Babeta told the story of her future mate, and promised pups to all that would listen to him, she became the most venerated personality. Sopranos with two hemispheres at their feet fed Ophelia the best sweets of the continent, and a justly celebrated baritone brought her a collar of pure silver, lined with costly fur. Nothing was too good for Ophelia, nothing too expensive for her.

From the river, a few hundred feet away, came the fog blasts of transport ships carrying thousands of men to a vortex of blood in which millions of men had already been crushed, pulverized and liquefied to check the rule of aristocracy, but back of that saloon near Eighth Avenue, Babeta, the anarchist-communist philosopher, was expounding the virtues of pure blood as exemplified in Ophelia and Prince, the Dane to which she was to be mated.

Many were the bottles of wine drunk to her health and the health of her offspring. Babeta actually experienced the joys of fatherhood when he made arrangements with a veterinarian, the best in town, for the great day. In the most comfortable corner of the kitchen a place was reserved for Ophelia's litter. A new soft mattress and warm woolen covers were prepared and only the privileged ones were shown all those preparations.

"I want a male puppy," said Sonori, "because I want to call it Hamlet."

"And I want a female one and I will call it Flora," said Mlle. Marienta, the great lyric soprano.

Babeta was happy. Thanks to his dog, he had obtained higgedly-piggedly more flattery than he ever craved for his famous food or for his philosophical discourses.

"Ophelia, you good girl, come for a walk," and master and dog went early every morning to breathe fresh air.

But spring was near. As the days went by it seemed to Babeta that Ophelia was gradually losing her haughtiness towards the common people, ordinarily along the wharves.

The hundred and one mongrel dogs roving there followed Ophelia and her master and she pulled at the leash with more insistence from day to day. Once she allowed one of the dogs to come so near that Babeta felt the fangs of the mongrel as he drove him away with a kick. And Ophelia stood meekly by. Homewards she bent her head in shame as the master censored her.

"Shame, Ophelia."

Ophelia was ashamed. She nestled close to Babeta as he sat down to bandage his leg and looked up to him and whined. Only when the whining threatened to turn into a howl did Babeta give a forgiving sign. The following days the morning walks were taken along the avenue; the leash was brought up shorter, as a precaution, and all was peaceful again. But during the day Ophelia showed signs of uneasiness, and Babetta watched the door because she tried twice to slink out.

"What's the matter with Ophelia? She has refused chocolate!" asked one of the guests.

"She has probably had enough sweets," answered Babeta off-handedly, but his heart sunk.

A few days later, a street dog slunk in through the door of the restaurant. Ophelia got up from her corner to meet the stranger. Her master sprung up and kicked the intruder so violently the dog's howl could be heard from the street.

"You treat the common people pretty roughly, Babeta!" observed Prosper.

Babeta was angry with Ophelia.

"Shame," he cried, "shame," and drove her to the kitchen. "Away from me, away."

In vain Ophelia tried to make up to him. Her eyes begged forgiveness. But when it was not given she turned about and barked and howled in righteous indignation as it just occurred to her that she was unjustly treated.

"Wherein have I sinned?" she seemed to question.

Sonori and others wanted to pat her, but she gave fair warning by snarling and snapping in the air.

"What's the trouble with Ophelia?" Sonori asked.

"To the kitchen, go, go," and Babeta pushed her away.

That night, after the guests were all gone, the master spoke to the dog.

"I am ashamed of you, Ophelia. You behaved miserably. You a pure Dane to permit and accept the courtship of a low-down street dog!—I am ashamed of you! Prince will soon come from Europe, and you want to associate with nondescripts that feed from garbage cans!"

Ophelia cried and whined and begged forgiveness, and was happy again only when Babeta allowed her to take the nightly piece of sugar from between his lips.

Yet Ophelia felt the misery of aristocratic loneliness. That streak of the dark blue sky she saw between the shutters at night and the snarling, howling and fighting of the dogs at the wharves caused her sleepless nights. It was early spring; the time when life asserts itself; when dog and man howl to the moon and snap at each falling star.

That dog Babeta had kicked out so violently from the restaurant came nightly under the window of his belle and called, begged, serenaded and pleaded in even more heartrending tones than the tenor in Bizet's "Pêcheurs des Perles." And it was Prosper again who brought the astonishing news "Ophelia was stolen!"

It was Babeta's version of what had happened. The lattices of the shutters were smashed, the window broken and the dog gone. Babeta was the most disconsolate of men.

"Put in an ad and offer a reward. Announce to the police. Go to the depot of S. P. C. A."

Such were the advices. But he cared not. He remembered the pulling at the leash, the meeting on the wharf, the dog he kicked out, and he despaired. He had promised pure blue puppies. He had been so good to Ophelia. He had given her the best there was to be had. But she left him, ran away like a thief in the dead of night.

Babeta could not touch any food the whole day. That night, when the tenors and sopranos came to eat, they cried and mourned the great loss.

"Dio, mio, oh. Dio, mio!" they all groaned.

Babeta found Ophelia the following morning. He recognized her from a distance. His attention was drawn to a pack of dogs fighting over something or other. There were two different groups, and Ophelia, not definitely attached to either of them, was keeping on the outskirts of the skirmish, snapping and snarling at individuals of both parties. Oh, what a glorious free time she had! Her wriggling tail expressed the joy of life and its mastery. They were all afraid of her. She was stronger than any of them, and she was so happy—so happy and free!

"Ophelia!" rang Babeta's voice. The dog turned about and, seeing the master, she started in the opposite direction, tail between hind legs and head down.

"Ophelia!" he called again. She took a few steps toward him, and as he approached nearer she laid down in the mud, closed her eyes and turned her head aside. Babeta had not taken the leash along, but he held on to the silver collar to bring her home.

Babeta hoped against hope that he would still be able to give pure Dane pups to his friends, but in a few weeks the shame could no longer be hidden. He opened his heart to every one and told where he had found her and in what company. The guests who had patted her and fed her the best sweets no longer looked at her. She was pushed away from near the table. With bowed head she nestled close to her master, her sole protector and friend, but he repulsed her. He did not understand. He did not sympathize.

"Fui, fui, get away, shameless creature, to the kitchen."

The ones that were promised pups became harsh to her and everybody scolded. And one of them remarked:

"Look, she is eating from the floor."

It was the most evident sign of her downfall. Before her escapade she had never eaten but what was given to her in a plate; and never the rests from the tables, but food especially prepared for her by Babeta himself.

"Shame," they all yelled, "shame, shame."

When she lifted her pleading head to her master, Babeta, in a fit of anger, spat at it. "Fui, fui!"

In vain she waited for forgiveness. She longed for the nightly piece of sugar from the lips of her master. She stretched her neck when he passed her by in his inspection of the kitchen. But he did not even look at her. What terrible thing had she done! If he were willing to forgive her she would feel as guilty as he wanted, but since he was so harsh and insulting she felt only his cruelty and not her shame.

Outside her friend was serenading again. The door was not even closed. The master no longer cared with whom she associated. Among humans no friend was left—she understood that—the door was wide open. She could do as she pleased. She had lost her master. He will only scold and never pat again. She understood that, too.

.   .   .   .   .

"Where is Ophelia?" Sonori asked the next evening.

"She has run away and committed suicide!" Babeta announced. "Actually committed suicide. She understood she was disgraced. I called and called, but she ran away—she surely committed suicide!" and he was flattered that Ophelia cared enough for him to commit suicide because she had lost his friendship. Only Prosper knows.

"She has gone to the dogs," he said. "The day of aristocracy is over. It's the people now. You are either with them; howling, fighting, getting ruffled and bitten, or you have to isolate yourself on an island at the mercy of much worse—like that other great aristocrat—and Ophelia understood and made her choice."

. . . . .

At Babeta's table they talk again about molecular physics, phonolites, chrystalloids, music and art.

Dogs and Scandinavian literature are taboo. And every time Prosper enters the place Babeta feels uneasy, as though he owes him an explanation.

THE FAITHFUL DOG

ONE MINUTE LONGER

BY *Albert Payson Terhune*

WOLF WAS A COLLIE, red-gold and white of coat, with a shape more like his long-ago wolf ancestors' than like a domesticated dog's. It was from this ancestral throwback that he was named Wolf.

He looked not at all like his great sire, Sunnybank Lad, nor like his dainty, thoroughbred mother, Lady. Nor was he like them in any other way, except that he inherited old Lad's staunchly gallant spirit and loyalty, and uncanny brain. No, in traits as well as in looks, he was more wolf than dog. He almost never barked, his snarl supplying all vocal needs.

The Mistress or the Master or the Boy—any of these three could romp with him, roll him over, tickle him, or subject him to all sorts of playful indignities. And Wolf entered gleefully into the fun of the romp. But let any human, besides these three, lay a hand on his slender body, and a snarling plunge for the offender's throat was Wolf's invariable reply to the caress.

It had been so since his puppyhood. He did not fly at accredited guests, nor, indeed, pay any heed to their presence, so long as they kept their hands off him. But to all of these the Boy was forced to say at the very outset of the visit:

"Pat Lad and Bruce all you want to, but please leave Wolf alone. He doesn't care for people. We've taught him to stand for a pat on the head, from guests—but don't touch his body."

Then, to prove his own immunity, the Boy would proceed to tumble Wolf about, to the delight of them both.

In romping with humans whom they love, most dogs will bite, more or less gently—or pretend to bite—as a part of the game. Wolf never did this. In his wildest and roughest romps with the Boy or with the Boy's parents, Wolf did not so much as open his mighty jaws. Perhaps because he dared not trust himself to bite gently. Perhaps because he realized that a bite is not a joke, but an effort to kill.

There had been only one exception to Wolf's hatred for mauling at strangers' hands. A man came to The Place on a business call, bringing along a chubby two-year-old daughter. The Master warned the baby that she must not go near Wolf, although she might pet any of the other collies. Then he became so much interested in the business talk that he and his guest forgot all about the child.

Ten minutes later the Master chanced to shift his gaze to the far end of the room. And he broke off, with a gasp, in the very middle of a sentence.

The baby was seated astride Wolf's back, her tiny heels digging into the dog's sensitive ribs, and each of her chubby fists gripping one of his ears. Wolf was lying there, with an idiotically happy grin on his face and wagging his tail in ecstasy.

No one knew why he had submitted to the baby's tugging hands, except because she *was* a baby, and because the gallant heart of the dog had gone out to her helplessness.

Wolf was the official watchdog of The Place; and his name carried dread to the loafers and tramps of the region. Also, he was the Boy's own special dog. He had been born on the Boy's tenth birthday, five years before this story of ours begins; and ever since then the two had been inseparable chums.

One sloppy afternoon in late winter, Wolf and the Boy were sprawled, side by side, on the fur rug in front of the library fire. The Mistress and the Master had gone to town for the day. The house was lonely, and the two chums were left to entertain each other.

The Boy was reading a magazine. The dog beside him was

blinking in drowsy comfort at the fire. Presently, finishing the story he had been reading, the Boy looked across at the sleepy dog.

"Wolf," he said, "here's a story about a dog. I think he must have been something like you. Maybe he was your great-great-great-great-grandfather. He lived an awfully long time ago—in Pompeii. Ever hear of Pompeii?"

Now, the Boy was fifteen years old, and he had too much sense to imagine that Wolf could possibly understand the story he was about to tell him. But, long since, he had fallen into a way of talking to his dog, sometimes, as if to another human. It was fun for him to note the almost pathetic eagerness wherewith Wolf listened and tried to grasp the meaning of what he was saying. Again and again, at sound of some familiar word or voice inflection, the collie would pick up his ears or wag his tail, as if in the joyous hope that he had at last found a clue to his owner's meaning.

"You see," went on the Boy, "this dog lived in Pompeii, as I told you. You've never been there, Wolf."

Wolf was looking up at the Boy in wistful excitement, seeking vainly to guess what was expected of him.

"And," continued the Boy, "the kid who owned him seems to have had a regular knack for getting into trouble all the time. And his dog was always on hand to get him out of it. It's a true story, the magazine says. The kid's father was so grateful to the dog that he bought him a solid silver collar. Solid silver! Get that, Wolfie?"

Wolf did not "get it." But he wagged his tail hopefully, his eyes alight with bewildered interest.

"And," said the Boy, "what do you suppose was engraved on the collar? Well, I'll tell you: *This dog has thrice saved his little master from death. Once by fire, once by flood, and once at the hands of robbers!* How's that for a record, Wolf? For *one* dog, too!"

At the words "Wolf" and "dog" the collie's tail smote the floor in glad comprehension. Then he edged closer to the Boy as the narrator's voice presently took on a sadder note.

"But at last," resumed the Boy, "there came a time when the dog couldn't save the kid. Mount Vesuvius erupted. All the sky was pitch-dark, as black as midnight, and Pompeii was

buried under lava and ashes. The dog could easily have got
away by himself—dogs can see in the dark, can't they, Wolf?
—but he couldn't get the kid away. And he wouldn't go without him. You wouldn't have gone without me, either, would
you, Wolf? Pretty nearly two thousand years later, some people
dug through the lava that covered Pompeii. What do you suppose they found? Of course they found a whole lot of things.
One of them was that dog—silver collar and inscription and all.
He was lying at the feet of a child. The child he couldn't save.
He was one grand dog—hey, Wolf?"

The continued strain of trying to understand began to get
on the collie's high-strung nerves. He rose to his feet, quivering,
and sought to lick the Boy's face, thrusting one upraised white
forepaw at him in appeal for a handshake. The Boy slammed
shut the magazine.

"It's slow in the house, here, with nothing to do," he said
to his chum. "I'm going up the lake with my gun to see if any
wild ducks have landed in the marshes yet. It's almost time for
them. Want to come along?"

The last sentence Wolf understood perfectly. On the instant
he was dancing with excitement at the prospect of a walk.
Being a collie, he was of no earthly help in a hunting trip;
but, on such tramps, as everywhere else, he was the Boy's
inseparable companion.

Out over the slushy snow the two started, the Boy with his
light single-barreled shotgun slung over one shoulder, the dog
trotting close at his heels. The March thaw was changing to
a sharp freeze. The deep and soggy snow was crusted over, just
thick enough to make walking a genuine difficulty for both
dog and Boy.

The Place was a promontory that ran out into the lake, on
the opposite bank from the mile-distant village. Behind, across
the highroad, lay the winter-choked forest. At the lake's north-
erly end, two miles beyond The Place, were the reedy marshes
where, a month hence, wild duck would congregate. Thither,
with Wolf, the Boy ploughed his way through the biting cold.

The going was heavy and heavier. A quarter-mile below the
marshes the Boy struck out across the upper corner of the lake.
Here the ice was rotten at the top where the thaw had nibbled

at it, but beneath it was still a full eight inches thick; easily strong enough to bear the Boy's weight.

Along the gray ice-field the two plodded. The skim of water, which the thaw had spread an inch thick over the ice, had frozen in the day's cold spell. It crackled like broken glass as the chums walked over it. The Boy had on big hunting-boots. So, apart from the extra effort, the glasslike ice did not bother him. To Wolf it gave acute pain. The sharp particles were forever getting between the callous black pads of his feet, pricking and cutting him acutely.

Little smears of blood began to mark the dog's course; but it never occurred to Wolf to turn back, or to betray by any sign that he was suffering. It was all a part of the day's work—a cheap price to pay for the joy of tramping with his adored young master.

Then, forty yards or so on the hither side of the marshes, Wolf beheld a right amazing phenomenon. The Boy had been walking directly in front of him, gun over shoulder. With no warning at all, the youthful hunter fell, feet foremost, out of sight, through the ice.

The light shell of new-frozen water that covered the lake's thicker ice also masked an air hole nearly three feet wide. Into this as he strode carelessly along, the Boy had stepped. Straight down he had gone, with all the force of his hundred-and-twenty pounds and with all the impetus of his forward stride.

Instinctively, he threw out his hands to restore his balance. The only effect of this was to send the gun flying ten feet away.

Down went the Boy through less than three feet of water (for the bottom of the lake at this point had started to slope upward towards the marshes) and through nearly two feet more of sticky marsh mud that underlay the lake bed.

His outflung hands struck against the ice on the edges of the air hole, and clung there.

Sputtering and gurgling, the Boy brought his head above the surface and tried to raise himself by his hands, high enough to wriggle out upon the surface of the ice. Ordinarily, this would have been simple enough for so strong a lad. But the glue-like mud had imprisoned his feet and the lower part of his legs; and held them powerless.

Try as he would, the Boy could not wrench himself free of

the slough. The water, as he stood upright, was on a level with his mouth. The air hole was too wide for him, at such a depth, to get a good purchase on its edges and lift himself bodily to safety.

Gaining such a finger-hold as he could, he heaved with all his might, throwing every muscle of his body into the struggle. One leg was pulled almost free of the mud, but the other was driven deeper into it. And as the Boy's fingers slipped from the smoothly wet ice-edge, the attempt to restore his balance drove the free leg back, knee-deep into the mire.

Ten minutes of this hopeless fighting left the Boy panting and tired out. The icy water was numbing his nerves and chilling his blood into torpidity. His hands were without sense of feeling, as far up as the wrists. Even if he could have shaken free his legs from the mud, now, he had not strength enough left to crawl out of the hole.

He ceased his uselessly frantic battle and stood dazed. Then he came sharply to himself. For, as he stood, the water crept upward from his lips to his nostrils. He knew why the water seemed to be rising. It was not rising. It was he who was sinking. As soon as he stopped moving, the mud began, very slowly, but very steadily, to suck him downward.

This was not a quicksand, but it was a deep mud-bed. And only by constant motion could he avoid sinking farther and farther down into it. He had less than two inches to spare, at best, before the water should fill his nostrils; less than two inches of life, even if he could keep the water down to the level of his lips.

There was a moment of utter panic. Then the Boy's brain cleared. His only hope was to keep on fighting—to rest when he must, for a moment or so, and then to renew his numbed grip on the ice-edge and try to pull his feet a few inches higher out of the mud. He must do this as long as his chilled body could be scourged into obeying his will.

He struggled again, but with virtually no result in raising himself. A second struggle, however, brought him chin-high above the water. He remembered confusedly that some of these earlier struggles had scarce budged him, while others had gained him two or three inches. Vaguely, he wondered why. Then turning his head, he realized.

Wolf, as he turned, was just loosing his hold on the wide collar of the Boy's mackinaw. His cut forepaws were still braced against a flaw of ragged ice on the air hole's edge, and all his tawny body was tense.

His body was dripping wet, too. The Boy noted that; and he realized that the repeated effort to draw his master to safety must have resulted, at least once, in pulling the dog down into the water with the floundering Boy.

"Once more, Wolfie! *Once more!*" chattered the Boy through teeth that clicked together like castanets.

The dog darted forward, caught his grip afresh on the edge of the Boy's collar, and tugged with all his fierce strength, growling and whining ferociously the while.

The Boy seconded the collie's tuggings by a supreme struggle that lifted him higher than before. He was able to get one arm and shoulder clear. His numb fingers closed about an upthrust tree-limb which had been washed downstream in the autumn freshets and had been frozen into the lake ice.

With this new purchase, and aided by the dog, the boy tried to drag himself out of the hole. But the chill of the water had done its work. He had not the strength to move farther. The mud still sucked at his calves and ankles. The big hunting-boots were full of water that seemed to weigh a ton.

He lay there, gasping and chattering. Then, through the gathering twilight, his eyes fell on the gun, lying ten feet away.

"Wolf!" he ordered, nodding towards the weapon. "Get it! *Get* it!"

Not in vain had the Boy talked to Wolf, for years, as if the dog were human. At the words and the nod, the collie trotted over to the gun, lifted it by the stock, and hauled it awkwardly along over the bumpy ice to his master, where he laid it down at the edge of the air hole.

The dog's eyes were cloudy with trouble, and he shivered and whined as with ague. The water on his thick coat was freezing to a mass of ice. But it was from anxiety that he shivered, and not from cold.

Still keeping his numb grasp on the tree-branch, the boy balanced himself as best he could, and thrust two fingers of his free hand into his mouth to warm them into sensation again.

When this was done, he reached out to where the gun lay, and pulled its trigger. The shot boomed deafeningly through the twilight winter silences. The recoil sent the weapon sliding sharply back along the ice, spraining the Boy's trigger finger and cutting it to the bone.

"That's all I can do," said the Boy to himself. "If anyone hears it, well and good. I can't get at another cartridge. I couldn't put it into the breech if I had it. My hands are too numb."

For several endless minutes he clung there, listening. But this was a desolate part of the lake, far from any road; and the season was too early for other hunters to be abroad. The bitter cold, in any case, tended to make sane folk hug the fireside rather than to venture so far into the open. Nor was the single report of a gun uncommon enough to call for investigation in such weather.

All this the Boy told himself, as the minutes dragged by. Then he looked again at Wolf. The dog, head on one side, still stood protectingly above him. The dog was cold and in pain. But, being only a dog, it did not occur to him to trot off home to the comfort of the library fire and leave his master to fend for himself.

Presently, with a little sigh, Wolf lay down on the ice, his nose across the Boy's arm. Even if he lacked strength to save his beloved master, he could stay and share the Boy's sufferings.

But the Boy himself thought otherwise. He was not at all minded to freeze to death, nor was he willing to let Wolf imitate the dog of Pompeii by dying helplessly at his master's side. Controlling for an instant the chattering of his teeth, he called:

"Wolf!"

The dog was on his feet again at the word; alert, eager.

"Wolf!" repeated the Boy. "*Go!* Hear me? *Go!*"

He pointed homeward.

Wolf stared at him, hesitant. Again the Boy called in vehement command, "*Go!*"

The collie lifted his head to the twilight sky with a wolf howl hideous in its grief and appeal—a howl as wild and discordant as that of any of his savage ancestors. Then, stooping first to lick the numb hand that clung to the branch, Wolf turned and fled.

Across the cruelly sharp film of ice he tore, at top speed, head down, whirling through the deepening dusk like a flash of tawny light.

Wolf understood what was wanted of him. Wolf always understood. The pain in his feet was as nothing. The stiffness of his numbed body was forgotten in the urgency for speed.

The Boy looked drearily after the swift-vanishing figure which the dusk was swallowing. He knew the dog would try to bring help, as has many another and lesser dog in times of need. Whether or not that help could arrive in time, or at all, was a point on which the Boy would not let himself dwell. Into his benumbed brain crept the memory of an old Norse proverb he had read in school:

"Heroism consists in hanging on, one minute longer."

Unconsciously he tightened his feeble hold on the tree-branch and braced himself.

From the marshes to The Place was a full two miles. Despite the deep and sticky snow, Wolf covered the distance in less than nine minutes. He paused in front of the gate-lodge, at the highway entrance to the drive. But the superintendent and his wife had gone to Paterson, shopping, that afternoon.

Down the drive to the house he dashed. The maids had taken advantage of their employers' day in New York, to walk across the lake to the village, to a motion-picture show.

Wise men claim that dogs have not the power to think or to reason things out in a logical way. So perhaps it was mere chance that next sent Wolf's flying feet across the lake to the village. Perhaps it was chance, and not the knowledge that where there is a village there are people.

Again and again, in the car, he had sat upon the front seat alongside the Mistress when she drove to the station to meet guests. There were always people at the station. And to the station Wolf now raced.

The usual group of platform idlers had been dispersed by the cold. A solitary baggageman was hauling a trunk and some boxes out of the express coop onto the platform, to be put aboard the five o'clock train from New York.

As the baggageman passed under the clump of station lights, he came to a sudden halt. For out of the darkness dashed a dog. Full tilt, the animal rushed up to him and seized him by the skirt of the overcoat.

The man cried out in scared surprise. He dropped the box he was carrying and struck at the dog, to ward off the seemingly murderous attack. He recognized Wolf, and he knew the collie's repute.

But Wolf was not attacking. Holding tight to the coat skirt, he backed away, trying to draw the man with him, and all the while whimpering aloud like a nervous puppy.

A kick from the heavy-shod boot broke the dog's hold on the coat skirt, even as a second yell from the man brought four or five other people running out from the station waiting-room.

One of these, the telegraph operator, took in the scene at a single glance. With great presence of mind he bawled loudly:

"MAD DOG!"

This, as Wolf, reeling from the kick, sought to gain another grip on the coat skirt. A second kick sent him rolling over and over on the tracks, while other voices took up the panic cry of "Mad dog!"

Now, a mad dog is supposed to be a dog afflicted by rabies. Once in ten thousand times, at the very most, a mad-dog hue-and-cry is justified. Certainly not oftener. A harmless and friendly dog loses his master on the street. He runs about, confused and frightened, looking for the owner he has lost. A boy throws a stone at him. Other boys chase him. His tongue hangs out, and his eyes glaze with terror. Then some fool bellows:

"Mad dog!"

And the cruel chase is on—a chase that ends in the pitiful victim's death. Yes, in every crowd there is a voice ready to raise that asinine and murderously cruel shout.

So it was with the men who witnessed Wolf's frenzied effort to take aid to the imperiled Boy.

Voice after voice repeated the cry. Men groped along the platform edge for stones to throw. The village policeman ran puffingly upon the scene, drawing his revolver.

Finding it useless to make a further attempt to drag the baggageman to the rescue, Wolf leaped back, facing the ever larger group. Back went his head again in that hideous wolf-howl. Then he galloped away a few yards, trotted back, howled once more, and again galloped lakeward.

All of which only confirmed the panicky crowd in the belief that they were threatened by a mad dog. A shower of stones hurtled about Wolf as he came back a third time to lure these dull humans into following him.

One pointed rock smote the collie's shoulder, glancingly, cutting it to the bone. A shot from the policeman's revolver fanned the fur of his ruff, as it whizzed past.

Knowing that he faced death, he nevertheless stood his ground, not troubling to dodge the fusillade of stones, but continuing to run lakeward and then trot back, whining with excitement.

A second pistol-shot flew wide. A third grazed the dog's hip. From all directions people were running towards the station. A man darted into a house next door, and emerged carrying a shotgun. This he steadied on the veranda rail not forty feet away from the leaping dog, and made ready to fire.

It was then the train from New York came in. And, momentarily, the sport of "mad-dog" killing was abandoned while the crowd scattered to each side of the track.

From a front car of the train the Mistress and the Master emerged into a bedlam of noise and confusion.

"Best hide in the station, Ma'am!" shouted the telegraph operator, at sight of the Mistress. "There is a mad dog loose out here! He's chasing folks around, and—"

"Mad dog!" repeated the Mistress in high contempt. "If you knew anything about dogs, you'd know mad ones never 'chase folks around,' any more than diphtheria patients do. Then—"

A flash of tawny light beneath the station lamp, a scurrying of frightened idlers, a final wasted shot from the policeman's pistol—as Wolf dived headlong through the frightened crowd towards the voice he heard and recognized.

Up to the Mistress and the Master galloped Wolf. He was bleeding, his eyes were bloodshot, his fur was rumpled. He seized the astounded Master's gloved hand lightly between his teeth and sought to pull him across the tracks and towards the lake.

The Master knew dogs. Especially he knew Wolf. And with-

out a word he suffered himself to be led. The Mistress and one
or two inquisitive men followed.

Presently, Wolf loosed his hold on the Master's hand and
ran on ahead, darting back every few moments to make certain
he was followed.

"*Heroism—consists—in—hanging—on — one — minute —
longer,*" the Boy was whispering deliriously to himself for the
hundredth time, as Wolf pattered up to him in triumph, across
the ice, with the human rescuers a scant ten yards behind.

THE HEDONIST DOG

POPI AND HUHUU

BY *Friedebert Tuglas*

I

THIS MORNING THE MASTER woke very early. A little
greenish-gray light entered through the round windowpanes. The room was still dark and the master lit the candle in
the brass candlestick. He put on a red jacket and blue trousers,
violently coughing as he did so. Then he drew on his shoes and
wrapped himself in a dark dressing gown which fell clear down
to the ground. As he fastened his shoes, a severe spell of
coughing overcame him.

He sighed, took out a necklace of red and black beads and
began to pass them between his fingers, his lips gently moving.

From his bed, Popi looked on at his master's movements
with his moist brown eyes. He knew the odor of those beads.
They seemed to be smooth and tender, and did not please Popi
at all. The master's face looked always sad and unwell whenever he rolled the beads.

The master suddenly stopped short and fixedly looked at the
candle flame. His head, white as snow, was bent forward and
his trembling fingers were joined together. The candle wick

continued to burn and then began to smoke, but the master did not notice it.

He had recently become very strange. He had been coming home late at night, would sit down near the light, would break his bread, but forget to eat it, and would only hold the bit of bread in his hand and talk to himself.

At night, Popi had been hearing his master sighing deeply in his sleep. Now he got up and approached his master. He wagged his tail, licked his poor master's hands, and sought to console him in his anxious, canine way. But the master paid no attention. He seemed to be having horrible dreams, like the dreams he, Popi, had when he dreamed of wandering along strange roads full of wild, mad dogs he did not know.

The master sighed again, rose, put on his leather cap with the big button on top, put out the light, and stooped down to pat Popi's back. "No, no, no," he murmured caressingly, slowly stroking the dog's soft head. Popi stretched himself out beneath that kindly hand, again wagged his tail, yawned and put his tongue out, very far indeed.

How good he was, this dear old master when thus sitting before Popi, his dark dressing gown falling in folds upon the floor! Popi could just make out his pale smile in the shadows of the early morning. Now the master rose and went to the corner where Huhuu's big cage was standing. "What does he have to go there for?" thought Popi enviously, as he ran to his master's side, wagging his tail furiously all the time.

But the master didn't give anything to Huhuu, as Popi had feared he would do. He only shook his finger at Huhuu, saying, in a tone of remonstrance, "No, no, come here, you!" Huhuu had just waked. He was very sleepy and seemed to be shivering. He rubbed his shoulders against the cage and held the back of his neck in his hand. As the master shook his finger at him, Huhuu growled with his deep, guttural voice.

Then the master put on his coat. Popi ran in front of him toward the big market basket which was hanging on the wall, but again the master did not notice him. With his head bent forward, he walked toward the door. Outside it was growing lighter. Through the open door one could see a crenelated wall, a slender, narrow tower and the green sky in the background.

The master closed the door in Popi's very face. Popi heard

the master walking slowly through the court, heard the outer door open, and then heard it close. Then all became silent again. For some moments Popi remained just behind the closed door, one ear pricked up, his head perked on one side, to listen. But he heard nothing at all, and left his post by the door. Popi was disappointed. "He isn't bringing any meat today," he thought. "He hasn't brought any for several days. And it would be so easy, too!"

He took several objectless turns about the room. His toenails scratched the smooth floor as he walked over it. His long tail and the tip of his muzzle almost touched the smooth, waxed floor. It was still so dark that his twisted knees collided with the furniture and other things within the room. He could smell the familiar odor of old leather and furniture. Many other things beside recalled to him the amiable memories he had of his master.

It was yet too dark, too cold and too gloomy to stay awake. Popi returned to his bed on the floor and lay down snugly. It was so good to be in bed, to warm himself through and through, to crouch well together and to dream. Now, he thought, the master is going through the streets, among many streets, many houses and many masters. But no house is as good as this one and no master as good as mine. He opened one eye and looked about. Outside it was really getting light. Two rows of dull windowpanes were colored a rosy red. Shadows were visible now on the floor.

"My master is better than any other master in the world," drowsily thought Popi, and closed his open eye. His master's goodness had, clearly, no limit. He might go out with an empty basket, but he always brought it back full of meat. Who would do that except the master?

Popi opened his eye again. The room was still lighter. It was now so light that the crocodile skin, impaled against the ceiling, was distinctly visible. It formed a dark mass above, the feet wide apart and the jaws gaping. Popi knew very well that the animal was dead and tranquilly closed his eyes again. His master was the only one he knew anything about, he reflected. He liked to go on an occasional stroll with his good master. It was great fun to plunge in among the enormous crowds filling the roadways and choking the market places. All these stran-

gers, though, could not be trusted and the master could be sure
of keeping Popi only by never letting him loose from his leash.

How had it happened that he had found so good a master?
Oh, the answer to that was not difficult. It was because he, Popi,
was good himself. He had deserved to have a good master.
Bad street dogs always have bad street masters. What chance
had brought him to this house? He knew nothing of his past.
It seemed to him that he had always existed. His present moments, though, all ended suddenly as if against a blank wall,
and he could hardly remember further back than yesterday.

He had not noticed his own growth at all. He thought, though
he was very doubtful on the point, that his paws had once been
softer and his skin and hair more supple and elastic than they
were now. That must have been at the time when the world
seemed so queer, when he could not tell living things from
inanimate objects, and when he used to wag his tail in front
of the furniture. All that was very far away, inconceivably far
away!

It was so good to reflect and dream! It was almost as good as
living, or, perhaps, even better than living. In dreams, you see,
the master was always good to him and cross to Huhuu, and
there was plenty to eat, more than he could eat.

He woke suddenly because a flea was biting him in the middle of his back. He made an enraged bite at the place. Then he
stretched out and yawned. He had slept for a long time. The
room was now filled with bright golden light. The upper half
of the window, bearing six diamond panes, each one framed
in tin or pewter, was open. It allowed one to hear the chattering
of the sparrows just outside.

Popi took several turns about the room, sniffed at the floor,
tested the air of the room, then went to the door and finally felt
sure that his master had not yet returned. He had been absent
for a long time, indeed. Popi strolled about some more, his
pointed muzzle continuing to sniff at the floor. His feet were not
bearing his head, it was rather his head which was dragging his
feet along, so close to the floor and so far forward did his sharp
nose protrude in front of him. He scratched at the sideboard,
at the base of the wall, at the little recess near the window and
at the bookshelves.

He smelled the same old odors which were new every morn-

ing and always taught him something. It was strange that all
these objects, seeming so much alike, were really so different.
Inside the sideboard he could smell old pewter plates and pots.
In the little recess he could detect the old bagpipe, the brushes,
the bellows and the two big beer mugs of different shape. Near
the books he could make out the odor of leather, of the insects
that ate the leaves of the books, and the smell which he always
knew meant Jews.

The best odors, though, were those of the kitchen. Popi followed his muzzle out to that famous place. His long tail glided
through the open kitchen door as a serpent might slip along.
The kitchen was high and narrow. In the middle there was a
square iron stove with a big stovepipe above, which grew
narrower and narrower as it mounted towards the ceiling. On
the stove there were pots, pans, kettles, flatirons and many
things which stood out like so many dark spots.

Popi raised his muzzle and moved his moist nostrils to and
fro. The kitchen unmistakably smelled of soot. The faint piping
of birds was audible through the chimney and stovepipe. There
were many good-for-nothing odors in this place. They were not
those of food or of anything else a body had any use for. It was
here that the master sometimes melted lead or copper, or cooked
queer porridge which he neither ate himself nor gave to any
one else. There were green jugs, small kegs, platters, pewter
bottles, pitchers and jars, little, long-handled stew-pans, and
iron utensils of all sorts.

Here and there, happily, Popi could get a sniff of delicate
odors of cheese, fat and meat. He smelled them through covers
placed over different pots and vessels. From the kitchen table
he got smells which made his nostrils vibrate violently and
caused his little heart to beat like mad. He could smell out a
mixture of earth, grasses and water. In one corner he recognized
the odor of squashes, of melons, of cabbage, of artichokes, of
carrots and of tomatoes. He found that this odd mixture came
out of a basket full of different vegetables, piled in it pellmell.

Popi had had enough of the kitchen and trotted back to the
other room. He stopped in the middle of it, quite suddenly, as
if something had occurred to him requiring a special effort of
his memory. Huhuu made an abrupt movement and then Popi

remembered what he had almost forgotten. His master was not at home. Huhuu moved about again, and another idea occurred to Popi. Perhaps his master was in the back room, asleep, or sitting silently beside the table. So he hurried into the back room.

In this room the windows were quite different from those of the room in front. They had very wide sashes, which were filled with tiny, many-colored panes set in pewter. The panes were of all sorts of different shapes and sizes. When the sun was shining brightly, the light passing through these little panes and falling upon the floor, the walls and the furniture made beautiful spots of lilac, purple, olive-green and soft crimson everywhere. The spots were shaped like men's heads, sheep, flowers and stars.

Popi had formed the habit of resorting to this room in the evening to get warm. Each particular color supplied a special degree of heat. Popi lifted up his muzzle and looked at the panes with his shining eyes. He found that there was a separate odor for each separate color. In a corner of this room, under a red canopy, from which were suspended heavy fringe and dull golden acorns, was placed the master's bed.

The room was nearly filled and running over with articles of furniture. Every kind of furniture imaginable was heaped together, so that walking about in the room was impossible. There were big wardrobes with mosaic doors, huge leather chairs, old clocks still in excellent order, marking the hours, days and months and showing representations of earth and sky. Old spinets stood against one wall. Music desks and racks, ancient guitars, Hebrew books with iron clasps, steel helmets, swords, glass mirrors, metal looking-glasses, rugs, cushions, and costumes in gold and purple, helped to complete the hodge-podge within the room.

From the ceiling, hung the model of a boat, covered with gilding and bearing carven figures of men, sitting in two rows on the deck. On the poop another man, in a red fez, was standing erect and pointing to the distant horizon. In the middle of the deck, among the other men grouped there, was a king, sitting on his throne, wearing a crown on his head and holding an apple and scepter in his hand. Popi often looked attentively at this model, with lifted muzzle and body crouched close against the floor. The model seemed to be a real thing. There was something extraordinarily lifelike about it.

However, many of the things in this room were extremely deceiving. As a matter of fact, it contained mostly visions, dreams and fancies. Here there were masters who were not masters at all. Elsewhere there were dogs, horses, and birds which did not really exist. The food in the room never made anyone hungry. This food was as unsatisfying and unreal as the food Popi dreamed about. It was painted on panels and canvases enclosed in frames which were slowly dropping to pieces. Some of the pictures represented odd corners full of skinned animals, entrails, lungs, tongues, heads and hides. Others showed tables bearing lambs, geese, swans, turkeys, trout, herrings, eels and shrimps. Still other paintings represented cornucopias full of tomatoes, parsley, onions, asparagus, artichokes, pumpkins and cabbages. Vines and grapes fauns with cloven feet and wearing clumsy sandals, and nymphs running away somewhere also shone out from some of the canvases.

A large tapestry represented a hunting scene. Young men with mandolins were looking at young girls holding doves, and in the air were peacocks and parrots. One picture showed churches, windmills and wood-sawyers. A dense forest lay close to a frozen marsh covered with a scanty fall of snow.

Each phantom was in its own place, all the masters with dreamy faces were smiling from the walls, everything suggested reality, but the real master was not there. Popi approached the bed. He sniffed at his master's dressing gown and his nightcap, and wagged his tail. These things recalled his master to him so vividly that, when he closed his eyes, the familiar smells almost made his master visible. However, it was all only illusory and deceptive, and Popi went sadly back to the front room.

Here the sun was shining through windowpanes shaped like the necks of bottles. A golden dust was floating about Huhuu's cage. The room was perfectly still. The sparrows were no longer chattering. Popi felt very uneasy all of a sudden. He began to hurry hither and thither in the room, never stopping, uttering plaintive cries, as if he were a lost and deserted child. Why didn't his master come back? He asked himself this question over and over. Where was he staying all this time? He had never been gone so long before. Where was he? Where was he? Popi sat down on his flat little bed, folded his tail about his legs, listened, listened, whined in a very low tone and his back bristled up and his skin shook all over as if he were shivering with cold.

II

Time passed, and still the master did not return. Noon was gone already. Still the master did not come. The sun marched over to the other side of the room. Its rays now touched the windows only obliquely and left them dark. Still, still the master did not come.

Huhuu began to move about uneasily in his cage. He seemed to be suffering from hunger. He gnawed the bars of the cage, stuck his paw out between them clear to the elbow, picked up a few stray leaves of lettuce from the floor of the cage and greedily put them in his mouth. The way he held himself crouched together was very, very strange. His face was close to the bars of the cage and his two thin paws were held out like those of an old woman holding a skein of yarn to be rolled into a ball.

Popi, his head well bent over, turned his shining eyes on this companion of his. His eyes wandered to those paws of Huhuu. Who was Huhuu, anyway? He had asked himself this question before. He had no doubts about himself. He was always surely himself. And he knew the master, too. He knew other dogs and masters, who were strangers. But who was this Huhuu, sitting there holding a lettuce leaf? Those fingers were thin, soft and black as coal. They made Huhuu look as if he were wearing specially fine gloves. His entire body was covered with grayish-brown hair. The skin at the back of his neck was stiff, and Huhuu often held his paw there as if he had a headache.

His face was also covered with hair, and to such a degree that it was impossible to tell whether he was gay or sad. His thoughts could never be read at all. He sometimes looked straight in front of him for hours, his gaze never ceasing to be fixed and unwavering. His temper was evidently very bad, otherwise he would not always be shut up in his cage. He was never taken out-of-doors and probably knew nothing at all of the streets, marketplaces or of any other master. Popi found, on the whole, that he deserved no more than he got. He was kept in his cage quite justly. Even his food was much worse than the food Popi received. They gave him nothing but green vegetables, fruit, and other inedible things.

It was odd, though, how much Huhuu resembled the master. Like the master, he walked erect or nearly so, and had hands and fingers. Who was he? A second master, perhaps? Could he be a malicious, sly and evil master who had to be always kept in confinement?

Hunger was now really tormenting Popi. He stirred himself, went to his porcelain bowl and took a bone from it. There was no longer any meat on the bone, but Popi could gnaw it, at any rate, and help to pass the time away. So he gnawed away for some moments, crouched flat on the floor, holding his bone between his forepaws. All the satisfaction he got, though, was a mouth full of water, so he left his bone on the floor, raised his muzzle, and looked at the window. Anguish, and a vague and terrible presentiment oppressed his heart.

Suddenly the sun disappeared behind a cloud. The room became yellow and then ashen gray. The wind whistled loudly in the chimney several times, and two or three large raindrops struck against the windowpanes. Popi uttered loud and plaintive barks, raising his forepaws one after the other, bending them and relaxing them as if he had chilled them by sitting for a long time on ice. This horrible cold silence lasted for some moments. Only Popi's gentle whining was heard in the room.

Huhuu had seated himself and was listening. Then, suddenly, he stood up straight, strutted across his cage, then jumped up and down on his four elbows, stopped, listened again and burst out into a sinister laugh, jumping about until his bones fairly clattered together. Popi was much frightened at this, and contracted his big, drooping ears close to his head. How very disquieting all this was! How very disquieting! Where could the master be?

Huhuu began to run about his cage, grasping now one bar of the cage, now another, and shaking them violently. A few yellowish, feathery clouds were passing across the sunlight and the light within the room was continually changing. All that

Popi could see in this ashen sort of twilight was the odd way in which Huhuu's dark shadow was projected here and there.

The doorframe of Huhuu's cage suddenly snapped and gave way. Huhuu remained within the cage for a moment. The wind was roaring at the windows. Then Huhuu gave his door a push, and it opened. Huhuu was frightened. He had not expected such a thing and did not know what to do. He approached the open door and sat down at the threshold, waiting very prudently until he could well reflect, holding firmly to the frame of the doorway.

From his bed on the floor Popi, frightened at all this, looked up at Huhuu. He was half sitting up, his hind legs drawn well up in front and his skin was very taut. Huhuu's astonishment remained only a moment. He slipped his chest forward, pressed his chin down on his chest, turned up his tail and, still sitting on his haunches, dragged himself towards Popi by two little steps. Then he suddenly strutted up again, coughed and jumped.

Popi disappeared under the sideboard like a tennis ball, howling as he went. He had to lie down, for the sideboard was low, and close to the floor. His heart was beating so hard that his nails clicked against the floor, although he was holding himself perfectly still. All was silent for some moments. Then he saw and heard Huhuu walking about on his soft paws, heard him stop, and then all was silent again. Popi carefully slid up to the edge of the sideboard, to see what was going on. Evening was falling outside, and twilight was creeping into the room.

In the middle of the shadowy expanse was crouched Huhuu, gnawing a lettuce leaf, which he held in his hands. It did not take him long to swallow the lettuce leaf. Then, looking about him, he discovered the great purple rug hanging above the door of the back room. He approached the rug, pulled its fringe and drew it toward him. The rug fell down and covered Huhuu up in it. He was frightened, groped about within the rug for a while, finally dragged himself out and crept away, glancing back with distrust at the rug as he fled from it.

He began a search for food. On the table he found a few beans, and ate them. Then he went to the threshold of the kitchen door, and was soon investigating the basket of vegetables. Popi heard him gnawing at the carrots. Then Huhuu seemed to have another idea. He seized the basket by the handle and dragged it into the other room, where he spilled its contents out on the floor. Pumpkins, melons and tomatoes rolled pellmell everywhere.

Huhuu sat down in the midst of it all and ate away, first attacking the apples and then trying the cabbages. Popi was only a few paces away, his chin pressed down on the chilly floor and his two forepaws placed beside his chin. His frightened thoughts were much upset and confused. He stared hard at Huhuu with his violet eyes and the skin at the back of his neck bristled up rigidly.

Huhuu soon ceased to eat and began to roll a large pumpkin across the floor. The room, growing darker in the twilight, was quite silent except for the noise made by the rolling pumpkin, and the pattering of Huhuu's paws. The pumpkin rolled under the table and Huhuu lost it in the darkness. He stopped. The room was becoming very dark, and he seemed afraid.

Through the rosy panes of the window of the back room the setting sun was now throwing only a few feeble gleams. This room was lighted best at evening. From it a beam of pale, faint rays entered the front room through the open doorway. Huhuu stood on the threshold of the back room, waiting cautiously. Then he made a few steps within it, and Popi saw his thin, hairless tail disappearing beyond the doorsill. The rustling of garments could be heard, then Huhuu laughed aloud several times, and then everything was quiet.

Popi waited for a long time, his heart beating hard with fear. However, everything remained perfectly calm. So he gently came out from under the sideboard and slowly approached the entrance of the back room. Through the parti-colored window a narrow beam of dark red and deep violet light was entering the room. Huhuu was sitting on the master's bed beneath the red canopy. He had wrapped himself up in the master's dressing gown, had put the nightcap on his head, had pulled up the collar of the gown about his ears, and was fast asleep.

Popi remained motionless for some moments, lifting his muzzle toward the bed, and looking at Huhuu intently. Then he glided back beneath the sideboard, seeking the remotest corner he could find. Everything was whirling about within his little brain. Some frightful dream, some ghostly fancy, was revolving before him. He crouched as flat as he could below the sideboard, trembling with dread.

What had happened? He did not know at all. Something very unusual, very disquieting and very incomprehensible was surely occurring. How and why had it come about? Popi sought to recall the different events. The master had gone out. He had sat down to wait for the master. The sun had set, the wind had risen, the room had become yellow, and Huhuu had escaped from his cage. Had all this really occurred? What had happened later in the yellow twilight? Who had pulled the purple rug down on the floor? Where was Huhuu? Was it Huhuu who was sitting under the red canopy in a yellow gown and red cap?

Now it was quite dark, in the room and outside as well. The wind was blowing about the doors and windows. The rain was beginning to crackle, first slowly, then falling harder and harder for hours. Where was the master now? thought Popi. Where had he gone? When would he come back?

All night long Popi kept his vigil by the icy wall, trembling with fear and cold. He listened to the mournful beating of the rain and waited, waited for his master. But still the master did not come. He would never come.

Toward morning, Popi dropped asleep for a little while. He dreamed that it was evening and that he was with the master in the street outside the house. The sky was covered with ashen-gray clouds. The dark streets grew darker and darker as they stretched away in the distance. Popi did not know where they had come from. They had been wandering for a long time. After the street came the marketplace, after the market there was another street, but they seemed never to arrive at the house. Popi was trembling with fatigue, wavered from one twisted leg to another, and tottered about in these endless muddy streets. It was indeed very strange to see everything so gray and deserted.

The master was walking ahead, his head forward and his back bent. He seemed very tired as he led Popi onward with the leash. He did not stop or look behind him. How much smaller and thinner the master was! His black coat was dragging along the ground and his head could not be seen at all under his leather cap.

Popi was becoming more and more weary with this long walk. He dragged his tired feet behind his master. The leash was now stretched taut as he pulled upon it and his master's hand was drawn far behind. The master continued to walk along without stopping or looking behind. In the twilight, Popi looked at his master's hand. It was small and hairy. The fingers were black as coal and their nails were very long. Popi suddenly felt a strange uneasiness. Where had they come from? Where were they going to? Who was it at the other end of the leash? Was it the master?

In the midst of the gray and forsaken street a nameless fear tugged suddenly at Popi's heart. His whole body was trembling, and he could walk on no longer. That man who was leading him kept pulling him along without stopping or looking behind. They advanced a few steps more. Popi's strength was now rapidly failing him. He was dragging more and more at his leash. His collar was compressing his throat. The skin on his forehead was so wrinkled up that he could hardly keep his eyes open.

With a sudden access of terror, he realized that the man ahead was not the master. He stiffened his paws against the pavement and clung to the cold stones with clicking nails. The leash was almost pulling his head off.

The man ahead now turned for the first time to look behind. Popi saw his face. With a plaintive cry, he leaped from under the sideboard into the middle of the room, trembling in every nerve. At the very same instant, he saw the master standing at the threshold of the room, his hand upon the doorknob, dressed in his everyday clothes, his nightcap on his head.

Popi looked hard at him for a few brief moments, completely bewildered by this sudden quick moment of happiness. But suddenly the hair bristled up stiffly on his neck and infinite anguish came into his eyes. The face he saw was the one he had seen when the man turned round in his dream!

Their life together began from that day. The reality was more fantastic than Popi's dream, and was a dream more terrible than reality. Popi could not tell where the boundaries of his life ended and where those of the dream began. He could no longer separate the two and lived from day to day, trembling between the two extremes of his existence. When he awoke in the morning, saw the sun shining into the room, and felt new strength within him, he still hoped to escape this ghostly existence.

The old master will come back to the house, he thought. He will subdue Huhuu, put him back in the cage, and the happy life of old will begin again. This hope was vain. He soon heard the sharp cry made by Huhuu, coming from another room, and then Huhuu himself appeared at the threshold. He wore a new costume every day. He opened the wardrobes, rummaged about in the sideboards and put on any clothes which pleased him. He strutted for hours before the mirror, like a child at play. Placing three mirrors in a corner, he examined himself now from before, now from behind.

He poured hair oil over his back and rubbed his face like a woman applying cosmetics. Then he turned his back toward the mirror and squinted his eyes around to see the back of his neck. He was as gay and happy as a child. At such times he was good-natured, and Popi could scent, without danger, the remains of food left upon the floor. Huhuu would not incommode himself for anything.

He had a strange taste in selecting clothing. He sometimes put on three coats, one over the other. Sometimes he put the overcoat on first, and the shirt outside. Sometimes he put on nothing whatever except a hat upon his head and a lace collar around his neck. Sometimes he appeared in a black velvet coat with wide sleeves, striped collar, big shiny buttons and a dagger at the waist.

Again, he was clad like a comedian in a dark red coat, beneath which a fat belly was protruding, on his head a bright red, three-cornered hat, the three tips ringing like little bells. He might appear dressed like the king of the little model of the boat, in a purple mantle trimmed with fur, and provided with a long train and a heavy chain about the neck. And lastly, he sometimes showed himself abruptly, seeming like a corpse brought to life in a yellow linen tunic, with a black cross upon his breast and a hood pulled down over his forehead.

All these costumes were worn without the slightest care or pains. He tore them fiercely, snatched them from his body in an hour, and left them lying forgotten on the floor. He was continually discovering things which interested him. He was always eating. He opened the closets in the kitchen and took out all the food within his reach. He gnawed the biscuits. Scraps which remained he threw on the floor. It was these scraps which formed Popi's food during those dark, gloomy nights when he ventured outside his corner, slipping furtively along by the wall. Huhuu liked vegetables best. He stuffed his mouth with loose tobacco and all sorts of spices. He liked those things. The saliva dripped plentifully from his mouth and he spat about him like a sailor.

He passed his days in play. He gathered together bright balls, pretty things, knives, forks and spoons, and placed them all on the purple rug. He rolled the whole collection for hours between his fingers, as a child plays with pebbles. From time to time he tried working at the table. But he had not the perseverance of the old master. He broke the spectacle lenses to pieces, smashed the base of the terrestrial globe, and tore the books to bits.

He would sit down on the floor to unroll a lot of parchments, but instead of examining them with his eyes he would try them with his teeth. Then he would throw the roll of parchments away as a thing of no value. He broke the great wall clock to bits. He smashed the hands and tore out all the mechanism. Shading his eyes with his hand, he carefully examined all the little wheels and the rest of the movement. He destroyed everything he touched. He injured the pictures, the windows and the mirrors. He took away from the walls, and removed from the drawers, everything which he could reach. He left nothing untouched.

He seemed to be just like the old master and yet quite different. He might easily have been good and kind, but he did not wish to be. He was simply malicious and ill-tempered. He was most terrible at evening, after the fatigue of the day. He then delighted in tormenting Popi, and his malice was unbounded. He chased poor Popi across the room, threw kitchen utensils at him and pricked him with skewers when he fled under the furniture. He hit him on the head with a stick, threw liquids all over him and pierced his ears. All Popi now did was to whine and cry with fear and pain. Sometimes he tried to resist. From beneath the sideboard he snapped his teeth fiercely, yapped loudly, and growled at the skewer with which Huhuu was pricking him. All his efforts and resistance were vain. His sole refuge was the sideboard. The sideboard was so low that his legs became more and more twisted from his visits to its shelter. Since he often had to flee very quickly under it, the skin on his neck and back became torn and finally very sore. The food that he had was utterly insufficient, and he suffered all day long from agonizing thirst.

His restless sleep was filled with dire fancies and his dreams only restored the reality. His brain was darkening. His memory became feebler and feebler, and he could no longer distinguish between the past and his dreams. Every connection with former times was lost. Now he retained only a faint memory of his happy past life, his good master and the remote and vanished golden age through which he had lived. His memories were like phantoms. They were only dreams and floating images.

How long ago was it that he had seen the old master? An infinite period had passed since the master had gone away. Was it today, yesterday, or months or years ago that he had departed? More and more did he forget the face and voice of the good old master, as they disappeared in the mists on the far horizon.

In dreams, though, he could see him more clearly. There he could make out his snowy, white hair and his gentle smile. At such times he would wake up, thinking that his master had called him. When he was awake, though, only the reality was about him. All that existed were the malicious master and the devastated room.

From time to time, he had the expectation that somebody would come. He did not know whether it would be the master or somebody else. Sometimes he heard voices penetrating the walls. Sometimes he perceived the sound of heavy shoes, outside in the street, but nobody came.

He became satisfied with the new master. He became habituated to fear and respect. He was old, sick and foolish and the present master would do very well. He knew fully that it was Huhuu. He could have identified him by his odor, had other signs been lacking. He was losing his faith in odors, though, as he had lost it concerning other things. His sense of smell was getting weak and he was no longer sure about odors. Everything was deceiving him, even odors!

His two masters became confused in his mind. They melted into a single individual. Each formed only a half of the whole person. As he had once admired the goodness, kindness and beauty of his old master, he now admired the malice, capricious humor and ugliness of his new one. The new master was almost the exact opposite of the old one in everything, though he possessed a hidden intelligence and ability which Popi did not have.

The old master used to enter and leave by the door. The new master did so by the window. He would leap upon the table, climb to the window and disappear. While Popi was waiting for him to come back he would stay in the middle of the room, astonished. Huhuu sometimes remained away for hours. Popi had no idea what he was doing. The absence of the new master, though, seemed just as mysterious and important as the absences of the old one had seemed. Sometimes Huhuu dragged outside the house garments, books and cushions, bringing back in their place sticks, empty bottles and tiles. He filled the cupboards with straw and poured water from a jug into the interior of the room from the window.

His conception of the values of things seemed peculiar. He completely altered all the odors within the house. Sometimes he was absent for a long time and everything indoors was quiet. Then Popi would be wearied and wait for Huhuu impatiently. He would become uneasy, run from one room to another, and utter plaintive cries, as he had used to do for the old master. He wanted Huhuu to come back. He was willing to have Huhuu beat him all he wanted to, if only he would not leave him forsaken.

The most curious thing of all was that the new master seemed to take a certain care of Popi. He did this after his rough and capricious style, but Popi appreciated it, nevertheless. One day, in particular, he brought some meat back with him. He had remained absent for a long time, and had with him a market basket when he finally returned. Inside the basket were vegetables, bread and a little raw meat hidden below the other things.

Huhuu shook out the basket on the floor, became frightened when he saw the blood of the raw meat, and ran away. Popi seized the meat, ran under the sideboard with it and was able to chew it for several days. After that day, when Huhuu had brought the meat, Popi thought much more of Huhuu and now understood that he was really the master.

The master climbed up again on the wall. But this time he came back very soon, and all the dogs in the streets seemed barking outside. The master's clothes were in rags. His skin was torn and bleeding and his paws left a trail of blood wherever they were placed. He crouched in a corner, licked his wounds and murmured low complaints. He was ill for a long time.

Popi then realized how close he was to Huhuu. He went to him every night and morning, as he had done formerly to his old master, to show his sorrow and pity. The smooth, grayish-blue eyelids of the master were closed, but he was breathing so softly that his sleep seemed light and restless. His face wore an expression of the deepest gravity and his heavy jowls were singularly sad. Popi was seized with pity and sympathy. He took care of Huhuu as an old servant takes care of his master when that master has become old and childish. How old and awkward they both were! Their lives were becoming sadder and sadder. The days were shorter and there was but little sunlight. A cold rain fell, from morning to night.

Popi shivered as he lay upon his bed. Huhuu wrapped himself up in blankets. He was now clumsy and stiff in his play, trembled when he sat down, and looked before him without the least interest. One day he found a little keg in the kitchen and rolled it into the other room. He put his ear against the keg and heard gurgling as the keg rolled hither and thither. He smelled of the bung, which emitted a marvelous fragrance. It was at once heavy, mild, toothsome and bewildering. He removed the stopper and poured out some of the liquid from the keg.

From that time, Huhuu began to drink. The only joy and interest he now possessed was to drink and become drunk. When he woke in the morning, his head was heavy with the wine, his hair rough and bristling, his eyes red and weak. He would lift the keg to the level of his mouth, swallowing eagerly until he felt himself becoming good-natured. Then he would mutter and dance about, leaping and staggering until he was weary. Then he would sit down on the floor, lift the keg to his lips again and drink, the wine streaming from his mouth along his cheeks.

When he was drunk, he would go to sleep, holding the keg close to him in a fond embrace, his hands resting on the keg and his face twisted in a smile. Popi liked him this way. He reminded Popi of that other master, who used to sit down much in the same way in the evening, holding his glass up to the light and smiling as he talked to himself with a satisfied air. Popi no longer feared Huhuu. They slept together and helped keep each other warm.

The drunken Huhuu would grope for Popi's head, and Popi would lick Huhuu's hand. Both became intoxicated, Huhuu by drinking and Popi by smelling the odor of the wine which filled the room. Neither any longer remembered anything. When the keg was empty, Huhuu found another one. He developed a marvelous capacity for finding kegs. He scented out the wine, whose odor was sharpened by his imagination. He became able to open bottles and drink from them.

One day the snow began to fall. It alighted, thick as down. A pale glow was reflected from the ceiling, and the colors within the room changed their hues. Through the broken window the snow and the cold entered the room, and a light wind scattered snowflakes over the overturned furniture. The two old drunkards raised their heads and found everything covered with a white coating.

But there was no more wine. Huhuu had begun to drink as soon as he woke, but the wine lasted only a moment. He staggered into the kitchen to look for more. He groped about for a long time, but his search was vain. He rummaged about, turning the furniture over and over and throwing the room into a terrible confusion. Finally, beneath some of the overturned pitchers and pots into which the old master had formerly poured that queer porridge of his, Huhuu found something which surely might contain wine. It was a tin box, square in shape, and soldered along all its edges. Huhuu thought he could smell wine inside the box, and brought it back with him into the other room.

Huhuu was then wearing a red, quilted jacket. Popi sat down in front of him, his muzzle raised, and his long tail resting on the floor. Huhuu tried to open the box. He scratched it with his nails and tried it with his teeth. Then he raised the box high in the air and threw it down as hard as he could.

A terrible explosion followed. The flames mounted to the ceiling. Huhuu was thrown against one wall, Popi against another. The house collapsed with a mighty roar.

THE ETERNAL DOG

THE CURATE THINKS YOU HAVE NO SOUL

BY *St. John Lucas*

The curate thinks you have no soul;
 I know that he has none. But you,
Dear friend, whose solemn self-control,
 In our foursquare familiar pew,
Was pattern to my youth—whose bark
 Called me in summer dawns to rove—

Have you gone down into the dark
    Where none is welcome—none may love?
I will not think those good brown eyes
    Have spent their life of truth so soon;
But in some canine paradise
    Your wraith, I know, rebukes the moon,
And quarters every plain and hill,
    Seeking his master . . . As for me,
This prayer at least the gods fulfill:
    That when I pass the flood and see
Old Charon by the Stygian coast
    Take toll of all the shades who land,
Your little, faithful, barking ghost
    May leap to lick my phantom hand.

THE PATERNAL DOG

THE DEACON'S GRANDPA

BY *Havilah Babcock*

L AST THANKSGIVING I got a telegram from a young gradu-
ate student at the University of Virginia. He was not tele-
graphing me that he had been elected to Phi Beta Kappa or had
married a millionaire's daughter. The cryptic message read:
YOUNG MIKE POINTED HIS FIRST COVEY TODAY.

CONGRATULATIONS, I wired back. BRING HIM DOWN WHEN
YOU COME CHRISTMAS. Throughout the fall that young fellow
had been writing me about a starry-eyed pup he had kept alive
with a medicine dropper after its mother died. That's the way
it is with men who like to train puppies.

There are certain events which enshrine themselves in a
man's memory. As Virgil said two thousand years ago, and as
you and I declaimed with great fervor when the world was
young: "Perhaps it will delight you to remember these things
in days to come."

Maybe it is the ineffable sweetness of that first romance that your memory enshrines, maybe that first touchdown, or the opulence of that first paycheck. But if you had the good fortune to be brought up in the country—and it ought to be against the law to bring up a boy in the city—peradventure it was the first point your puppy made. There he stood alone and tremulous, but shining and resplendent, while you, excited and thumb-fingered, besought the Giver of All Gifts for one precious boon: that you might drop the neophyte's first bird for him.

In this Age of Surpluses, when too much seems to cause more trouble than too little, there is one acute shortage: well-trained bird dogs, hunters which my friend Mr. Whipple would call *"de bonus"* good. Mr. Whipple ought to know. He is still hunting birds at eighty-four, an age when most men have long since presented their credentials at the Pearly Gates. Or elsewhere.

He is about the spryest old fossil you can imagine, his little 28-gauge embarrassing me more than once last season. I often tell him that he will live to be 110 and be hanged for poaching. Two of Mr. Whipple's traits I have often noted: he invariably grins when he misses a bird, and he is always doing what he calls "projeckin' with a puppy."

"Why are good dogs so scarce, Mr. Whipple?" I asked him.

"Because everybody thinks his time is too valuable to train them. They ought to call this the Age of Impatience. Everybody talks about saving time, saving time. More people get killed trying to save time than any other way. And what do they do with all the time they save? Answer me that! Time is not something to be saved. It's something to be spent. That's what it was made for. Now when a man is projeckin' with a puppy . . ."

Like Mr. Whipple, I am always projeckin' with a puppy or two. Whether I need another dog or not, the advent of fall usually finds me bragging about a scion of something or other I have managed to acquire. Why I like to train puppies I don't know. Maybe it's just another defect in my character. Maybe it's because a puppy distracts me from the harassments which beset us all in this wondrous age. Maybe having a pup along keeps the day from being too perfect. Certainly no man can follow a rollicking, bungling, and overjoyous pup all day without laughing a lot and crying a little.

I am indulgent toward his mistakes because I have made so

many myself—and I hope I shall live to make a few more. I like to be around when a puppy discovers himself, when that compelling and imperious thing we call instinct smacks him between the eyes and he stands in trembling grandeur on his first point. No man can witness this tremendous little drama and feel old. If you want to stay young, if you bandy-legged old bird hunters would prolong your days on this pleasant planet, take a puppy hunting with you.

I like to think that experience has made me fairly proficient at puppy training. At least I have succeeded in some cases where others despaired. But from the outset Deacon, an eight-month-old pointer pup, was something of a problem child. After three weeks of almost daily hunting he persisted in one ruinous quirk of character, and it was not until mid-season that he finally achieved the summit of fool's hill. Then it was Mark Twain who gave me the idea.

Deacon's quirk was a disconcerting one. Possessed of a talented nose and a great zest for hunting, he was also an instant and joyous retriever. And when he found birds himself he was as stanch as you please. But when Preacher, his grandfather, found them first, Deacon unfailingly sprinted up and pounced on the covey with great gusto. This was altogether contrary to what my experience with Preacher had led me to expect.

Preacher was a tremendous rawboned pointer who had attained the circumspect age of nine. He was lemon and white in color, a combination I have always fancied. Wise in the ways of bobwhite and his ilk, he traversed the spacious flatwoods with the distance-consuming lope of an unhurried deer. And when he said yes, he didn't mean maybe.

Preacher was quiet-mannered and gentlemanly in his habits and of such a benevolent and patriarchal visage that people often commented on the aptness of his name. I have always liked to have a dependable older dog to help me in puppy-training, and for several seasons Preacher had been my competent assistant. It was a role he relished, and neighbors often borrowed him to lend a hand with their youngsters, whimsically dubbing him "the Professor." He kept a canny eye on any protégé entrusted to his care—and was not above taking a perverse youngster to task by roughing him up.

But in helping me with Deacon, Preacher proved a complete

washout for the first three weeks. Deacon was Preacher's grandson, and his very spit and image. A thoroughly spoiled and
impish grandson he was, continually tormenting old Preacher
and subjecting him to every thinkable indignity. He would nip
the old gentleman's tail, yank his ears, and badger him un-
ceasingly.

The scoundrelly Deacon spent half his time inventing new
tricks to play on his long-suffering grandpa. And Preacher, who
had never in his life taken "sass" from another dog, was
strangely indulgent toward his grandson. In fact, he seemed
to think that whatever the little rapscallion did was awfully
cute.

It was soon apparent that Preacher intended to humor the
brat in the field too. After sprinting up and catapulting himself
atop Preacher's birds, Deacon would caper and prance around,
yank Preacher's ear, and gleefully yip: "How'd you like that,
Grandpa? Wasn't that something now!"

And Preacher would wag his head and simper like an infatuated imbecile. Ordinarily he would have slit the throat of
any interloper who persisted in tampering with his birds. This
shameless exhibition happened not once but half a dozen times
a day—whenever Preacher found birds and the alert Deacon
spied him on point.

"Preacher, you backsliding old son of a gun, you unregen-
erate son of Belial!" I told him. "What in the devil has come
over you? I've never seen anybody's character deteriorate as
fast as yours. Time and again you've let that little show-off bust
your birds without lifting a finger to stop him. Have you no
sense of honor, no self-respect? Think of your reputation. Think
of your good name in the community. Think of——"

But I was wasting words. The old reprobate was clearly un-
impressed by the threatened loss of social standing or my ideas
regarding his morality. And as for public opinion, he didn't
care a nickel about that. Stalking away, he pretended to be
greatly concerned about the doings of a stink sparrow that had
flitted athwart his ken.

"All right, Preacher, if you won't help me discipline that
pampered brat, I'll do it myself. Let him bust your birds one
more time—just one more—and I'll tan his britches for him.
And when I tan somebody's britches——"

And I did, with a leaf-stripped aspen switch, for which every country-raised boy has a profound respect. There are few things that can bring such instant remorse to a penitent soul as a well-chosen aspen switch. But it caused the irrepressible Deacon to make only one minor adjustment in his behavior. When he flushed thereafter, he not only declined my invitation to come for another conference but adroitly maneuvered to keep his grandpa between him and the avenging aspen. He would even take refuge under Preacher himself, who was not above shielding the renegade, to such low estate had he fallen.

After three weeks of this tragicomedy I was baffled and discouraged. Deacon, for whom I had such high hopes before the season opened, had proved an ignominious flop. My pearl of great price had become a pain in the neck, mainly because thus far I had found no way of reaching him. And he might have wound up on the dump heap of half-trained self-hunters, abhorred and abjured by all self-respecting gunners, but for the timely intervention of Mark Twain.

One wakeful night I picked up a book at random. I would follow Alice's suggestion and read myself to sleep, forgetting about the antics of Preacher and Deacon. The book was *The Prince and the Pauper*, and half an hour later I chanced upon a passage that was nothing less than an inspiration. In my excitement I woke up Alice and told her about it. "If you don't mind," she informed me grumpily, "I wish you and your literary friends would quit waking me up in the middle of the night."

The passage described how Tom Canty, a street urchin, while temporarily subbing for the royal Prince, learned the function of the Whipping Boy attached to his court. Whenever the Prince faulted in his Greek lessons or committed other royal peccadilloes, the Whipping Boy was thrashed in his stead, the person of the Prince being inviolate.

I chuckled in unholy glee over the application I intended to make of this brilliant idea. I would use Preacher as my Whipping Boy, lambasting *him* every time Deacon busted his birds, and keep it up until—well, we would see what we would see.

The next morning when Deacon barged in on Preacher's birds, I ignored the puppy and gave Preacher himself a lusty trouncing. I used a branch of dried oak leaves, and it was more sound than fury, but Preacher considered himself whipped. His reaction was one of puzzlement. Surely I didn't think—didn't imagine for one moment—that *he* had busted those birds! Obviously it was just a mistake on my part. He pondered the matter for a while, generously conceded everybody the right to make one mistake, and resumed his hunting.

An hour later Deacon jumped his grandpa's birds again, and Preacher got another shellacking. This time he was not only puzzled but indignant, the picture of injured innocence. Did I mean to stand there and tell him that *I didn't know who it was that flushed those birds?* Did I mean to stand there and tell him . . . But after a while he quit trying to unscrew the inscrutable and was ready to go again.

"Preacher," I said, "I wish I could explain things to you. If you will excuse my using a seven-dollar word, the punishment you are getting is vicarious. I admit it's not very ethical, but I don't know what else to do. Honestly, it hurts me more than it hurts you."

But his stand-offish demeanor showed that he wasn't falling for that line, and I can't say I blamed him.

Four times that morning I lambasted Preacher with great ardor, keeping up a verbal bombardment that resounded through the flatlands, and by noon he was becoming irritable and morose. When at lunchtime Deacon gave his tail a tentative nip, Preacher didn't think it was funny and told him so. Good, I said. The old boy is beginning to figure out who's getting him into hot water, and he's not happy about it. If I can just make him mad enough . . .

During the afternoon Preacher got three other brushing-downs, and by nightfall I had cause to hope that my system of pedagogy was working. On the last point, as Deacon bunched himself to spring forward, there issued from Preacher a deep-throated warning. It was a soft, half-pleading disapprobation, a grandfatherly shake of the head, which of course Mister Know-It-All disregarded. But it had made him hesitate a moment, hesitate, and glance curiously about him before jumping. We had at least raised a question in his mind, and that was something.

Back in the kennel that night, Preacher ate alone and in dour silence, rejecting Deacon's advances. When Deacon persisted in his horseplay, an ominous growl warned him away. The old boy was nursing his wrath to keep it warm.

"Deacon," I said the next morning, "something tells me there's going to be a man-sized earthquake in these parts soon, and you're going to be slapdash in the middle of it. If I were you, I'd sure be on my P's and Q's this day!"

But the blithesome brat swaggered off as usual, having fully persuaded himself that the world was his oyster. "That cocky little idiot is sure riding for a fall!" I said, as I saw old Preacher lift his big muzzle and sniff the wind. But it was Deacon rather than Preacher who discovered gold first. Sweeping around a ragged peafield, he almost slid into a stylish point, with flags flying. And there he stood, a lemon-and-white statuette, awaiting my pleasure. From the beginning I had loved the dash and derring-do of that little scapegrace. If I could just teach him to honor a point . . .

"Deacon," I grinned, "half the time I want to put a load of birdshot into that precious fundament of yours, the other half I want to hug you. Right now I want to hug you." And I did. But half an hour and two hundred yards later I fell out of love with him fast. There was Preacher standing in his pulpit and Deacon sprinting joyously toward him to break up the meeting.

But as he came abreast, there issued from Preacher a deep-throated and cavernous growl. Deacon glanced around in slight puzzlement but saw no reason for reconsidering matters. The cavernous growl became a snarling crescendo, and the puissant Deacon bethought himself a second time.

For a moment it looked as if discretion would have the better part of valor. But at this critical juncture in history either the doctrine of original sin prevailed or it occurred to a pampered grandson that grandfatherly precepts may be taken lightly. I know not which. But certain it was that Deacon, after a quick survey of the pros and cons, launched himself forward with at least a stout fraction of his customary verve.

This time I hardly had the heart to go through with my Whipping-Boy program, and I made only a bluff of trouncing old Preacher. He took his medicine without complaint, skipping his usual references to the injustice of mankind. There was about him a grim and preoccupied air I had not detected before. "Go ahead," he seemed to say. "Lay it on. Right now I've got my mind on a piece of business that needs looking after bad."

A segment of the covey which Deacon exploded had circled back and pocketed down a hundred and fifty yards away. It comported with my immediate purpose for Preacher to find it first. He did and hoisted the flag of sovereignty. Up bounded Deacon, the blithesome bushwhacker. And that suited me too.

"Deacon," I said, "if I'm worth two cents as a sign-reader, here's where old Preacher is going to jump down your throat and ball the jack on your chitterlin's. As for me, I'm going to prop my gun against a sapling and get myself a reserved seat atop that stump. This is one show I don't mean to miss."

Preacher was strangely silent as the impetuous bouncer raced up. Not a sound of protest issued from him even as Deacon reached his flank, but he was narrowly eying the renegade and biding his time. Emboldened by this seeming acquiescence, Deacon marshaled his forces for his assault on the citadel.

It was at this precise and strategic second, when the redoubtable Deacon was partly airborne, that Preacher hit him a whopping broadside. Events of the next few seconds were somewhat confused. Under the impact, Deacon went hurtling through the air with the greatest of ease, executing a few involuntary somersaults in the progress of his journey.

When the fracas subsided, he was some fifteen feet from his point of origin. Flat on his back in a brier patch he lay, and Preacher was astraddle the prostrate foe and engaged in a very earnest and grandfatherly conversation. I noted that his tremendous jaws half encircled Deacon's throat, and Deacon was listening with great intentness.

Preacher continued his discourse as long as he thought necessary, tentatively released his hold, and slaveringly asked Deacon whether he wished to pursue the discussion further. Deacon didn't. In fact, he thought he was dead, and it took several minutes—and several experimental movements on his part —to discover that he wasn't. He finally achieved a standing position, but he was about the most chastened pup in the history of chastened pups.

Preacher hadn't hurt the little rapscallion. He had just roughed him up, and we were all back hunting half an hour later. And an hour or so later I came upon Preacher in his pulpit again. This time I invited Deacon to attend the services, and he was nothing loth. But as he reached Preacher's rear guard, I heard a soft admonition. I could hardly hear it, but Deacon had no such trouble. It said: "All right, you don't take no for an answer, do you? Evidently you're just tired of living. Well, if you want all your miseries ended suddenly, just take one more step. Just one more. *Please!*"

But Deacon was nobody's fool. It must be recorded that he knew when he had enough. Nervously lolling his tongue, he glanced at Preacher with profound respect. Then he gingerly backed two steps until his head was even with Preacher's rump, the proper place for a grandson, after all. There he planted himself for the whole world to see. As I watched the tableau with swelling heart, the menace in Preacher's throat subsided into a soft murmur of approbation.

For five minutes I let them stand. I am no longer a young man, I reminded myself. In the span that may be vouchsafed me by the Bountiful Giver, I may not walk this path again. I will hang this picture in the gallery of my mind to enliven my fancy in days to come. And if I felt the taste of salt in my mouth, it was nobody's damned business but mine.

After a while I quietly told Preacher that I was ready whenever he was, and he strode gravely in and put the skulkers to wing. Preacher brought me one bird and indulgently permitted Deacon to bring the other.

I could make this story much longer, but there would be little point in my doing so. Deacon never flushed Preacher's birds thereafter. In fact he was most punctilious in seconding any motion that his mentor made. On that day Deacon attained his manhood and discovered his mission in life.

But back in the kennel that night, Deacon lay unhappily in one corner, old Preacher in another. I got to feeling sorry for the old boy. I'm a grandpa myself. But after a while Preacher went over to the crestfallen Deacon and playfully nipped his tail. Five minutes later Preacher was lying contentedly on his back, with eyes half closed, and with the waggish Deacon astraddle him and making a great show of devouring old Grandpa alive.

I guess there is nothing else to tell, except that during the remainder of the season Preacher, Deacon, and I frolicked and hunted so much that my faithful secretary was continually posting notices: *Professor Babcock will be sick for the next two days.* We hunted so much, in fact, that I had to give the illustrious president of our university several messes of birds to keep him from getting somebody else to look after the English Department for him.

THE SCHIZOID DOG

DESCENT TO THE BEASTS

BY *C. G. Learoyd*

THERE WAS ONCE in a little country town, called Market Citron, a journalist, and he was a great lover of dogs. He had a very special fox-terrier of his own called Jorrocks, and he was so keen about dogs that he used to read all the dog stories he could lay his hands on. Most of these stories, although they were very pleasant, were perhaps just a little bit slushy— sob-stuff and fidelity and humble servant of man sort of business—so being a journalist he couldn't help wondering whether any of them ever remotely approximated to the truth.

Now one night the journalist had to go to the annual dinner of the National Farmers' Union at the "Rose and Billycock" in Market Citron to report the speeches. It was a wonderful dinner. Colonel Carlton, who was in Scotland, had sent several haunches of venison, and Major Eistein, who was in Hatton Garden, had sent several barrels of caviare, and there was much meeting of old friends, old whisky and old ale, and toasting of Agriculture—that came early on the list because it is rather hard to say—and the King and Empire and the turnip crop and mangel-wurzels, which is so easy to say under certain circumstances that it was the very last toast.

Now when the journalist was going home in the not too early hours of the morning he met in High Street a wizened-up old

charwoman, probably going to clean the office of some super-
summertime fiend, and when she noticed his eccentric behavior
she called him a "low animile," then a "dirty dog," and finally,
when he had tried to explain his honorable intentions, a "bestial
beast."

This rather stung the journalist and, although when he got
home he got a great welcome from Jorrocks, yet he felt distinctly insulted and started to look up "bestial" in the dictionary.

Then it was that the Great Idea struck him. What a glorious
opportunity! Here he was, practically one of the lower animals
—she'd said so three times—so that, with his journalist's notebook and pencil in his pocket, he could sally forth and listen in
to his canine friends on their own level. Get in on the ground
floor, so to speak, hearken unto their vows of fealty and devotion, take them down in shorthand, and immortalize them
in a canine saga! Only once in a thousand centuries did such a
chance come to man. Nebuchadnezzar had it and apparently
utterly wasted it. What staggering headlines he could have had:
"Seven Years as a Cow." But perhaps he was a bull, he'd
hardly be a bullock one would think. Better still: "Cows I've
conquered and men I've tossed," by A Bull. Let's see who else
had had the chance? Wasn't somebody turned into a serpent
once, or was he thinking of Beauty and the Beast? He was a bit
vague about that. At any rate the Beast was asleep, wasn't he?
Wonder if he dreamt like a beast. Perhaps—as you were, as
you were. He was a journalist and had the most gorgeous opportunity, simply waiting to be grasped; he was the only man
who had had this wonderful chance since the time of Beauty—
no, the Beast, and Nebu—that fellow. He wondered which came
first. Did Beauty, no the Beast, live before Nebu? As you were,
as you were. Where's my hat? Come, Jorrocks, come.

.   .   .   .   .

"Come on, Jorrocks. Why do you always spend such a devil
of a time sniffing at that wall?"

"Well, that's pretty cool from a newspaper man! You like
to know what's going on, don't you? So do I. And what do I find
here? Bingo was here last, probably took his bloke to the post
last thing. Before him was old Max and that sap Sandy. And

before him that well-behaved young lady Dorothea the Dachshund. Her message is not quite complete—she was probably as usual on a string. And before her—oh, it's myself. And if you weren't in such a blasted hurry I could tell you what they'd all been eating."

"Come on, do come on," said the journalist. "I want to meet all your friends and listen-in to the faithful servants of man."

"Gosh, some faith," said Jorrocks. "One minute—I must just make sure. Most of the lads have been here this morning, but not Sambo. Probably they locked him up when you were having that gorge last night and now they're sleeping it off, and poor old Sambo's still locked up. That's a nice way to treat a faithful servant of man, what? Well, if you want to meet some of my friends, we'd better go up to the Memorial."

"Righto," said the journalist. "I've often noticed you dogs like the Memorial, but I've never understood why."

"Good heavens!" exclaimed Jorrocks. "And you do crossword puzzles. Well, the Memorial on market day is better than any crossword you've ever seen. Everyone goes there. Most of us have our favorite places. Mine's under 'Presented by the Mayor, J. L. Stubbs, Esq.' Bingo's is under the motto on the other side. Sambo's is under that part about the Duchess laying the foundation stone. On market days when the farmers bring their 'faithful servants' in, why the Memorial must be one of the most interesting places in the world; something like that place London that you talk about I should think."

They walked smartly down Church Street, which except for one or two early step-cleaners was deserted, and turned into High Street, Jorrocks scouring the lamp-posts and walls for sign of friend or foe.

Sure enough, there were half a dozen dogs sniffing round the Memorial at the top of the street, and Jorrocks ran on ahead out of earshot to join them. When the journalist arrived they were all deeply immersed in conversation about an individual called Gertie. They took no notice of the journalist, who seated himself on one of the steps of the Memorial, got out his notebook, and prepared to report proceedings. He found it hard at first to pick up the thread of conversation. Gertie—Gertie—Gertie—the name kept recurring.

"May I ask," interrupted the journalist, "who is this Gertie?"

"By the great St. Bartholin!" exclaimed Clarence the Collie. "Who is Gertie!"

"The appalling ignorance of man——" began Sandy.

"Shut up, you tykes," said Jorrocks loyally. "My old Smell knows Gertie all right, but not by that name. She's the butcher's bitch—you know, the one you wrote a par about: Killed 154 rats in an afternoon. 'Best ratter in Market Citron,' don't you remember?"

"What, that cur!" exclaimed the journalist.

"Pardon me," said the Collie, "but you are speaking of the mother of my children."

"And mine," said Mac, with aggressive Scotch dignity.

"Yes, but they drowned your little lot," interrupted Jorrocks, "and I don't wonder."

"She was also the mother of at least one of my children," said Stanley the Spaniel sententiously. "If you remember in that litter of which Clarence was supposed to be the father there was one with beautifully spotty legs, and——"

"Oh, bilge!" exclaimed Jorrocks. "You're superstitious and believe in superfoetation! You and your spots!"

"Anyway," said the journalist, tactfully changing the subject, "why are you all so keen about this Gertie?"

"Because she's the only eligible young lady round here," explained Jorrocks. "Curious shortage of women! Of course there is Dorothea the Dachshund, who lives with Miss Barley, but when she becomes matrimonially eligible she's guarded like the Crown Jewels—cooks, housemaid, and Miss Barley herself—triple guards!"

"A seething nest of virginity," snapped Mac.

"Let them keep it for all I care," said Clarence. "I don't want children like earthworms. By the way, I heard an amusing anecdote about Dorothea the other day."

"Is it the old chestnut," said Bingo, "about when Miss Barley took her to the railway station and we were all following behind, and the station master said to Miss Barley, 'If I was you, Miss, I'd keep that animal locked up in that condition,' and she answered, 'Oh no, Mr. Payne, he's no trouble at all. *He* never fights. He's such a popular little chappie!' Why, that was years ago."

"It is not my habit to tell what you are pleased to call chestnuts, and that was not the anecdote I was about to relate," said Clarence with dignity, "when I was so rudely interrupted. You will remember that red-haired maid Miss Barley had, the one who had an objectionable habit of throwing water at us if we went up that side passage? Well, Miss Barley dismissed her last week—and I think quite rightly—for keeping her waiting for a quarter of an hour for her early morning tea. Two or three hours afterwards Miss Barley took our precious Dorothea for a walk on the string. Now you know what with all that bread and milk muck she gets our Dorothea is inclined to be a little costive; no roughage at all. Now twice during their passage down High Street—I timed it by the church clock—Miss Barley had to wait ten minutes at one end of the string while poor Dorothea did agonizing expressions at the other. Twenty minutes in all. Was Dorothea dismissed? Was she! Dear little Tootsyootsums!"

"Anyway," said Jorrocks, "to revert to the point. When is Gertie putting the banns up and saying 'Come hither'?"

"How ever can you tell that?" asked the journalist.

"Don't show your ignorance," said Jorrocks in a whisper. "You know the song, don't you?

"The 'Angelone' is stronger
And it cannot be much longer
Till the wedding bells are tinkling . . .

'Angelone' is from the sacral glands and is a sort of external hormone."

The other dogs were not listening. They had all turned to old Maximillan the Mongrel. He had the best catalogued, cross-referenced turbinates in the town—some said in the county. Wonderful stories were told of his prowess. How a farmer from Elmash had once brought his dog in on market day—only once and ten years ago. Then one day old Max had gone into Cambridge and spotted this stranger's pup on Parker's Piece from a family cystin! How once he had said to Sambo, the dog at the "Rose and Billycock," "I see they have changed your biscuits." And Sambo said, "No, they're just the same. I saw the label on the bag this morning and they taste just the same. You're wrong for once, Max." Then later it had turned out that that scoundrel Perkins the grocer had run short of Pratts, so had filled up an old Pratts' bag with something very similar. On questions of marriage dates like this of Gertie he was almost infallible.

"Gertie's glad days will start on the sixteenth," said Maximillan sadly. He was an old dog now, and although mentally and turbinately still in his prime, his libido was distinctly on the chain, and as every dog within miles knew, he had something which was terribly like a Bence-Jones proteose.

Sunny, the Sealyham pup who had been hanging about on the outskirts of the pack listening to his elders, broke in:

"I should have thought it would have been nearer the thirteenth," he said, pathetically trying to imitate a grown dog's gruffness.

"You!" said Clarence, advancing to administer chastisement. "You who can't yet balance yourself on three legs! You— why you still reek of your mother's angelone!"

"You, you little tapeworm!" growled Jorrocks. "I've got something to say to you. You dug up my innominate bone last Friday and then, you little swine, you hadn't even got the acidity to digest it. I keep on coming across bits of it all over the place."

Sunny beat a hasty retreat with tail reversed and several of the pack followed half playfully in pursuit.

Suddenly they were recalled by the sound of excited barking coming from the opposite direction. It grew louder, and in a moment an agitated ball of white, Dr. Graver's cairn, Constantine, was seen coming like a comet up High Street.

All the dogs round the Memorial stiffened to attention. He had strange tidings in his mouth. That bark meant an emergency—taut muscles and keen turbinates would be required. They waited thus.

He burst upon them.

"One of the animals—a lion or a tiger or a panther—from the menagerie that went through to Cambridge the other day has escaped," he announced breathlessly. "I picked up the scent in Market Square. Here, smell my nose." He turned to Maximillan. "You can smell where I smelt him."

Maximillan rose to his feet and smelt carefully; the others awaited the verdict.

"There's something strange here," said Maximillan gravely.

"The intruder is young and virile, exclusively carnivorous, very fierce, and—and—there is something here I've never come across before."

Something Maximillan had never come across before!

The others gathered round Constantine's nose as men might round a newspaper bearing grievous news.

What should they do? They turned instinctively to old Max.

"Our women—our woman—our very sustenance will not be secure with this ferocious monster at our doors. We must pick up the scent, we must follow, we must attack."

Having said this, Maximillan set off at a dignified trot down High Street.

"Come on, boys," barked Clarence. "For God and Gertie!"

The pack followed, and the journalist, who had been taking down the conversation in shorthand, was left with Jorrocks to bring up the rear.

"Come on, old Smell," said Jorrocks joyfully. "This is exciting. Much blood will flow this day!"

"What shall we do?" asked the journalist.

"Oh, our general plan of campaign on these occasions is to send a man on ahead as a sort of bait, and when the brute's got his teeth well into him, we rally round on the flanks and chew him up. It's fairly safe that way."

Led by the warlike Constantine the pack picked up the scent by the lamp-post outside the "Rose and Billycock" in Market Square, and infuriated by its pungent fleshiness, galloped at half-cry to a fresher and more contemptuous stench at the well-known calling stone on the corner of Church Street and Prior's Walk.

Back hair bristled and canines bared, a low growl ran through the pack, the instincts of a thousand centuries took control, and in a moment the pack was in full cry down Prior's Walk, to check at the entrance of that narrow passage, Prior's Prudence. Here was another insult, fresher, more bitingly feral, and full of lustful fierceness. A hurried council of war, and then they were off again, the journalist, notebook in hand, at their heels, down Prior's Prudence, the cloistered stillness of which echoed to their bedlam.

Now at the end of Prior's Prudence is the Monks Garden, a

secluded public garden with an old sundial and many bushes and old-time flowers and pleasant shadowings. Its gate (with "Dogs not Admitted" on it) stood ajar.

With one accord the pack burst in and hesitated. This they knew was a cul-de-sac, surrounded by high old walls, and it behoved them to go warily lest their retreat should be cut off. They scouted in silence round the bushes till a low insistent growl from Maximillan brought them to his side.

"He's in there," he said in a low, excited voice, directing his nose to a circular clump of bushes with standard roses growing in the bed around them. "Those bloody flowers confuse me, blast them, but almost certainly he comes from the coast—probably Brightsea. I smell the sea in him. He lays gorged in there. Let us surround it and advance cautiously."

"Look here," said Jorrocks. "I'll send my old *homo sap.* in first. The brute may not like his stench and bolt."

Egged on by Jorrocks, the journalist advanced hesitatingly towards the bushes.

"Whooa there," he said, cautiously flapping them with his notebook. "Burr. Get out of it. Whhssst."

Not a leaf stirred.

Jorrocks at his heel and the other dogs in a circle round the clump growled menacingly.

The journalist now took up a clod of earth and threw it into the bushes. The pack barked defiantly. Suddenly came the moving of leaves and parting of branches. The journalist retreated a few steps and the snarling pack tautened on their haunches, and with teeth now bared to the last molars prepared to attack or retreat as the crisis demanded.

Then suddenly, with a sheepish yet self-assured smirk on his plebian features, Sambo, the half-breed dog from the "Rose and Billycock," emerged bashfully.

As storm clouds pass suddenly, leaving the friendly warmth of the sun, so was the fury of the pack. In a second they were all around him, smelling him from Dan even to Beersheba, enviously, lasciviously, and with a host of comment.

"Well I'm damned." "My Gawd, what a feed the old boy's had." "Holy Tripehounds, Sambo, you must have broken into the butcher's after Gertie, found you were ten days too soon, and eaten the whole blinking shop."

"No," said Maximillan. "It's not butcher's meat. More likely the fish shop. But it's not that either."

"If you'll leave me alone for a minute I'll tell you all about it, boys. You see—excuse me belching—they locked me in the outhouse when they had that feed with all those farmer fellows last night. Pretty putrid behavior that. I got all the food smells and nothing else. Well, I was pretty annoyed, I can tell you. I did a scratch about for a bit and then did a prolonged whine, but I knew from the start it was hopeless, so after a time I lay down and tried to sleep. Of course that was almost impossible with all those savory and tantalizing smells about. Well, about eleven I heard the steps of a lot of these farmers going out to their Memorial and wandering back again in a few minutes. That of course made sleep quite impossible, because I kept hoping it was my old Stench coming to let me out. They kept coming in ones and twos and threes and each time they had to pass my outhouse and I got a whiff of their filthy gluttony. I tell you I was getting pretty weary of this, when very late indeed I heard an unsteady step getting nearer and nearer, and instead of going past me I think he must have mistaken my prison for his Memorial. At any rate he fumbled about with the bolts, and let me out! Well, the show was nearly over and my old Stink was three-quarters asleep and soon went to bed, leaving the dining-room door open! My boys, believe me or believe me not, there was enough meat on that table to feed all Mr. Cruft's little outfit. Huge joints of savory, half-decomposed deer meat and some most extraordinary good black fish eggs. I'm telling you. Did I fairly let myself go? Did I not. Without the word of a lie —excuse me belching——"

"Venison and caviare!" said Maximillan sadly. "I have been misled, but it isn't every day a dog gets his fill of these. Perhaps I was overhasty, but the combination certainly made him smell very strange and fresh and fruity." He turned sadly away; his first mistake!

"I tell you boys, when I got that second joint on the floor, the black-green spots showing in the beautiful red flesh—excuse me belching—I fairly—"

Jorrocks and the journalist followed Max.

"Sambo's quite a good fellow, but it is rather revolting having to listen to him gloating like that," said Jorrocks. "Let's go home."

"And it doesn't end here," he continued when they were out in the street again. "If Gertie gets to hear of this, it will give him an enormous pull on the sixteenth. Very virile and stimulating, venison and caviare."

"What an unpleasant little dog you are!" said the journalist.

"Unpleasant? How do you make that out?"

As the journalist threw himself on his bed, to get if possible an hour's sleep before going to the office, he felt vaguely disgusted at the olfactory and excretory world in which he had been. Softly he muttered: "O Freud, where is thy sting!"

THE DOG AND THE FOX

BY *John Gay*

A shepherd's Dog, unskilled in sports,
Pick'd up acquaintance of all sorts:
Among the rest a Fox he knew;
By frequent chat their friendship grew.
　　Says *Renard*, 'tis a cruel case,
That man should stigmatize our race.
No doubt, among us, rogues you find,
As among dogs and human kind;
And yet (unknown to me and you)
There may be honest men and true.
Thus slander tries, whate'er it can,
To put us on the foot with man.
Let my own actions recommend;
No prejudice can blind a friend:
You know me free from all disguise;
My honour as my life I prize.
　　By talk like this from all mistrust
The Dog was cur'd, a thought him just.
　　As on a time the Fox held forth
On conscience, honesty, and worth,
Sudden he stopt; he cock'd his ear;
Low dropt his brushy tail with fear.
　　Bless us! the hunters are abroad.
What's all that clutter on the road?
　　Hold, says the Dog, we're safe from harm:
'Twas nothing but a false alarm.
At yonder town, 'tis market-day;
Some farmer's wife is on the way:
'Tis so, (I know her pye-ball'd mare,)
Dame *Dobbins*, with her poultry-ware.
　　Renard grew huff. Says he, This sneer

From you I little thought to hear;
Your meaning in your looks I see.
Pray, what's dame *Dobbins*, friend, to me?
Did I e'er make her poultry thinner?
Prove that I owe the dame a dinner.
 Friend, quoth the Cur, I meant no harm:
Then why so captious? Why so warm?
My words, in common acccptation,
Could never give this provocation.
No lamb (for ought I ever knew)
Maybe more he knows than you.
 At this, gall'd *Renard* winc'd and swore
Such language ne'er was giv'n before.
What's lamb to me? This saucy hint
Shows me, base knave, which way you squint.
If t'other night your master lost
Three lambs; am I to pay the cost?
Your vile Reflections would imply
That I'm the thief. You dog, you lye.
 Thou knave, thou fool, (the Dog reply'd,)
The name is just, take either side;
Thy guilt these applications speak:
Sirrah, 'tis conscience makes you squeak.
 So saying, on the Fox he flies.
The self-convicted felon dies.

THE PRIMORDIAL DOG

THE SOUNDING OF THE CALL

BY *Jack London*

WHEN BUCK EARNED sixteen hundred dollars in five minutes for John Thornton, he made it possible for his
master to pay off certain debts and to journey with his partners
into the East after a fabled lost mine, the history of which
was as old as the history of the country. Many men had sought

it; few had found it; and more than a few there were who had never returned from the quest. This lost mine was steeped in tragedy and shrouded in mystery. No one knew of the first man. The oldest tradition stopped before it got back to him. From the beginning there had been an ancient and ramshackle cabin. Dying men had sworn to it, and to the mine the site of which it marked, clinching their testimony with nuggets that were unlike any known grade of gold in the Northland.

But no living man had looted this treasure house, and the dead were dead; wherefore John Thornton and Pete and Hans, with Buck and half a dozen other dogs, faced into the East on an unknown trail to achieve where men and dogs as good as themselves had failed. They sledded seventy miles up the Yukon, swung to the left into the Stewart River, passed the Mayo and the McQuestion, and held on until the Stewart itself became a streamlet, threading the upstanding peaks which marked the backbone of the continent.

John Thornton asked little of man or nature. He was unafraid of the wild. With a handful of salt and a rifle he could plunge into the wilderness and fare wherever he pleased and as long as he pleased. Being in no haste, Indian fashion, he hunted his dinner in the course of the day's travel; and if he failed to find it, like the Indian, he kept on traveling, secure in the knowledge that sooner or later he would come to it. So, on this great journey into the East, straight meat was the bill of fare, ammunition and tools principally made up the load on the sled, and the time-card was drawn upon the limitless future.

To Buck it was boundless delight, this hunting, fishing, and indefinite wandering through strange places. For weeks at a time they would hold on steadily, day after day, and for weeks upon end they would camp, here and there, the dogs loafing and the men burning holes through frozen muck and gravel and washing countless pans of dirt by the heat and the fire. Sometimes they went hungry, sometimes they feasted riotously, all according to the abundance of game and the fortune of hunting. Summer arrived, and dogs and men packed on their backs, rafted across blue mountain lakes, and descended or ascended unknown rivers in slender boats whipsawed from the standing forest.

The months came and went, and back and forth they twisted

through the uncharted vastness, where no men were and yet where men had been if the Lost Cabin were true. They went across divides in summer blizzards, shivered under the midnight sun on naked mountains between the timber line and the eternal snows, dropped into summer valleys amid swarming gnats and flies, and in the shadows of glaciers picked strawberries and flowers as ripe and fair as any the Southland could boast. In the fall of the year they penetrated a weird lake country, sad and silent, where wildfowl had been, but where then there was no life nor sign of life—only the blowing of chill winds, the forming of ice in sheltered places, and the melancholy rippling of waves on lonely beaches.

And through another winter they wandered on the obliterated trails of men who had gone before. Once, they came upon a path blazed through the forest, an ancient path, and the Lost Cabin seemed very near. But the path began nowhere and ended nowhere, and it remained mystery, as the man who made it and the reason he made it remained mystery. Another time they chanced upon the time-graven wreckage of a hunting lodge, and amid the shreds of rotted blankets John Thornton found a long-barreled flintlock. He knew it for a Hudson Bay Company gun of the younger days in the Northwest, when such a gun was worth its height in beaver skins packed flat. And that was all—no hint as to the man who in an early day had reared the lodge and left the gun among the blankets.

Spring came on once more, and at the end of all their wandering they found, not the Lost Cabin, but a shallow placer in a broad valley where the gold showed like yellow butter across the bottom of the washing-pan. They sought no farther. Each day they worked earned them thousands of dollars in clean dust and nuggets, and they worked every day. The gold was sacked in moose-hide bags, fifty pounds to the bag, and piled like so much firewood outside the spruce-bough lodge. Like giants they toiled, days flashing on the heels of days like dreams as they heaped the treasure up.

There was nothing for the dogs to do, save the hauling in of meat now and again that Thornton killed, and Buck spent long hours musing by the fire. The vision of the short-legged hairy man came to him more frequently, now that there was little work to be done; and often, blinking by the fire, Buck wandered with him in that other world which he remembered.

The salient thing of this other world seemed fear. When he watched the hairy man sleeping by the fire, head between his knees and hands clasped above, Buck saw that he slept restlessly, with many starts and awakenings, at which times he would peer fearfully into the darkness and fling more wood upon the fire. Did they walk by the beach of a sea, where the hairy man gathered shellfish and ate them as he gathered, it was with eyes that roved everywhere for hidden danger and with legs prepared to run like the wind at its first appearance. Through the forest they crept noiselessly, Buck at the hairy man's heels; and they were alert and vigilant, the pair of them, ears twitching and moving and nostrils quivering, for the man heard and smelled as keenly as Buck. The hairy man could spring up into the trees and travel ahead as fast as on the ground, swinging by the arms from limb to limb, sometimes a dozen feet apart, letting go and catching, never falling, never missing his grip. In fact, he seemed as much at home among the trees as on the ground; and Buck had memories of nights of vigil spent beneath trees wherein the hairy man roosted, holding on tightly as he slept.

And closely akin to the visions of the hairy man was the call still sounding in the depths of the forest. It filled him with a great unrest and strange desires. It caused him to feel a vague, sweet gladness and he was aware of wild yearnings and stirrings for he knew not what. Sometimes he pursued the call into the forest, looking for it as though it were a tangible thing, barking softly or defiantly, as the mood might dictate. He would thrust his nose into the cool wood moss, or into the black soil where long grasses grew, and snort with joy at the fat earth smells; or he would crouch for hours as if in concealment, behind fungus-covered trunks of fallen trees, wide-eyed and wide-eared to all that moved and sounded about him. It might be, lying thus, that he hoped to surprise this call he could not understand. But he did not know why he did these various things. He was impelled to do them, and did not reason about them at all.

Irresistible impulses seized him. He would be lying in camp, dozing lazily in the heat of the day, when suddenly his head would lift and his ears cock up, intent and listening, and he would spring to his feet and dash away, and on and on, for hours, through the forest aisles and across the open spaces where the niggerheads bunched. He loved to run down dry watercourses, and to creep and spy upon the bird life in the woods. For a day at a time he would lie in the underbrush where he could watch the partridges drumming and strutting up and down. But especially he loved to run in the dim twilight of the summer midnights, listening to the subdued and sleepy murmurs of the forest, reading signs and sounds as man may read a book, and seeking for the mysterious something that called—called, waking or sleeping, at all times, for him to come.

One night he sprang from sleep with a start, eager-eyed, nostrils quivering and scenting, his mane bristling in recurrent waves. From the forest came the call (or one not of it, for the call was many-noted), distinct and definite as never before—a long-drawn howl, like, yet unlike, any noise made by husky dog. And he knew it, in the old familiar way as a sound heard before. He sprang through the sleeping camp and in swift silence dashed through the woods. As he drew closer to the cry he went more slowly, with caution in every movement, till he came to an open place among the trees, and looking out saw, erect on haunches, with nose pointed to the sky, a long, lean, timber wolf.

He had made no noise, yet it ceased from howling and tried to sense his presence. Buck stalked into the open, half crouching, body gathered compactly together, tail straight and stiff, feet falling with unwonted care. Every movement advertised commingled threatening and overture of friendliness. It was the menacing truce that marks the meeting of wild beasts that prey. But the wolf fled at sight of him. He followed, with wild leapings, in a frenzy to overtake. He ran him into a blind channel, in the bed of the creek, where a timber jam barred the way. The wolf whirled about, pivoting on his hind legs after the fashion of Joe and of all cornered husky dogs, snarling and bristling, clipping his teeth together in a continuous and rapid succession of snaps.

Buck did not attack, but circled him about and hedged him in with friendly advances. The wolf was suspicious and afraid; for Buck made three of him in weight, while his head barely reached Buck's shoulder. Watching his chance, he darted away, and the chase was resumed. Time and again he was cornered and the thing repeated, though he was in poor condition or Buck could not so easily have overtaken him. He would run till Buck's head was even with his flank, when he would whirl around at bay, only to dash away again at the first opportunity.

But in the end Buck's pertinacity was rewarded; for the wolf, finding that no harm was intended, finally sniffed noses with him. Then they became friendly, and played about in the nervous, half-coy way with which fierce beasts belie their fierceness. After some time of this the wolf started off at an easy lope in a manner that plainly showed he was going somewhere. He made it clear to Buck that he was to come, and they ran side by side through the sombre twilight, straight up the creek bed, into the gorge from which it issued, and across the bleak divide where it took its rise.

On the opposite slope of the watershed they came down into a level country where were great stretches of forest and many streams, and through these great stretches they ran steadily, hour after hour, the sun rising higher and the day growing warmer. Buck was wildly glad. He knew he was at last answering the call, running by the side of his wood brother toward the place from where the call surely came. Old memories were coming upon him fast, and he was stirring to them as of old he stirred to the realities of which they were the shadows. He had done this thing before, somewhere in that other and dimly remembered world, and he was doing it again, now, running free in the open, the unpacked earth underfoot, the wide sky overhead.

They stopped by a running stream to drink, and, stopping, Buck remembered John Thornton. He sat down. The wolf started on toward the place from where the call surely came, then returned to him, sniffing noses and making actions as though to encourage him. But Buck turned about and started slowly on the back track. For the better part of an hour the wild brother ran by his side, whining softly. Then he sat down, pointed his nose upward, and howled. It was a mournful howl, and as Buck held steadily on his way he heard it grow faint and fainter until it was lost in the distance.

John Thornton was eating dinner when Buck dashed into

camp and sprang upon him in a frenzy of affection, overturning him, scrambling upon him, licking his face, biting his hand— "playing the general tom-fool," as John Thornton characterized it, the while he shook Buck back and forth and cursed him lovingly.

For two days and nights Buck never left camp, never let Thornton out of his sight. He followed him about at his work, watched him while he ate, saw him into his blankets at night and out of them in the morning. But after two days the call in the forest began to sound more imperiously than ever. Buck's restlessness came back on him, and he was haunted by recollections of the wild brother, and of the smiling land beyond the divide and the run side by side through the wide forest stretches. Once again he took to wandering in the woods, but the wild brother came no more; and though he listened through long vigils, the mournful howl was never raised.

He began to sleep out at night, staying away from camp for days at a time; and once he crossed the divide at the head of the creek and went down into the land of timber and streams. There he wandered for a week, seeking vainly for fresh sign of the wild brother, killing his meat as he traveled and traveling with the long, easy lope that seems never to tire. He fished for salmon in a broad stream that emptied somewhere into the sea, and by this stream he killed a large black bear, blinded by the mosquitoes while likewise fishing, and raging through the forest helpless and terrible. Even so, it was a hard fight, and it aroused the last latent remnants of Buck's ferocity. And two days later, when he returned to his kill and found a dozen wolverenes quarreling over the spoil, he scattered them like chaff; and those that fled left two behind who would quarrel no more.

The blood-longing become stronger than ever before. He was a killer, a thing that preyed, living on the things that lived, unaided, alone, by virtue of his own strength and prowess, surviving triumphantly in a hostile environment where only the strong survived. Because of all this he became possessed of a great pride in himself, which communicated itself like a contagion to his physical being. It advertised itself in all his movements, was apparent in the play of every muscle, spoke plainly in speech in the way he carried himself, and made his glorious furry coat if anything more glorious. But for the stray brown on his muzzle and above his eyes, and for the splash of white hair that ran midmost down his chest, he might well have been mistaken for a gigantic wolf, larger than the largest of the breed. From his St. Bernard father he had inherited size and weight, but it was his shepherd mother who had given shape to that size and weight. His muzzle was the long wolf muzzle, save that it was larger than the muzzle of any wolf; and his head, somewhat broader, was the wolf head on a massive scale.

His cunning was wolf cunning, and wild cunning; his intelligence, shepherd intelligence and St. Bernard intelligence; and all this, plus an experience gained in the fiercest of schools, made him as formidable a creature as any that roamed the wild. A carnivorous animal, living on a straight meat diet, he was in full flower, at the high tide of his life, overspilling with vigor and virility. When Thornton passed a caressing hand along his back, a snapping and crackling followed the hand, each hair discharging its pent magnetism at the contact. Every part, brain and body, nerve tissue and fiber, was keyed to the most exquisite pitch; and between all the parts there was a perfect equilibrium or adjustment. To sights and sounds and events which required action, he responded with lightning-like rapidity. Quickly as a husky dog could leap to defend from attack or to attack, he could leap twice as quickly. He saw the movement, or heard sound, and responded in less time than another dog required to compass the mere seeing or hearing. He perceived and determined and responded in the same instant. In point of fact the three actions of perceiving, determining, and responding were sequential; but so infinitesimal were the intervals of time between them that they appeared simultaneous. His muscles were surcharged with vitality, and snapped into play sharply, like steel springs. Life streamed through him in splendid flood, glad and rampant, until it seemed that it would burst him asunder in sheer ecstasy and pour forth generously over the world.

"Never was there such a dog," said John Thornton one day, as the partners watched Buck marching out of camp.

"When he was made, the mold was broke," said Pete.

"Py jingo! I t'ink so minself," Hans affirmed.

They saw him marching out of camp, but they did not see the instant and terrible transformation which took place as soon as he was within the secrecy of the forest. He no longer marched. At once he became a thing of the wild, stealing along softly, cat-footed, a passing shadow that appeared and disappeared among the shadows. He knew how to take advantage of every cover to crawl on his belly like a snake, and like a snake to leap and strike. He could take a ptarmigan from its nest, kill a rabbit as it slept, and snap in midair the little chipmunks fleeing a second too late for the trees. Fish, in open pools, were not too quick for him; nor were beaver, mending their dams, too wary. He killed to eat, not from wantonness; but he preferred to eat what he killed himself. So a lurking humor ran through his deeds, and it was his delight to steal upon the squirrels, and, when he all but had them, to let them go, chattering in mortal fear to the treetops.

As the fall of the year came on the moose appeared in greater abundance, moving slowly down to meet the winter in the lower and less rigorous valleys. Buck had already dragged down a stray part-grown calf; but he wished strongly for larger and more formidable quarry, and he came upon it one day on the divide at the head of the creek. A band of twenty moose had crossed over from the land of streams and timber, and chief among them was a great bull. He was in a savage temper, and, standing over six feet from the ground, was as formidable an antagonist as ever Buck could desire. Back and forth the bull tossed his great palmated antlers, branching to fourteen points and embracing seven feet within the tips. His small eyes burned with a vicious and bitter light, while he roared with fury at sight of Buck.

From the bull's side, just forward of the flank, protruded a feathered arrow-end, which accounted for his savageness. Guided by that instinct which came from the old hunting days of the primordial world, Buck proceeded to cut the bull out from the herd. It was no slight task. He would bark and dance about in front of the bull, just out of reach of the great antlers and of the terrible splay hoofs which could have stamped his life out with a single blow. Unable to turn his back on the fanged danger and go on, the bull would be driven into paroxysms of rage. At such moments he charged Buck, who retreated craftily, luring him on by a simulated inability to escape. But when he was thus separated from his fellows, two or three of the younger bulls would charge back upon Buck and enable the wounded bull to rejoin the herd.

There is a patience of the wild—dogged, tireless, persistent as life itself—that holds motionless for endless hours the spider in its web, the snake in its coils, the panther in its ambuscade; this patience belongs peculiarly to life when it hunts its living food; and it belonged to Buck as he clung to the flank of the herd, retarding its march, irritating the young bulls, worrying the cows with their half-grown calves, and driving the wounded bull mad with helpless rage. For half a day this continued. Buck multiplied himself, attacking from all sides, enveloping the herd in a whirlwind of menace, cutting out his victim as fast as it could rejoin its mates, wearing out the patience of creatures preyed upon, which is a lesser patience than that of creatures preying.

As the day wore along and the sun dropped to its bed in the northwest (the darkness had come back and the fall nights were six hours long), the young bulls retraced their steps more and more reluctantly to the aid of their beset leader. The down-coming winter was harrying them on to the lower levels, and it seemed they could never shake off this tireless creature that held them back. Besides, it was not the life of the herd, or of the young bulls, that was threatened. The life of only one member was demanded, which was a remoter interest than their lives, and in the end they were content to pay the toll.

As twilight fell the old bull stood with lowered head, watching his mates—the cows he had known, the calves he had fathered, the bulls he had mastered—as they shambled on at a rapid pace through the fading light. He could not follow, for before his nose leaped the merciless fanged terror that would not let him go. Three hundredweight more than half a ton he weighed; he had lived a long, strong life, full of fight and struggle, and at the end he faced death at the teeth of a creature whose head did not reach beyond his great knuckled knees.

From then on, night and day, Buck never left his prey, never gave it a moment's rest, never permitted it to browse the leaves of trees or the shoots of young birch and willow. Nor did he give the wounded bull opportunity to slake his burning thirst in the slender trickling streams they crossed. Often, in desperation, he burst into long stretches of flight. At such times Buck did not attempt to stay him, but loped easily at his heels, satisfied with the way the game was played, lying down when the moose stood still, attacking him fiercely when he strove to eat or drink.

The great head drooped more and more under its trees of horns, and the shambling trot grew weaker and weaker. He took to standing for long periods, with nose to the ground, and dejected ears dropped limply; and Buck found more time in which to get water for himself and in which to rest. At such moments, panting with red lolling tongue and with eyes fixed upon the big bull, it appeared to Buck that a change was coming over the face of things. He could feel a new stir in the land. As the moose were coming into the land, other kinds of life were coming in. Forest and stream and air seemed palpitant with their presence. The news of it was borne in upon him, not by sight or sound, or smell, but by some other and subtler sense. He heard nothing, saw nothing, yet knew that the land was somehow different; that through it strange things were afoot and ranging; and he resolved to investigate after he had finished the business in hand.

At last, at the end of the fourth day, he pulled the great moose down. For a day and a night he remained by the kill, eating and sleeping, turn and turn about. Then, rested, refreshed and strong, he turned his face toward camp and John Thornton. He broke into the long easy lope and went on, hour after hour, never at loss for the tangled way, heading straight home through strange country with a certitude of direction that put man and his magnetic needle to shame.

As he held on he became more and more conscious of the new stir in the land. There was life abroad in it different from the life which had been there throughout the summer. No longer was this fact borne in upon him in some subtle, mysterious way. The birds talked of it, the squirrels chattered about it, the very breeze whispered of it. Several times he stopped and drew in the fresh morning air in great sniffs, reading a message which made him leap on with greater speed. He was oppressed with a sense of calamity happening, if it were not calamity already happened; and as he crossed the last watershed and dropped down into the valley toward camp, he proceeded with greater caution.

Three miles away he came upon a fresh trail that sent his neck hair rippling and bristling. It led straight toward camp and John Thornton. Buck hurried on, swiftly and stealthily, every nerve straining and tense, alert to the multitudinous details which told a story—all but the end. His nose gave him a varying description of the passage of the life on the heels of which he was traveling. He remarked the pregnant silence of the forest. The bird life had flitted. The squirrels were in hiding. One only he saw—a sleek gray fellow, flattened against a gray dead limb so that he seemed a part of it, a woody excrescence upon the wood itself.

As Buck slid along with the obscureness of a gliding shadow, his nose was jerked suddenly to the side as though a positive force had gripped and pulled it. He followed the new scent into a thicket and found Nig. He was lying on his side, dead where he had dragged himself, an arrow protruding, head and feathers, from either side of his body.

A hundred yards farther on, Buck came upon one of the sled-dogs Thornton had bought in Dawson. This dog was thrashing about in a death-struggle, directly on the trail, and Buck passed around him without stopping. From the camp came the faint sound of many voices, rising and falling in a sing-song chant. Bellying forward to the edge of the clearing, he found Hans, lying on his face, feathered with arrows like a porcupine. At the same instant Buck peered out where the spruce-bough lodge had been and saw what made his hair leap straight up on his neck and shoulders. A gust of overpowering rage swept over him. He did not know that he growled, but he growled aloud with a terrible ferocity. For the last time in his life he allowed passion to usurp cunning and reason, and it was because of his great love for John Thornton that he lost his head.

The Yeehats were dancing about the wreckage of the spruce-bough lodge when they heard a fearful roaring and saw rushing upon them an animal the like of which they had never seen before. It was Buck, a live hurricane of fury, hurling himself upon them in a frenzy to destroy. He sprang at the foremost man (it was the chief of the Yeehats), ripping the throat wide open till the rent jugular spouted a fountain of blood. He did not pause to worry the victim, but ripped in passing, with the next bound tearing wide the throat of a second man. There was no withstanding him. He plunged about in their very midst, tearing, rending, destroying, in constant and terrific motion which defied the arrows they discharged at him. In fact, so inconceivably rapid were his movements, and so closely were the Indians tangled together, that they shot one another with the arrows; and one young hunter, hurling a spear at Buck in mid-air, drove it through the chest of another hunter with such force that the point broke through the skin of the back and stood out beyond. Then a panic seized the Yeehats, and they fled in terror to the woods, proclaiming as they fled the advent of the Evil Spirit.

And truly Buck was the Fiend incarnate raging at their heels and dragging them down like deer as they raced through the trees. It was a fateful day for the Yeehats. They scattered far and wide over the country, and it was not till a week later that the last of the survivors gathered together in a lower valley and counted their losses. As for Buck, wearying of the pursuit, he returned to the desolated camp. He found Pete where he had been killed in his blankets in the first moment of surprise. Thornton's desperate struggle was fresh-written on the earth, and Buck scented every detail of it down to the edge of a deep pool. By the edge, head and forefeet in the water, lay Skeet, faithful to the last. The pool itself, muddy and discolored from the sluice boxes, effectually hid what it contained, and it contained John Thornton; for Buck followed his trace into the water, from which no trace led away.

All day Buck brooded by the pool or roamed restlessly about the camp. Death, as a cessation of movement, as a passing out and away from the lives of the living, he knew, and he knew John Thornton was dead. It left a great void in him somewhat akin to hunger, but a void which ached and ached, and which food could not fill. At times, when he paused to contemplate the carcasses of the Yeehats, he forgot the pain of it; and at such times he was aware of a great pride in himself—a pride greater than any he had yet experienced. He had killed man, the noblest game of all, and he had killed in the face of the law of club and fang. He sniffed the bodies curiously. They had died so easily. It was harder to kill a husky dog than them. They were no match at all, were it not for their arrows and spears and clubs. Thenceforward he would be unafraid of them except when they bore in their hands their arrows, spears, and clubs.

Night came on, and a full moon rose high over the trees into the sky, lighting the land till it lay bathed in ghostly day. And with the coming of the night, brooding and mourning by the pool, Buck became alive to a stirring of the new life in the forest other than that which the Yeehats had made. He stood up, listening and scenting. From far away drifted a faint, sharp yelp, followed by a chorus of similar sharp yelps. As the moments passed the yelps grew closer and louder. Again Buck knew them as things heard in that other world which persisted in his memory. He walked to the center of the open space and listened. It was the call, the many-noted call, sounding more luringly and compelling than ever before. And as never before, he was ready to obey. John Thornton was dead. The last tie was broken. Man and the claims of man no longer bound him.

Hunting their living meat, as the Yeehats were hunting it, on the flanks of the migrating moose, the wolf pack had at last crossed over from the land of streams and timber and invaded Buck's valley. Into the clearing where the moonlight streamed, they poured in a silvery flood; and in the center of the clearing stood Buck, motionless as a statue, waiting their coming. They were awed, so still and large he stood, and a moment's pause fell, till the boldest one leaped straight for him. Like a flash Buck struck, breaking the neck. Then he stood, without movement as before, the stricken wolf rolling in agony behind him. Three others tried it in sharp succession; and one after the other they drew back, streaming blood from slashed throats or shoulders.

This was sufficient to fling the whole pack forward, pellmell, crowded together, blocked and confused by its eagerness to pull down the prey. Buck's marvelous quickness and agility stood him in good stead. Pivoting on his hind legs, and snapping and gashing, he was everywhere at once, presenting a front which was apparently unbroken so swiftly did he whirl and guard from side to side. But to prevent them from getting behind him, he was forced back, down past the pool and into the creek bed, till he brought up against a high gravel bank. He worked along to a right angle in the bank which the men had made in the course of mining, and in this angle he came to bay, protected on three sides and with nothing to do but face the front.

And so well did he face it, that at the end of half an hour the wolves drew back discomfited. The tongues of all were out and lolling, the white fangs showing cruelly white in the moonlight. Some were lying down with heads raised and ears pricked forward; others stood on their feet, watching him; and still others were lapping water from the pool. One wolf, long and lean and gray, advanced cautiously, in a friendly manner, and Buck recognized the wild brother with whom he had run for a night and a day. He was whining softly, and, as Buck whined, they touched noses.

Then an old wolf, gaunt and battle-scarred, came forward. Buck writhed his lips into the preliminary of a snarl, but sniffed noses with him. Whereupon the old wolf sat down, pointed nose at the moon, and broke out the long wolf howl. The others sat down and howled. And now the call came to Buck in unmistakable accents. He, too, sat down and howled. This over, he came out of his angle and the pack crowded around him, sniffing in half-friendly, half-savage manner. The leaders lifted the yelp of the pack and sprang away into the woods. The wolves swung in behind, yelping in chorus. And Buck ran with them, side by side with the wild brother, yelping as he ran.

And here may well end the story of Buck. The years were not many when the Yeehats noted a change in the breed of timber wolves; for some were seen with splashes of brown on head and muzzle, and with a rift of white centering down the chest. But more remarkable than this, the Yeehats tell of a Ghost Dog that runs at the head of the pack. They are afraid of this Ghost Dog, for it has cunning greater than they, stealing from their camps in fierce winters, robbing their traps, slaying their dogs, and defying the bravest hunters.

Nay, the tale grows worse. Hunters there are who fail to return to the camp, and hunters there have been whom their tribesmen found with throats slashed cruelly open and with wolf prints about them in the snow greater than the prints of any wolf. Each fall, when the Yeehats follow the movement of the moose, there is a certain valley which they never enter. And women there are who become sad when the word goes over the fire of how the Evil Spirit came to select that valley for an abiding place.

In the summers there is one visitor, however, to that valley, of which the Yeehats do not know. It is a great, gloriously coated wolf, like, and yet unlike, all other wolves. He crosses alone from the smiling timberland and comes down into an open space among the trees. Here a yellow stream flows from rotted moose-hide sacks and sinks into the ground, with long grasses growing through it and vegetable mold overrunning it and hiding its yellow from the sun; and here he muses for a time, howling once, long and mournfully, ere he departs.

But he is not always alone. When the long winter nights come on and the wolves follow their meat into the lower valleys, he may be seen running at the head of the pack through the pale moonlight or glimmering borealis, leaping gigantic above his fellows, his great throat a-bellow as he sings a song of the younger world, which is the song of the pack.

THE SUPERHUMAN DOG

BUDDY

BY *Dickson Hartwell*

T HE DOGS of The Seeing Eye are not unlike their masters in their variations of personality, temperament and size. They are completely different from their masters in that all of them must meet rigid standards for intelligence and performance, which, in terms of human understanding, are just two or three points short of genius. There are usually about a hundred dogs at The Seeing Eye at one time and they have much the same attitude toward doing their jobs as a candidate for a position on the freshman football team has toward the varsity squad.

When they leave the school with their blind masters they begin to adapt the fundamentals they have learned to widely divergent conditions. One will guide its master about a farm in a quiet rural countryside, going into a small town once a week on Saturday nights. Another, the guide of a salesman of household appliances, will be with his master on the sidewalk, calling on block after block of housewives, continually throughout the working day. Still another dog, whose master is a commuting lawyer, will find itself using bus, taxi, train and street car, and amassing a broad knowledge of the intricacies of a large country courthouse. Another will find itself on the campus of a large university—a campus where there are no sidewalks but only smooth pathways which have no identifying curbs to mark each intersection and inform a blind man of where he is.

These are the everyday problems to which dog and master together gradually adjust themselves. These conditions, like the weather, or the rules of play in football, are accepted for what they are and treated accordingly. They do not affect the spirit, the character or the individuality of the dog any more than the regulations, or the condition of the playing field, affect the individuality of an athlete.

But with all their individual differences, Seeing Eye dogs have certain common features which run like a backbone through their character. There is a vast difference in the detail of their makeup, but there is a true likeness in fundamentals. In these fundamentals Morris Frank's beloved Buddy was typical of all Seeing Eye dogs.

Man, even with his capacity for mental creation, a few years ago could not have imagined a guide for the blind such as Buddy was. Considered merely as a substitute for eyes, in getting a man from place to place, Buddy was magnificent. When she guided Morris past a building they had entered once before, no matter in what city it was, she always slowed imperceptibly but enough to indicate to him alone that here was a place where he might have some business. When they went into a hotel she headed first for the desk, realizing that it was both a place for registration and a source of information. When getting off a train she would stand near Morris's bags until a porter picked them up, and then, at the command from her master to go forward, would follow those bags, guiding her master to wherever the porter took them.

In an office building Buddy knew an elevator button from a wall decoration. She knew the significance of a uniform—

whether on a policeman, doorman, elevator starter, bell boy or Boy Scout. When there seemed to be doubt in Morris's mind she would guide him over to the nearest uniform and stand there until he got his directions. An especially neat piece of guiding was as exhilarating to Buddy as a long run around the end is to a fast halfback. Third Avenue and Twenty-third Street was one New York intersection which she especially enjoyed. There was heavy traffic at this crossing complicated by two street car lines. But the real zest came from the Elevated which ran above Third Avenue.

Occasionally when Buddy was in the center of this inter-section, picking her way carefully across with Morris beside her, with a crashing roar an express train would thunder over-head, blotting out sounds on which Buddy depended for her own and Morris's safety. Then her ears would go fully forward and her eyes would dart back and forth, alert not to miss a moving thing. After an experience of this kind, when Morris returned to the nearby hotel where he often stayed when in New York, Buddy would jump around him to show how pleased with herself she was for the fine job she had done. If they went home to The Seeing Eye at Morristown, Buddy would go the rounds of the offices; to Mrs. Eustis, Jack Humphrey, Willi Ebeling and other members of the staff, tail wagging, eyes shining, budging them with her nose until they gave her a pat on the head or some other sign that she was recognized and her splendid qualities fully appreciated.

Sometime a writer with a descriptive prose worthy of the subject will attempt a character sketch of Buddy. When that person comes along he may find useful some notes made from first-hand observation.

For Buddy was a truly great dog. It is not difficult to find in her a character which is both rich and noble and yet possessing those endearing qualities which all people, in defense of their frailties, commonly describe as human. Buddy had unusual opportunities and she made the most of them. She had the un-doubted advantage of extensive travel and she was constantly meeting people of superior intellect. It may have put her on her mettle but she invariably rose to the occasion.

Buddy could measure her rights in mathematical fractions which carried to three places beyond the decimal point. She could measure to an even finer degree how far she could advance beyond the limit of those rights and still not be challenged. She was astute, always conscious of her own natural charm, and ready to use her wiles to enhance its effectiveness when the occasion required.

Though ordinarily regal in appearance and attitude, there were times, while not guiding, when Buddy would permit herself the commoner's luxury of being a tramp. When in one of these moods and out slumming, she was not above a roll in the muck or the thorough inspection of a neighborhood garbage can. At other times she was a downright thief, imagining herself, perhaps, as a sort of canine Jimmy Valentine, robbing the rich to help the hungry poor—although in Buddy's case the hunger invariably proved to be Buddy's own. In this as in all things, Buddy was expert. If someone set down a tray of canapés or cookies near her, she could silently filch half a dozen without seeming to move her head. Buddy would steal her hostess blind, as the saying goes, but she would never beg. Buddy had character and with it dignity. She knew that begging was mean.

On matters in which there was a possibility of doubt Buddy was her own supreme court. She would never have refused for a moment to obey Morris Frank on anything she felt was really important or clear-cut. But on things that she considered trivial, mere whims of her master, or open to reasonable interpretation, she did exactly as she pleased. When Morris was endeavoring to make a particularly good impression on an audience, which was not infrequently, Buddy might completely nullify his efforts by screwing up her face into a look of ferocity and barking at the audience at inopportune moments with all the menace she could muster. She enjoyed hearing Morris apologize for her, explaining that shepherd dogs weren't at all fierce really, that Buddy just liked to bark to show she was present.

Buddy must have enjoyed these feeble attempts at an explanation. She wanted to bark because she wanted to bark. It amused her to bark. And as far as getting recognition for her presence, she could tell, if her blind companion could not, that every eye in the audience was focused on her, whether she barked or not. It was she they had come to see. In order to watch her they would tolerate what her sometimes stuffy master had to say to them.

There were some people who twitted Morris, telling him that Buddy was spoiled, and that he ought to be more firm with her. Buddy wasn't spoiled; Buddy was smart and knew her role. If she climbed up on a silk bedspread in a house where she and her master were staying it was because in her position she felt it was important that she should. Of course ordinary dogs should sleep on the floor. That was because they were ordinary dogs. If all dogs were to climb on beds, no one would have them around and that would be very bad for dogdom.

But it was practically mandatory for Buddy to be on a bed because it helped to show people that there was a difference in dogs, just as there was a difference in people. People who were important; people who had done things; people who had shown capacity for leadership, were accorded privileges as a matter of course. Buddy was all these things. She maintained the propriety of her position by making certain that there were no errors of omission on her part.

Buddy would have lived up to her royal blood with any master who did not completely crush her spirit. With Morris Frank it was perhaps a little easier than it might have been with another because, as Morris had been told the first day he met Buddy, he did not own her; she owned him. Morris did nothing in particular to encourage Buddy's assumption of sovereign privileges nor did he do anything consistently to discourage it. He was somewhat in the position of an aide-in-waiting who often found it necessary, if somewhat trying, through constant repetition, to explain patiently to crude commoners who had lived too long in a democracy, the full meaning of the phrase "The Queen can do no wrong."

On at least one occasion, however, Buddy carried her prerogative of independent action a little too far. Morris was giving a talk at a fashionable girls' school and took Buddy out for a run on the lawn. Ignoring Morris's admonition to stay close, Buddy ran off some distance and came upon a beautiful black and white kitten which needed inspection. Investigation quickly proved, however, that the kitten was the offspring, not of a cat, but of a skunk, and that despite its tender years it had already developed to the full its time-honored powers of defense.

Redolent and horrified Buddy rushed back to where Morris stood surrounded by admiring young ladies. Crashing into the middle of the group, Buddy ran from one person to the other, trying to rub off the terrifying smell. The attempt didn't succeed, but before the young ladies became fully aware of what was happening, they smelled just as Buddy did.

Later that evening, when Buddy was being scrubbed and one or two of the more courageous faculty members had the temerity to question Buddy's behavior, Morris pointed out what seemed to him to be the only logical view to take of the situation. It was, he stoutly maintained, entirely the skunk's fault. It should have known Buddy intended no harm. Be that as it may, Buddy never returned to that college, although doubtless the skunk did.

Morris claimed for Buddy certain gifts which verge on the supernatural and probably had no basis in fact in even such a remarkable dog. Whenever Morris went to a clothing store to pick out a suit of clothes, he would feel the texture of the several offered for his selection and discuss each of them with the salesman. Then when the time came to pick out one, he would call Buddy over and let her sniff carefully at each. The one she sniffed at the longest was the one he decided she thought was best for him and that was the one he would buy. Whatever Buddy's capacity may have been for judging either the style, color or cut of men's clothing, even Morris's worst enemies wouldn't have said of him that he wasn't well dressed.

During their first years together Morris was also inclined to judge people by Buddy's reaction to them. If Buddy was obviously hostile, it would take a great deal of tact, persuasion and charm to put Morris in a frame of mind which could be described as anything more than coldly civil. If Buddy was friendly and showed approval when meeting someone, Morris would welcome him as a bosom friend. This inclination could be as quickly dissipated, however, if any annoyance was shown at Buddy's unexpected exuberance. Such a reaction Morris was inclined to put down as a lack of good breeding or, if in his more tolerant moods, merely to a lack of understanding of who Buddy was.

But Buddy's tendency vigorously to express her friendliness finally got out of bounds. Whenever she felt particularly affectionate, which occurred frequently, Buddy would greet an unsuspecting friend by jumping up and putting her front paws against his, or her, chest and making a valiant and usually successful effort to plant a kiss on whatever uncovered portion of anatomy came within reach. Occasionally Buddy would thus express her attachment for some lady in a fragile evening dress. The resulting disaster was sometimes total. At best Buddy left unwelcome footprints which stubbornly resisted efforts at eradication. In such a circumstance the reaction of the lady was not likely to be pleasant.

Prodded into action by several persistent friends, Morris finally decided that something had to be done to cure Buddy of jumping up on people. He reached this decision with reluctance and, because he was a sensible young man, with trepidation.

It is very simple to stop a dog from committing the malfeasance of which Buddy was guilty. It is also a very kind and considerate thing to do. For, from the animal's point of view, once this method of greeting people becomes a fixed habit, any punishment seems harsh and unwarranted. But in polite society —in Buddy's social circle—jumping on people causes an immediate and continued diminishing of popularity. This, too, a dog finds difficult to understand when its intent is so friendly.

In breaking the animal of the practice, when it jumps up on a friend who has been forewarned what to do, the friend merely inches his foot forward and steps lightly on the dog's hind feet. The resulting discomfort comes as a complete surprise to the animal, which, ever trustful of man, blames the discomfort on the fact that its front paws are not down where they should be. As a consequence, after two or three repetitions of the deception, the dog ceases to jump up. It is all done with the same neatness and dispatch with which the visiting trainer taught the pup not to "chicken" at Fortunate Fields.

In order to break Buddy of the habit, Morris asked his cousin to undertake the small task of stepping on Buddy's toes the next time she jumped up on him. The cousin obligingly agreed and when opportunity afforded, did so. To his great amazement, Buddy did not immediately jump down. Apparently she was not aware of the formula. She merely took his wrist firmly in her teeth and held it until he took his foot off her toes. A cure was effected all right, but it wasn't the one Morris had anticipated. Thereafter, the cousin kept his feet well curled up under him. Buddy kept greeting people by jumping on them and nothing further was done to teach her otherwise. It was less work, Morris reflected, to mold the world to Buddy than Buddy to the world.

Morris learned from experience to make only the most considered statements when he lectured on The Seeing Eye. Once when he was speaking at a convention, he made the unqualified statement, in answer to a question, that Seeing Eye dogs never engaged in fights with other dogs—they were too well educated!

After the talk, Morris went to the check room, got his hat, and he and Buddy went about their business. A score of people from the audience followed to see what happened when he got out on the street in traffic. Suddenly a fox terrier joined the crowd, yapping at Buddy as if to challenge the right of the big shepherd to walk on its block. When Buddy didn't respond, the terrier became courageous and finally got close enough for Buddy to retaliate. She nipped a piece out of the terrier. The terrier yowled murder. Immediately some of his lecture audience pounced on Morris.

"I thought you said your dog didn't fight," they challenged.

"Well, I don't call that a fight," Morris replied. "Do you?"

They agreed it wasn't.

Morris had silenced his onlookers, but thereafter he was careful to qualify his claims regarding Buddy's capacity to resist annoyance.

Morris maintained that Buddy was so peaceful that she must have some Quaker blood in her. "Why, she's only been in ten fights in her life. That's only one a year and that's an awful lot less than I've had," he said.

Because Morris and Buddy worked together as smoothly as if they had been cast from one mold, not infrequently people thought that he received a special training or that perhaps he could "see a little." On one occasion a lady in a Queen Mary hat had stopped at The Seeing Eye and wanted to be shown about. Though it was not during visitors' hours, because she was an older person and had come a long way Morris courteously took her around himself, explaining as they went along how the organization functioned.

After a bit, she asked if she could see some of the blind students working with their dogs. Morris politely told her that it was impossible and mentioned the school's inflexible rule against placing the students on public exhibition. But to be obliging, Morris walked with the lady out to where she could see the kennels—from a distance. That special privilege, he felt, ought to satisfy anyone. But the lady was not satisfied.

"I think it's outrageous," she said, "to come all the way to this school and then find that you are not able to see even one blind person."

"But, madam," Morris replied, "I'm blind."

The woman looked at him closely for a minute then said, "Oh no you're not. Your right eye looks perfect."

The opening was too inviting to ignore. As Morris said later, he could have driven a chariot through it.

"It ought to be," he replied. "It cost me $25.00."

Many a dog has at one time or another been credited with saving his master from fire, and sometimes along with him a whole houseful of people. Buddy is no exception. One morning in an Eastern hotel, Morris was awakened by Buddy licking his face, in the cold dark hours before dawn. It was obvious that Buddy wanted something and though normally she would have been good for several more hours, Morris naturally assumed that she wanted to take a walk. He took up the telephone on the table beside his bed and called the porter. He got up to get Buddy's leash and when he opened the closet door a cloud of smoke billowed out at him. He gave the alarm. But by the time the hotel fire staff had reached his room, Buddy had guided Morris down to the lobby and safety. The linen-room on the floor below Morris's room was ablaze and was rapidly being consumed when Buddy's sensitive nose was aroused to the danger of fire. For years afterwards Buddy was a hero at that hotel.

Buddy lived up to her position in the dog world by proving she was equal to the ordeal by fire. She also showed she was equal to the ordeal by water. Morris enjoys swimming and will plunge into anything bigger than a bathtub. Ordinarily, when there was room in a pond for both of them, and even if there wasn't, Buddy would come in after him. When he was in deep water, she would swim around him in circles, standing by, as it were, in case of need.

Morris's friends thought this stunt of Buddy's was "cute" rather than practical, especially whenever Morris swam in the friendly atmosphere of Mr. Ebeling's lake at Openaka. But on one occasion when Morris had been swimming alone for an hour or so in a large lake he unexpectedly found that all at once he was exhausted. As he started to swim ashore, he suddenly realized that he had lost his sense of direction. He didn't know where the nearest shore was!

There was no sun and he could not learn his direction by feeling its warmth on his face. The light breeze he dared not trust; he knew the vagaries of the wind. He knew that even if his fading strength held out he might swim in circles for hours without ever touching the shore. For a moment he was panic-stricken, then he remembered and relaxed.

"Buddy," he called. "Come."

And Buddy paddled over and Morris reached out and felt her shaggy coat and took hold of the tip of her tail.

"Buddy, forward," Morris commanded, and then swam along behind her as she paddled off.

In five minutes, Buddy had him back exactly at the place where they had entered the water together. Buddy never got any Carnegie medals for heroism—she just did her job.

Yes, Buddy just did her job. Her life was filled to the brim with happiness of a kind few are privileged to know, the joy of appreciated service. Now Buddy II directs Morris Frank's energetic steps, and Buddy has gone to whatever special heaven is reserved for the faithful and the brave in heart. But her spirit still guides.

Hundreds of other guide dogs outside the spotlight that followed Buddy are today, and every day, doing their jobs. From the deserts of Arizona to Montana's Little Big Horn; from fog-wrapped Puget Sound to the deep blue water of Florida's Boca Grande; day in and day out these devoted animals joyfully lead men and women out from the bondage of blindness into a world where the only barriers are those of space and time.

They and those twoscore people of The Seeing Eye and the

thousands of that organization's members who make possible this great humanitarian achievement have begun a new chapter in the history of freedom. The first page is now written. Through endless tomorrows the record will grow—the record of animal sagacity combined with human intelligence—the story of dogs against darkness.

THE PROTECTIVE DOG

THE SHEPHERD AND HIS DOG

BY *Yehuda Yaari*
(*translated by Israel Schen*)

I

IT WAS TWILIGHT, and over the valley had begun to descend the mute blue-tinged shadow that heralds evening. The overlooking height had donned a veil of dark purple as Avshalom came down the mountainside with his flock of sheep. Avshalom went first, staff in hand and a gold-coated sheep dog frisking at his feet, and the sheep followed, streaming down in two long, white rows, like strings of pearls on the mountain's bosom.

The flock was a new acquisition. Only a week before the *kibbutz* had decided at the general meeting to add sheep breeding to its many activities. Thereupon Zvi and Avshalom had set out for the Jordan Valley to purchase a flock from the Bedouin living there. Zvi went because he managed all the affairs of the *kibbutz*, and it was inconceivable that an event of such major importance as the purchase of a new flock should take place without his having a hand in it; Avshalom went because he had been chosen to be shepherd from the very earliest days of the settlement, when a flock of sheep had been no more than a remote dream.

Avshalom was born in Palestine, in a mountain settlement in Upper Galilee. He had a sturdy body and a frank and open nature. His face was full and tan, and his clear, deep eyes were like pools in the heart of the forest, and the eyebrows above them wistful and gentle, like an innocent ewe's. He had joined the *kibbutz* in the early days of the settlement in the valley. He had come with his father to lend a hand in the many arduous tasks of those early days. When his father completed his task he returned to Upper Galilee, but Avshalom stayed on in the *kibbutz* as a member. Bred of the open spaces was Avshalom, tutored of the free-rolling hills—a born shepherd. Indeed, the very idea of buying a flock of sheep had been suggested for his sake, so he could become its shepherd. Even those *haverim* who were skeptical about the advisability of undertaking a new venture, one in which they had no experience and whose success was problematical, did not have the courage to oppose the motion when it was put to the general meeting. For everyone knew how Avshalom longed to become a shepherd, and how well he was suited to the task.

A week earlier, the day after the general meeting, Zvi and Avshalom had set out. Staff in hand and revolver on hip they climbed the mountain that stood like a mighty wall before the camp. When the workers in the fields paused to have breakfast, they could see their figures silhouetted on the mountaintop against the rising sun and then disappearing over the other side.

Excitement had been mounting ever since. The settlement was going into a new enterprise. And not just an ordinary business venture, but one that would bring a new spirit, new color to the life of the entire *kibbutz*—a flock of sheep. Anticipation ran highest among the children, who, having been told by their parents about the approaching event, could hardly wait for the flock to arrive. Each day they went out as far as the path on the mountainside to see if it was coming. As soon as they saw a shepherd and his flock in the distance, they were sure that it must be Avshalom, and began hallooing with all their might and jumping and waving their hats; but when, on drawing nearer, he proved to be merely an Arab grazing his sheep on the mountainside, which was quite a common occurrence, they returned to the camp disappointed. The children went on this way every day for a week.

Meanwhile a sheepfold had been built in the yard, from planks. It was put up near the poultry run, so the sheep and the fowl would be neighbors. It was made well, but not so well as to pamper the hardy Arab sheep that had never known what it was to be under a roof.

Zvi returned to the camp one morning, and excitedly told all about the flock—how it had been bought and what it was like. Never since becoming business manager of the *kibbutz* had Zvi been known to show such enthusiasm. Many new ventures had been undertaken since then, and he had had a hand in them all, but he had always talked about them dryly, without wasting words. Not this time. His face flushed with eagerness as he spoke, and his eyes sparkled with pleasure. In his enthusiasm, his voice broke into a kind of singsong, almost as if he were reading the Portion of the Law in synagogue on a Saturday. A flock of sheep was, indeed, a very different matter.

"Three days we sat in Sheikh Hassan's tent," Zvi related, "before we found an opening to say why we had come. We ate roast mutton with rice, we drank black, bitter coffee, and we exchanged stories. Hassan and his people told some, and so did we. But Avshalom really outdid himself. Really, I never dreamed what an imagination he has; he can tell the tallest stories. Hassan and company just took it all in. . . . On the third day, when another roast sheep stuffed with rice was set before us, I got up and said, the way it's in the Bible, 'We will not eat until we have told our errand; we have come to buy sheep.' Then Hassan and his people got up and showered us with greetings, as if we had only then entered the tent. That's the way the Bedouin do—the minute you begin talking about the business that brought you to them, they treat you as if you've just come into their tent, even though you've been there for days. 'Sheep?' said Hassan when the exchange of compliments was over, 'all my sheep are before you; take what you will!' Well, to make a long story short, we did all right by that roast sheep. We ate quietly and leisurely; then we drank the thick, bitter Bedouin coffee, and spiced the meal with stories. When the meal was over, we went out into the field and picked ourselves a flock from among Sheikh Hassan's best sheep. And what a flock, let me tell you! Seventy year-old ewes, all solid colored; two big horned rams; five old, but lively, she-goats to lead the flock among the rocks in the mountains and a beauty of a sheep dog. But a dog I tell you! You won't find the likes of him in this country no matter how hard you look. He's a real devil! You should see him bring in the flock. One short whistle from Avshalom and he rounds them up, barking wildly, and has the sheep clustering round him, their heads buried in each other's wool. Now that's a dog for you! At first Hassan didn't want to let us have him! He would rather give up his young wife, whom he married only a year ago, than that dog. By Allah, without that dog there was no living! By day he guards the sheep in the field, while by night he stands watch over Hassan against the members of the neighboring tribe, who have a blood feud with him. That dog, he said, is the light of his eyes. He was a gift from a German farmer. Only they, the Allemani, know how to breed such dogs. The Arab dogs are flea bags compared to him. No, nothing could make Sheikh Hassan give us the dog—but Avshalom's talk did it. He drew the most flowery expressions from his rich stock of Galilean Arabic. On and on he spoke, and every word a gem, until he had completely won Hassan over. 'Whatever I possess is thine,' said he finally, his spirit broken, with a sad smile in his eyes. 'And this dog, too, is thine. He has cleaved to the honey of thy tongue, for thy tongue is as sweet as honey.' Anyone who speaks Arabic with real elegance can get not only a fine sheep dog out of Hassan, and not only his youngest wife, but his very soul. Never have I seen a man who loves style as much as Sheikh Hassan."

Zvi eagerly repeated his story over and over that morning. First he told it to Yehudit, Avshalom's wife, who worked with the chickens; and then to those on kitchen duty. After that he repeated it with the same zest to the men who were taking their showers after the morning's work. Finally he went through it once again in the dining-hall, during lunch. Asked why Avshalom had not returned with him, he said in surprise:

"Avshalom? Would he be likely to bring in the sheep at high noon, before their bellies are full? If you think so, you don't know that Avshalom of ours. He found some good grazing on the other side of the mountain, near the springs, so he said, 'I'll graze them here all day, and toward evening I'll water them at the spring and then I'll come back to camp. You'll see how fat and round they are when we get back in the evening; so help me you'll be able to roll them along like barrels!' That's what he said. I tried to get him to come back with me. But not him! Yes, *haverim*, he's a born shepherd, our Avshalom."

The bluish shadow of twilight was spreading over the valley as the members of the *kibbutz*, who had just returned from their day's work, assembled in the middle of the yard to welcome Avshalom and his sheep. They were all there, young and old. The tots had been in the children's house, getting ready for supper, but as soon as they heard that Avshalom was coming down the mountainside with his sheep, they left their food untasted and gleefully dashed toward the yard to see the sight. Everyone was there but Yehudit, Avshalom's wife, who was in the poultry run.

Yehudit longed to be there and witness Avshalom's entry into the yard at the head of his new flock. Earlier, when she saw him far off, as he was starting down the mountainside with two white strings of sheep drawn out behind him and a dog frisking and capering at his side, she had suddenly felt jealous of the dog. Yehudit realized that this was a great moment in Avshalom's life, and she very much wanted to be with him. But he had chosen twilight to come back, when she had to feed the chickens and get them into the roosts, and she felt that she could not abandon her work in order to go and meet him. She was devoted to her work and loved her chickens. There was something sacred for her about this hour of twilight, when she fed the birds and put them to roost. No, she could not forgo this hour, even to gratify her longing. She stood in the poultry yard, scattering grain to her chickens, which clustered around her, looking like a giant mother dispensing from her bounty of food to her tiny tots. Her head was bowed in sadness; the dull gold of the twilight was reflected in her eyes and gave them a beautiful dark luster. The birds crowding around her warmed her feet, and her yearning for Avshalom warmed her heart and brought a soft blush to her cheeks. She heard the children shouting excitedly and the adults cheering as Avshalom approached the yard, and she saw the cloud of dust raised by the flock of sheep, and excitement welled up within her. At that moment she felt like flying to the spot, but she could not move. She simply could not bring herself to disperse the birds that clustered round her so thickly and warmed her feet with their soft bodies.

Avshalom, too, wanted very much to have Yehudit with him just then. As a conquering hero returning from battle with the wreath of victory on his brow might yearn to have his beloved at his side, to share his joy and his triumph, so did Avshalom yearn for Yehudit. He wanted very much to see her coming toward him. But he knew that his wish would not be fulfilled, and that she would not come. He knew his Yehudit and what feeding the chickens and bringing them to roost at twilight meant to her and nothing could induce her to neglect this task. . . . Then, knowing all this, why didn't Avshalom return earlier? Being a devoted shepherd, it never occurred to him to bring in his sheep before they had eaten their fill. Especially not today, his first day at work.

When Avshalom saw the crowd that had gathered in the yard to greet him, he decided to show off some of his prowess. He put two fingers in his mouth, and gave a short whistle. Immediately his dog bounded up, barking furiously, and in a trice had rounded up the sheep and herded them into a compact mass around him until he stood there half-swallowed up by his flock, only the upper part of his body and staff visible. Thus he entered the yard—like a picture come to life. The onlookers were much impressed, and cheered loudly. The dog, intoxicated by the shouting, cavorted wildly, running around the flock several times, letting go triumphant, savage barks. Avshalom was pleased, and laughed proudly.

Avshalom did not tarry in the yard; he wanted to reach the poultry run. He knew that Yehudit was there, and he wanted her to see him as he was just then, in the midst of the animated tableau. He urged his flock on, quickly passed by the tents, and made his way to the back yard, where the sheepfold and poultry run were. Catching sight of Yehudit in the distance, he put his hat on his staff and waved excitedly. Yehudit tossed the last of the grain backward to the birds and rapturously stretched her hands out to him as if meaning to embrace him from afar.

Then it happened. The door of the poultry run was open, and the dog, still intoxicated with excitement, burst in upon the chickens like a whirlwind, and within a second the whole place was in an uproar. The frightened birds clucked in terror and scattered in all directions, leaving behind them a cloud of dust and feathers. Yehudit clapped her hands to her head and shrieked with all her might, as if her whole world had collapsed around her. The bedlam lasted for only a moment, as Avshalom dashed in, seized the dog by the scruff, dealt him several blows on the head and carried him out of the poultry run. Then he went up to Yehudit, who stood in a cloud of dust, her body taut with fear and her face as white as her chickens' feathers, and took her hand in his, stammering:

"Never mind, Yehudit—he didn't mean any harm . . . He only wanted to play . . . That's a dog's way of playing . . . A dog's a dog . . . He won't do it again, really. I gave him a good beating. . . ."

Yehudit did not answer. Her lips were trembling and she could not utter a sound. Avshalom's confusion mounted; he did not know what to do. When a strong man becomes confused he is helpless as a child. Yehudit, seeing his embarrassment, withdrew her hands from his.

Meanwhile it had turned dark in the yard. The dog was somewhere in a corner, whining with shame and pain, and the other dogs in the neighborhood answered him sympathetically with their barks. The sheep, left without their shepherd, were bleating with fear of their strange surroundings, while the

chickens were still clucking with fright. Yehudit began to round
them up and take them into the roosts, and Avshalom helped
her. They worked in silence, she because she was so upset, he
out of embarrassment.

When they had finished, Yehudit went to her tent without a
word, and Avshalom put the sheep into the fold and tied the dog
up at the entrance. At first he had thought of letting him sleep
in his tent, but in view of what had happened, he thought it
better not to do so that night. Yehudit was still in a nervous
state, and he did not want to do anything to irritate her further.
The dog, sensing that Avshalom was not treating him properly,
jumped up at him, licking his face and whimpering softly with
resentment. The sound of that whimper sent a shudder through
Avshalom.

The camp was dark when Avshalom left the sheep fold. He
did not go straight to the tent, but walked about for a while
in the gloom. He walked with the heavy tread of one returning
home after long wandering, only to find that it is no longer his
home. There was the usual evening bustle about the camp. The
horses, just out of harness, were neighing in their stalls, and the
heifers were lowing in the cow shed, while from the washroom
came snatches of lighthearted song from the men under the
showers. Gay chatter could be heard from the tents, and there
was a great to-do in the kitchen. The girls had prepared a
special meal that evening in honor of the new flock. There was
a festive atmosphere in the camp, but Avshalom felt despondent. Fallen was the laurel wreath from the conquering hero's
brow when he arrived at the gate of his beloved. Wearily Avshalom wended his way toward the tents. His tent was dark.
He stood motionless before it for a long time; he meant to wait
till Yehudit lit the lamp. It was, he thought, only fitting that on
that evening she should welcome him with a lighted tent. God
knows he would have preferred their meeting now to take place
in the dark, but all the same . . . He understood what Yehudit
must be feeling, and was even able to justify her strange
behavior. If the same sort of thing happened to him—if a dog
had attacked his flock so viciously and frightened his sheep—
he would also have been very upset and angry. Yes, he understood her; but he also felt some resentment against her. After
all, it was not every day that a man came home bringing a new

flock with him. But to run away like that, without a word, without even a smile? . . . No, in her place he would not have acted like that.

Avshalom stood there for a long time and when he saw that Yehudit was not going to light the lamp, he finally walked into the tent.

The sheep smell emanating from him immediately filled out the whole tent. Yehudit, sitting glumly on the bed, let out a cough at the sharpness of the smell and said nothing. Quite at a loss, Avshalom stood hesitating a while, and then asked her, with a note of mingled embarrassment and complaint in his voice:

"What's the matter, Yehudit? Can't you even say hello to me?"

"It's your dog," said Yehudit weakly. "I don't like your dog."

"What a pity," muttered Avshalom with a soft sigh. "What a great pity. I do like him so much and I thought you would too. Such a dog! . . . I was thinking—"

But the dinner bell stopped him in the middle of his sentence. Yehudit got up from the bed and took him by the arm.

"Come, Avshalom," she said, "there's the dinner bell. The girls have got up a regular feast in honor of your flock."

Together they left the oppressive gloom of the tent for the spacious darkness outside. They entered the dining hall arm in arm, their faces beaming, as if nothing had happened.

II

During the summer Avshalom pastured his sheep in the valley fields. He would follow the reapers and let the sheep feed on the stubble and ripe ears of corn left by the mechanical harvesters. The machines left rich gleanings behind them, enough to feed several flocks of sheep. Avshalom's sheep fattened, and their tails hung down heavily with the weight of fat.

It was a hot summer. Avshalom's face was scorched, sunken and drowsy—a shepherd who does not roam the hilltop with his sheep gets no pleasure from his calling. Drive a flock through fields strewn with ears of corn—even a child could do that. Wearily and spiritlessly Avshalom made his way among the parched, harvested fields of the valley. He was like a

strong-winged bird that is forced to walk. The sheep would
spread out, dotting the fields in little groups as they tracked
down the ears of wheat turning golden under the burning sun.
When they had eaten their fill, they would line up in rows,
each sheep sheltering its head in the shadow of its neighbor.
Thus they stood until they were ready to graze again, while
Avshalom would cover up his face in his Bedouin cloak and
lie down, like someone pausing to rest from carrying a heavy
burden. His dog would lie in his shadow. The dog's face, too,
was sunken and weary during those days.

It is amazing how much the dog's face resembled his master's. But then, it really isn't so amazing. For we know of a
man spending much of his time in the company of beasts until
his face comes to resemble theirs and their faces come to resemble his. In Avshalom's face could be discerned a kind of
blending of a dog's face and a sheep's, just as the face of the
dog showed something of a sheep's face blended with a suggestion of Avshalom's face.

Wearily and lethargically the two of them wended their way
in those days. It was as if they were superfluous, the dog and
his master. As a rule there is not much for a shepherd to do
during the summer, when there is neither lambing nor shearing
to occupy him. But this summer there was especially little for
Avshalom to do, pasturing his flock as he did in the plains,
where there was more than enough grazing. He watered his
sheep morning and evening, and took them out of the sheepfold at dawn and brought them back again at dusk. That was
all. And the dog was almost completely useless. The sheep
were spread all over the field, every single one within sight of
the shepherd, and his call was enough to bring them in in the
evening. Every day at sunset Avshalom would wake out of his
drowse and call several times. In answer to his summons the
bellwether would come, with the other sheep following almost
at once. The dog had nothing to do. The sheep had eaten their
fill, and were thirsty for the water that filled the troughs in the
yard—having eaten nothing but dry ears of wheat all day—
and they needed no dog to urge them back to the camp.

As the summer drew to a close, the tractors and plows came
to plow up the soil of the valley: the golden stubble was turned
underneath and the black soil came to the top. There was no

more pasture left in the fields, and Avshalom had to go and
graze his sheep on the other side of the mountain, near the
springs. There was a large stretch of well-watered land near
the springs where green grass could be found at all seasons
of the year. Eagerly the sheep grazed upon the grass, but there
was not enough to sate them, for the spot was a favorite grazing
ground for the shepherds of the district at the end of summer,
and there was not enough pasturage for all. The sheep would
return to the fold in the evening hungry and tired, and Avshalom had to give them fodder to appease their hunger. But
he took the fodder from the barn by stealth, so the *kibbutz*
skeptics shouldn't be able to say, "See? We've been telling you
all along that it doesn't pay to have sheep on the farm; they're
not worth the fodder they eat."

During this time the sheep grew thin, and their tails shriv-
eled, but the spirits of Avshalom and his dog had revived somewhat. Avshalom began to feel once again that there was some
pleasure in being a shepherd, and the dog no longer felt superfluous. Grazing was poor, and the hungry sheep would stray
far afield in search of tufts of grass hidden away between the
rocks of the hillside or among the undergrowth. Avshalom's
call was no longer enough to round them up at sunset: the dog
had to do the job. Now Avshalom's and the dog's spirits rose
somewhat, though there was still a shadow of despondency
upon their faces. And no wonder; for a shepherd who cannot
find sufficient pasturage for his flock cannot be completely happy
and carefree, even though he breathes wholesome mountain air
all day long and bathes in the light of the hilltops. And when
the shepherd is not completely happy, neither is his dog. And
especially Avshalom's dog, whose freedom of movement about
the camp Avshalom had restricted, and whom, every evening,
he tied up for the night at the entrance to the sheepfold. Avshalom had not forgotten what happened the first time he
brought the flock home, and he didn't want the dog roaming
about the yard.

So passed the season between the Palestinian summer and
winter. There was mountain air a-plenty, but pasturage was
scarce. There was much to do, and little reward, until the
first rain fell.

The first rain that falls at the eastern end of the Emek

Jezreel no more than moistens the earth's parched lips and
smoothes out the wrinkles caused by the intense summer heat;
it does not quench its thirst or make the grass grow. That is
why, as soon as winter sets in, the shepherds of the Emek
move to the slopes of Mount Carmel, where the grass grows
thick after the first rain—tender, succulent grass that is very
much to a sheep's taste. Avshalom saw what the other shepherds
did and followed suit.

On the day the first rain fell, Avshalom's face lit up with
joy. He came back to camp earlier than usual, as though this
were a festival eve. He cleaned out the sheepfold, washed, put
on clean clothes, and walked out in the rain outside the settlement for a long time. By the time he got back supper was over,
and the committee was discussing the next day's work schedule.
Avshalom gulped down his meal in the kitchen and went into
the dining hall. The Bedouin cloak he was wearing covered him
like a tent, and his woolly hair was full of raindrops glistening
like silver spangles in the lamplight. He walked up and down
the dining hall several times, finally went up to the table where
the work roster was being drawn up, and announced his in-
tention of taking his flock west for a while, to the slopes of
Carmel, where there was plenty of pasturage. That's what the
other shepherds do. . . . Avshalom's eyes had glowed with
happiness that time when the general meeting decided to get
him the flock. But, "Now the work really begins. Now I'll show
you what sheepherding is," he said eagerly, as if he had only
just been appointed shepherd. "To go roaming with the flock
far from home, sleep in caves or in fields—that's sheepherding.
Up until now it's just been a game. . . . It's almost lambing time
and every ewe of mine will produce at least twins. You'll
see . . . I'll leave here with seventy-seven sheep and bring back
a hundred and seventy-seven. The fold won't be big enough to
hold them. You'll see . . ."

Of course, no objection was raised to Avshalom's proposal.
It's for the good of the sheep? Then he goes. Who is more concerned for the welfare of the sheep than the shepherd? He
probably knows what he's doing. But when they suggested that
he take someone along to help him—to protect the flock against
thieves, and to give him a hand at lambing time—he scouted
the idea, and was almost offended.

"What! An assistant? What do I need an assistant for? Didn't I have a slack enough time during the summer for me to be able to do all the work at lambing time myself? Did you ever hear of the shepherd of a flock of seventy-seven sheep needing help during lambing? And protection—well, if you have your doubts about me, then you can count on my dog. There isn't a better or truer watchdog in the country."

Next morning Avshalom was up before daybreak, and got everything ready for his departure. Yehudit was up with him to help. Out of an old tent flap he made a large, waterproof haversack, into which Yehudit put some clothes and food she had prepared. After breakfast, Avshalom released the dog and let the sheep out of the fold, while Yehudit let the chickens out of the coops and fed them. Then Avshalom set out with his flock, and Yehudit went with him a little way.

It was not so early when they set out. On dry days at that hour the yard is full of men and beasts setting about their daily tasks. But that day the place was deserted. It was a rainy, lazy morning, and during the rainy season the members of the *kibbutz* gorge themselves on the sweet pleasure of oversleeping.

Not a creature stirred. Sleepy and rain-washed the tents stood, and they were steaming slightly, like campfires that have just been doused. A dim light showed from the kitchen, and the drowsy voice of the watchman, who was late in going off duty that morning, could be heard in the stable.

The sheep bleated as they passed through the yard, and those whom the sound had awakened out of their winter drowse put tousled heads round the tent flaps and bade Avshalom a sleepy good-by.

The gate of the yard was shut. Hardly did Avshalom get the gate open than the dog was outside, barking joyfully, while the sheep crowded behind him. And thus they set out; the dog first, the flock following, and Avshalom and Yehudit bringing up the rear. Avshalom's eyes were glistening, and his heart brimmed; Yehudit was gloomy and silent.

By the time they reached a small hill near the camp, the sun had broken through a ragged cloud that lay as if flung across the northeastern corner of the sky, while light gray clouds scudded from the west like magnificent horses galloping on high. The rain, which had stopped a short while ago, began to fall again. Rain and sunlight were mingled, and a mighty rainbow formed above the horizon. The sheep stood and gazed at the rainbow in admiration, and the dog came bounding toward Avshalom, as if to say, "See what they've prepared for us there in the west!" Avshalom smiled, but not wishing to have the dog near him just then, he threw his stick as far as he could. While the dog ran off to fetch it, Yehudit took leave of Avshalom.

"Good-by," she said in a voice full of yearning. "I'll go back to camp now."

Avshalom spread his Bedouin cloak over her and hugged her to him.

"Be careful, Avshalom, and don't take any chances," she added as she went. "And when you come home, you'll let me know beforehand so I can come and meet you?"

"Of course."

The rain lashed the earth with myriad wet flails, and Yehudit ran back to camp like a ewe that had left a newborn lamb behind. Reaching the yard gate, she looked back and saw Avshalom and his flock being swallowed up in a bright cloud that had settled upon the hilltop.

III

For some two and a half months Avshalom and his flock became an inseparable part of the landscape. In sunshine or in rain, they could be seen wending their way slowly over the expanses of grass that covered the slopes of the Hills of Ephraim and Carmel. They looked as if they had grown there, together with the grass. Avshalom himself did not know how long he had been there. The time that had passed seemed to him like one long day with many sunrises and sunsets. To a shepherd roaming the open spaces far from home, the whole world becomes a home, and whoever calls the whole world "home" does not mark the passage of time. By day Avshalom would lead his flock over the grass-covered hillsides; the nights he spent together with Arab shepherds in rocky caves round the open fire. The ewes bore quite a few lambs, and they yielded milk in plenty, which, together with wild herbs, constituted the whole of Avshalom's diet throughout that period.

After lambing, which more than doubled the size of the flock, Avshalom took his sheep back to camp.

It was a lovely, clear day toward the end of winter. The air was full of the smell of rain-soaked, fertile earth. Flowers glittered in the fields like lighted candles, and the dew-covered rocks on the hillsides sparkled from afar like mounds of snow. In the early morning, at the hour when the members of the *kibbutz* were going out to their work, Avshalom's voice could be heard hallooing from the mountaintop the way shepherds do: "Ya-hoo! Ya-hoo! A-oo-a-oo-a-oo!" His cries were accompanied by the insistent barking of his dog. Avshalom had spent the night in the open air, on the other side of the mountain, so as to make the top just as the members of the *kibbutz* started out for the day's work.

At that moment Yehudit was entering the poultry run to take care of her usual morning chores, and when she heard Avshalom's hail, her heart warmed, for she knew that it was meant for her. She recalled their parting two and a half months ago, and remembered the promise she had made him, "When you come home you'll let me know beforehand, and I'll be out to meet you." Yehudit finished her work as quickly as she could, changed into her off-duty dress, went into the kitchen and took food for two, and set off for the mountain to meet Avshalom.

Slowly Yehudit walked up the mountainside, like one who knows that a great pleasure is in store, but does not wish to hurry toward it, enjoying the anticipation as much as the pleasure itself. From time to time she would therefore leave the beaten track to stop and pick cyclamens, which did not grow in the valley at all but grew in profusion on the hillside; or else she would bide behind a rock for a few minutes so that Avshalom, not being able to see her, would come all the quicker to meet her. But she had no desire to hasten the hour of their meeting; anticipation was sweet to Yehudit.

Avshalom and his sheep came down the mountainside slowly, and every now and then he would send a few notes from his flute into the clear, sweet-scented air. On the way down he grazed the sheep upon the grass on the slopes, as if that were what he had come there for in the first place. A shepherd has the eyes of a hawk, and Avshalom soon made out the white shape that left the camp in the early morning and walked with light, springy steps toward the mountain. He knew whose steps they were, and where they were going, and his heart filled with longing. But when he actually saw Yehudit coming toward him, he no longer felt like hastening the moment of their meeting. He, too, wanted to prolong the anticipation and to drink his fill of sweet expectancy. Besides, the sheep have to graze today too. Just because he's coming home today and Yehudit is on her way to meet him, is that any reason for him to drive the sheep and let them go hungry? A good shepherd has to know how to mix pleasure with work to take his pleasure without neglecting his work.

It was almost noon when they met halfway down the mountainside. Yehudit was carrying a bunch of flowers she had picked on the way and the food she had brought to eat together with Avshalom. He had in his arms two lambs that had been born that very morning and could not yet walk with the flock. Their meeting was one of quiet, restrained joy.

"Shalom, Yehudit."

"Shalom, Avshalom. You see, I've come."

After that no word passed between them for some time. One whose heart is brimming over with joy speaks little, so as not to diminish the joy. The dog also seemed to realize that the occasion was one of solemn gladness, and refrained from barking; slowly, almost guiltily, he went up to Yehudit, and licked her hand ingratiatingly. Yehudit was startled, and shrank back; but in an instant she recovered her composure, smiled and stroked the dog on the head. Avshalom's face beamed with satisfaction.

Avshalom sent the dog on ahead to keep the sheep from straying too far, and put the two lambs down before their mother, who had been following him closely all morning, bleating all the way. When the lambs had begun to suck at the ewe's distended udders Avshalom spread his cloak on the ground, took some cheese made of sheep's milk from his haversack, and Yehudit took out the food she had brought with her, and they sat down to eat.

"Well, Avshalom," said Yehudit as they began their meal, "it's a long time since you were here, isn't it?"

"Time? What's time?" said Avshalom innocently. Then, seeing that his surprise had brought a cloud to Yehudit's face, he hastily added, "Yes, Yehudit, a very long time."

Yehudit looked at him in silence for a while, and said:

"How you've changed, Avshalom. Now I see it. At first I didn't notice at all."

"I've changed. Of course I've changed. When I left I didn't have a beard, and now I've got one. And my hair is as wild as a Bedouin's. I suppose—"

"No, that's not what I meant," Yehudit broke in. "You're changed altogether—your whole nature's different."

"Listen, Yehudit. When a man lives with a dog and a flock of sheep, between hills and sky—outside of time and space, if you can put it that way—his nature is bound to change. It can't be helped."

Yehudit saw that the conversation was taking too serious a turn, and she changed the subject, saying vivaciously:

"Tell me the truth, Avshalom, where have you been all the time? What did you eat, where did you sleep?"

"Where have I been? I told you: over there, between the hills and the sky. I ate sheep's milk cheese like this and green herbs, and sometimes the Arabs gave me some bread. On fine nights I slept outdoors, and when it rained, in caves. There are lots of caves all over Carmel; you ought to see them some time."

"And wasn't there ever any danger?" Yehudit continued, still half in jest. "You know, Avshalom, I was often very, very worried about you and your flock."

"What was there to worry about? Me? The devil himself couldn't touch me! And the flock? A shepherd with a dog like this has to worry about his flock? He's a marvelous dog, let me tell you! You know, once he actually saved the flock from robbers. It had been pouring all day, and I was standing at the mouth of a cave, watching the sheep as they grazed on the slope below. Toward evening two Arab travelers came alone. They told me that they were from Transjordan, and that they were on their way to Haifa, on business. They asked me whether they could spend the night in my cave, and I told them they were welcome. On such a night not even shepherds like to be alone. I took them into the cave and made up a fire out of wood that I had prepared beforehand. The strangers were happy, because they were drenched to the skin and frozen stiff with the cold. Then I brought the sheep in and sat down by the fire with my guests. We ate and then we talked for a long time. They offered me *pittah* and dates, and I gave them sheep's cheese. They were pleasant and friendly, and it never entered my mind that they were up to anything. It was getting late and we all went to sleep. Suddenly, in the middle of the night, I was wakened by the dog pawing at my head—you know how hard it is to get me up. By the light of the dying fire I saw that my guests had disappeared and that the flock was gone. I was frantic. I took my revolver and ran out of the cave. By the light of a bit of moon showing through a gap in the clouds I saw the two Arabs driving the sheep down the slope with their sticks. I fired several shots in the air to scare them. But the dog had already caught up with them and gotten his teeth into them— to judge by their cries of pain. A minute or two later I could see them both making for the mountain as fast as they could run. Their screams and curses echoed through the night like black snakes striking. The dog brought the sheep back to me at the mouth of the cave. He was bleeding, but jubilant with victory. It had been a hard fight and he had won. Not a lamb had been hurt or lost. I tell you he's quite a dog. Here, watch!"

He blew a short note on his flute, and in a flash the dog was at his side. Then he had him leap through the air several times, and put him through all kinds of tricks, at the same letting go loud, almost savage, laughter that reverberated through the hills like crashing rocks. He then sent the dog back to the sheep and sat down beside Yehudit on the cloak. Yehudit leaned her head against his shoulder, as if overcome by giddiness. His story, and the way he played with the dog, had upset her and made her feel completely worn out. Avshalom thought it was a sudden surge of affection that had made her lean against him, and he hugged her close. For a moment they sat in silence and then Avshalom stirred himself from his reverie.

"Look at that, Yehudit. Here I've been raving about myself and about the dog, and I haven't even asked you how you are or what you've been doing all the time. I'm really awful. It's years since I last saw you! Tell me, Yehudit, please. Tell me what's been happening in camp all this time. How are things in the poultry run? Have you many new chickens?"

At the mention of the chickens Yehudit immediately became herself again. Her tiredness passed away, and her momentary annoyance vanished completely. Her eyes glowed with excitement as she started telling about her work. It's the hatching season, and the poultry run is teeming with chicks. Five incubators had been installed that year, and the eggs are hatching beautifully. Even she herelf doesn't know the exact number of chicks hatched, there are so many; there must be thousands of them! But she must confess that she isn't too fond of the chicks that came out of the incubators. Not that she hates them; she just hasn't taken to them. Every time she takes one of them in her hands she is surprised to feel that its body is warm. She always had the idea that an incubator chick must be as cold as a fish. Really . . . she prefers chicks that have been hatched by a hen; they are alive and healthy. . . . There's one hen that is really a marvelous hatcher: she sat her on twenty-four eggs, and nearly all of them had hatched. She loves those chicks with all her heart. Funny, those chicks have a mother of their own, and don't need her attention, while the incubator chicks— they have no mother, they're born orphans, and are more in need of attention. By rights, and according to the maternal instinct that women are supposed to have, she should feel sorry for them and love them the more. But that's not the case. Really. Seems you don't feel sorry for an artificial creature that never knew what "mother" meant. This thought has been occupying her mind a great deal lately. Oh yes, she has plenty to worry about in the poultry run; but it also gives her a lot of pleasure. How happy she feels every morning as she goes in and thousands of chicks surround her, chirping merrily away. As if she were their mother. She feeds them all and tends them. And there, in a place especially set aside for her, stands the hen with her chicks, proudly queening it over the whole poultry run. Oh, how she loves them!

For a long time Yehudit sat there, giving her excited account of life in the poultry run. Avshalom listened, at first with interest, then with boredom. At the end it was only with difficulty that he succeeded in suppressing his yawns.

When the shadows began to lengthen in the valley, and the afternoon train whistled in the distance, they got up. Avshalom signaled to the dog to round up the sheep. When the sheep had

been collected around him, he picked up the two lambs, gave
one to Yehudit and took the other in his arms, and thus they
descended into the valley. He and Yehudit walked in front
and the sheep stretched out in a long line behind them.

IV

That evening, after a festive supper, Avshalom and Yehudit
sat up late in their tent. There was a great deal they had not
yet managed to say to one another. The tent was filled with
light from the polished lamp and was bright with flowers. The
intoxicating scents of spring, of sheep and of fowl mingled in
the air. For a long time the two of them sat and talked, quietly
and happily, Avshalom sitting on his bed, Yehudit on hers.

At the first cockcrow they both left the tent. Yehudit went
to the poultry run to check the thermometers of the incubators,
as she did every night during the hatching season, while Avshalom went to look at his sheep in the fold. Two ewes were
due to give birth, and he thought that they might do so that
night. He had only just succeeded in singling them out among
the rest of the sheep when he heard a short, agonized cry,
immediately after which the dog rushed into the fold and hid
in a corner. Avshalom took no notice of the dog, but hurried
to the poultry run, for the cry had been Yehudit's!

A terrible sight awaited Avshalom in the poultry run.
Yehudit lay unconscious on the ground, near her lay the lighted
lamp where it had fallen from her hand, while all around her
was a shambles: blood, feathers and the limbs of chicks. Avshalom realized at once what had happened; but for the
moment his one thought was for Yehudit. First he must attend
to her and revive her; later he would see about the dog. He
took Yehudit up in his arms as easily as if she were an infant,
carried her to the tent and laid her on her bed. A minute or
two later she came to, opened her eyes and breathed deeply.

"How do you feel now, Yehudit?" Avshalom asked anxiously.

But instead of answering his question Yehudit flew at him:
"Oh, the dog, the dog—look what he's done, that dog of
yours! Killed the chicks—the best—the ones the hen hatched
. . . They were like my own children . . . I can't stand it any
more . . . I can't . . ."

Avshalom sat by her side trembling like someone who had been caught at a crime. As if it were he, and not the dog, who had killed the chicks. He was silent for a moment, then murmured helplessly:

"Well, what can I do to him?"

"What can you do to him?" Yehudit flared up again. "You want to know what you can do to him? Tie him up! Drive him away! As far as I'm concerned you can kill him!"

On hearing these words, Avshalom felt the blood freeze in his veins. He got off the bed slowly, as if a boulder were sitting on his head. Without another word he took his revolver out of the haversack hanging on the tent pole and went outside. He made straight for the poultry run. The dog is sure to come back there tonight. A dog that has once tasted chicks is sure to come back for more.

He sat down to wait for him; he was prepared to stay there all night if necessary. Just let him try and attack the chicks again; just let him try . . .

The poultry run was silent in the moonlight. An upturned crate, filthy with chicken droppings, lay in the yard, and Avshalom sat down on it, placing his revolver across his knees. Then he took out a cigarette and lit it, inhaling deeply. The glow of the cigarette lit up the fear and sorrow on his face. As a rule Avshalom did not smoke, and he only carried cigarettes with him so as to be able to offer them to his Arab fellow shepherds. He himself was not in the habit of smoking, unless he was unusually nervous or excited, or for social reasons. He sat quiet and absorbed on the filthy crate, gazing at the bereaved hen on her perch in her special compartment. The clear moonlight bathed the white hen as she dozed peacefully, while around her huddled the chicks that had escaped the dog's teeth. Suddenly he felt a surge of vicious anger against the hen. He took his gun off his knees, and just at that moment the dog came in; probably he had scented his master and wanted to be petted. Avshalom stroked his head lovingly, and murmured to him in pained voice:

"Look over there, my boy. See that hen? Look how calm and peaceful she sits there dozing away as if nothing has happened. You know, she's the mother of the chicks you killed. She's sleeping there without a worry, while Yehudit is lying in the tent almost mad with grief. . . . But it was you who killed the chicks. Yes, my boy, it's because of you that Yehudit is lying there now in such a state. Do you realize that Yehudit was like a mother to those chicks? It wasn't the children of that hen that you killed, but Yehudit's children. . . . Yes, damn you, you blasted hound!"

As he uttered the curse, a shot rang out and a bullet entered the dog's throat. The dog gave a hoarse whine and reared his head; but before he collapsed on the ground another shot was heard, and the hen rolled off her perch like a bundle of feathers, while the chicks, waking up, began to flutter with fright.

"What happened? Who fired?" came the cries of alarm from all quarters. But Avshalom heard nothing. His heart suddenly became empty, and his mind grew confused. He only knew one thing: he had fired twice, not once. He got up, left the poultry run and went directly to his tent. He staggered along like a drunkard. In the yard he was met by the excited watchman, who saw the revolver in his hands, and realized that the shots had come from it.

"What happened," he asked, "why did you fire?"

Avshalom muttered vaguely, "I don't know—the dog—the dog—he killed the chicks, and the hen was dozing. I don't know, the dog . . . He killed the chicks—and the hen was dozing—I don't know anything . . ."

It was dark in the tent. When Avshalom left for the poultry run Yehudit had put the light out. He stood a while at the opening of the tent and gazed at Yehudit, who lay huddled on her bed like a woman in labor.

"Yehudit, are you asleep?"

There was no reply. He knew she wasn't asleep. She couldn't have failed to hear what all the others had heard—that there had been two shots instead of one. No, she wasn't asleep, she couldn't be . . .

"Are you asleep, Yehudit?" he asked again, and his voice was thick and indistinct.

Still there was no reply. Avshalom waited for another minute and, seeing that she did not stir, turned and went out into the night whose silence had been shattered. He went to the sheepfold. He walked heavily, as if his feet were rocks. The people who were about in the yard already knew what had happened, and were afraid to approach him.

When he entered the fold the sheep clustered round him and warmed his legs with their fleeces. But Avshalom no longer felt anything; as if he had suddenly dissolved into nothingness.

THE INGRATIATING DOG

APRIL DAY

BY *Mazo de la Roche*

IT WAS SEVEN IN THE MORNING and the Scottie and the Cairn knew that soon it would be time to get up. They heard stirrings in the house below. They slept on the top floor in a dressing room between the bedrooms of their mistresses, Zia and Cara. The two round dog baskets, with the cretonne cushions exactly alike, stood side by side. Dan, the Scottie, was able to look straight into Robbie's face.

Out of his almond-shaped eyes that were set high in his hard brindle head, Dan gazed lovingly into Robbie's face, veiled in fine gray hair which stood in tremulous half-curls on his brow, curved into a tiny mustache on his lip, and turned velvet and close on his ears.

Robbie knew that Dan was staring at him but the love did not matter, for, at this moment, he wanted nothing but to be let alone. He was savoring the last delicious doze before the moment when he would spring out of his basket. He kept his eyes shut tight. His head rested against the side of the basket helpless-looking, like a little child's.

Dan stared and stared. A quiver ran down his spine, making the tip of his tail vibrate. He was sixteen months old and Robbie had had his first birthday last week. Dan seemed much the older, for he often had a dour look. He poured out his soul in love to Robbie all day long.

Now a felt-slippered step shuffled outside the door and it opened a little way. The cook put in her head. "Come, boys, come now, time to get up," she said, and held the door open wide enough for them to pass through.

Dan jumped from his basket and reared himself on his hind legs. He waved his forepaws at the cook but she had barely a word for him. Robbie was her charmer.

Now, as he coyly descended the stairs behind her, she encouraged him with endearments. At each landing he lay on his back and rolled, talking to himself in a low pleasant growl.

"Come along, darling, do," urged the cook, halfway down the stairs, but she had to plod back to the landing to persuade him.

Dan had gone down the two flights of stairs like a bullet. Now he stood waiting by the open front door, looking back over his shoulder. When Robbie reached the bottom step, Dan ran out and Robbie after him.

They went to their usual place under the weeping rose tree that was newly in leaf. The sun had just risen above the great shoulder of the nearest hill. The spring morning lay spread before them, to the distant mountains of Wales.

Shoulder to shoulder they trotted round the house and up

the slope, pushing aside the faces of daffodils and narcissus, hastening a little as they neared the denseness of trees. Among the trees there was a moist mossy twilight and across it flitted the brown hump of a young rabbit. Dan saw it first. He gave a cry, as of agony, and hurled himself into the wood. With a little moan of bewilderment Robbie flew after him, not yet knowing what he chased.

Head to tail, they dived into the green twilight. The rabbit whirled beneath the prickly fortress of a holly bush. Out at the other side it flew, skimming the wet grass, its ears flat in stark terror. Dan circled the holly bush, screaming.

Now Robbie was sure that what they were pursuing had escaped, though he had never known what it was. He stood pensive a moment, listening to Dan's screams, then drifted back toward the house. He found the front door shut—the cook always did this against their return—so he went to the green knoll outside the kitchen window and sat there under the green-and-white spread of the sycamore tree. He looked imploringly, from under his fine fringe, into the window at the cook bending over the range, at the maid putting on her cap, tucking her curls beneath it.

He heard the clump of a step on the cobbled path and saw the milkman coming with his carrier of milk. It was a shock to find that he had drawn so near without molestation. Robbie hurled himself down the knoll, screaming and champing at the milkman's legs. The cook came out of the kitchen calling:—

"Robbie Robbie! He won't hurt you! He's as gentle as a lamb!"

She said this every morning to the milkman, who never believed her but came on grumbling. The cook picked Robbie up and he let his head rest against her bosom. She still held him a moment after the milkman had gone. He was patient but he wanted to go upstairs.

As soon as she put him down he glided along the hall and up the two flights of stairs. He scratched on the door of the dressing room. Zia opened it and she and Cara told him how good and beautiful he was. He lay on his back looking up at them gently but haughtily, savoring their homage. His pointed gray paws hung quiet.

He saw the gas fire burning and stretched himself before it.

At first Dan did not miss Robbie, then suddenly realized that he had gone back to the house. What might not Robbie be doing without him? He tore across the grass, found the front door shut, and barked insistently till it was opened by the maid.

On his short legs he pulled himself up the stairs and scratched peremptorily on the door of the dressing room. Inside he reared and walked on his hind legs for a few steps with the sturdy grace of a pony stallion. He rolled his eyes toward the cupboard where the big glass marble lived. Zia went to the cupboard.

"Oh, must he have that?" said Cara. "It makes such a noise!"

"He says he must," said Zia. She laid the glass marble, with the silver bear in its middle, on the floor.

With a growl of joy, Dan pounced on it. He struck it with his paw, then bounded after it. Up and down the room he chased it, pushing it swiftly with his nose, then panting after it, banging it against the wall and, at last, between Robbie's paws.

Robbie hated the marble with a bitter hatred. The rolling and the noise of it made him feel sick. Now he lay, with half-closed eyes, guarding it between his paws.

Dan looked up into Zia's face. "Robbie's got my ball," his look said.

"Get it, then," said Zia.

Dan approached Robbie tremblingly, pretending he was afraid or really being afraid.

Zia gave him back the marble. He struck it with his muzzle, then flew after it growling. After a little he began to gnaw it.

"Enough!" said Zia, taking it from him. "You'll ruin your teeth."

The four went down to breakfast. The dogs' plates stood waiting, filled with bits of hard-toasted brown bread. They crunched in delight, Dan's tail waving, Robbie's laid close. The moment they had finished they ran to the table to beg. Dan sat staring up out of glowing eyes. Cara dropped bits of bacon to him, which he caught with a snap. Robbie mounted the arm of the settee behind Zia's chair. He put his paws on her shoulder and his cheek close to hers, so that she gave him bits of roll and honey.

At the first whiff of cigarette smoke Dan clambered into his basket and Robbie established himself on the fender stool, with his back turned to the table. He wore a look of disdain.

The children came in on their way to school. The dogs suffered themselves to be caressed, but they wanted to doze.

As the sun shone warmer they went to the drive and stretched themselves at ease, ready for what might happen. Each time an errand boy came through the gate they went after him, exploding in barks as they ran. Cara or Zia or the gardener called to them, apologized for them, petted them for coming when they were called. They felt fearless and proud and obedient, wagging their tails after each sortie.

After a while the cook brought bones to them. She chose the biggest, hardest bone for Dan and the one with the most juicy meat on it for Robbie. But it was Dan who looked up at her in an ecstasy of gratitude, Robbie who took his haughtily, as though it were no more than he had expected. They settled down with the bones, eyeing each other distrustfully before they began to gnaw.

Dan gnawed his bone in long steady grinds, wearing it down with his strong teeth, exposing its granular interior, arching his muscular neck above it. Robbie ripped the red meat from his, gnawed at the end where the marrow was, grew tired, and rose with the bone in his mouth, looking about for a place to bury it.

Dan saw this with dismay. To bury so soon! It could not be done! He darted at Robbie and tried to take the bone from him. Robbie lifted his lip in a defensive sneer. He growled in his throat. Dan returned to his own bone.

After a little while Robbie glided into the shrubbery and began to dig in the moist mossy earth. He buried the bone well, drawing the earth over it with paws and delicate nose. He came out of the shrubbery just as Cara came out of the house.

"Too much bone," she said; "you're having too much bone." She went toward Dan.

He wagged his tail at her to take the sting from his ferocious growl. "Don't touch my bone!" he shouted. "Don't touch my bone!"

"You'd growl at me!" cried Cara, and she made a dart for the bone.

He caught it up and romped away from her.

Zia came out of the house with collars and leads in one hand and a dog brush in the other.

"Walkee, walkee," she said as she came. "Walkee, walkee!"

Dan dropped his bone and ran to her. Robbie danced toward her. Jealously Dan shouldered him away, pulling him gently by the ear. He loved him, but he did not want him making up to Zia.

She took Dan in her hands and laid him flat. She began vigorously to brush him. He stretched himself at full length, giving himself to the brush in delight, kicking joyfully when it touched a sensitive spot. He showed his teeth in a grin of love and beamed up at Zia.

When Dan was brushed Zia stretched out her hand for Robbie, but he slid from under it like water. He looked at her coyly from over his shoulder. He kept always just out of reach, as she followed him on her knees across the grass.

"Walkee, walkee," she cooed. "Brushee, brushee!"

He bowed politely and touched her hand with his nose, but was gone before she could catch him.

"Very well," said Zia, "we'll go without you."

She and Cara went into the house, ignoring Robbie. When they came down with their coats and hats on he was sitting on the pink best chair. Zia caught him up, sat down with him on her lap, and began to brush him. He could tolerate this. He sat resigned as she brushed his long delicate hair first up, then down, then in a swirl to follow the streamline of his spine. But when she put the harness and lead on him he stiffened himself and an icy aloofness came into his eyes. He looked as aloof as a carved unicorn on the top of a stone gateway. He was not Robbie at all.

But he was himself again as he and Dan trotted down the drive and through the gate shoulder to shoulder, their mistresses on the other end of the leads. They turned from the main road into a country road, past the fields where the new lambs were being suckled and the glossy hunters were nibbling the grass, past the duck pond. Robbie averted his eyes from the ducks with a bleak look as though he could not bear the sight of them, but Dan, now off the lead, looked at them with beaming interest. He beamed up at Zia. "What about it?" his eyes asked.

"Don't dare!" said Zia.

On and on they walked, the great hills always rising before them, the primrose wreaths palely blooming on the banks. But hills and flowers meant nothing to the dogs. The thousand scents of road and ditch meant much. A rabbit had passed this way. A weasel had passed that. Only an hour ago the Hunt had crossed the road.

Dan never wearied of the pleasures of the road. He jogged jauntily on and on as though he would go forever. From a front view, one saw first his pricked ears, with the tail appearing exactly between them, then the strong shoulders, the bent elbows, and the round paws that padded one over the other as though he were climbing a ladder.

Now Robbie was bored. He wanted to go home. He drifted along the road like a resigned little old lady with her gray shawl draped about her. He looked neither to right nor to left.

They took the short cut home through the lane where the holly berries still shone bright among the prickly leaves. They found the break in the hedge. Zia lifted Dan over first, then followed him. Cara handed Robbie over and came last. She took off his harness and lead.

He stood crouching while it was undone, then sped forward like a slim gray arrow, past the house, past the stables, into the wildwood. Each breath was a protest against restraint. He felt free and cruel as a fox.

Now he was chasing a rabbit, all his boredom gone. Through the green twilight of the wood they sped, terror in one, joy in the other. Under the thick clammy leaves of rhododendrons, under the prickling boughs of holly, through horny undergrowth that tore out locks of Robbie's hair and scratched his face. Neither he nor the rabbit uttered a sound. They flew silently, as though in a dream.

Then suddenly the rabbit was gone, swallowed up in a burrow. Robbie lay panting, his heart throbbing. He pulled some of the burrs from his paws and his tail. After a while he remembered his dinner, his home. He trotted along a path and was passing the orchard when he saw that the hens had been let out of their run and were strutting about among the daffodils.

He hesitated by a hole in the hedge and peered through at them. His eyes were bleak, as when he had turned his gaze away from the ducks. But now he did not turn away. He stared and stared. He was alone. There was no one to stop him.

He glided through the hedge and sprang fiercely on the nearest hen. She flapped her big red wings and ran squawking, with him on her back. She fell and, still holding her by the neck, he threw her from side to side till she stopped struggling. All the other hens and the cock were in a panic, running here and there among the trees, each thinking it was its turn next. Robbie, with the face of a little gargoyle, ran after them. He whimpered in his delight.

The red feathers were scattered over the grass. Five bundles of them lay still and two more huddled in weakness and fear. The rest of the flock were safe in their run. Robbie stood looking in at them. They were all right there. That was where they belonged. In the orchard they were wild things to be pursued.

The front door stood open. He glided into the sitting room. Dan was curled up in his basket, asleep after a good dinner, but he jumped out and came to meet Robbie. He sniffed Robbie's mouth and his tail quivered in recognition of the scent there. He grinned joyfully at Robbie.

But Robbie wanted his dinner. He went to the kitchen and found the maid. He danced about her, gently nipped her ankles in their black cotton stockings. She snatched him up and rocked him in her arms.

"Oh, baby, baby, little baby!"

His beautiful eyes pleaded but she could not bear to put him down. She snuggled her rosy cheek against him, then held him at arm's length in her hands, adoring him. He looked at her, docile yet roguish. When she put her face near enough he gave her nose a swift nip. She hugged him close.

At last his plate was set in front of him—boiled cod mixed with vegetable. He ate less daintily than usual, for he was very hungry. Dan stood watching him and, when he had finished, came to his plate and licked it thoroughly. Robbie took a big drink out of the brown earthen dish, then went back to the sitting room and stretched himself at length on the settee. Dan returned to his basket.

For some reason the settee did not satisfy Robbie, though generally it was his favorite spot. He jumped down and came to the basket and gazed in at Dan. Dan turned up his belly and rolled his eyes at Robbie, but after a little he scrambled out of the basket and onto the settee. Robbie drifted into the basket.

While they were still drowsy Zia came with brush and comb and began to groom them. They were to go to the photographer's and already they were late for the appointment, but they must look their best. The car was at the door and now Zia slid under the wheel and Cara sat in the seat behind with a little dog on either side of her. They were as pretty as pictures, she told them.

They sat looking noble, till the car went into low gear on the steep hill and they felt the threat of the engine's vibration. They yawned and drooped, then hid their faces in Cara's lap and gave themselves up to misery. But on the level their spirits returned and they began to romp in exhilaration, growl at each other, stand upright on the seat, breast to breast.

What grand puppies, the photographer said, and placed them side by side on a settee and hid his head in the camera. That was only the beginning.

Dan jumped to the floor and, when he was lifted to the settee, Robbie jumped down. They did this till they were excited and panting and spoken to severely. Then they cowered on the settee, looking like curs. The photographer barked loudly and they had hysterics. Robbie suffered the photographer to put him on the settee and admonish him, but Dan raised his voice and barked "Don't touch me, man!" He showed his teeth in a threatening grin. Then suddenly he was well-behaved and posed nobly, sometimes in profile, sometimes full-faced, but always fine, like the prize winner at a dog show.

Now there was only Robbie to cope with, but Robbie had become all wriggles and gayety. Being photographed was funnier than he could bear. He lay on his back and kicked his joy in it.

Then, at last, he sat still. But now Dan was tired. He curled himself into a tight ball and fell asleep. When he was raised he had no backbone, but lolled and looked imbecile. Zia produced toffee and fed them. The trick was done! The camera clicked.

Now there was shopping and they sat alone in the car while Zia and Cara went into the shops. It was lonely in the car. Dan attended to his paws, licking them till his nails shone like ebony, sometimes, by mistake, licking the cushion of the car.

Robbie never licked his paws. He ignored sore spots which Dan
would have licked incessantly. So, to pass the time, Robbie
gnawed the polished wood of the window frame. It was awkward to get at but he managed it. They were nearly home when
Cara discovered the tooth marks. "Which of you did this?" she
demanded sternly.

Dan looked guilty, contrite, but Robbie knew nothing about
it. His eyes spoke innocence from under his silken fringe.
Cara smacked the top of Dan's lean flat skull. He burrowed
into a corner, ashamed.

Presently Robbie's thoughts returned to the window frame
and he gave it a last gnaw as they passed through the gate.

"So—it was you, Robbie!" cried Cara. "Oh, poor Dan, why
were you so silly?" She pulled Dan from his corner and patted
him. Robbie leaped lightly from the car when it stopped and,
pursued by Dan, sped into the wilderness. Soon they were
chasing a rabbit and Dan's screams echoed among the trees.

They came back in time for tea. They stood shoulder to
shoulder, yearning toward the teapot. They had their saucers
of weak tea, then got into the basket together and slept.

The gardener stood, strong and bent, in the corner of the
room, the loam scraped from his boots, his hands washed clean.

"Thur's been fowls killed," he said, "seven of 'em. Some
time this marnin', it were. I think one o' our little fellers
done it."

Cara turned pale. "How awful! Are you sure it was one of
ours?"

"Thur's been no other on t' place, ma'am. T' gates is all
shut fast."

He bent over the basket and with his gentle thick hand lifted
Dan's lip and looked at the double row of white teeth laid
evenly together, a little underhung but not much.

"Nubbut thure."

As gently but less cautiously he looked in Robbie's mouth.
Quickly he folded down the soft lip. " 'Tis him, for sartin,"
he said quietly. "Thure's a bit o' feather between his teeth.
I'm not surprised, ma'am. He killed one once afore. I caught
him at it. He thinks they didn't orter be runnin' in t' orchard.
But 'tis only a puppy. Don't you fret. He'll not do it again."

Robbie looked coyly up at them. He laid a pointed paw on

each side of his face and looked up lovingly into Cara's eyes.

"He'll never do it again," comforted the gardener.

As the sun slanted in at the west window and the children were getting ready for bed, Dan and Robbie went to the nursery for their evening play. Dan romped with the children. He was rough with them, but they must not pull him about. "Have a care how you handle me!" his warning growl came.

Robbie drifted about, always just outside the game. But when the children caught him, he surrendered himself to be held uncomfortably in small arms, to be dandled on small hard knees.

Toward evening the air had become warmer. Without question the birds and flowers opened their hearts to summer. Starlings walked about the lawn, staring into daisy faces. Dan and Robbie lay before the door serenely facing the great spread of hills unrolled before them. Their sensitive nostrils put aside the smell of the wallflower and drank in what rich animal scents came their way.

They lay as still as carven dogs except for the faint fluttering of the hair on Robbie's crown. Dan faced the breeze with head stark, neck arched and thick like a little stallion.

When two gypsy women clumped up the drive selling mimosa the dogs did not bark but watched their coming and their going tranquilly. They were steeped in the new sweet warmth of the evening.

But when they were turned out for a last run before bedtime, it was different. The air came sharply from the highest hill. The earth sent its quickness up into them. Robbie ran into the wildwood, but Dan found a hedgehog and worked himself into a rage before its prickles. Cara and Zia found him in the blackness beneath a yew tree and turned the beam of an electric torch on him. On the bright green of the grass the hedgehog sat like a bundle of autumn leaves, impervious.

"Open up! Open up!" shouted Dan, his teeth wet and gleaming.

Robbie came drifting out of the shrubbery and sat down watching the pair, knowing the hopelessness of the onslaught. Dan put his nose against the prickles and started back, shouting still louder—"Open up! Open up!"

But the hedgehog held itself close, impervious as a burr.

"Enough!" said Zia and tucked Dan under her arm.

Cara pounced on Robbie. The hedgehog was left to his dreams.

Snug in their baskets they lay in the dressing room, the velvet darkness pressing closer and closer. Dan lay stretched as though running, but Robbie's four feet lay bunched close together. His head was thrown back, his ears tilted alert for the whispering of dreams. What did he hear? The cry of a rabbit in a trap? Or some ghostly cackle from the poultry yard?

He woke. He sat up in his basket and uttered a loud accusing bark at what had disturbed him. His own voice was comforting. He had never before barked so sonorously, so much like Dan. The comfort of the barking gave him deep peace. He kept on and on. Cara came in at the door. She turned on the light.

Robbie looked at her wonderingly, his little head pillowed on his pointed paw. Dan gave a sheepish grin and hung his head. He had got out of his basket to meet her.

"Naughty, naughty, naughty!" said Cara. "Back to your bed, Dan! Not another bark out of you!"

Dan slunk back to his basket, curled himself close. . . .

The shadows would not let Robbie be. Out of them came mysterious things to disturb him. He went to the open window and sat on the ledge, framed in ivy. He barked steadily on an even more sonorous note. He had lovely sensations. He felt that he could go on till dawn.

But he heard the door of Cara's room open and, in one graceful leap, he was back in his basket. Small and stern, Cara entered the room. In her room Zia was lying with the blankets over her head. In shame Dan went to meet Cara.

"It is the end, Dan," she said mournfully. "You must go into the box room by yourself."

She took his basket and he humbly followed her, stopping only to nozzle Robbie as he passed. She put him in the farthest, darkest corner of the box room where, if he did bark, he would scarcely be heard. She went back to bed. There was beautiful quiet. Zia uncovered her head.

Robbie was alone now and he gave full vent to the trouble that was in him. He forgot all but the mournful majesty of his barking, as he sat on the window ledge.

When Cara came into the room he disregarded her till she

took him into her arms. Then he laid his head confidingly on her shoulder and gave himself up to what might befall. It befell that he was laid on the foot of her bed. It seemed almost too good to be true. Everywhere there was peace and slumber.

At half-past seven the cook heavily mounted the stairs. She opened the door of the dressing room and saw the one empty basket. She knocked on Cara's door and opened it.

"Half-past seven, madam," she said, "and I can't find the puppies at all!"

"Dan is in the box room. Robbie is here."

Dan and Robbie met in the passage. They kissed, then pranced about each other joyfully. They nipped the cook's ankles as they descended the stairs. Another April day had begun!

THE DEFIANT DOG

AN EPITAPH

BY *William Watson*

His friends he loved. His fellest earthly foes—
    Cats—I believe he did but feign to hate.
My hand will miss the insinuated nose,
    Mine eyes the tail that wagg'd contempt at Fate.

THE SNOBBISH DOG

COUPLET

BY *Alexander Pope*

I am His Highness' dog at Kew;
    Pray, tell me, Sir, whose dog are you?

THE PEERLESS DOG

QUATRAIN

BY *George Crabbe*

With eye upraised, his master's look to scan,
  The joy, the solace, and the aid of man;
The rich man's guardian, and the poor man's friend,
  The only creature faithful to the end.

THE PURSUING DOG

EPITAPH ON FOP

BY *William Cowper*

Though once a puppy, and though Fop by name,
Here moulders one whose bones some honour claim.
No sycophant, although of spaniel race,
And though no hound, a martyr to the chase—
Ye squirrels, rabbits, leverets, rejoice,
Your haunts no longer echo to his voice;
This record of his fate exulting view,
He died worn out with vain pursuit of you.
    "Yes—" the indignant shade of Fop replies—
"And worn with vain pursuit Man also dies."

354

THE MALEMUTE

BY *Frank J. Cotter*

He's a real chum with things coming easy,
    He's a pal with things breaking tough,
He's a hell-roaring fighting companion
    When somebody starts something rough.
He's a true friend in sorrow and sickness
    And he doesn't mind hunger or cold,
And he's really the only one pardner
    You can trust when you uncover gold.

THE EXEMPLARY DOG

EPITAPH ON A FAVORITE LAP DOG

BY *Thomas Blacklock*

I never barked when out of season;
I never bit without a reason;
I ne'er insulted weaker brother;
Nor wrong'd by force nor fraud another;
Though brutes are plac'd a rank below,
Happy for man could he say so!

Acknowledgments

WE WISH to thank the authors, publishers, and literary agents for granting us permission to use the following works in this book. Every effort has been made to contact the copyright owners of the works included herein to obtain their permission to reprint them and acknowledge them herewith. Any error of omission in this acknowledgment will be corrected in subsequent printings, provided written notification is made to the publisher.

ABELARD-SCHUMAN LIMITED for "The Shepherd and His Dog" by Yehuda Yaari from *Tehilla and Other Israeli Tales*, translated by Israel Schen, copyright 1956.

SHOLOM ALEICHEM ESTATE for "Rabchik" by Sholom Aleichem from *A Treasury of Jewish Humor*, Doubleday, 1951, published with permission of Crown Publishers, Inc.

EDWARD ARNOLD (PUBLISHERS) LTD. for "Descent to the Beasts" by C. G. Learoyd from *Physician's Fare*.

HAVILAH BABCOCK for "The Deacon's Grandpa" from his book *I Don't Want to Shoot an Elephant*.

KONRAD BERCOVICI ESTATE for "Babeta's Dog" from *Dust of New York* by Conrad Bercovici, published by Boni and Liveright.

CASSELL AND COMPANY LTD., PUBLISHERS for "Voltaire, Tono and Dulcibel" by G. B. Stern from *The Ugly Dachshund*.

CAROLINE CLEMENT, Estate of Mazo de la Roche, for "Tiny Tim" and "April Day" by Mazo de la Roche from *The Sacred Bullock*.

CONSTABLE AND COMPANY LIMITED for "Dog's Happiness" by Alexander Kuprin from *A Slav Soul and Other Stories*.

DODD, MEAD AND COMPANY for "Buddy" by Dickson Hartwell from *Dogs Against Darkness*, copyright 1942 by Dickson Hartwell.

DOUBLEDAY AND COMPANY, INC. for "Being a Public Character" by Don Marquis, from his book *The Revolt of the Oyster*, and copyright 1917 by The Crowell Publishing Co.

HARCOURT, BRACE AND WORLD, INC. for "Flush in Love" by Virginia Woolf from her book *Flush*, copyright 1933 by Harcourt, Brace and World, Inc.; renewed © 1961 by Leonard Woolf.

MACKINLAY KANTOR for "That Greek Dog," copyright 1961 by Curtis Publishing Company.

P. J. KENEDY AND SONS for "What Yuni Thinks of His Master," by Jean Gautier from *A Priest and His Dog*, translated by Salvator Attanasio, copyright by P. J. Kenedy and Sons, Inc.

MANUEL KOMROFF for his story "A Dog from Nowhere," first published in *Esquire Magazine*, then in *All In Our Day* by Manuel Komroff, published by Harper and Brothers, 1942.

LITTLE BROWN AND COMPANY for "The White Dog of the Ojibways" by Sheila Burnford from her book *The Incredible Journey*, copyright 1961 by Sheila Burnford. And for "Mutt Makes His Mark" by Farley Mowat from his book *The Dog Who Wouldn't Be*, and copyright 1957 by Curtis Publishing Company, copyright 1957 by Farley Mowat.

THE MACMILLAN COMPANY for "Kashtanka" by Anton Chekhov, translated by Constance Garnett, from *The Cook's Wedding and Other Stories*, copyright 1922 by The Macmillan Company; renewed 1950 by David Garnett.

HAROLD OBER ASSOCIATES, INC. for "Home Is the Hero" by Corey Ford from *A Man of His Own and Other Dog Stories*, published by Whittlesey House and copyright 1949 by Corey Ford.

PRESTON QUADLAND for his story "Setter and Terrier."

ALBERT PAYSON TERHUNE, INC. for "One Minute Longer" by Albert Payson Terhune from his book *Buff: A Collie and Other Stories*.

THE VANGUARD PRESS, INC. for "MacDonald" by John Held, Jr., from his book *John Held, Jr.'s Dog Stories*, copyright 1930 by The Vanguard Press, Inc.